Sadlier-Oxford

Master the Conventions

GRAMMAR FOR WRITING

Grades 9–12

COMPOSITION
USAGE
GRAMMAR
MECHANICS

COMPOCOMPOCOM
USAGESUSAGESUSAG

"Research studies clearly and consistently show that the most effective way to help students use the conventions of writing is to teach grammar in the context of writing."

Beverly Ann Chin

welcome to
Grammar for Writing

Grammar for Writing is a new program for today's secondary school students. It offers a complete course in grammar, usage, and mechanics—with an emphasis on writing—intended to help build the communication skills needed in a rapidly changing world.

The program takes the "mystery" out of grammar and helps develop better and more confident writers.

Grammar for Writing illustrates how the rules of grammar, usage, and mechanics—the conventions of standard English—can help students develop writing that is not just "correct" but powerful and persuasive, too.

Grammar for Writing has been designed with today's students in mind. Grammar rules are presented and explained in a clear and simple manner so that students can grasp them quickly and apply them to their writing immediately.

AUTHORSHIP

A broad-based team of experienced curriculum specialists and professional writers, working under the direction of *Beverly Ann Chin*, professor of English at the University of Montana and past-president of the National Council of Teachers of English (NCTE), developed the new *Grammar for Writing* series to help prepare today's secondary students to be effective writers in school, on writing assessments, on standardized tests, for college admission and placement, and for the workplace.

COMPOCOMPOCO
USAGEUSAGEUS

COMPOSITION
USAGE
GRAMMAR
MECHA

Sadlier-Oxford introduces *Grammar for Writing*, Grades 9–12:
a course in grammar, usage, and mechanics with an
emphasis on writing at each grade level.

Program Features

- **Informal, student-friendly tone**
- **Practical, two-page lesson format**
  Rules + Examples + Practice Exercises
- **Strong emphasis on writing**

- **Composition** unit (Chapters 1–3) at each grade level provides seven writing workshops teaching the types of writing often required of students.

- **Abundant exercises** include cooperative activities and practice with revising, editing, and proofreading.

- **Flexible lesson format** allows students to write exercises alone, with a partner, in small groups, or with the whole class.

- Emphasis on **persuasive writing** in *Write What You Think* exercises encourages critical thinking.

- Mid-chapter **reviews**, chapter reviews, and cumulative reviews reinforce lesson concepts.

- Four-page **tests** in standardized test format follow the grammar, usage, and mechanics sections in each student book.

- Chapter openers feature striking **photos** as writing prompts and real **student writing models**.

- **Teacher's Edition** includes answers to exercises and valuable teaching tips.

new!

fourth course Gr. 9

fifth course Gr. 10

sixth course Gr. 11

complete course Gr. 12

Begin with Writing

"Grammar for Writing helps students communicate effectively with a variety of audiences and for different purposes."

Beverly Ann Chin

Enriching Your Vocabulary

Just as word knowledge aids students' listening and reading comprehension, an effective speaking and writing vocabulary is critical to developing writing skills.

Authentic Writing

Models of published works set the expectation that students will learn to write clearly, coherently, and expressively.

Student Writing ▶

Authentic student models make writing relevant.

COMPOSITION
Lesson 3.4

Enriching Your Vocabulary

Voracious comes from the Latin verb *vorare*, meaning "to swallow up, eat greedily, or devour." This versatile adjective may be used in both a literal [concrete] and a figurative [an abstract] sense. A person who has a *voracious* appetite is likely to eat huge quantities of food. Someone with a hunger for knowledge may be a *voracious* reader.

Reference to the poem "The Rime of the Ancient Mariner" by Coleridge

Thesis statement

Example

An

Gen

N

52

Writing About Literature: Analyzing Fiction

When you write about a story or novel, you usually create one of three kinds of essays. The three serve very different purposes.

1. In a **personal response** essay, you write about how you felt and what you thought as you read, about the passages that seemed particularly meaningful, and about the other works that the story reminded you of.

2. In an **evaluation**, you write about how good or bad the work is. Your evaluation is based on objective **criteria**, or standards, that are used to measure the excellence of a literary form. For example, here are two criteria for measuring a short story:

   • The characters are believable.

   • The plot engages the reader's interest.

3. In a **literary analysis**, you discuss one or more of the **elements of fiction**: characters, plot, setting, point of view, and theme.

The following excerpt is from a long literary analysis of Ernest Hemingway's novel *The Old Man and the Sea*. Here, Carlos Baker discusses the feelings that the main character, Santiago, has for birds and fish while he is battling a marlin.

Hemingway's Ancient Mariner
an excerpt from an essay by Carlos Baker

[1]According to the ancient mariner of Coleridge, "[h]e prayeth best who loveth best all things both great and small." [2]Along with humility, pride, and piety, Hemingway's ancient mariner [Santiago] is richly endowed with the quality of compassion. [3]Of course, he is not so foolish as to love all creatures equally. [4]He dislikes, for example, the Portuguese men-of-war, whose beautiful "purple, formalized, iridescent, gelatinous" bubbles serve to buoy up the "long deadly purple filaments" which trail a yard behind them in the water and contain a poison which will paralyze the unwary passersby. [5]He has another set of enemies in the water of the tropic sea.

Internet

Visit us at
www.sadlier-oxford.com

STUDENT WRITING
Expository Essay

What I Learned About Life from Selling Shoes
by Katherine Ivers
high school student, Meriden, Connecticut

I know you're asking, "What could you possibly learn from selling shoes?" But the vast knowledge I have acquired from this minimum-wage job will last a lifetime.

Hired right before Christmas, I was about to receive a crash course in responsibility. Amid the decorations, elevator music, and hordes of customers, I learned my first lesson—patience. This virtue, unbeknownst to the six million crazed customers waving and shoving shoes in my face, is the only reason many of them were not bludgeoned to death by a high heel.

Another very important lesson is stress management. I faced the triple necessity of balancing honors courses at school, holding down a part-time job, and retaining a social life. . . .

I also learned to master quickly the art of budgeting time. I eat dinner, talk to my boss, and study for a trig quiz in fifteen minutes. Going to the bathroom can wait. In the shoe department, I learned something else that surprised me: Men and women are different! I never saw a man try on a pair of shoes and inquire whether they made his ankles look fat. On the other hand, I never saw a woman so anxious to get out of the mall that she purchased any shoe without trying it on. I learned to appreciate and adapt to these differences.

I learned, too, that physical fitness plays an important role. How many people get

---

Writing Workshops

In-depth lessons set the stage for students to see themselves as readers, writers, and communicators.

Writing About Literature:
Analyzing Fiction

Exercise 19 Organize and Draft Your Essay

Before you start writing, review your notes. Choose two or three of your most important points. Then sit down and start writing—anywhere in the essay. Do not worry about perfect sentences. Just get your ideas down in sentences and paragraphs so that you will have something to revise.

• **Introduction, body, conclusion** Make sure you have included everything that belongs in each of the three basic parts.

• **Title** Think of a possible title; try out several. Your title should suggest both the work and your essay's focus.

> **A Literary Analysis**
> INTRODUCTION
> • Author and title of work
> • Brief plot summary
> • Thesis statement
> BODY
> • Major point 1
> Support, support
> • Major point 2
> Support, support
> CONCLUSION

Exercise 20 Revise and Edit Your Essay

Let the draft sit awhile. Then use the four revising strategies suggested in Lesson 1.3. Read for accurate content, clear organization, and appropriate style for your purpose and audience. As you and your peer editors revise, ask these questions:

• Is the essay coherent, or well-organized?

• Are the general statements clearly expressed bu[t]

• Have you elaborated enough to support or "pro[ve]

• Is everything unified, or directly related to, the

Exercise 21 Edit, Proofread, and Pub[lish]

Double-check each quotation for accuracy and al[so] satisfied that you have corrected all errors in gram[mar] papers with a partner to check for any you may h[ave]

You might form two reading-and-discussion grou[ps] novels. Take turns reading aloud papers to the ap[propriate group] have read the work you have written about, see i[f] they have comments or ideas to add. Your group [could recommend] novels that members might enjoy.

You might also compile a "lit crit" anthology of e[ssays] Then share the anthology with other English clas[ses].

Step-by-Step Exercises

Lessons lead students through the writing process with exercises providing hands-on practice. Students develop and use strategies for assessing their final compositions before presenting their writing to different audiences.

COMPOSITION
Lesson 2.3

Coherence

✎ Each of your paragraphs should be **coherent**; that is, its sentences should be sensibly organized so that your reader can follow your thoughts easily.

STRATEGIES FOR WRITING COHERENTLY

1. **Be Clear** Express your thoughts simply and directly.

2. **Guide the Reader** Use signposts that show the reader what lies ahead and how thoughts relate to one another. Some signposts are transitional expressions like those on page 27. Others are pronouns and synonyms (words that mean almost the same thing), which refer to terms you have already used. Repeating key words or terms also improves coherence.

3. **Put Your Thoughts in Order** Arrange information so that "first things come first."

The following list includes four common ways of organizing paragraphs and essays. Unless you have a good reason not to do so, choose one of these orders as a framework.

• **Chronological Order** Organizing your writing chronologically means telling about events in the order in which they occurred. Use chronological order for narrative paragraphs, which may tell a true story or a fictional one; for writing about a historical event; and for describing steps in a process.

• **Spatial Order** Organize your paragraph spatially when you want to describe a person, an animal, a place, or an object. Include details in an orderly way; moving from left to right, top to bottom, near to far, or inside to outside.

• **Order of Importance** Organize your paragraph by degree of importance when trying to persuade your audience. State the least important reasons and other details first, and end with the most important ones—or the reverse.

Writing Strategies

Detailed strategies point out critical writing suggestions, enabling students to communicate clearly in many different situations.

"Grammar for Writing helps students use writing strategies and the writing process to communicate with different audiences for a variety of purposes."

Beverly Ann Chin

Writing Hints

Students learn practical advice for applying the skills of grammar, usage, and mechanics to their own paragraphs and essays.

Strengthen Grammar and Usage Skills

GRAMMAR
Lesson 6.6

Combining Sentences: Inserting Phrases

✦ Combine related sentences by inserting a phrase from one sentence into another sentence.

Sometimes, you must alter the words from one sentence to create a phrase for another sentence. Sometimes, you can simply pick up a phrase from one sentence and move it to another sentence.

ORIGINAL   Benny was traveling through Europe. He visited several circuses.
COMBINED   **Traveling through Europe**, Benny visited several circuses. [participial phrase]

ORIGINAL   Lisa plays in a band. The band is in New York. Janet and Rebecca are the other members of her band.
COMBINED   Lisa plays **in a band in New York with Janet and Rebecca**. [prepositional phrases]

ORIGINAL   We have time. We will buy the tickets at the ticket window. The ticket window is by the third-base line.
COMBINED   We have time **to buy the tickets at the ticket window by the third-base line**. [infinitive phrase containing two prepositional phrases]

ORIGINAL   My uncle enjoys something. He enjoys walking briskly.
COMBINED   **Walking briskly** is something my uncle enjoys. [gerund phrase]

Often there is more than one way to combine sentences. Here are two other versions of the last sentence.

COMBINED   To walk briskly is something my uncle enjoys. [infinitive phrase]
COMBINED   My uncle enjoys walking briskly. [gerund phrase at end]

In addition to creating a verbal or a prepositional phrase to put in another sentence, you can convert a sentence to an appositive phrase (see Lesson 6.2) and transfer it to another sentence.

ORIGINAL   My uncle lives in St. Louis now. He is an immigrant from Russia.
COMBINED   My uncle, **a Russian immigrant**, lives in St. Louis now.

Enriching Your Vocabulary

The adjective *apt* comes from the Latin *aptus*, which means "suited, fitted, or appropriate." The class valedictorian offered *apt* advice to the new graduates. *Aptitude*, as used on page 162, is derived from *aptus* and the suffix *-tudo* (condition or quality). Do you have an *aptitude* for a particular sport?

Writing Hint

Too many prepositional phrases in sentences can make them confusing and singsongy. Avoid this problem by breaking apart and rewording sentences.

The cashmere sweaters are **on the rack next to the ties on display in front of the shirt counter**.

The cashmere sweaters are displayed **on a rack**. They're **next to the ties**. You'll find the ties displayed **in front of the shirt counter**.

Chapter 6 • Phrases **161**

Sentence Combining ▲

Frequent lessons teaching sentence combining give students the practice they need to master this valuable skill.

Skill Building

Thorough and clear presentation of grammar and usage concepts builds skills that students apply to their own writing.

Cross References

References help students find related material throughout the book.

Complete Course, page 239

Using Object Pronouns

Object Pronouns	
SINGULAR	**PLURAL**
me, you, him, her, it	us, you, them

🖊 Use an **object pronoun** when the pronoun functions as the direct object (DO), indirect object (IO), or object complement (OC) of a sentence or a clause.

        IO   IO   DO
My father gave Dolores and **me** the keys to the car.

        DO
We thanked **him** for the keys.

        DO   DO OC
The family counselor made **you** and **me us.**

🖊 Use an object pronoun when the pronoun functions as the object of a preposition (OP) in a sentence or clause.

        OP   OP
Dad handed the keys to Dolores and **me.**

     OP   OP
For both of **us**, driving Dad's car was a big responsibility.

P.S. Don't become confused by the many terms that include the word *object*. Just get a general sense of how an object differs from a subject.

Exercise 4 **Choosing the Correct Pronoun**

Underline the pronoun in parentheses that correctly completes each sentence.

1. Every actor in his heart believes everything bad that's printed about (he, him). —Orson Welles

2. There is nothing which (we, us) receive with so much reluctance as advice. —Joseph Addison

3. Everything intercepts (we, us) from ourselves. —Ralph Waldo Emerson

4. A man in passion rides a horse that runs away with (he, him). —Thomas Fuller

5. We shape our buildings; thereafter, they shape (we, us). —Winston Churchill

■ See **Grammar,** Lesson 5.7, for more on direct and indirect objects and Lesson 5.9 for more on object complements.

USAGE
Lesson 10.2

Editing Tip

Avoid this common error: "between you and I." Always say or write, "between you and me."

P.S. Features

Students begin to recognize that some rules and definitions are more important than others.

Step by Step

Strategies familiarize students with an alternate presentation of the more complex concepts of grammar.

Step by Step

To decide whether to use a subject pronoun or an object pronoun:

1. Decide what function the pronoun performs in the sentence.

2. If th[e] predi[cate] subje[ct]

3. If the an i[ndirect] com[plement] prep[osition]

Working Together

Frequent opportunities for students to work cooperatively help them realize that there are many ways to revise, edit, and proofread the same material.

Working Together

Exercise 14 **Writing Paragraphs**

The information in the table is about mean, or average, verbal and math scores of college-bound seniors from 1988 to 1997. Use the information in the table to write one or more paragraphs about trends in the Scholastic Aptitude Test (SAT) scores over that ten-year period. Exchange papers with a partner, and make suggestions for improving each other's paragraphs. Try combining related sentences by inserting phrases.

■ Refer to **Composition,** Lessons 3.4 and 3.5, to find strategies for writing an expository paragraph and essay.

SAT Mean Verbal and Math Scores of College-Bound Seniors										
	1988	1989	1990	1991	1992	1993	1994	1995	1996	1997
VERBAL SCORES	505	504	500	499	500	500	499	504	505	505
Males	512	510	505	503	504	504	501	505	507	507
Females	499	498	496	495	496	497	497	502	503	503
MATH SCORES	501	502	501	500	501	503	504	506	508	511
Males	521	523	521	520	521	524	523	525	527	530
Females	483	482	483	482	484	484	487	490	492	494

Source: The College Board

162 *Chapter 6 • Phrases*

Complete Course, page 162

Master the Mechanics of Writing

"Grammar for Writing helps students apply knowledge of writing conventions — punctuation, capitalization, and spelling — to their own writing and to the writing of others."

Beverly Ann Chin

Mechanics ▶

The conventions of mechanics include punctuation, capitalization, and spelling.

Thematic Practice Sets

Thematically related exercises encourage students to apply their new skills.

Semicolons

A **semicolon** can show that two or more ideas are closely related.

🖊 Use a semicolon to join independent clauses in a compound sentence *without* a coordinating conjunction.

Claude McKay was a great poet and essayist of the Harlem Renaissance; McKay did not write much after 1930. [Semicolon alone joins two independent clauses.]

Claude McKay had few equals as a poet; **however**, his novels were not as well crafted. [Semicolon (before conjunctive adverb) joins two independent clauses.]

Claude McKay had few equals as a poet; **as a result**, his poems still appear in textbooks. [Semicolon (before transitional expression) joins two independent clauses.]

Claude McKay was a great poet and essayist of the Harlem Renaissance, **but** he did not write much after 1930. [With a coordinating conjunction, a comma joins two independent clauses.]

You may use a semicolon between independent clauses joined by coordinating conjunctions if either clause contains a comma. But you don't have to.

She was the last one to read; but when she recited her poems, we were glad we'd stayed.

🖊 Use a semicolon to separate items in a series when one or more of the items contain a comma.

McKay was born in Upper Clarendon Parish, Jamaica; Langston Hughes was born in Joplin, Missouri, but grew up in Lawrence, Kansas; and Countee Cullen, born in Louisville, Kentucky, and adopted by a Methodist minister, grew up in New York City.

Common Conjunctive Adverbs

accordingly	meanwhile
also	moreover
besides	nevertheless
consequently	otherwise
furthermore	still
however	then
indeed	therefore

Common Transitional Expressions

as a result	in fact
for example	in other
for instance	words
from that	on the other
point on	hand
in addition	that is

Editing Tip

Do not use a semicolon between an independent clause and a dependent clause or phrase.

We read poems by Langston Hughes, who is probably the best known of the Harlem Renaissance poets.

Exercise 3

Some of th...
colons. Re...
proper pu...

1. Khalil...
   poets...
2. Jean T...
   his lat...

Exercise 4 Combining Sentences into Compound Sentences

On a separate piece of paper, combine each set of independent clauses into a compound sentence. Do *not* use coordinating conjunctions. You may introduce conjunctive adverbs and transitional expressions. Check your combined sentences for proper punctuation.

1. Zora Neale Hurston believed that folklore was priceless. It constitutes the art of the people, who never recognized it as art.

2. Hurston was a self-styled literary anthropologist. She used literary techniques to shape oral narratives.

3. She created a new literary language. The language reflected the poetry in the oral culture of rural blacks in the South.

4. Hurston wrote four novels, a memoir, and more than fifty shorter works. She was more prolific than any black woman writer had been before.

5. Hurston grew up in Eatonville, Florida. Eatonville was the first incorporated black community in the United States.

6. Hurston's mother was a teacher in Eatonville. Hurston's father served three terms as mayor there.

7. Hurston worked while in high school and college. She worked as a maid, waitress, and manicurist.

8. As an English major at Howard University, Hurston began writing short stories and poems. She joined the literary club there.

316 *Chapter 14 • Punctuation: All the Other Marks*

Skills Instruction

Concrete instruction focusing on relevant mechanical skills helps improve students' understanding of writing conventions.

Complete Course, page 319

MECHANICS
Lesson 14.4

Quotation Marks

Lesson 14.3 shows italics (underlining) for certain works of art. This lesson tells when to use quotation marks for shorter works and for other purposes as well.

🖋 Use **quotation marks** for titles of short works.

POEMS	"Ode to a Grecian Urn" "The Lake Isle of Innisfree"
SHORT STORIES	"Araby" "The Fall of the House of Usher"
ARTICLES	"Going Out of Our Gourds Over Pumpkins"
SONGS	"The Star-Spangled Banner" "Penny Lane"
SINGLE TV PROGRAMS	"Rescue at Sea" (an episode of *American Experience*)
PARTS OF BOOKS	Part I, "Essays and Memoirs"

🖋 Use quotation marks at the beginning and end of a direct quotation, but not with an indirect quotation.

Introduce a short, one-sentence quotation with a comma or a colon; introduce a quotation that is a long sentence or more than one sentence with a colon.

> Of T. S. Eliot, critics wrote, "Eliot was better equipped than any other poet to bring free verse into the twentieth century."

When only a word or two is quoted, use a lowercase letter if the quoted words do not begin the sentence.

> T. S. Eliot referred to W. B. Yeats as "the greatest poet."
> [no capital letter in quotation]

🖋 Use single quotation marks for titles or quotes within a quotation.

> Brenda asked, "Have you read T. S. Eliot's poem 'Gerontion'?"

🖋 The following rules apply to quotation marks with other marks.

Commas and periods These marks g...
> "Dinner is ready," he announced.

Semicolons and colons These marks...
quotation mark.
> Here are three reasons I like "Araby": ...

Question marks and exclamation...
quotation marks if the quotation is a d...
go outside if the whole sentence is a q...
> "Did everyone read the poem?" she a...
> Was she surprised when you said, "No...

Editing Tip

Don't use two question marks with a single quotation mark.

Do you know the line after "Where have all the flowers gone"?

Don't use quotation marks for nicknames or slang.

His nickname is "Spike"; he's a "yuppie."

Editing Tips

Features help students avoid the pitfalls of writing by alerting them to possible problem areas and common errors.

after death.

10. Eavan Boland dedicated her 1967 book of poems, "New Territory," to her mother.

Working Together **Exercise B** **Write Your Own Exercise**

On a separate piece of paper, write one or more complete sentences for each item below. Mention actual titles wherever possible, but leave out all punctuation marks. Then exchange papers with a classmate. See if you agree on how to punctuate each sentence.

1. Your thoughts about an episode of a TV program you watched recently (Make up a name for the episode if you don't remember it.)
2. A song that you've heard recently
3. A direct quotation (actual or made up) at the beginning of a sentence
4. A quotation within a quotation
5. A short story or magazine article you've read and your thoughts about it
6. A poem you've read and your thoughts about it
7. A title of a chapter of a book you are reading and a summary of that chapter

Abundant Practice ▶

Thorough exercises reinforce lesson concepts.

320 *Chapter 14 • Punctuation: All the Other Marks*

Instructional Support

Teacher's Edition

- **Presents ideas and prompts for students' writing**
- **Includes strategies for effective grammar instruction**
- **Provides assessment rubrics for evaluating students' writing**
- **Supplies checklists for revising, editing, and proofreading**
- **Provides answers on the page and in the Answer Key**

▼ **Annotated Teacher's Edition Pages**

Provide convenient on-page answers and annotations

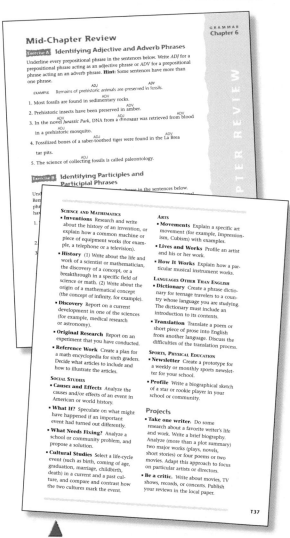

GRAMMAR
Chapter 6

Mid-Chapter Review

Exercise A Identifying Adjective and Adverb Phrases

Underline every prepositional phrase in the sentences below. Write *ADJ* for a prepositional phrase acting as an adjective phrase or *ADV* for a prepositional phrase acting an an adverb phrase. **Hint:** Some sentences have more than one phrase.

EXAMPLE   Remains of prehistoric animals are preserved in fossils.

1. Most fossils are found in sedimentary rocks.
2. Prehistoric insects have been preserved in amber.
3. In the novel *Jurassic Park*, DNA from a dinosaur was retrieved from blood in a prehistoric mosquito.
4. Fossilized bones of a saber-toothed tiger were found in the La Brea tar pits.
5. The science of collecting fossils is called paleontology.

Exercise B Identifying Participles and Participial Phrases

SCIENCE AND MATHEMATICS

- **Inventions** Research and write about the history of an invention, or explain how a common machine or piece of equipment works (for example, a telephone or a television).
- **History** (1) Write about the life and work of a scientist or mathematician, the discovery of a concept, or a breakthrough in a specific field of science or math. (2) Write about the origin of a mathematical concept (the concept of infinity, for example).
- **Discovery** Report on a current development in one of the sciences (for example, medical research or astronomy).
- **Original Research** Report on an experiment that you have conducted.
- **Reference Work** Create a plan for a math encyclopedia for sixth graders. Decide what articles to include and how to illustrate the articles.

SOCIAL STUDIES

- **Causes and Effects** Analyze the causes and/or effects of an event in American or world history.
- **What If?** Speculate on what might have happened if an important event had turned out differently.
- **What Needs Fixing?** Analyze a school or community problem, and propose a solution.
- **Cultural Studies** Select a life-cycle event (such as birth, coming of age, graduation, marriage, childbirth, death) in a current and a past culture, and compare and contrast how the two cultures mark the event.

ARTS

- **Movements** Explain a specific art movement (for example, Impressionism, Cubism) with examples.
- **Lives and Works** Profile an artist and his or her work.
- **How It Works** Explain how a particular musical instrument works.

LANGUAGES OTHER THAN ENGLISH

- **Dictionary** Create a phrase dictionary for teenage travelers to a country whose language you are studying. The dictionary must include an introduction to its contents.
- **Translation** Translate a poem or short piece of prose into English from another language. Discuss the difficulties of the translation process.

SPORTS, PHYSICAL EDUCATION

- **Newsletter** Create a prototype for a weekly or monthly sports newsletter for your school.
- **Profile** Write a biographical sketch of a star or rookie player in your school or community.

Projects

- **Take one writer.** Do some research about a favorite writer's life and work. Write a brief biography. Analyze (more than a plot summary) two major works (plays, novels, short stories) or four poems or two movies. Adapt this approach to focus on particular artists or directors.
- **Be a critic.** Write about movies, TV shows, records, or concerts. Publish your reviews in the local paper.

T37

The Writing Process	
Steps	**Tasks**
PREWRITING (Lessons 1.1 and 1.2, pp. 9-13)	▪ Use brainstorming, freewriting, class discussion, newspaper articles, clustering and other graphics, listing, and *5W-How?* questions to generate topic ideas. ▪ Choose and limit topic. ▪ Gather details, information; do research, if needed. ▪ Organize details (make an outline). ▪ Specify purpose and audience.
DRAFTING (Lesson 1.2, pp. 13–14)	▪ Put prewriting notes into sentences and paragraphs. ▪ Draft thesis statement (main idea of paper). ▪ Draft attention-grabbing title and introduction. ▪ Draft strong conclusion.
REVISING (Lesson 1.3, pp. 15–17)	▪ Read draft for coherence, unity, content. See four-readings strategy (page 15). ▪ Peer editors comment on draft. ▪ Consider peer editors' comments. ▪ Do additional drafts (second, third, fourth).
EDITING (Lesson 1.3, pp. 16–17)	▪ Check for sentence completeness. ▪ Find and correct errors in subject-verb agreement, verb forms, pronoun usage, and other errors in grammar and usage.
PROOFREADING (Lesson 1.4, pp. 18–19)	▪ Find and correct errors in mechanics: spelling, punctuation, capitalization. ▪ Utilize peer proofreading.
PUBLISHING (Lesson 1.4, p. 19)	▪ Find a way to share writing with intended audience.

Resources

Atwell, Nancie. *In the Middle: Writing, Reading, and Learning with Adolescents.* Portsmouth, NH: Boynton/Cook, 1987.

Merriam-Webster's 3rd Edition.

Powell, David. *What Can I Write About? 7000 Topics for High School Students.* Urbana, IL: National Council of Teachers of English, 1981.

Random House Roget's Thesaurus. New York: Ballantine, 1996.

Strunk, William, Jr. and E. B. White. *The Elements of Style,* 3rd ed. New York: Macmillan, 1979.

T33

Writing Process Guidelines ▲

- List the steps of the writing process
- Provide strategies for teaching each of the steps
- Help customize instruction for varying ability levels

▲

Writing Across the Curriculum

- Gives teachers a variety of writing ideas and projects

Introduction and Conclusion
☐ Does the introduction make you want to read more? What suggestions can you make for improving it?

☐ Does it introduce the topic and the main idea?

☐ Does the conclusion end the essay strongly?

You may want to offer students variations on peer checklists from time to time. One option is to generate mode-specific checklists such as the ones below or even assignment-specific checklists. (See also the discussion of rubrics on pp. 52–55.)

Mode-Specific Checklists	
Checklist for Persuasive Writing	☐ Is the writer's opinion clearly stated? ☐ Does the writer give at least two reasons to support that opinion? ☐ Are the reasons themselves supported by convincing evidence (facts, statistics, examples, anecdotes, quotations, and so on)? ☐ Do you understand what the writer wants the reader to do? ☐ Has the writer persuaded you? Why or why not?
Checklist for Narrative Writing	☐ Does the beginning make you want to read more? ☐ Does the writer *show* characters in action and let you hear what they say, or does the writer simply *tell* you about characters? ☐ Does the writing include sensory details? ☐ Are the writer's comparisons relevant and illuminating? ☐ Has the writer used specific nouns and vivid verbs (especially, as alternatives for *said*)? ☐ Is the ending satisfying?
Checklist for Descriptive Writing	☐ Can you picture the setting? ☐ Does the writing include specific sensory details? ☐ Are the comparisons fresh? ☐ Does the organization of details (for example, proceeding from near to far, left to right, or top to bottom) make sense? ☐ Does the description establish an overall mood? What is it?

T42

Editing and Proofreading

As previously mentioned, this series separates the revising task (which focuses on content, style, and organization) from the editing task (which focuses on grammar and usage). Proofreading is the stage of the writing process when students look for mechanical errors in spelling, punctuation, and capitalization. These checklists provide references either for the teacher or the student.

Editing Checklist

☐ Is every sentence grammatically complete (not a fragment or a run-on)? *Lesson 5.1*

☐ Do subjects and verbs agree in number and gender? *Chapter 9*

☐ Are the correct forms of pronouns used? *Chapter 10*

☐ Does each pronoun clearly refer to an antecedent? *Lesson 10.5*

☐ Are verb tenses used consistently, unless there is good reason to vary them? *Chapter 8*

☐ Are the correct forms of irregular verbs used? *Chapter 8*

☐ Are the correct forms of plural nouns and the comparative forms of adjectives and adverbs used? *Chapter 4*

Proofreading Checklist

☐ Is every word spelled correctly? Check a dictionary if you're unsure. *Chapter 16*

☐ Have homonyms been confused (*their* instead of *there*, for example)? *Chapter 16*

☐ Do proper nouns and proper adjectives begin with capital letters? *Chapter 15*

☐ Does every sentence begin with a capital letter and end with an end punctuation mark? *Chapters 13 and 14*

☐ Are commas used correctly in all of their many uses? *Chapter 13*

☐ Is dialogue punctuated correctly? *Lesson 14.6*

Resources

In the classroom, students should have access to several copies of a good college dictionary and a dictionary-style thesaurus.

T43

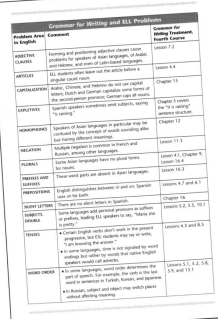

Grammar for Writing and ELL Problems		
Problem Area in English	**Comment**	**Grammar for Writing Treatment, Fourth Course**
ADJECTIVE CLAUSES	Forming and positioning adjective clauses cause problems for speakers of Asian languages, of Arabic and Hebrew, and even of Latin-based languages.	Lesson 7.2
ARTICLES	ELL students often leave out the article before a singular count noun.	Lesson 4.4
CAPITALIZATION	Arabic, Chinese, and Hebrew do not use capital letters; Dutch and German capitalize some forms of the second-person pronoun; German caps all nouns.	Chapter 15
EXPLETIVES	Spanish speakers sometimes omit subjects, saying "Is raining."	Chapter 5 covers the "It is raining" sentence structure.
HOMOPHONES	Speakers of Asian languages in particular may be confused by the concept of words sounding alike but having different meanings.	Chapter 12
NEGATION	Multiple negation is common in French and Russian, among other languages.	Lesson 11.3
PLURALS	Some Asian languages have no plural forms for nouns.	Lesson 4.1, Chapter 9, Lesson 16.4
PREFIXES AND SUFFIXES	These word parts are absent in Asian languages.	Lesson 16.3
PREPOSITIONS	English distinguishes between in and on; Spanish uses en for both.	Lessons 4.7 and 6.1
SILENT LETTERS	There are no silent letters in Spanish.	Chapter 16
SUBJECTS, DOUBLE	Some languages add personal pronouns as suffixes or prefixes, leading ELL speakers to say, "Maria she is pretty."	Lessons 5.2, 5.5, 10.1
TENSES	• Certain English verbs don't work in the present progressive, but ESL students may say or write, "I am knowing the answer." • In some languages, time is not signaled by word endings but rather by words that native English speakers would call adverbs.	Lessons 4.3 and 8.5
WORD ORDER	• In some languages, word order determines the part of speech. For example, the verb is the last word in sentences in Turkish, Korean, and Japanese. • In Russian, subject and object may switch places without affecting meaning.	Lessons 5.1, 5.2, 5.8, 5.9, and 13.1

T51

▲ Practical Teacher Checklists
- Checklists for evaluating types of writing
- Checklists for monitoring the writing process

◀ Support for English Language Learners
- Shows how specific content in English might pose difficulties in another language and where to find help within *Grammar for Writing*

visit us at www.sadlier-oxford.com **T11**

Assessment

Ongoing Assessment ▶ in the Student Edition

- **Mid-Chapter and Chapter Review Exercises**
- **Cumulative Review of Units**
- **Grammar, Usage, and Mechanics Tests**

...in the ▶ Teacher's Edition

- **Rubrics for Evaluating Students' Writing**

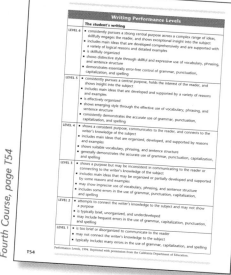

...and in the Student Test Booklet ▶

Also available is a student Test Booklet for each grade level. The Test Booklets extend testing and assessment opportunities and include comprehensive standardized chapter tests that review and reinforce new concepts. A Diagnostic Test and a Mastery Test help teachers identify problem areas and place students within the program.

to order call toll free **1-800-221-5175**

Technology

www.sadlier-oxford.com

Portfolio Projects

At the beginning of each chapter of *Grammar for Writing*, an Internet prompt directs students to the Sadlier-Oxford website, where they will find a portfolio project suggestion incorporating the concepts from the chapter. Teacher suggestions support each project with assessment suggestions and teaching guidelines.

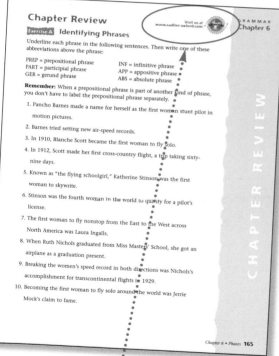

Complete Course, page 165

STUDENT WRITING
Narrative Essay

Working Pride
by Lacey Waldron
high school student, El Cajon, California

As I drove to my job interview on a sunny Saturday afternoon, my palms began to sweat. This was my first job interview, and I wanted to make sure I did everything perfectly. I thought to myself, "What should I say? How should I act?" As I came up to a white duplex that read "DR. McDONALD'S OFFICE," I started to panic. Looking at the clock, I realized I had ten minutes until I had to be in the office. I kept reminding myself that everything would be okay, but that was very hard to believe as my stomach began to turn in circles. After parking my car and fixing myself up, I slowly walked up to the office. Turning the knob of the large, oak door, it was time—time to suck up my fear and put my best foot forward. The first person that I met as I walked through the door was a lady named Mary. Mary seemed like she was a very kind hearted woman. She made me feel at home instantly. Before I knew it, a man who was skinny and had gray hair came walking out; it was Dr. McDonald.

I walked over and met him halfway, and he said, "You must be Lacey." I shook his hand firmly and remembered to make eye contact. I also remembered what my mom had advised me minutes earlier and told myself to relax. After a short interview, Dr. McDonald finished by saying, "I will call you and tell you when I want you to start working." I thanked him, shook his hand again, and walked out to my car.

"I GOT IT!" I said, "I GOT THE JOB!!" I couldn't wait to tell my mom the good news!

Getting my first job has really affected my life; it teaches me responsibility and gives me something to do rather than to get into trouble. My parents also seem to look at me as more responsible, and that's enough of a reward for me. Having money of my own has its ups and downs at times. But having the job that I am proud of is a valuable achievement that can never be forgotten.

Lacey Waldron organizes her personal narrative chronologically—in the order the events happened. She uses transition words and expressions such as *after*, *first*, and *before*. She also includes dialogue to make the reader feel close to the action. In the last paragraph, Lacey explains the significance of the event—what the incident meant to her.

Reread Lacey's essay and notice that each sentence is a little different from the one before. As you work on sentences in this chapter, think about how you can manipulate them communicate your ideas in an interesting way.

124 *Chapter 5 • Parts of a Sentence*

Complete Course, page 124

Chapter Review

Exercise A **Identifying Phrases**

Visit us at
www.sadlier-oxford.com

GRAMMAR
Chapter 6

Underline each phrase in the following sentences. Then write one of these abbreviations above the phrase:

PREP = prepositional phrase
PART = participial phrase
GER = gerund phrase

INF = infinitive phrase
APP = appositive phrase
ABS = absolute phrase

Remember: When a prepositional phrase is part of another kind of phrase, you don't have to label the prepositional phrase separately.

1. Pancho Barnes made a name for herself as the first woman stunt pilot in motion pictures.

2. Barnes tried setting new air-speed records.

3. In 1910, Blanche Scott became the first woman to fly solo.

4. In 1912, Scott made her first cross-country flight, a trip taking sixty-nine days.

5. Known as "the flying schoolgirl," Katherine Stinson was the first woman to skywrite.

6. Stinson was the fourth woman in the world to qualify for a pilot's license.

7. The first woman to fly nonstop from the East to the West across North America was Laura Ingalls.

8. When Ruth Nichols graduated from Miss Masters' School, she got an airplane as a graduation present.

9. Breaking the women's speed record in both directions was Nichols's accomplishment for transcontinental flights in 1929.

10. Becoming the first woman to fly solo around the world was Jerrie Mock's claim to fame.

Chapter 6 • Phrases **165**

CHAPTER REVIEW

Publishing Hyperlinks

In each Chapter Review, an Internet prompt directs students to discover hyperlinks to student writing and publishing websites, as well as a list of creative ways for students to publish their writing, both on-line and in print publications.

ALTERNATE ASSESSMENT OPPORTUNITIES

ON THE INTERNET

- Chapter-specific portfolio project assignments
- Opportunities for long-term projects

TEACHER SUPPORT

- Suggestions for providing support for projects

Content Overview

	UNIT I: COMPOSITION										UNIT II: GRAMMAR																	
	Writing Workshops										Parts of Speech								Phrases					Clauses				
	The Writing Process	Writing Paragraphs	Writing Essays	Narrative Writing	Persuasive Writing	Expository Writing	Writing About Literature	Research Paper	Special Writing Tasks	Combining Sentences	Parts of a Sentence	Subjects and Predicates	Sentence Fragments	Run-on Sentences	Direct and Indirect Objects	Predicate Nominatives and Adjectives	Object Complements	Prepositional Phrases	Participial Phrases	Gerund Phrases	Infinitive Phrases	Appositive Phrases	Adjective Clauses	Adverb Clauses	Noun Clauses	Sentence Structures	Parallel St...
Fourth Course Grade 9	■	■	■	■	■	■	■		■	■■	■	■	■	■	■	■	■	■	■	■	■	■	■	■	■	■	
Fifth Course Grade 10	■	■	■	■	■	■	■		■	■■	■	■	■	■	■	■	■	■	■	■	■	■	■	■	■	■	■
Sixth Course Grade 11	■	■	■■	■	■			■		■■	■	■	■	■	■	■	■	■	■	■	■	■	■	■	■	■	■
Complete Course Grade 12	■	■	■	■■	■	■■	■		■	■■	■	■	■	■	■	■	■	■	■	■	■	■	■	■	■	■	■

UNIT III: USAGE

Using Verbs	Agreement	Using Pronouns	Using Modifiers

UNIT IV: MECHANICS

Punctuation	Capitalization	Spelling

Column topics (left to right):

Unit III — USAGE
- Using Verbs: Verb Tenses · Active Voice · Mood
- Agreement: Person and Number, Compound Subjects · Indefinite Pronouns
- Using Pronouns: Subject and Object Pronouns · Who or Whom? · Agreement with Antecedents
- Using Modifiers: Degrees of Comparison · Double Negatives · Misplaced and Dangling Modifiers · Usage Handbook

Unit IV — MECHANICS
- Punctuation: End Marks and Abbreviations · Commas in a Series · Compound Sentences and Phrases · Colons and Semicolons · Italics · Quotation Marks · Dashes, Parentheses, Brackets, Ellipses
- Capitalization: Titles · Organizations, Religions, School Subjects · Historical Events, Documents, Periods · Calendar Items, Brand Names · Business Writing
- Spelling: Spelling Rules · Prefixes and Suffixes · Noun Plurals · Commonly Misspelled Words

Topic	Row 1	Row 2	Row 3	Row 4
Verb Tenses	■	■	■	■
Active Voice		■		■
Mood		■		■
Person and Number, Compound Subjects	■	■	■	■
Indefinite Pronouns		■		■
Subject and Object Pronouns	■	■	■	■
Who or Whom?		■		■
Agreement with Antecedents		■		■
Degrees of Comparison	■■	■	■■	■■
Double Negatives	■	■	■	■
Misplaced and Dangling Modifiers		■		■■
Usage Handbook	■	■	■	■
End Marks and Abbreviations	■	■	■	■
Commas in a Series	■	■	■	■
Compound Sentences and Phrases	■	■	■	■
Colons and Semicolons	■	■	■	■
Italics	■	■	■	■
Quotation Marks	■	■	■	■
Dashes, Parentheses, Brackets, Ellipses	■	■	■	■■
Titles	■	■	■	■
Organizations, Religions, School Subjects	■	■	■	■
Historical Events, Documents, Periods	■	■	■	■
Calendar Items, Brand Names	■	■	■	■
Business Writing	■	■	■	■
Spelling Rules	■	■	■	
Prefixes and Suffixes	■	■	■	■
Noun Plurals	■	■	■	■
Commonly Misspelled Words	■	■	■	■

KEY
■ = Lesson(s) dedicated to listed topic

Master the Conventions

GRAMMAR FOR WRITING
Grades 9–12

COMPOSITION
USAGE
GRAMMAR
MECHANICS

Sadlier-Oxford
A Division of William H. Sadlier, Inc.
New York, NY 10005-1002
www.sadlier-oxford.com

*to order call toll free **1-800-221-5175***

fourth course
grade 9

SADLIER-OXFORD

GRAMMAR FOR WRITING

Teacher's Edition

Sadlier-Oxford
A Division of William H. Sadlier, Inc.

CONTENTS

N O T E

The Student Text for the Fourth Course (Grade 9) of *Grammar for Writing* is available in a softcover edition and in a hardcover edition. This Teacher's Edition is intended to accompany both editions of the Student Text. Students may, with the teacher's permission, write in the softcover texts, but are directed in the Dear Student letter in the hardcover edition not to write in those texts.

Introduction to Fourth Course

Grammar for Writing Fourth Course is one part of a new grammar and composition program for high school students, grades 9–12. This book provides a full year's work—all the grammar and writing that students need to know plus assignments and exercises to fill the school year. Used together with a literature program and literature-based writing assignments, this book gives you a powerful component to a complete language arts program for students.

This series emphasizes grammar as it applies to writing. It has a user-friendly tone. Its minilessons zoom right to the essentials. Its teaching is prescriptive—with easy-to-follow rules, definitions, instruction, and examples. Students are encouraged to view good grammar not as a list of rules that must be memorized for their own sake but as a valuable tool that can help them improve their writing.

Grammar for Writing prepares students for standardized testing.

The grammar, usage, and mechanics sections address the conventions of standard English that students need to know for state assessment tests and national tests, such as the PSAT and SAT. The three Grammar, Usage, and Mechanics Tests in standardized test format (error recognition and error correction) prepare students for the writing exam in the PSAT test. Two-page Mid-Chapter, Chapter, and Cumulative Reviews reinforce and test students' understanding of writing and grammar concepts. In addition, there is a separate forty-eight page Test Booklet.

Grammar for Writing helps students meet the standards for writing.

In the writing sections and throughout the text, students learn to express and develop their ideas coherently and concisely. In Chapter 3 "Workshops," students proceed step-by-step through the writing process as they write for a variety of audiences and for different purposes. They conduct research on issues that interest them, using libraries and electronic databases. The text gives students repeated practice in revising and editing samples of poor writing. Students correct errors in grammar, usage, and mechanics; they use sentence-combining strategies to improve the flow of their writing.

Use *Grammar for Writing* with students of varying ability levels.

Exercises can be done individually by students needing to learn, review, and practice a particular grammar, usage, or mechanics concept. Frequently, exercises are done cooperatively with a partner or small group. You might pair LEP (Limited English Proficiency) students with more proficient students to create an informal tutoring-buddy system. Give mainstreamed ELL (English Language Learner) students many opportunities to *hear* standard English used correctly. You might have them read aloud corrected exercise sentences and paragraphs, for example, and use small-group activities to give ELL students speaking and listening practice. Advanced students might go over lessons and exercises with less advanced students. Challenge these students to do more writing, create new exercises, and turn their "Write What You Think" exercises into longer papers.

Use *Grammar for Writing* with a variety of schedules.

At the beginning or end of a class period, students can work on minilessons (the teaching text and exercises). You might go over the teaching text in class and assign the exercises to be started in class and finished as homework. Students can also meet in writing groups or with partners to work on both cooperative-learning exercises marked by the "Working Together" label and ongoing writing projects, such as the exercises in Chapter 3. Students can meet regularly in writing groups and in peer editing sessions.

If the whole class shows repeated weakness in one grammar concept (say subject-verb agreement), set aside a block of time to go over the appropriate lesson(s) carefully. Assign the exercises as group, partner, or individual work; and meet as a class or in small groups to compare exercise answers. Comparing finished writing is especially useful when students do a Revising and Editing Worksheet exercise (see page 94). Since there are no single right answers to these worksheets, students will learn even more by seeing and discussing how other groups or teams have revised the flawed writing samples.

Grammar for Writing improves students' critical thinking skills.

The "Write What You Think" exercises throughout the book give students practice in developing, supporting, and evaluating arguments on real-life issues. Students develop and strengthen their persuasive skills by giving logical reasons and evidence to support their opinions.

In most of the lessons in Chapter 3, a series of questions, marked by a "Critical Thinking" label, leads students to analyze professional models of writing. These questions might be used as an assignment or as a prompt for class discussion.

Features and Benefits of Grammar for Writing

Throughout the book, *Grammar for Writing* honors its commitment to teach the fundamentals of grammar through the context of writing. The following charts itemize how both the unit called "Composition" and the units called "Grammar," "Usage," and "Mechanics" incorporate features that help today's students express their thoughts clearly and succinctly.

Unit: Composition	
Feature	**Benefit**
LESSONS	Students spend more time working on writing assignments than reading about writing.
EASY-TO-SCAN LISTS OF ADVICE	Students can locate strategies, directions, and other help faster than is possible with extensive, run-on instruction.
WRITING HINTS	Students learn that writers consider not only important, general principles—such as coherence—but also practical, specific problems—such as "How can I figure out if this topic is too broad?" and "How should I publish this piece?"
"WRITING WORKSHOP" SETUP	Students realize that regardless of what they write, they can *always* apply the multistage writing process.
COOPERATIVE-LEARNING EXERCISES *Working Together*	Students learn that *every* writer needs an editor; students learn that a writing prompt may stimulate many different responses.
Modes of Writing	**Benefit**
NARRATIVE	Students tell a story—a fictional or true narrative. They use steps, critical events, or chronological order.
EXPOSITORY	Students explain or inform; state the main idea. They use facts, examples, quotations, statistics, and definitions presented in a logical order.
PERSUASIVE	Students learn to convince a reader. They use well reasoned arguments, persuasive language, and emotional appeals in order of importance.

Units: Grammar, Usage, Mechanics

Feature	Benefit
SUCCINCT INSTRUCTION	Students quickly move on to exercises.
COOPERATIVE-LEARNING EXERCISES	Students realize that a particular sentence-level problem may yield a variety of solutions.
"WRITE WHAT YOU THINK" EXERCISES	Students doing these persuasive-writing activities get ongoing practice in supporting an opinion with reasons and examples.
WRITING HINTS	Students learn that the end purpose of grammar, usage, and mechanics is applying those skills to paragraphs and essays.
EDITING TIPS	Students, forewarned of common errors, have a head start in working through exercises instead of feeling trapped or tricked by them.
STEP-BY-STEPS	Students exposed to an alternative presentation of the more complex concepts have a greater chance of understanding them.
P.S. NOTES	Students begin to recognize that some rules and definitions are more important than others.
REVISING AND EDITING WORKSHEETS	Students get opportunities to see that all drafts need revising and editing—and that multiple solutions exist.
REVIEWS, REVIEWS, REVIEWS	Students learn, through mid-chapter, chapter, and cumulative reviews, that in reviewing any written material they must be on the lookout for several potential sentence-level problems—that real writing doesn't neatly present only one problem at a time.
TESTS IN STANDARDIZED FORMATS	Students lose some fear of test taking by developing competence in error-recognition and error-correction question formats.
ENRICHING YOUR VOCABULARY	Students develop vocabulary skills by being exposed to words used in context and by immediately reading their meanings in a sidebar.

The Role of Grammar in Improving Students' Writing

by Beverly Ann Chin

Grammar is the sound, structure, and meaning system of language. All languages have grammar, and each language has its own grammar. People who speak the same language are able to communicate because they intuitively know the grammar system of that language—that is, the rules of making meaning. Students who are native speakers of English already know English grammar. They recognize the sounds of English words, the meanings of those words, and the different ways of putting words together to make meaningful sentences.

However, while students may be effective speakers of English, they need guidance to become effective writers. They need to learn how to apply their knowledge of grammatical concepts from oral language to written language.

Effective grammar instruction shows students what they already know about grammar, and it helps them use this knowledge as they write. By connecting their knowledge of oral language to written language, teachers can demystify abstract grammatical terminology so that students can write—and read—with greater competence and confidence.

What does Research Say About Grammar and the Teaching of Writing?

Strong research evidence suggests that the most beneficial way of helping students improve their command of grammar in writing is to use students' writing as the basis for discussing grammatical concepts. Researchers agree that it is more effective to teach punctuation, sentence variety, and usage in the context of writing than to approach the topic by teaching isolated skills (Calkins, 1980; DiStefano and Killion, 1984; Harris, 1962).

As students revise and edit their writing, teachers can provide grammar instruction that guides students in their attempts to identify and correct problems in sentence structure and usage. For example, if a teacher sees that many students are writing sentences containing misplaced modifiers, the teacher can present a mini-lesson on this concept using examples from student writing. The teacher can have students edit their own and each others' drafts for this problem.

Integrating grammar instruction into the revising and editing process helps students make immediate applications, thus allowing them to see the relevance of grammar in their own writing.

To What Specific Aspects of Writing Does Grammar Contribute?

Because writing is a complex activity for many students, teachers should focus on the grammatical concepts that are essential for the clear communication of meaning.

Research on the teaching of grammar since the early 1900s shows that grammar instruction that is separate from writing instruction does not improve students' writing competence (Braddock and others, 1963; Hillocks, 1986). In addition, research indicates that the transfer of formal grammar instruction to writing is not applicable to larger elements of composition. Through detailed studies of students' writing, Shaughnessy (1977) concludes that the best grammar instruction is one that gives the greatest return for the least investment of time. Shaughnessy advocates four important grammatical concepts: the sentence, inflection, tense, and agreement. She recommends that teachers encourage students to examine grammatical errors in their own writing. She also cautions teachers not to overemphasize grammatical terminology to the detriment of students' ability to understand and apply the concepts.

Weaver (1998) proposes a similar approach to teaching grammar in the context of writing. She writes, "What all students need . . . is guidance in understanding and applying those aspects of grammar that are most relevant to writing." In a chart as reproduced here, Weaver proposes five grammatical concepts that enable writers to show improvement in sentence revision, style, and editing.

A minimum of grammar for maximum benefits

1. Teaching concepts of subject, verb, sentence, clause, phrase, and related concepts for editing

2. Teaching style through sentence combining and sentence generating

3. Teaching sentence sense through the manipulation of syntactic elements

4. Teaching both the power of dialects and the dialects of power

5. Teaching punctuation and mechanics for convention, clarity, and style

(Weaver, 1998, pp. 21–23)

Rather than striving to teach all grammatical concepts to all students, teachers should prioritize and provide instruction on the grammatical elements that most affect their students' ability to write effectively. Teachers should also be sensitive to individual students' readiness to learn and apply grammatical concepts.

How Does Sentence-Combining Improve Writing?

Sentence combining is the strategy of joining short sentences into longer, more complex sentences. As students engage in sentence-combining activities, they learn how to vary sentence structure in order to change meaning and style. Numerous studies (Mellon, 1969; O'Hare, 1973; Cooper, 1975; Shaughnessy, 1977; Hillocks, 1986; Strong, 1986) show that the use of sentence combining is an effective method for improving students' writing. The value of sentence combining is most evident as students recognize the effect of sentence variety (beginnings, lengths, complexities) in their own writing.

Hillocks (1986) stated that "sentence combining practice provides writers with systematic knowledge of syntactic possibilities, the access to which allows them to sort through alternatives in their heads as well as on paper and to choose those which are most apt" (150). Research also shows that sentence combining is more effective than freewriting in enhancing the quality of student writing (Hillocks, 1986).

Hillocks and Smith (1991) show that systematic practice in sentence combining can increase students' knowledge of syntactic structures as well as improve the quality of their sentences, particularly when stylistic effects are discussed as well. Sentence-combining exercises can be either written or oral, structured or unstructured. Structured sentence-combining exercises give students more guidance in the ways to create the new sentences; unstructured sentence-combining exercises allow for more variation, but they still require students to create logical, meaningful sentences. Hillocks (1986) reports that, in many studies, sentence-combining exercises

produce significant increases in students' sentence-writing maturity.

Given Noguchi's (1991) analysis that grammar choices affect writing style, sentence combining is an effective method that helps students develop fluency and variety in their own writing style. Students can discover sentence variety, length, parallelism, and other syntactic devices by comparing their sentences with sentences from other writers. They also discover the decisions writers make when they revise sentences for their effect on readers.

Teachers can design their own sentence-combining activities by using short sentences from student writing or other appropriate sources. For example, teachers who notice many choppy sentences in students' writing can place these sentences on an overhead for all their students to read. Teachers can then ask different students to combine orally the short sentences in a variety of ways. As students share their different sentence combinations, their teacher can show students how they are naturally applying grammatical concepts such as clauses, phrases, modification, conjunctions, appositives, antecedents, and verb forms.

By participating in oral and written sentence-combining activities, students discover the relationships among meaning, sentence structure, usage, and punctuation. When presented as a revising strategy, sentence-combining activities help students identify short, choppy sentences in their own writing, leading them to combine their ideas in more fluid and sophisticated ways. As students generate more complex sentences from shorter sentences, they discover how the arrangement of phrases and clauses affects meaning and their readers.

What Strategies Can Teachers Use to Teach *Grammar for Writing*?

Grammar instruction is most naturally integrated during the revising, editing, and proofreading phases of the writing process. After students have written their first drafts and feel comfortable with the ideas and organization of their writing, teachers may wish to employ various strategies to help students see grammatical concepts as language choices that can enhance their writing purpose.

For example, teachers can help students revise for effective word choices in a writing conference. As the teacher and student discuss the real audience(s) for the writing, the teacher can ask the student to consider how formal or informal the writing should be. The teacher can remind the student that all people vary their level of language (formal to informal) in oral conversations, depending on their listeners and the speaking context. The teacher can then help the student identify words that change the level of formality of the writing.

Teachers can help students revise boring, monotonous sentences by having a partner read aloud the writing to the student writer. As the partner reads the writing aloud to the writer, both the partner and the writer

can recognize when too many sentences begin with "It is" or "There are." Both the partner and the writer can discuss ways to vary the sentence beginnings. After the writer revises the sentences, the partner can read the sentences aloud, and both can discuss the effectiveness of the revision.

Teachers can help students edit from passive voice to active voice by presenting a minilesson. In editing groups, students can exchange papers and look for verbs that often signal the passive voice, such as "was" and "been." When students find these verbs, they can read the sentence aloud to their partners and discuss whether the voice is passive and, if so, if the sentence might be strengthened with an active-voice verb. The student writer can decide which voice is most effective and appropriate for the writing purpose and audience.

Teachers can help students become better proofreaders through peer editing groups. Based on the writing abilities of students, teachers can assign different proofreading tasks to specific individuals in each group. For example, one person in the group can proofread for spelling errors, another person for agreement errors, another person for fragments and run-ons, and another person for punctuation errors. As students develop increasing skill in proofreading, they can become responsible for more proofreading areas. Collaborating with classmates in peer editing groups helps students improve their own grammar skills as well as understand the importance of grammar as a tool for effective communication.

As teachers integrate grammar instruction into writing instruction, they should use the grammar terms that make sense to the students. By incorporating grammar terms naturally into the processes of revising, editing, and proofreading, teachers help students understand and apply grammar purposefully to their own (student) writing. Strategies such as writing conferences, partnership writing, grammar minilessons, and peer response groups are all valuable methods for integrating grammar into writing instruction.

Standard 4: "Students adjust their use of spoken, written, and visual language (e.g., conventions, style, vocabulary) to communicate effectively with a variety of audiences and for different purposes" (p. 3).

Standard 5: "Students employ a wide range of strategies as they write and use different writing process elements appropriately to communicate with different audiences for a variety of purposes" (p. 3).

Standard 6: "Students apply knowledge of language structure, language conventions (e.g. spelling and punctuation), media techniques, figurative language, and genre to create, critique, and discuss print and nonprint texts" (p. 3).

How Does the Teaching of Grammar Relate to the National Content Standards for Students?

The National Council of Teachers of English and the International Reading Association (1996) published *Standards for the English Language Arts*, which defines "what students should know and be able to do with language" (p. 1). While the twelve content standards are presented as a list, they are closely intertwined and emphasize the complex interactions among language skills. Standards 4, 5, and 6 most directly address students' ability to write.

According to the standards:

> *By closely observing students' writing processes and carefully reading their work, teachers can see which aspects of language structure are giving students trouble and help them learn these concepts through direct instruction and practice. It is also important for students to discover that grammar, spelling, and punctuation are useful not only in the context of fixing problems or mistakes; they can be studied effectively in a workshop context in which students work together to expand their repertoire of syntactic and verbal styles. When students connect the study of grammar and language patterns to the wider purposes of communication and artistic development, they are considerably more likely to incorporate such study into their working knowledge (p. 37).*

The national content standards for English language arts are based on professional research and the best classroom practices. While the standards acknowledge the importance of grammar concepts, they clearly recommend that students learn and apply their knowledge of grammar for the purpose of effective communication. By embedding grammar instruction into writing instruction, teachers can positively affect students' actual writing skills.

References

Braddock, R., Lloyd-Jones, R., & Schoer, L. *Research in Written Composition*. Urbana, IL: National Council of Teachers of English, 1963.

Calkins, L. M. "When Children Want to Punctuate: Basic Skills Belong in Context." *Language Arts* 57 (1980): 567–73.

Cooper, C. "Research Roundup: Oral and Written Composition." *English Journal* (1975): 64, 72.

DiStefano, P. & Killion, J. "Assessing Writing Skills Through a Process Approach." *English Education* 16, no. 4 (1984): 203–7.

Harris, R. J. "An Experimental Inquiry into the Functions and Value of Formal Grammar in the Teaching of Written English to Children Aged Twelve to Fourteen." Ph.D. diss., University of London, 1962.

Hillocks, G., Jr. *Research on Written Composition: New Directions for Teaching*. Urbana, IL: ERIC Clearinghouse on Reading and Communication Skills and the National Conference on Research in English, 1986.

Hillocks, G., Jr., & Smith, M. "Grammar and Usage." In *Handbook of Research on Teaching the English Language Arts*, edited by J. Flood, J. M. Jensen, D. Lapp, & J. R. Squire, 591–603. New York: Macmillan, 1991.

Mellon, J. C. *Transformational Sentence-Combining: A Method for Enhancing the Development of Syntactic Fluency in English Composition*. NCTE Research Report No. 10. Urbana, IL: National Council of Teachers of English, 1969.

National Council of Teachers of English and the International Reading Association. *Standards for the English Language Arts*. Urbana, IL: National Council of Teachers of English, 1996.

Noguchi, R. R. *Grammar and the Teaching of Writing: Limits and Possibilities*. Urbana, IL: National Council of Teachers of English, 1991.

O'Hare, F. *Sentence-Combining: Improving Student Writing Without Formal Grammar Instruction*. Urbana, IL: National Council of Teachers of English, 1973.

Shaughnessy, M. P. *Errors and Expectations: A Guide for the Teacher of Basic Writing*. New York: Oxford University Press, 1977.

Strong, W. *Creative Approaches to Sentence Combining*. Urbana, IL: ERIC and the National Council of Teachers of English, 1986.

Weaver, C. *Lessons to Share on Teaching Grammar in Context*. Portsmouth, NH: Heinemann, 1998.

Why Grammar?

The definitions of grammar vary. In this series, the term *grammar* means not only the description of parts of speech and parts of a sentence but also the topics often labeled usage and mechanics.

The questions about whether to teach grammar—and, if so, how—have confronted secondary-school English teachers for years. From the 1960s through the 1980s, university-level scholarship argued against formal grammar instruction. But teachers at middle school and high school levels had to face several unsettling realities that have surfaced in the wake of this argument.

- Some students—even native English speakers—haven't mastered the conventions of standard written English.

- Some students are not scoring well on standardized tests that require recognizing and correcting sentence-level errors.

- Some parents have demanded that schools teach their children writing skills that will get them into college, land them better entry-level jobs, and advance them in a chosen career.

In this age of raising standards, it is the philosophy of this series that all students need to know and use the conventions of standard English. To accomplish this goal, students need thorough and coherent teaching and practice. The random coverage of grammar in integrated literature anthologies is not sufficient to help students meet the standards.

How to Engage Students in the Study of Grammar

The following suggestions will help improve the study of grammar in secondary-school classrooms.

Tell Students Why They Are Using *Grammar for Writing*

To succeed in high school, on tests, and in college, students must be able to use conventions of standard English. They are learning skills and habits to last a lifetime. In jobs that require them to deal with the public (such as customer service representatives, sales personnel, and professional jobs), employees need to be able to use standard English. Companies require that their white-collar employees write and speak correctly because they represent the company. In business letters, memos, and e-mail, employees must express themselves according to the conventions of standard English.

Acknowledge That Students Already Know Grammar

Native speakers of English start speaking at a very early age. They learn where to place which words. *Grammar for Writing* helps students get around the spots that give most of us writers trouble. Students will be more open to embarking on a study of grammar if they realize there really is a limited number of concepts to deal with in order to improve their writing.

"P.S." Feature

The P.S. feature that appears in many lessons reassures students that they don't need to memorize or remember all of the terms in the lesson. It tells them which terms are important—and why.

Grammar Concepts

1. subject-verb agreement
2. verb forms and tenses
3. pronoun-antecedent agreement
4. pronoun reference and case
5. degree of modifiers
6. positioning of modifiers
7. run-on sentences and fragments
8. spelling
9. punctuation
10. commonly confused words

The Writing Process

The writing process movement dates back to the early 1970s, when Donald Murray published his article "Teaching Writing as a Process Not a Product." Faculty members at the University of New Hampshire (including Donald Murray, Donald Graves, Lucy Calkins, Nancie Atwell, and Thomas Newkirk) gave the writing process movement a home, training teachers and reporting on writing process theory in action. "Children want to write," Donald Graves wrote in 1983 (*Writing: Teachers and Children at Work,* Heinemann). "They want to write the first day they attend school." Today, the writing process movement dominates English classrooms from kindergarten through college.

Writing Workshops

At the core of the writing process are minilessons, peer response groups, and writing workshops (see Chapter 3). In a writing workshop, students complete a sustained writing activity in stages that involve planning, drafting, and revising. Prewriting (the planning stage) and revising (the improving stage) are most heavily emphasized.

You will find a writing workshop in each of the lessons in Chapter 3 of the Fourth Course book. All of these workshops deal with the following common types of writing that students are asked to do throughout their school career:

Writing Workshops

- Narrative Writing: Autobiographical Incident (pp. 36–40)

- Persuasive Writing (pp. 41–45)

- Expository Writing: Compare and Contrast Essay (pp. 46–51)

- Writing About Literature: Analyzing Fiction (pp. 52–57)

- Expository Writing: Research Paper (pp. 58–66)

- Special Writing Tasks: Essay Tests (pp. 67–70)

How to Use Them These writing workshops are flexible and can be used in different ways to meet your classroom needs. With the whole class, you might read and discuss the professional model and go over the Strategies for Writing that appear in each workshop. Notice that in each workshop the exercises take students step-by-step through the writing process. By the time they complete all of the exercises, students will complete a finished piece of writing of the type specified in the workshop. Students may work in small groups or with partners to talk about the critical thinking questions following the model and to give each other feedback on the exercises. If you prefer, students can work through the exercises individually—in class or as homework.

Writing Groups Try to make the writing groups heterogeneous, with a mixture of students of different ability levels. You might even try to have a mix of different learning styles in each group. A comfortable number for a writing group is four to six students. ELL students who are mainstreamed into regular English classes will benefit from speaking/listening interactions with members of their small writing groups.

Using the Writing Process

Emphasize to students that the writing process isn't the same for everyone. Some students like to outline carefully; others just plunge ahead from rough notes and start writing. Some begin writing with a title and introduction; others find it easier to start with the body and do an introduction and conclusion later.

Explain also that the process is recursive; that is, students can return to an earlier stage to gather more information, for example. Or they may try out a topic and find that it just doesn't work, so they discard that topic and start over again in the topic selection process. Some teachers require students to do several drafts, revising each one. Others focus on just one draft. Many teachers don't separate revising and editing; they consider all the tasks to be revising.

Steps in the writing process may have different names, but basically it goes like this:

The Writing Process

Steps	Tasks
PREWRITING (Lessons 1.1 and 1.2, pp. 9-13)	■ Use brainstorming, freewriting, class discussion, newspaper articles, clustering and other graphics, listing, and *5W-How?* questions to generate topic ideas. ■ Choose and limit topic. ■ Gather details, information; do research, if needed. ■ Organize details (make an outline). ■ Specify purpose and audience.
DRAFTING (Lesson 1.2, pp. 13–14)	■ Put prewriting notes into sentences and paragraphs. ■ Draft thesis statement (main idea of paper). ■ Draft attention-grabbing title and introduction. ■ Draft strong conclusion.
REVISING (Lesson 1.3, pp. 15–17)	■ Read draft for coherence, unity, content. See four-readings strategy (page 15). ■ Peer editors comment on draft. ■ Consider peer editors' comments. ■ Do additional drafts (second, third, fourth).
EDITING (Lesson 1.3, pp. 16–17)	■ Check for sentence completeness. ■ Find and correct errors in subject-verb agreement, verb forms, pronoun usage, and other errors in grammar and usage.
PROOFREADING (Lesson 1.4, pp. 18–19)	■ Find and correct errors in mechanics: spelling, punctuation, capitalization. ■ Utilize peer proofreading.
PUBLISHING (Lesson 1.4, p. 19)	■ Find a way to share writing with intended audience.

Resources

Atwell, Nancie. *In the Middle: New Understandings about Writing, Reading & Learning,* 2nd ed. Portsmouth, NH: Boynton/Cook, 1998.

Powell, David. *What Can I Write About? 7000 Topics for High School Students.* Urbana, IL: National Council of Teachers of English, 1981.

Random House Roget's Thesaurus. New York: Ballantine, 1996.

Strunk, William, Jr., and E. B. White. *The Elements of Style,* 4th ed. New York: Simon & Schuster, 1999.

Merriam-Webster's Collegiate Dictionary, 10th ed. Springfield, MA: Merriam-Webster, 1999.

Purposes of Writing

Help students see that there are many reasons for writing—now and in the future. Basically, these can be broken down into three categories: personal writing (self-expression), real-life writing, and writing for school.

Personal Writing

Writing as self-expression began to be emphasized in the mid-1960s, when progressive teachers introduced journals, freewriting, and other kinds of personal writing into the classrooms. James Moffett (1973) sees self-expressive modes of writing as a way of engaging student writers, even those with limited English proficiency. Everyone has stories to tell, ideas and feelings to communicate.

Journals/Diaries Encourage students to start a special notebook in which they record ideas and experiences. They might also include a list or description of "things I like"; or they can tape into their notebook excerpts from articles, poems, songs, cartoons/comic strips, photos, and ads that they find appealing. Over the course of months, such a journal becomes a rich source of topic ideas and details. Remind students to include in these journals or diaries only those things they're willing to share with their classmates.

- **Writing Logs** Prewriting notes, ideas for writing topics, proofreading logs, reflections on their writing experiences

- **Reading Logs** A record of books they've read and their comments, questions, and responses; responses to particular stories and poems, novels, essays they've read

- **Learning Logs** A record of important ideas and concepts they've learned

Sketchbooks Some students may want to create a sketchbook. They might sketch people, places, objects, and events from memory or direct observation. Encourage them to express what they've sketched in words, too. They might write on the back of a sketch or, if they're using a looseleaf notebook, interleave sketches and written descriptions.

Creative Writing Encourage students to write original poems and stories in conjunction with their study and discussion of literature genres. These may be individual, partner, or group efforts. Share finished works in class—on bulletin boards, in oral readings, or in a class newsletter or literary magazine. Tell students who are interested in creative writing to look for student writing contests and magazines (print and electronic) that publish student writing.

Real-life Writing

Experienced teachers know that students are motivated when they write for a real-life purpose and a specific audience. Here are just a few of the real-life writing situations students may engage in.

Forms, Applications, Résumés
Students must follow directions and develop the ability to summarize and express ideas clearly and concisely.

All Kinds of Letters Some letters are social (thank you notes, friendly letters, and pen-pal letters) and chatty. Others are business letters (order letters, complaint letters, letters to the editor) and formal. Students need to write in the appropriate form and language.

Research As part of their research projects, students may write letters requesting information or interviews. They may need to write letters of acknowledgment and thanks.

E-mail Students may write formal e-mail messages (requesting information, asking questions of an expert) and informal messages to friends and family. They need to learn the "netiquette"—the accepted conventions for writing e-mail messages.

Persuasion Students express and support their opinions when they write letters to the editor (see the writing workshop, p. 43), proposals for solving a school or community problem, and letters to elected representatives. The Write What You Think exercises throughout the Pupil's Edition (see, for example, p. 96) give them repeated practice in writing for persuasive purposes.

Work At work, students may write letters, memos and reports. Their writing must communicate ideas clearly and concisely.

Writing for School

Students know how important writing skills are in all their classes. Here are just a few of the reasons to write in school.

Reports In history, science, math, and other classes, students are asked to research, organize, and communicate ideas in written and oral reports. (See "Writing Across the Curriculum," pp. T36–T37.)

Paragraphs Paragraph practice helps students gain skill in expressing and developing their ideas. (See Chapter 2, pp. 21–34, for lessons devoted to developing paragraph-writing skills.) In the minicontext of writing a single paragraph, students develop all of the following:

- a natural voice
- flow (sentences that read smoothly in a sequence)
- coherence (ideas that are easy to follow)
- unity (ideas and supporting details that stick to a topic).

Essays By the Fourth Course, students should be applying their paragraph-writing skills to longer papers. (See Chapter 3, the "Writing Workshops, pp. 36–70.) Encourage students to write as much as they need to in order to express what they want to say.

Writing for Tests Increasingly, an essay question or two appear as part of standardized tests. This is part of the performance assessment movement— students are graded on how well they accomplish a writing task in the given time frame. They must formulate, develop, organize, and express their ideas in a limited time. The skills they learn in practicing paragraph development (Chapter 2) and in the writing workshops (Chapter 3) will stand them in good stead on essay tests.

Writing for a Wider Audience
Within the context of school, students have many opportunities to use their writing for a real purpose and audience.

- school paper (articles, letters to the editor, critical reviews)

- literary magazine or classroom newsletter of students' creative writing

- speeches for school-wide campaigns (elections, assemblies, rallies)

- scripts (school radio broadcasts and theater productions)

- press releases and publicity (school events and productions)

Writing Across the Curriculum in *Grammar for Writing*

Writing-across-the-curriculum programs began in the late 1960s with several researchers at the University of London Institute of Education. They proposed that writing should be an essential part of students' learning in all classes, not just in English, from kindergarten through university level. In some American schools, this policy manifests itself by encouraging teachers in all subject areas to give writing assignments, which they then help their students carry out according to the writing-process paradigm with, at times, advice from English-teacher colleagues. In other American schools, writing across the curriculum remains the purview of the language arts department in hopes that students' interest will be sparked with a variety of writing opportunities.

The following are some cross-curricular writing assignments—in addition to those that can be found throughout *Grammar for Writing*—that students can explore either under your guidance in English classes or under the guidance of subject-area teachers.

Writing Ideas

All of the following suggestions can be done as individual projects, or students can work with partners or small groups. Students should be willing to publish—that is, share—what they've written, making sure it's the best writing they can produce.

Science and Mathematics

- **Inventions** Research and write about the history of an invention, or explain how a common machine or piece of equipment works (for example, a telephone or a television).

- **History** (1) Write about the life and work of a scientist or mathematician, the discovery of a concept, or a breakthrough in a specific field of science or math. (2) Write about the origin of a mathematical concept (the concept of infinity, for example).

- **Discovery** Report on a current development in one of the sciences (for example, medical research or astronomy).

- **Original Research** Report on an experiment that you have conducted.

- **Reference Work** Create a plan for a math encyclopedia for sixth graders. Decide what articles to include and how to illustrate the articles.

Social Studies

- **Causes and Effects** Analyze the causes and/or effects of an event in American or world history.

- **What If?** Speculate on what might have happened if an important event had turned out differently.

- **What Needs Fixing?** Analyze a school or community problem, and propose a solution.

- **Cultural Studies** Select a life-cycle event (such as birth, coming of age, graduation, marriage, childbirth, death) in a current and a past culture, and compare and contrast how the two cultures mark the event.

Arts

- **Movements** Explain a specific art movement (for example, Impressionism, Cubism) with examples.

- **Lives and Works** Profile an artist and his or her work.

- **How It Works** Explain how a particular musical instrument works.

Languages Other Than English

- **Dictionary** Create a phrase dictionary for teenage travelers to a country whose language you are studying. The dictionary must include an introduction to its contents.

- **Translation** Translate a poem or short piece of prose into English from another language. Discuss the difficulties of the translation process.

Sports, Physical Education

- **Newsletter** Create a prototype for a weekly or monthly sports newsletter for your school.

- **Profile** Write a biographical sketch of a star or rookie player in your school or community.

Projects

- **Take one writer.** Do some research about a favorite writer's life and work. Write a brief biography. Analyze (more than a plot summary) two major works (plays, novels, short stories) or four poems or two movies. Adapt this approach to focus on particular artists or directors.

- **Be a critic.** Write about movies, TV shows, records, or concerts. Publish your reviews in the local paper.

- **Write your memoirs.** Write not just about one autobiographical incident—but several (see pp. 36–40). Give the book of memoirs to family members, or put it in a drawer and take it out in the year 2025.

- **Write about your heritage.** What holidays do you celebrate, and how do you celebrate them? What customs and traditions do you follow? What sayings did you hear as you were growing up? Work with other students to write a multicultural memoir about holidays.

- **Interview relatives or neighbors who are senior citizens.** Ask what they remember about their early days, what life was like where and when they grew up. Summarize your interview into discrete articles and send them to the local paper of the senior citizen's home town.

- **Do a Foxfire project.** Interview students, teachers, family members, and neighbors. Find out what they know how to do well. Get step-by-step directions to do a particular project; add photographs, diagrams, and drawings. Publish a how-to flyer or booklet.

- **Make life better.** Work to solve an actual school or community problem. Do some research. Consider possible solutions. Write a proposal to someone in charge, and lobby whoever is in power. Write editorials and letters to the editor in support of your issue.

- **Write creatively.** Set some parameters on content and language.

Encourage interested students to write original short stories, poems, or essays. Have an open mike (microphone) night or day in class with students reading what they've written. Invite other classes, parents, and families. Have students research places that publish student writing, and have them send in their work. Counsel them in advance about rejection slips.

- **Make up writing prompts on topics that will interest students.** Have students clip newspaper articles, summarize local news, and so on. Post these in the classroom and discuss them with students. This activity is a great way to interest students in community events, government, and voting. Make up brief prompts you're sure students can respond to in writing without further research. For example:

> You've been asked by the principal to come up with a proposal that will improve the school. Write your proposal and defend it.

Resources

"Ideas for Teachers" column in *English Journal*. Urbana, IL: National Council of Teachers of English, 1996.

Fulweiler, Toby, and Art Young, eds. *Programs That Work: Models and Methods for Writing Across the Curriculum.* Portsmouth, NH: Boynton/Cook, 1990.

Moffett, James. *Student-Centered Language Arts and Reading, K–13: A Handbook for Teachers.* Boston: Houghton Mifflin, 1973.

Step-by-Step Revising, Editing, and Proofreading

Many of your students would probably be happy turning in their first draft as a final paper. Help them to understand that the revising, editing, and proofreading stages in the writing process raise the standards for their own writing. What they learn from repeated practice in revising and peer editing sticks: Over the course of a year, students produce better organized, better written first drafts based on what they've learned through revising and editing.

Note that this series distinguishes between revising and editing—two steps that many teachers lump together as revising. We've separated these steps because it's hard for students to look critically at a piece of writing and see everything at once:

- **Revising** is concerned with content, organization, style, and word choice (see p. 15 in the Pupil's Edition and the four-step strategy for revising).

- **Editing** involves grammar and usage concerns.

- **Proofreading** refers to checking for errors in spelling, capitalization, and punctuation.

Self-Editing

Encourage students to let their first draft sit a while so they can approach it with "fresh eyes." Before they share their drafts with one or more peer editors, encourage them to do a round of self-editing. They can use the Revising and Editing checklists (see pp. T41–T43) that you gave them as handouts at the beginning of the year. They can also refer to the four-step revision strategy on p. 15 of the Pupil's Edition.

Peer Editing

In the days before peer editing, teachers spent a lot of their evenings marking up student papers with red pen or pencil, filling margins with abbreviations such as *Awk* (Awkward), *Frag* (Fragment), and *Sp* (Spelling). Peer editing has not only helped lighten your paper load; it is also one of the most powerful tools of the writing process. Whether students comment on each other's papers in **writing groups** or one on one as a single writer and **peer editor**, they develop skills and strategies that transfer to their own writing:

- They learn what to look for in evaluating a draft.
- They learn to ask questions about organization and content.
- They learn from others' approaches to the same assignment.
- They even learn to be tactful in expressing their comments.

It's important to get the peer editing process underway as soon as students have completed and have had a chance to do some self-evaluation of their first draft—so writers don't lose momentum. If margins are at least an inch on either side, peer editors may write comments directly on their own copy (printed or photocopied) of the draft. In some high-tech classrooms, drafts are posted on a computer. Students might write their comments directly under the draft or even e-mail their comments to the writer.

Forming Writing Groups

Writing process expert Nancie Atwell reports that in her classes she lets students choose the classmate or classmates they think can help them on the part of a paper they are struggling with at the time. "In the writing workshop," she says, "small groups form and disband in the minutes it takes for a writer to call on one or more other writers, move to a conference corner, share a piece or discuss a problem, and go back to work with a new perspective on the writing" (*In the Middle: Writing, Reading, and Learning with Adolescents*, p. 41).

You may want to organize students into groups that stay together for several weeks or throughout the time devoted to one writing workshop. Such stable groups work well with block scheduling and with ongoing projects. Students get to know and trust each other as they try out topic ideas,

discuss specific writing problems, and share their drafts and revisions.

The same group might work together on a writing project—for example, a compare and contrast paper or any of the project ideas mentioned on pages T37–T38. Think of having a writing group do speaking/listening and media projects, too: perhaps a panel discussion with a question-and-answer period on a problem or issue that the group researches, or maybe a multimedia project.

Peer Editing Abbreviated

Depending on your class, you might use a brief peer editing checklist like the following; or the longer, more detailed checklists that follow:

Brief Peer Editing Checklist

What Are the Strong Points?
- What are the best parts of the paper?
- What has the writer done especially well?

What Are the Weak Points?
- What parts of the paper need more work?
- Do you have any questions about the paper?
- Can you make any specific suggestions for improving the writing?

Revising in Greater Depth

Here is a much more detailed Revising Checklist, one that students may refer to in revising their own work and when commenting on each other's papers. You might want to produce another version of this checklist (and the editing and proofreading ones as well) for students to refer to throughout the year. This checklist applies to expository writing, the kind of writing that students are most often asked to do in school (a comparison and contrast essay, for example, or a critical review). In addition, see the boxed revising questions, which refer specifically to persuasive, narrative, and descriptive writing.

Revising Checklist

Purpose and Audience
❏ How well does the writing accomplish its intended purpose?

❏ Are the language and details appropriate for the intended audience?

Main Idea
❏ What is the main idea? Is it clearly and directly stated?

Supporting Details
❏ How well does the writer develop the main idea and major points? Are there enough interesting supporting details?

❏ Would the writing be improved by dropping or by adding information? Where? What's missing?

❏ Do you have unanswered questions? What are they?

❏ Would adding details make the writing more interesting? Where? What kind of details would you suggest?

Organization
❏ How well can you follow the writer's ideas?

❏ Would a different organization help?

❏ Do any parts of the draft stray from the main idea?

Sentence Style
❏ Do transitions help the reader follow ideas?

❏ Can unnecessary words, details, and sentences be dropped?

❏ Do sentences read smoothly? Can some be combined?

❏ Do sentence lengths, beginnings, and structures vary?

Voice
❏ Does the writing sound natural? Are word choice and sentence structures awkward and difficult?

❏ Is the writing appropriate for the intended audience?

Word by Word
❏ Are words used precisely? Can you find vague, overused words that should be replaced? Would vivid verbs and specific nouns improve the writing? Where?

❏ Are the sentences overloaded with too many modifiers or too many prepositional phrases?

❏ Can you spot any clichés?

Title
❏ Does the title capture the reader's interest? Does it accurately reflect the paper's content?

Introduction and Conclusion

❏ Does the introduction make you want to read more? What suggestions can you make for improving it?

❏ Does it introduce the topic and the main idea?

❏ Does the conclusion end the essay strongly?

You may want to offer students variations on peer checklists from time to time. One option is to generate mode-specific checklists such as the ones below or even assignment-specific checklists. (See also the discussion of rubrics on pp. T52–T55.)

Mode-Specific Checklists	
Checklist for Persuasive Writing	❏ Is the writer's opinion clearly stated? ❏ Does the writer give at least two reasons to support that opinion? ❏ Are the reasons themselves supported by convincing evidence (facts, statistics, examples, anecdotes, quotations, and so on)? ❏ Do you understand what the writer wants the reader to do? ❏ Has the writer persuaded you? Why or why not?
Checklist for Narrative Writing	❏ Does the beginning make you want to read more? ❏ Does the writer *show* characters in action and let you hear what they say, or does the writer simply *tell* you about characters? ❏ Does the writing include sensory details? ❏ Are the writer's comparisons relevant and illuminating? ❏ Has the writer used specific nouns and vivid verbs (especially, as alternatives for *said*)? ❏ Is the ending satisfying?
Checklist for Descriptive Writing	❏ Can you picture the setting? ❏ Does the writing include specific sensory details? ❏ Are the comparisons fresh? ❏ Does the organization of details (for example, proceeding from near to far, left to right, or top to bottom) make sense? ❏ Does the description establish an overall mood? What is it?

Editing and Proofreading

As previously mentioned, this series separates the revising task (which focuses on content, style, and organization) from the editing task (which focuses on grammar and usage). Proofreading is the stage of the writing process when students look for mechanical errors in spelling, punctuation, and capitalization. These checklists provide references either for the teacher or the student.

Editing Checklist

❑ Is every sentence grammatically complete (not a fragment or a run-on)? *Lesson 5.1*

❑ Do subjects and verbs agree in number and person? *Chapter 9*

❑ Are the correct forms of pronouns used? *Chapter 10*

❑ Does each pronoun clearly refer to an antecedent? *Lesson 10.5*

❑ Are verb tenses used consistently, unless there is good reason to vary them? *Chapter 8*

❑ Are the correct forms of irregular verbs used? *Chapter 8*

❑ Are the correct forms of plural nouns and the comparative forms of adjectives and adverbs used? *Chapter 4*

Proofreading Checklist

❑ Is every word spelled correctly? Check a dictionary if you're unsure. *Chapter 16*

❑ Have homophones been confused (*their* instead of *there*, for example)? *Chapter 16*

❑ Do proper nouns and proper adjectives begin with capital letters? *Chapter 15*

❑ Does every sentence begin with a capital letter and end with an end punctuation mark? *Chapters 13 and 14*

❑ Are commas used correctly in all of their many uses? *Chapter 13*

❑ Is dialogue punctuated correctly? *Lesson 14.6*

Resources

In the classroom, students should have access to several copies of a good college dictionary and a dictionary-style thesaurus.

Vocabulary

In many lessons, you'll find an extra feature: Enriching Your Vocabulary. One word from an example or exercise sentence is explored in depth. These vocabulary side features give the word's origin, meanings, related forms, and some information about how and when the word is used. Some of them also offer an example sentence that uses the vocabulary word. In the fourth course, words highlighted in the Vocabulary side features have been drawn from Sadlier's *Vocabulary Workshop* program.

How to Use These Vocabulary Features

Make sure students digest these features by taking a few minutes to go over each one—whenever you can fit these features in—with the whole class. Here are some suggested activities for using these side features and for helping students to acquire new vocabulary words:

- **Create your own exercise.** This type of exercise appears occasionally in the Grammar, Usage, and Mechanics chapters. Ask students to think of other example sentences using the word in the Enriching Your Vocabulary feature. They might do this as an individual writing assignment or, better yet, ask volunteers to write example sentences on the board. Discuss with the class as a whole or in small groups whether the example sentences use the words precisely.

- **Check a dictionary.** Try to have several good dictionaries in class (an unabridged dictionary and two or three different college dictionaries). Ask students to compare the etymologies and meanings given in several dictionaries: Do they agree with the vocabulary note in the text and with each other? This kind of activity gives students practice in dictionary skills, which will help them work independently to discover the meanings, origins, and usage of unfamiliar words they find in their reading.

- **Create new vocabulary features.** Once you've covered several of the vocabulary features, ask students to imitate the approach. Have each student write an original Enriching Your Vocabulary feature for one unfamiliar word they come across in a literature selection, newspaper, or magazine—even one that they hear on television or radio. Have students share their features with the class or a small group. You might do this on a weekly basis.

- **Keep a vocabulary notebook.** Have students keep a notebook (or part of a notebook) devoted to new words they encounter in their reading. Encourage them to include words from other subjects, too. For each entry, they might list brief definitions and example sentences. On a regular basis, you might have students get together in small groups to teach each other the words they've recorded in their notebooks.

- **Compile a dictionary.** As an ongoing cooperative activity, you might have students work in small groups to create their own minidictionaries for a field that interests them: computer jargon, sports terms, music terminology, and so on. Give students a choice of which group to join, but limit group size to four or five.

- **Introduce word puzzles and games.** Enrich your classroom with word puzzles and games (crossword puzzles from the newspaper, anagrams, and so on) that students can use when they've completed their classwork. Encourage students to work together in teams to make up other puzzles, word games, and puns.

Other Approaches to Vocabulary Study

Here are some other tried-and-true ways to enlarge students' vocabulary:

Reading and More Reading Many studies show that the most effective way for students to enlarge their vocabulary is through the sustained silent reading of books that they choose. Assemble a classroom library that includes a wide range of materials for students with varying abilities. You might work with a school or public librarian (media specialist) to create a minilibrary containing books

designed to appeal to your students. Emphasize multicultural content and authors, popular young adult (YA) fiction, and high-interest nonfiction. Add the classics that you think will appeal to your students. Students might meet in reading groups to discuss what they're reading and to recommend books to each other. You might have them write critical reviews or present oral reports. They can write in reading logs—noting their informal responses and questions about what they have read.

Context clues Teach or review the skills needed to use **context clues**, the words and sentences surrounding the unfamiliar word that help students guess the meanings of unfamiliar words. Give students example sentences showing the following kinds of context clues: definitions, appositives, synonyms, comparison/contrast, and other kinds of clues embedded in surrounding sentences.

Internet Explain to students that another tool for improving vocabulary might be using recommended internet sites:

http://www.m-w.com/netdict.htm The thesaurus link gives related words, contrasted words, and antonyms. Recommended for all four grade levels.

http://www.thesaurus.com/ This is Roget online. It offers extensive lists. No antonyms are given. It is a fairly sophisticated site and best for the higher grades.

Connecting Technology to Grammar for Writing

Computers make both writing and researching so much easier. Students love working—as well as playing—on computers, but if your students and classrooms do not have access to computers, that fact won't affect the quality of their writing. Assure them that excellent writing still arrives in longhand on ruled paper (or however you require that it be turned in).

Word Processing: Writing on the Computer

The positive side of word processing is that both revising and editing is a snap and printed papers are clean and legible. The negative side of word processing is that it's easy for students to copy others' papers and turn in the work as their own. You can avoid plagiarism by requiring students to hand in various stages of their work, such as prewriting notes, outlines, and lists of sources.

Here are the basic skills students must know in order to produce papers on a word processing program:

- how to create and save documents
- how to set margins and line spacing
- how to select fonts (encourage them not to get too fancy)
- how to print documents

Writing Process

Word processing can be used for every stage in the writing process. Here are some specific suggestions:

Prewriting

- To gather ideas for topics, students can use the computer for freewriting, brainstorming, and listing. For freewriting, tell students to turn down the brightness on the monitor so they're not distracted by what they've already written.

- Students can take notes on the computer instead of on note cards. Encourage them to set up separate documents for each source. When they organize their notes, they'll work from printouts of their notes and can highlight the information they find most useful. Just as note cards should have a heading and note the page number of the source, tell students to put in headings and note page numbers whenever they take notes.

- Working with printouts of their notes, students can easily draft and rework an outline on a computer, using tabs for indenting.

Drafting

- Remind students how important it is to save their work regularly and to back up their documents in case of a power failure or computer crash.

- Assure students that there is no "right" way to write on a computer. Some students (those who say they "think better" writing in longhand and those who are new to keyboarding) may prefer writing and revising in longhand. That's acceptable, too. Remind them to leave wide margins and extra space around their handwritten drafts so that there's room to revise. As preparation for revising, double spacing is a good idea so that there is room to revise on printouts.

Revising

The best part of word processing is revising. It's easy to replace, insert, move, and delete words, sentences, and paragraphs.

- Encourage students to try out changes and various different versions and to read aloud to themselves what they've written. If they don't want to "lose" a version of their writing, they can keep the original, make a copy, and revise on the copy.

- Some students find it easier to print out a draft, revise in longhand in pencil or pen, and then keyboard their changes. Others prefer revising directly on-screen. Any way that works is fine.

Proofreading

Most word processing programs have built-in grammar and spell checkers. Make sure students realize that these aren't foolproof. Students still must proofread their own papers carefully; exchanging papers with a peer proof-

reader is an extra safeguard. Students should proofread first drafts, revised drafts, and the final paper.

- Advise students to proofread by reading the whole paper slowly. Reading aloud to themselves might help.

- Warn students that a spell checker won't detect extra words, missing words, and words used incorrectly. As long as a word is spelled correctly, the spell checker approves. For instance, it lets the two errors in this sentence pass unnoticed:

  Mickey order too pizzas with peppers, mushrooms, and olives.

- Grammar checkers will alert students to errors in capitalization, commonly confused words, hyphenation errors, misused words, double negatives, passive construction, punctuation, sentence structure, subject-verb agreement, wordiness, and so on. However, no grammar checker is foolproof. A grammar checker may indicate an error when there is no error, and it may make suggestions that are incorrect. Tell students that the responsibility for correct grammar in their writing is theirs alone.

- Encourage proofreading skills in your class by insisting that students who use word processors turn in a clean final paper—without ink corrections or whiteout.

Harnessing Software for *Grammar for Writing*

Invite students to list and discuss the features of software that make writing easier for them. Raise their consciousness about the connections between technology and their writing assignments. Make sure that at least the following dozen features are at the top of your students' lists:

1. networking and e-mail For helping one another generate ideas during prewriting and for sharing responses to one another's drafts; for distribution—that is, publishing—of finished documents across the aisle or around the world

2. outlining software For help in organizing main ideas and details during prewriting and later

3. cut-and-paste function of a word processor For moving words, sentences, paragraphs, and sections during revising and editing

4. find-and-replace function of a word processor For global replacement of one term or spelling for another at any stage

5. save and save-as functions of a word processor For easily comparing and contrasting drafts

6. thesaurus tool on a word processor For quickly finding alternative vocabulary during any stage

7. spelling tool on a word processor For superficial proofreading (Students must do their own proofreading if they want to catch problems with homonyms, typographical errors, and so on.)

8. grammar tool on a word processor For sentence-level analysis (Students must decide whether to accept the tool's suggested revision.)

9. drawing programs, page-design programs, and other features of desktop-publishing software For professional formatting and the inclusion of nontext material (e.g., photographs, drawings) in reports

10. online searches to locate pertinent documents For getting information and facts for research projects

11. discussion groups Whether synchronous or not, to provide access to people seriously interested in and often well informed about topics students are researching

12. hypertext links For direct access to online sources that a student has used in putting together a research report and that readers may want to review for themselves

Evaluating Internet Information

Emphasize to students that they should not believe everything they read, see, or hear on the Web. Information gleaned from a Web site could be coming from a twelve-year-old, a university library, or a business. Students must learn to evaluate information they find on the Web for bias, accuracy, and current information. They should get in the habit of double-checking what they find on the Web in additional sources.

To evaluate information, students need to know where it is coming from—literally. They must notice and make deductions based on the top-level domain, the three letters at or toward the end of a Web site's address. The letters have meaning.

- **.gov** A local, state, or national government [Information from such a source is generally reliable.]

- **.edu** An educational institution [The source may be a research department at an eminent university or a fourth-grade class.]

- **.org** An organization [Any organization may have an agenda—that is, a bias—which students must take into consideration.]

- **.com** A commercial—that is, business—source [Students must consider whether the site's information is biased to encourage purchases or other commercial interaction.]

- **.net** A network [Anyone can create a home page and post it here.]

Reliable Sites for Teachers and Students

You and your students may enjoy identifying Web sites helpful to class work by searching with key terms such as *standard English*, *grammar*, and *OWL* (for "online writing lab"). Here are sites that have been checked for reliability and suitability. Remember that Web sites are in constant flux and sites change overnight. Do your own screening before recommending them to your students.

English as a Second Language
http://www.comenius.com This site includes "Fluency through Fables" and "The Weekly Idiom." There are interactive features. There are links for many languages.

Grammar, Usage, Mechanics
http://andromeda.rutgers.edu/~jlynch /Writing/ The site is very clear and helpful on relevant grammatical issues.

http://webster.commnet.edu/HP/pages /darling/original.htm This takes the student to a site called "Guide to Grammatical Writing." There are features on sentences, paragraphs, essays, forms of communication (e.g., business letters), and grammar.

Research on the Web
http://www.marlboro.edu/~jsheehy/ writing/ This site is called the Clear Writing Program. It is full of useful information and includes links for *writing* as well as research.

http://ipl.org/teen/aplus/aplus.htm Here, students can access the writing process pages, the Web research pages, and a variety of links. This site is geared to teens.

Writing Process
http://owl.english.purdue.edu This site is geared more toward teachers than toward students, though students will find the writing links useful. These include over 130 handouts on the writing process, grammar, punctuation, job searches, business letters, ESL, and so on. There are extensive lists of Web research links and links to the Purdue libraries.

Using *Grammar for Writing* with English Language Learners

Variously called ESL (English as a Second Language) students, EFL (English as a Foreign Language) students, nonnative speakers, English-language learners (ELL), and multilingual writers, students for whom English is not a first language give you a chance to raise everyone's consciousness about the respect that all languages and dialects deserve. Here are some strategies for giving ELL students a chance to talk about languages and demonstrate what languages other than English sound and look like:

- Conduct an informal survey at the beginning of the term, asking students

  - What other languages do you speak, read, and write besides English?

  - What language(s) do you speak at home?

  - What language(s) besides English have you studied in school? How well do you speak it? Write it? Read it? Understand it when it is spoken to you?

  - How did you learn the rules for forming sentences in your first language? In the other language(s)?

- Give native English speakers a chance to hear the sounds of other languages by asking ELL students to translate into their native language and orally deliver conversational sentences based on the following English ones:

  - Hi. My name is _____.

  - I am _____ years old.

  - My hobbies are _____.

  - The kind of music I like best is _____, and _____ is one of my favorite songs.

  - Good-bye for now.

- Ask ELL students to identify ways in which their first language differs from English. Encourage them to talk about what is giving them the most trouble in learning to speak and write English.

Recognizing Problem Areas for ELL Students

The following table identifies some of the problems ELL students have with English. It lists chapters and lessons from the *Grammar for Writing* series to which you can direct students with those problems.

Grammar for Writing and ELL Problems

Problem Area in English	Comment	Grammar for Writing Treatment, Fourth Course
ADJECTIVE CLAUSES	Forming and positioning adjective clauses cause problems for speakers of Asian languages, of Arabic and Hebrew, and even of Latin-based languages.	Lesson 7.2
ARTICLES	ELL students often leave out the article before a singular count noun.	Lesson 4.4
CAPITALIZATION	Arabic, Chinese, and Hebrew do not use capital letters; Dutch and German capitalize some forms of the second-person pronoun; German caps all nouns.	Chapter 15
EXPLETIVES	Spanish speakers sometimes omit subjects, saying "Is raining."	Chapter 5 covers the "It is raining" sentence structure.
HOMOPHONES	Speakers of Asian languages in particular may be confused by the concept of words sounding alike but having different meanings.	Chapter 12
NEGATION	Multiple negation is common in French and Russian, among other languages.	Lesson 11.3
PLURALS	Some Asian languages have no plural forms for nouns.	Lesson 4.1, Chapter 9, Lesson 16.4
PREFIXES AND SUFFIXES	These word parts are absent in Asian languages.	Lesson 16.3
PREPOSITIONS	English distinguishes between *in* and *on*; Spanish uses *en* for both.	Lessons 4.7 and 6.1
SILENT LETTERS	There are no silent letters in Spanish.	Chapter 16
SUBJECTS, DOUBLE	Some languages add personal pronouns as suffixes or prefixes, leading ELL speakers to say, "Maria she is pretty."	Lessons 5.2, 5.5, 10.1
TENSES	▪ Certain English verbs don't work in the present progressive, but ESL students may say or write, "I am knowing the answer." ▪ In some languages, time is not signaled by word endings but rather by words that native English speakers would call adverbs.	Lessons 4.3 and 8.5
WORD ORDER	▪ In some languages, word order determines the part of speech. For example, the verb is the last word in sentences in Turkish, Korean, and Japanese. ▪ In Russian, subject and object may switch places without affecting meaning.	Lessons 5.1, 5.2, 5.8, 5.9, and 13.1

Assessment in *Grammar for Writing*

The *Grammar for Writing* series has assessment built right in. In this age of assessment and accountability, you'll want some ongoing measures of how well students are doing in the course of the term. The series offers the following different types of assessment in each Pupil's Edition and Test Booklet:

Objective Evaluation

- **Mid-Chapter and Chapter reviews** In each book, Mid-Chapter Reviews and Chapter Reviews help students review the grammar, usage, and mechanics concepts learned in the preceding lessons. Each review is broken down into exercises that focus on one lesson or one particular grammar, usage, or mechanics problem.

- **Cumulative Reviews** At the end of Chapters 7, 12, and 16, a two-page Cumulative Review covers the preceding chapters in that section. Use these Cumulative Reviews as mastery tests or diagnostic tests depending on your classroom needs.

- **Grammar, Usage, and Mechanics Tests** These objective tests differ from the Cumulative Reviews; the tests incorporate the standardized test format of the PSAT writing exam. Test items include both error recognition and error correction. Again, you may use these materials either as mastery tests or diagnostic tests. Note that the optional assessment component of *Grammar for Writing*, the *Grammar for Writing Test Booklet*, contains test items in standardized-test formats, as well as other kinds of items.

Lightening the Paper Load

Consider letting students help you in scoring objective tests. Have students exchange papers and score them as you go over answers in class; ask for volunteers to give the answers. A whole-class discussion of test items gives students a chance to ask questions. This will reinforce understanding and help students who may still be confused.

Evaluating Responses to Writing Exercises

Grammar for Writing includes many writing exercises that can't be scored objectively, such as the exercises in the Composition Unit (Chapters 1–3), as well as the exercises based on notes, exercises with paragraphs needing revision, and the Revising and Editing Worksheets in the grammar, usage, and mechanics sections (Chapters 4–16). It's up to you to decide whether—and how—to grade these writing exercises or simply to check that students have completed them.

Revising and Editing Worksheets

These one-page themed exercises are examples of poor writing. Students are directed to work individually or with a partner or group to improve the writing. Typically, instructions ask students to correct errors covered in the preceding lessons and to combine sentences and eliminate fragments and run-ons. *There is no single correct answer to any of the revision exercises in the pupil's edition.*

What students will learn from these exercises—especially by comparing their revisions and edits with those of their classmates—is that there are many workable solutions to writing problems and many different ways to communicate the same idea. This empowering insight should make students more confident as they revise and edit their own writing. To get the most benefit from the Revising and Editing Worksheets, direct students to compare revisions (sentence-by-sentence or paragraph-by-paragraph) in a whole-class session.

It is impossible to give students' work on the Revising and Editing Worksheets a percentage score; they contain many errors and invite many ways to revise and edit. Also, remember that students may be working with partners or a group, so the final result is a shared effort. If you feel you must record a number score, try judging the revisions on a 1–4 scale (with four being "excellent"). Give students points for each of the following criteria, and then find the average score.

The revised and edited version:

- communicates ideas and information clearly.
- is made up of complete sentences (no fragments or run-ons) that read smoothly and naturally.
- has no errors related to the chapter content.
- has no (or very few) errors in grammar and usage.
- uses punctuation correctly.
- spells words correctly.

Rubrics for Evaluating Students' Paragraphs and Essays

You can measure students' original writing using the rubrics on p. T54, which help to identify students' performance levels. Note that the rubrics are generic (they apply to all types of essays) and are based on a six-level scale. (You may find that in your classroom a four-level scale, beginning at Level 4, is more suitable.)

At the beginning of the term, share these (or your own) rubrics with students as a handout that they can keep in their notebooks. Let students know exactly what your standards are, so that they know what to aim for. You might also give students copies of essays from unidentified writers as an example of each level of performance. Reading and discussing these sample essays will clarify for students what you expect of them.

Writing Performance Levels

	The student's writing
LEVEL 6	• consistently pursues a strong central purpose across a complex range of ideas, skillfully engages the reader, and shows exceptional insight into the subject • includes main ideas that are developed comprehensively and are supported with a variety of logical reasons and detailed examples • is skillfully organized • shows distinctive style through skillful and expressive use of vocabulary, phrasing, and sentence structure • demonstrates essentially error-free control of grammar, punctuation, capitalization, and spelling
LEVEL 5	• consistently pursues a central purpose, holds the interest of the reader, and shows insight into the subject • includes main ideas that are developed and supported by a variety of reasons and examples • is effectively organized • shows emerging style through the effective use of vocabulary, phrasing, and sentence structure • consistently demonstrates the accurate use of grammar, punctuation, capitalization, and spelling
LEVEL 4	• shows a consistent purpose, communicates to the reader, and connects to the writer's knowledge of the subject • includes main ideas that are organized, developed, and supported by reasons and examples • shows suitable vocabulary, phrasing, and sentence structure • generally demonstrates the accurate use of grammar, punctuation, capitalization, and spelling
LEVEL 3	• shows a purpose but may be inconsistent in communicating to the reader or connecting to the writer's knowledge of the subject • includes main ideas that may be organized or partially developed and supported by some reasons and examples • may show imprecise use of vocabulary, phrasing, and sentence structure • includes some errors in the use of grammar, punctuation, capitalization, and spelling
LEVEL 2	• attempts to connect the writer's knowledge to the subject and may not show a purpose • is typically brief, unorganized, and underdeveloped • may include frequent errors in the use of grammar, capitalization, punctuation, and spelling
LEVEL 1	• is too brief or disorganized to communicate to the reader • may not connect the writer's knowledge to the subject • typically includes many errors in the use of grammar, capitalization, and spelling

Performance Levels, 1994. Reprinted with permission from the California Department of Education.

Writing Portfolios

The movement for performance assessment has gained strength over many years. Today, writing portfolios, an essential part of performance assessment, are part of most English classrooms. Writing portfolios give students tangible evidence that their efforts pay off. The portfolios can be made available for review by students' new teachers in subsequent terms.

Many teachers have students create two different kinds of writing portfolios:

- **A works-in-progress portfolio** For every finished piece of writing, students include prewriting notes, outlines, early drafts, revised drafts, and even a brief reflection on their writing experience. Students may also include journals, sketches, logs, and notes about their reading.

- **A best-efforts portfolio** This portfolio shows only the *finished pieces of writing*, examples of what students think are their best writing efforts.

Teacher-Student Conferences

An integral part of performance assessment is teacher-student conferences. One-on-one conferencing helps you assess performance and motivates students to raise their own standards.

Test Booklet

For every course of *Grammar for Writing*, a separate Test Booklet is available for purchase. The Test Booklet contains a separate test for every chapter as well as a Diagnostic Test and a Mastery Test. Items take standardized test formats: error-recognition and error correction. Here is an example of an error recognition question from the Fourth Course Mastery Test.

Directions: Fill in the circle for each sentence that contains an error.

1. Ⓐ Ⓑ Ⓒ Ⓓ
   A. He and I are on the school paper together.
   B. Of the two of them, she is the best skater.
   C. Just between you and me, our band needs work.
   D. Michel or Suki are representing our grade at the conference.

Note that there are two incorrect sentences, both B and D.

Here's why:

B is incorrect. The sentence should use the word *better*, not *best*, because only two people are being compared, so the comparative form is needed.

D is incorrect. The verb should be *is*, not *are*. Two singular subjects connected by or take a singular verb.

Diagnostic Test

A four-page Diagnostic Test appears at the beginning of each Test Booklet. You may use this test at the beginning of the school term to determine students' strengths and weaknesses. Each question on the Diagnostic Test is devoted to a single problem area.

Tallying class results will also reveal the grammar, usage, and mechanics skills that the class as a whole needs to learn and review. Use the Diagnostic Test scores and the errors on students' first batch of papers to decide which textbook lessons to use with the whole class and which lessons should be reserved for individuals or small groups.

Mastery Test

Use the four-page Mastery Test to assess the progress students have made during the term. You might plan to hold brief individual conferences with each student to discuss the student's work as a whole and to identify those skills that still need work.

Students whose Mastery Test scores indicate that they are still having trouble (with subject-verb agreement, for example) might work together in small groups to review appropriate lessons and to go over the exercises together.

You might ask these students to create their own exercise items in the style of exercise items in the Pupil's Edition. For example, a pair of students working together might write ten sentences that test knowledge of subject-verb agreement (similar to Exercise 2 on page 192 of Fourth Course, for example). Exercise writers can then exchange exercises with another team and work together to answer the exercise questions. Finally, both teams (writers and exercise takers) can get together to see if their answers agree.

Chapter Tests

Most Chapter Tests are four pages; a few are two pages long. The Chapter Test focuses entirely on concepts taught in the chapter lessons. In addition to error recognition and error correction items in a standardized-test format, many Chapter Tests end with a writing prompt. Four-page tests may also contain a paragraph to be revised.

Writing Prompts

These are a variety of writing exercises that are similar to the Write What You Think exercises in the Pupil's Edition. Students are asked to express an opinion on a topic or issue related to the content of a preceding exercise. They don't need any additional information to express and support an opinion.

Paragraph Revision

Some of the four-page Chapter Tests contain paragraphs that students are to revise. These are similar to the revision exercises found in the pupil's edition.

Test Book Answer Key

A separate Answer Key is provided with each package of Student Test Booklets.

Answer Key

Chapter 5

Exercise 8 Combining Sentences

1. Photography developed in the 1820s and became a new art form.

2. The scenes and faces in photographs can be both moving and powerful.

3. During the Civil War, Mathew Brady and his assistants photographed soldiers and battle scenes.

4. In 1888, George Eastman's box camera and roll film made photography easy for everyone.

5. Margaret Bourke-White, Walker Evans, and Dorothea Lange photographed Americans during the Great Depression of the 1930s.

Exercise 13 Editing Run-on Sentences

Answers will vary. Sample answers are given.

1. Freedom Riders rode buses in the South. Their goal was to end racial segregation on public buses.

2. Alaska became the forty-ninth state in 1959, and Hawaii became the fiftieth state in that same year.

3. Anthropology is the scientific study of human beings; similarly, archaeology is the scientific study of ancient societies.

4. Lewis Carroll wrote *Alice in Wonderland*, but in real life he was Charles Lutwidge Dodgson, a mathematics lecturer at Oxford.

5. Butterflies, cockroaches, and fleas are insects. Scientists have identified more than a million species of insects.

CHAPTER REVIEW

Exercise C Combining Sentences

Answers will vary. Sample answers are given.

1. Ellen and her sister left at 5 A.M. for a bike ride at Shark Valley.

2. The baseball stadium holds fifty thousand people, and every seat was sold.

3. When Li Jian finished playing Beethoven's "Moonlight Sonata," the audience applauded enthusiastically.

4. Joe, Amy, and Columbus are counselors at a summer camp.

5. Lori lost her driver's license and applied for a new one.

6. Either Jed or his brother will return the library book and pay the fine.

7. The speed limit near a school is fifteen miles an hour and is strictly enforced.

8. Weekends, Jo and her friends go to the mall.

9. The meeting was scheduled for 9 A.M., but by 8:30 every seat was taken.

10. Lee wants to attend the U.S. Military Academy at West Point and has written to her senator.

Chapter 6

MID-CHAPTER REVIEW

Exercise C Editing Sentence Beginnings

Sentences will vary. Sample answers are given.

1. On Thursday, Harvey hiccupped for hours, including all through his algebra final. PREP, PART

2. At the graduation assembly, Mrs. Gittleson handed out the achievement awards. PREP

3. Wailing and sobbing, the child refused to leave the toy department. PART

4. Kneeling in the hot sun, the elderly couple weeded the vegetable garden behind their house. PART

5. Turning once for a last look and a wave, Josie boarded the train. PART

Exercise 15 Combining Sentences with Appositives

1. Geronimo, an Apache leader, attended Teddy Roosevelt's inauguration.
2. The reformer Susan B. Anthony worked to obtain the vote for women.
3. This ancient Greek statue, *Venus de Milo*, is famous for its beauty.
4. Portuguese is spoken in Brazil, the largest South American country.
5. World War II ended in Europe on V-E Day, May 8, 1945.
6. Sean's dog Sniffles disappeared three days ago.
7. I play my favorite CD, Vivaldi's "The Four Seasons," loudly.
8. Diana got an *A* on Friday's test, her algebra final.
9. This postcard is from my friend Jerrie in London.
10. Ben's job, working in a bookstore, starts today after school.

CHAPTER REVIEW

Exercise C Combining Sentences
Students' sentences will vary. Do not penalize them if they use a technique that's different from the suggested phrase.

1. Many people prefer reading the original novel to watching a movie version.
2. *The Adventures of Huckleberry Finn*, Mark Twain's greatest novel, has been made into a movie and a musical.
3. Songs were written for a 1974 movie version of *The Adventures of Huckleberry Finn*.
4. Ron Howard, playing the role of Huckleberry Finn, starred in a TV adaptation.
5. *Big River*, another musical version of *The Adventures of Huckleberry Finn*, was unsuccessful on Broadway.

6. *Les Misérables* was a very successful musical based on a long novel by the French novelist Victor Hugo.
7. The musical's writers decided to cut the novel to the bare bones of its plot.
8. Adapted from poems by T. S. Eliot, *Cats* is the longest-running Broadway musical.
9. You can meet the original cats in T. S. Eliot's *Old Possum's Book of Practical Cats*.
10. Many movies adapted from great novels have been unsuccessful.

Chapter 7

Exercise 9 Sentences with Adjective Clauses
Even though the directions ask students to turn the second sentence into an adjective clause, many sentences can also be combined by turning the first sentence into a clause.

1. Blood plasma is a colorless liquid which contains red blood cells, white blood cells, and blood platelets.
2. George Washington Carver, who was a chemist and a botanist, developed hundreds of uses for the peanut.
3. Mary Cassatt is an American Impressionist painter whose paintings often portray mothers with children.
4. In 1947, an observer who saw strange objects in the sky near Mt. Rainier coined the term *flying saucer*.
5. Nitrogen is a chemical element which makes up almost 80 percent of Earth's atmosphere.

Exercise 10 Sentences with Adverb Clauses
Answers may vary. Accept any combined sentence that contains an adverb clause.

1. The Beast turns into a handsome prince when Beauty agrees to marry him.
2. Don Quixote attacks a windmill because he thinks it is a giant.
3. As soon as Dorothy clicks her ruby-red shoes together, she finds herself back in Kansas.
4. According to Aesop's fable, the ever-plodding tortoise won the race even though the sleeping hare could run much faster.
5. The giant chased Jack down the beanstalk after Jack stole the goose that laid golden eggs.

MID-CHAPTER REVIEW

Exercise C Combining Sentences: Using Subordinate Clauses
Answers will vary somewhat. Make sure students have put a comma after an introductory adverb clause.
1. Laura volunteers at a nursing home where her mother works.
2. Howie, who is my older brother, coaches a Little League team.
3. Julie's poem, which she wrote in Mr. Li's class, will appear in the literary magazine.
4. I have a great idea that you will like.
5. Nora, who lives in Hawaii, and Ben, who lives in California, send each other e-mail every night.
6. The Spraggs had to leave their house for two days while their street was flooded. [or . . . because their street was flooded.]
7. Unless it's pouring, we'll leave for the beach at eight o'clock.
8. Kris and Jenny are best friends, although they don't like the same movies.
9. Until he met Gwen, George didn't have many friends.

10. Ralph takes his dog for a long walk every day after he gets home from work.

GRAMMAR TEST: CHAPTERS 4–7

Exercise 3 Combining Sentences
Students' sentences may vary.
1. She was born on June 14, 1811, in Litchfield, Connecticut.
2. Have you read Harriet Beecher Stowe's famous novel, *Uncle Tom's Cabin*?
3. *Uncle Tom's Cabin* was first published serially, from 1851 to 1852, in an abolitionist newspaper.
4. In her novel, Stowe, who was violently opposed to slavery, powerfully portrays the suffering of slaves.
5. Stowe's novel was extremely popular, selling more than 300,000 copies in a single year and increasing antislavery sentiments in the North.

Chapter 8

Exercise 12 Using the Active Voice
1. Sadat and Begin signed the Camp David agreements in 1978.
2. Keep the passive voice. The sentence has no "performer" of the action.
3. Joe Louis won sixty-three of his sixty-six professional fights.
4. Edgar Allan Poe wrote "The Raven" in 1845.
5. Keep the passive voice. The sentence has no "performer" of the action. *Also accept,* One finds the koala bear only in eastern Australia.
6. Linus Pauling won both the Nobel Prize for Chemistry and the Nobel Peace Prize.
7. The Incas built the city of Machu Picchu about 1500 A.D.
8. The Rio Grande forms the border between Mexico and the United States.

9. Keep the passive voice. The sentence has no "performer" of the action. *Also accept*, Scientists have identified nearly 8,500 species of birds.
10. Jonathan Swift wrote *Gulliver's Travels*, a satire.

Chapter 9

MID-CHAPTER REVIEW

Exercise A Writing Complete Sentences

Students' sentences will vary. Sample sentences are given.

1. Nobody in the room has a calculator.
2. One of my favorite movies is *Titanic*.
3. A few of my best CDs are missing.
4. All of my teachers give a lot of homework.
5. None of my friends have dogs.
6. Few of the people in the room wear eyeglasses.

Chapter 11

Exercise 9 Editing Sentences

1. Driving toward Colorado, we could see the mountains in the distance.
2. Jim tried to stop the kitten from scrambling wildly up the drapes.
3. To arrive at the airport in plenty of time, we set the alarm for 6 A.M.
4. Before leaving for the movies, she showed us pictures of the wedding.
5. While we were eating dinner, the power went off.
6. During the eclipse, Shelley could see a faint light surrounding the moon.
7. A tern flying just above the canal plunged into the water and came up with a fish.
8. She kept having a recurring dream of forgetting the combination to her locker.
9. Reiko read about a new star at the far reaches of the solar system.
10. Although well prepared, she found that the algebra test was difficult.
11. The little girl wearing jeans and a red-striped T-shirt held a garter snake.
12. To change a flat tire, you'll need the jack in the trunk.
13. Hoping for the best, he mailed the application.
14. Annoyed by the constant interruptions, she turned off the phone.
15. Jacques is the tall forward sitting on the bench and wearing the number twenty-seven.

CHAPTER REVIEW

Exercise B Correcting Misplaced and Dangling Modifiers

1. Looking for information for her research paper, Helen found 106 Web sites on the extinction of dinosaurs.
2. Trying to evaluate the information, she printed articles from museums and scientific organizations.
3. Reading a natural history museum's home page, she discovered some new information.
4. After exploring the Internet for several days, she had a stack of note cards piled high on her desk.
5. Before writing her first draft, Helen sorted the piles of note cards.
6. Helen tried to evaluate the accuracy of information taken from Internet sources.
7. She discarded articles printed from possibly unreliable Web sites. C
8. Proofreading for errors, she checked the punctuation of her Works Cited list.
9. She read aloud her first draft, listening to the sound of the sentences.
10. Congratulating herself, Helen turned in her paper by the due date.

Exercise A Using Verbs Correctly

1. Carey set a new school record when she swam the race in fifty-eight seconds.
2. After Flora dived [*or* dove] a dozen times, she became dizzy. [Accept the present tense also.]
3. Flora drank a glass of water and lay down beside the pool.
4. The coach, who told her to sit awhile and rest, brought her a towel.
5. All of the girls on the swimming team knew that drinking plenty of water is important; the coach has spoken about it many times.
6. The coach has taught them about the dangers of dehydration.
7. Haven't you done some research and written a paper on heat exhaustion?
8. Once I wore heavy clothes and did hours of gardening on a very hot, dry day.
9. When I rose from my knees, I began to feel weak, and then I fainted.
10. Fluids should be given to people with heat exhaustion, and they should lie flat or with their heads down.

Exercise D Using Modifiers Correctly

Sentences will vary. Sample answers are given.

1. The most expensive car isn't always the best one to buy.
2. Searching for a good used car, Ryan found some bargains.
3. The most desirable used car has had a single owner who has taken good care of it.
4. Some cars are driven fewer than ten thousand miles a year.
5. Suppose you are trying to decide which of two used cars is better.
6. Ask a mechanic experienced in fixing used cars to check both cars.

7. A skilled mechanic can hear and feel problems better than you can.
8. Car repair and maintenance, more important than any other class, should be a required course.
9. Lauren is buying a 1986 blue convertible being sold by a friend.
10. The convertible is cleaner and shinier than any other car she looked at, but it needs a new transmission, brakes, and four tires.

Chapter 13

Exercise 6 Revising Sentences

Answers may vary. Sample answers are given. In sentence 7, accept either a comma or no comma following the single introductory prepositional phrase.

1. In Dayton, Ohio, from 1892 to 1904, the brothers Orville and Wilbur Wright owned a bicycle repair shop.
2. Using the tools in their shop, the brothers experimented with different designs for an airplane.
3. Although people had flown balloons and gliders successfully, no one had flown a craft that was heavier than air.
4. Attaching a homemade engine to a glider, the Wright brothers designed a power-driven biplane.
5. On December 17, 1903, at Kitty Hawk, North Carolina, Orville Wright flew the plane 120 feet.
6. Setting new aviation records, the Wright brothers made four flights that day.
7. During the next few years the Wrights became world famous as they made longer flights.
8. In 1909, when the U.S. government ordered army planes, the two brothers founded the Wright Company.
9. If you go to Greenfield Village, Michigan, you can visit the restored house where Orville was born as well as the Wrights' bicycle shop.

10. In 1927, the government established the Wright National Monument on more than four hundred acres in Kitty Hawk.

Chapter 14

Exercise 6 Using Punctuation in Compound Sentences

1. An immigrant is someone who comes to live in a new country; an emigrant is someone who leaves a country.

2. American Indians are native Americans; every other American is an immigrant or a descendant of immigrants.

3. The first colonists were English; later immigrants came from other Western European countries.

4. Some came to escape religious persecution; however, most sought a better economic opportunity.

5. As the country expanded, immigrants moved west to find land; for instance, Danes, Norwegians, and Swedes staked out farms on the Great Plains.

6. During the 1840s and 1850s, about 1.5 million Irish arrived; they came to escape the potato famine.

7. From the 1880s to the 1920s, 4.5 million Italians arrived; during the same period 2.5 million Jews immigrated.

8. Communists took over Cuba in 1959; as a result, about 700,000 Cubans moved to the United States.

Exercise 11 Write Your Own Exercise
Students' sentences will vary. Sample sentences are given.

1. I dislike the popular song "Believe" by Cher, because it is played too frequently on the radio.

2. "We are all precious in God's sight—the real rainbow coalition," said Jesse Jackson at the July 1988 Democratic National Convention.

3. Chapter 5, "Parts of a Sentence," reviews all of the basic sentence parts.

4. Wallace Stevens's "Sunday Morning," like all of Stevens's poems, is filled with beautiful images.

5. No one who's seen *The Wizard of Oz* can forget Judy Garland singing "Over the Rainbow," a song that expresses the hope of wishes coming true.

6. "Ten Tips for Improving Your Test Scores" is a really helpful article; I plan to test its advice during my next test.

7. I think "The Cask of Amontillado" by Edgar Allan Poe is strange because the murderer gets away and is never punished.

8. I thought the TV drama "The Speckled Band," based on a Sherlock Holmes short story, was a terrific mystery. It made me want to read some of Arthur Conan Doyle's stories about Holmes.

9. In 1956, Nelson Mandela said that only free men can negotiate.

10. Eileen says that what everyone really wants and needs is "inner peace."

Exercise 13 Punctuating Dialogue

¶¹Tina and Lou are waiting for the school bus. ²"Last night I read an article about a girl who's the kicker on her high school football team," Tina told Lou.

¶³"Really!" he exclaimed. ⁴"I don't believe you!"

¶⁵"Really," Tina insisted. ⁶"Her name is Anna Lakovitch, and she goes to a private high school. ⁷She's the captain of the school soccer team, too, which is probably why she's such a good kicker."

¶⁸"Hmphhh!" Lou snorted. ⁹"I can't believe they'd let girls play on a school varsity team."

¶¹⁰Tina's voice rose. "And why not, Lou?"

¶11"If girls want to play football, they should play with other girls, not guys. 12They don't belong on a guy team," he growled.

¶13"Well, her teammates like having her there. 14She scores points for them. 15And do you know what?" she asked.

¶16Lou grunted, "What?"

¶17"Her football team nominated her as homecoming queen," Tina announced, "and she won. 18She was crowned during half-time—wearing her football uniform!"

CHAPTER REVIEW

Exercise C Adding Punctuation to Dialogue

Students continuation of the dialogue will vary.

¶1"Have you seen my sneakers?" Laura asked.

¶2"No, I haven't seen them," her younger brother Gabe answered. 3"Why?" he added sarcastically. 4"Do you think I've hidden them?"

¶5"Don't be so smart, Gabe," she sighed. 6"I know I left them right here by the couch."

¶7"So, Laura," he asked, "why don't you put your shoes in the closet when you take them off—like I do?"

¶8"Everyone can't be as neat and perfect as you are, Gabe." 9Laura's voice had an edge to it. 10How did Gabe always manage to be so annoying?

¶11"Will you two please stop arguing all the time!" Mom called from the kitchen. 12"You left your sneakers under the kitchen table, Laura. 13And Gabe's right. 14Stop leaving your clothes all over this apartment."

Chapter 15

Exercise 8 Create Your Own Exercise

Students' answers will vary. Sample sentences are given.

1. I plan to take advanced algebra, world history, English, Spanish, and biology.

2. I like to watch basketball and baseball on TV. My favorite teams are the New York Knicks and the San Francisco Giants.

3. In Spanish, *de buenas a primeras* means "all at once."

4. I'd donate money to CARE and Save the Children, because both charities help feed hungry people around the world and help them in other ways, too. I'd also give money to the United Way, which helps people in our community in many different ways.

5. I follow the New York Knicks and the Chicago Bulls. The Knicks have an outstanding team this year, but the Bulls will take years to rebuild a great team.

6. My mother's parents were born in Matanzas, Cuba, on the northern coast of Cuba and not far from Havana. My father's parents were born in Puerto Rico. My grandmother was born in the capital, San Juan, and my grandfather was born in a small city in the south named Playa de Ponce.

7. In his autobiography, Malcolm X wrote, "I would just like to *study*. I mean ranging study, because I have a wide-open mind. I'm interested in almost any subject you can mention."

8. Malcolm X said that he would just like to study because he has a wide-open mind and is interested in almost every subject.

9. The Jewish holiday of Succoth comes in the fall. It's a celebration of the harvest, and for eight days people are supposed to eat outdoors in booths that are open to the sky.

10. I think the census form should list many different categories, such as African American, Asian/Pacific American, European American, and Hispanic American.

Chapter 16

Exercise 3 Remembering Spelling Rules

Students' answers will vary. Sample answers are given.

1. If you wish to *succeed*, *proceed* with your plans but don't *exceed* the speed limit.

2. bleed, creed, deed, feed, greed, heed, need, reed, seed, speed, steed, teed, treed, weed

3. Several of these words have additional meanings. Accept other meanings and sentences.
   concede: to admit that a statement is true. She *conceded* that she had been careless.
   intercede: to step in to settle an argument. When a peer mediator *interceded*, both parties agreed to talk about their dispute calmly.
   precede: to come before. Months of negotiation *preceded* the settlement.
   recede: to move back. The shoreline has *receded* dangerously close to two houses on the beach.
   secede: to withdraw formally from an organization. How many states *seceded* from the Union at the beginning of the Civil War?

CHAPTER REVIEW

Exercise A Spelling with Prefixes and Suffixes

Sample answers are given. Students may think of others.

admirable	excited
admiration	excitement
admired	exciting
admiring	imaginable
amazed	imagination
amazement	imagined
amazing	imagining
appearance	likable
appeared	liked
appearing	liking
disappear	reappear
disappearance	reappearance
disappeared	reappearing
disappearing	reexcite
dislike	unimaginable
disliked	unimagined
disliking	unlikable
excitable	unlike

fourth course
grade 9

SADLIER-OXFORD
GRAMMAR
FOR WRITING

Phyllis Goldenberg

Carol Domblewski

Elaine Epstein

Martin Lee

Senior Series Consultant

Beverly Ann Chin
Professor of English
University of Montana

Series Editor
Phyllis Goldenberg

Sadlier-Oxford
A Division of William H. Sadlier, Inc.

Reviewers

Dr. Muriel Harris
Writing Lab Director
English Dept.
Purdue University
West Lafayette, IN

Keith Yost
Program Director,
Humanities and
Language Arts
Tomball, TX

**Ellen Young
Swain**
English Teacher
Cimarron High
School
Cimarron, NM

Mel Farberman
Asst. Principal
of English
Cardozo High School
Bayside, NY

Galen Rosenberg
English Dept.
Coordinator
Los Altos High School
Los Altos, CA

Patricia Stack
English Teacher
South Park School
District
Library, PA

Donald L. Stephan
Retired English
Dept. Chair
Sidney High School
Sidney, OH

Rose F. Schmitt
English Teacher
Florida Air Academy
Melbourne, FL

Cary Fuller
English Teacher
Rye Country
Day School
Rye, NY

Roxanne Hoblitt
English Teacher
Belgrade High School
Belgrade, MT

Brad Rinn
English Teacher
Roseville High School
Roseville, CA

Barbara A. Mylite
UFT Teacher Center
Specialist
New York City Board
of Education

Patrick O'Reilly
English Teacher
Freeport High School
Freeport, NY

Peter J. Accardi
English Teacher
Chaminade High
School
Mineola, NY

John Manear
English Dept. Chair
Seton-La Salle
High School
Pittsburgh, PA

Carolyn Phipps
English Teacher
Wooddale High
School
Memphis, TN

Wanda Porter
English Dept. Head
Kamehameha
Secondary School
Honolulu, HI

Student Writers

Damian Acosta
Coral Gables, FL

Jonathan Dewbre
Dallas, TX

Hugh Field
San Diego, CA

Leslie Harrell
Grosse Pointe
Farms, MI

Anna Markee
Tacoma, WA

Leslie Miller
Pottsville, PA

Mandy Kiaha
Kamehameha, HI

Greg Ruttan
Lake Oswego, OR

Dorothy Schardt
Darien, IL

Emma Sheanshang
New York, NY

Sarah Swenson
The Woodlands, TX

**Peter
Tanpitukpong**
Wilmington, DE

Joshua Vinitz
Queens, NY

Acknowledgments

Every good faith effort has been made to locate the owners of copyrighted material to arrange permission to reprint selections. In several cases this has proved impossible.

Thanks to the following for permission to reprint copyrighted materials.

"Arthur Ashe" from *Boys Will Be* by Bruce Brooks, © 1993 by Bruce Brooks. Reprinted by permission of Henry Holt & Company, Inc.

Days of Grace by Arthur Ashe and Arnold Rampersad Copyright © 1993 by Jeanne Moutoussamy-Ashe and Arnold Rampersad. Reprinted by permission of Alfred A. Knopf, Inc.

"Grant and Lee: A Study in Contrasts" from *The American Story* by Bruce Catton. Copyright © 1956 U.S. Capitol Historical Society

"Hemingway's Ancient Mariner" by Carlos Baker. Excerpted with permission of Scribner, a Division of Simon & Schuster, from *Ernest Hemingway: Critiques of Four Major Novels*, Carlos Baker, Editor. Copyright © 1962 Charles Scribner's Sons

Market Audit Survey Database. Reprinted with permission of Claritas, Inc.

"The Cuban Missile Crisis" by Leslie Porter. Copyright © 1997 by Leslie Porter. Reprinted with permission of the author.

Photo Credits

FPG International/ Kevin Laubacher: Ch. 11
Graphistock/ Todd Haiman: Ch. 14
The Image Works/ M. Antman: Ch. 9

International Stock/ Michael Agliolo: Ch. 5
Richard B. Levine: Ch. 4
Photodisc: Ch. 10
Photonica/ Erik Rank: Ch. 3; Deborah Raven: Ch. 8;

Arthur Selbach: Ch. 15; Tony Cordoza: Ch. 16
The Stock Market/ Gabe Palmer: Ch. 12
Tony Stone Images/ Warren Bolster: Ch. 1; Aldo Brando:

Ch. 2; Dennis O'Clair: Ch. 6; Barry Rowland: Ch. 7; Garry Hunter: Ch. 13

Dear Student:

This book is designed to take the mystery out of grammar and to help you become a better, more confident writer. *Grammar for Writing* does just what its title suggests: it shows how the rules of grammar, usage, and mechanics—the conventions of standard English—can make your writing not just correct but more powerful and persuasive, too.

As a student, you are being challenged to write correctly and effectively not only in your English classes but also in social studies, science, and history classes as well. High schools all over America have raised their expectations for graduates. If you have taken a standardized test recently or are preparing to take one soon, you know this only too well. The writing sections of these tests have grown more rigorous and more demanding than ever.

However, there are reasons to speak and write well other than to score well on standardized tests. People judge you by the way you write and speak. Your use of English is evaluated in the writing you do in school, on job and college applications, and in many different kinds of careers. That doesn't mean that you have to say, "To whom am I speaking?" when a friend calls, but you should be able to speak and write correctly when the situation calls for it—in a formal speaking or writing assignment, on a test, and in an interview. The more you practice using standard English, the more comfortable and confident you will become when you write and speak.

As you become a more confident writer, you will find new excitement in recording your thoughts, ideas, opinions, and experiences. You will also see that communicating effectively is the most important way to influence others. As you write about the topics you care about, you will find that people in every part of your life—your teachers, your peers, your bosses, your parents, and your community—gain respect for you and are influenced by the things you write and say.

No textbook can make writing easy. Good writers work hard and revise their work often to find just the right words to move their audience. Consequently, in *Grammar for Writing* you will find a lot of exercises called "Write What You Think." These exercises are designed to help you develop clear, logical arguments to persuade people that your opinion is right. These exercises will sharpen your thinking as well as your writing skills.

Of course, you already know how to write. You've been doing it for years. No one has to prove to you that writing is important—it just *is*. But your writing can always be improved, and the best way to improve it is to learn and practice the skills and strategies in this book. In *Grammar for Writing*, we have tried to present the rules of grammar as simply as possible; whether you are merely refreshing your memory or are learning the concepts for the first time, you'll be able to understand the rules and apply them to your writing.

All of the skills you learn and practice in this book—grammar, writing, thinking—will last you a lifetime.

Good luck, and study well!

CONTENTS

COMPOSITION

GRAMMAR

USAGE

MECHANICS

The Writing Process

Prewriting

◖ **Prewriting** is all the thinking, planning, and organizing you do before you actually start writing.

"What shall I write about?" Every writer wrestles with this question. As you start to think about writing, choose a topic (a) that interests you (b) that's important to you or (c) that you know a lot about.

Narrow your topic to one that is limited, thus allowing you to cover it adequately in the number of words or pages you're expected to write.

TOO BROAD	new cars
LIMITED	How new cars are named
	Who rates new cars, and how?
	Shopping for a car on the Internet

It may take you several revisions to get a topic that fits your assignment. Use the five prewriting strategies below, both to discover topics and main ideas to write about, and to help you gather supporting details that elaborate on the topics.

PREWRITING STRATEGIES

1. Writer's Notebook Keep a separate notebook or folder in which you jot down experiences and thoughts about anything that interests you.

Later you can convert these jottings into effective paragraphs, essays, stories, and so on. You might put such things in your notebook as quotations, cartoons, and poems that "speak" to you; then explain why you like them. Think of your notebook entries as memory joggers.

Tues. 4/7. Arch Creek office for driver's license test. My appointment was for 8 A.M., waited till almost 10. So nervous I felt sick. Examiner—a woman, never smiled. Do this, do that; left turn, right turn; parallel park. Heavy rains and wind. What did she write on the forms?? I have to wait—results come in the mail.

2. Brainstorming Focus on a single word, and list everything that pops into your head.

Don't *think* about what you've written; just get every idea down on paper. If you brainstorm with a partner or group, have one person do the writing. When you run out of thoughts, go back over your list, and check or circle the ones that seem most usable.

TOPIC: Driving

BRAINSTORMING NOTES:

red convertible	huge trucks, accidents	ticket for speeding
changing flat tire	Jeff's collision with stop	rolling stop
time we went camping	sign safety belts	insurance cost?

3. Freewriting This strategy is similar to brainstorming, but it involves nonstop writing.

Focus on a word or topic, and write continuously for three to five minutes. Don't worry about complete sentences, grammar, or spelling. If you can't think of anything new to write, write the same word over and over until a new thought appears. Keep moving forward; do not back up and reread.

TOPIC: Car safety
What kinds of things do they look for during car inspections? Do they check tires? How? How often do you need to take a car in for an inspection? I'd better keep up regular maintenance. Maintenance. Of what? Of seat belts? What's to maintain? Doesn't matter. Point is to wear seat belts? Why? Dumb question. . .

4. Clustering (also called **Mapping** or **Webbing**) Create a cluster diagram to explore a topic, to break a large topic into smaller parts, or to gather details.

First, write your topic (or any word or phrase) in the middle of a piece of paper, and then circle it. Around the circled topic, write subtopics—related words and phrases. Circle each new word or phrase, and connect it to your original topic. Each new word or phrase may have subtopics, too. Keep going until you run out of thoughts.

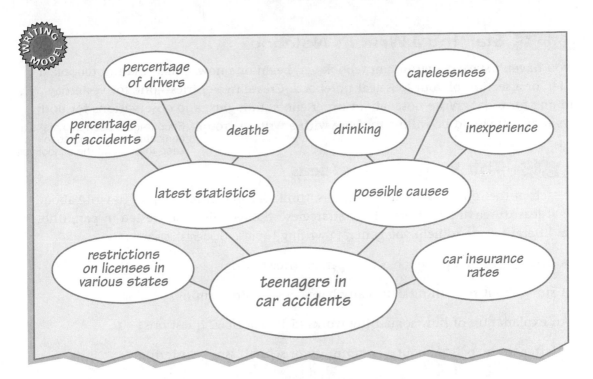

5. **5-*W and How?* Questions** Asking the questions *Who*? *What*? *When*? *Where*? *Why*? and *How*? about any topic will help you narrow, or limit, your essay.

For some topics, not every question will apply; for other topics, you may think of several questions beginning with the same word. Here are one writer's questions about the Model T, one of the early automobiles.

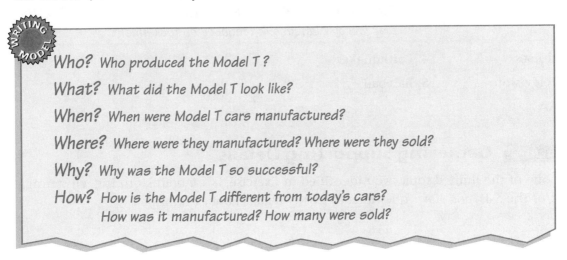

Who? Who produced the Model T?

What? What did the Model T look like?

When? When were Model T cars manufactured?

Where? Where were they manufactured? Where were they sold?

Why? Why was the Model T so successful?

How? How is the Model T different from today's cars?
How was it manufactured? How many were sold?

Exercise 1 Starting a Writer's Notebook

If you haven't started a writer's notebook yet, begin one now. Use a small notebook, a folder, or a section of your looseleaf notebook. Create two entries—one for yesterday and one for today. Write notes about experiences, thoughts, and observations for both days that you would be willing to share with a writing group. Encourage students to make a dedicated writer's notebook to keep throughout the school year.

Exercise 2 Thinking of Topic Ideas

For each of the following numbered items, think of three or four topics to write about. Use at least three different prewriting strategies—the technique suggested in parentheses or a different one—to help you generate writing topics. Students' lists will vary.

1. A description of a place, object, or person (freewriting)

2. A story about something that really happened (brainstorming)

3. An explanation of how something works (*5-W and How?* questions)

4. A letter to the editor about a community or school issue (clustering)

Exercise 3 Narrowing a Topic

Choose two of the broad, general topics below. For each topic, suggest three limited topics that you could cover in a three-page paper. Students' topics will vary.

EXAMPLE	TOO BROAD	LIMITED
	Rock music	*A visit to the Rock 'n' Roll Hall of Fame in Cleveland, Ohio*
		The earliest recordings by Elvis Presley
		Disc jockey Alan Freed's influence on rock music

1. Horses   4. Earthquakes

2. Television   5. Baseball

3. Art

Exercise 4 Gathering Supporting Details

For one of the limited topics you identified in Exercise 3, use brainstorming, clustering, and/or the *5-W and How?* questions to gather details about that topic. Students' details will vary.

Prewriting and Drafting

🖋 Use your prewriting notes to create an **outline**. An outline is a writing plan consisting of the most important points. An outline forces you to make two important decisions about your prewriting notes: (1) which main ideas and details to include in support of your topic and (2) what order to present them in.

Outlines work well for writing that explains, persuades, or describes. A model of a brief, informal outline is at the right.

🖋 Before you begin writing, decide on your writing style. **Style** is the manner in which you express your ideas. Your writing style is determined by your audience and your purpose. Your **audience** is the person or persons who will read what you write. Your **purpose** may be to describe, to inform, to tell a story, to persuade, to entertain, or a combination of these.

Thinking about your audience helps you to decide how much background information and which supporting details you should include. Ask yourself questions such as, "Does my audience need definitions of the technical terms or proper nouns that I'm going to use?" Thinking about your purpose also helps you to sift through the supporting details and to choose the most appropriate ones.

🖋 **Drafting** is the step in the writing process when you start putting your thoughts into sentences and paragraphs.

When you have a limited topic, prewriting notes, a rough outline, and a clear idea of whom you're writing for and why, use the strategies below for writing a first draft.

DRAFTING STRATEGIES

1. Focus Find a quiet place, and concentrate on the task.

2. Start Early Allow enough time to let your draft sit awhile (overnight is ideal) before you revise, edit, and proofread it.

WRITING MODEL

A Rough Outline: Chinese Immigration

Early Chinese immigration to US

California gold rush (1849)

Transcontinental railroad

Exclusion of Chinese laborers

Chinese Exclusion Act (1882)

Wave of immigration after San Francisco fire (1906)

Angel Island immigration station, 1910-40

Writing Hint

Write in your own voice —that is, sound like yourself. Don't try to sound "intelligent" by using words you don't know and by lengthening or writing complicated sentences. Express your ideas clearly and simply.

---

3. **Think in Sentences** Write complete sentences, and vary their structures and lengths. You may wish to refer to Lesson 7.7: Varying Sentence Beginnings and Structure.
4. **Stay Flexible** Follow the general direction of your outline, but feel free to make appropriate changes and add or drop details.

■ See **Grammar Chapter 5** for more on sentences, including suggestions for varying sentence structures.

Exercise 5 Drafting Part of a Report

The outline at the beginning of this lesson grew out of the information on the note card below. Draft two or more paragraphs using some or all of this information. The purpose of this writing exercise is to inform. Suppose that the audience is your history class. You do not have to use all of the information. First drafts will vary.

Angel Island—Ellis Island of the West

First Chinese immigrants came to "Gold Mountain" (U.S.) after Calif. gold rush (1849). Built railroads @ 12 cents an hour.

Then high unemployment → passage of Chinese Exclusion Act, 1882: stopped all Chinese laborers from entering; no Chinese could become U.S. citizen

Great San Francisco fire (1906)—birth & business records totally destroyed. American Chinese claimed nonrelatives in China as "paper sons and daughters"

Angel Island, California—in San Francisco Bay, U.S. immigration station, 1910–40: New immigrants held there & questioned intensely

On walls of men's barracks—anonymous poems by desperate immigrants detained there

---

Exercise 6 Drafting a Paper

Draft a paper using the prewriting notes you made for a limited topic in Exercise 4 on page 12. Decide on an audience and purpose, and make a rough outline. Before you start drafting, talk with a partner or small group about what you're planning to write. See if you can clearly summarize your topic, the main idea(s), and the supporting details. When you're ready to start drafting, follow the four strategies suggested in this lesson. Students' papers will vary. Students will be asked to revise this draft on page 17 in Lesson 1.3, Exercise 9.

Revising and Editing

🔸 When you **revise** and **edit**, you shape your draft into its almost-final form.

At this stage in the writing process, you try to make your written thoughts clearer. Add new information, cut words or sentences, change the order of sentences and paragraphs, and replace weak words with stronger ones. You should also fix sentences that have grammar or usage problems—such as lack of subject–verb agreement.

REVISING STRATEGIES

When you **revise**, you look for ways to eliminate problems in content, organization, and style. To begin revising, try this four-step strategy. Reread your first draft four separate times, concentrating on something different with each reading.

1. **Content** Can you summarize your main idea(s)? (In a narrative, you need to ask yourself whether you can summarize the event or events rather than the main idea or ideas.) Do you have enough supporting details or too many? Will adding or cutting details improve your paper? Do you need more background information? Is everything relevant, or related, to your main idea(s), or have you wandered off track?

2. **Organization** Does the opener grab the reader's attention? Can you improve your draft by moving paragraphs? by moving sentences? Is information presented in a logical order, an order that makes sense to the reader? Would adding transition words help?

3. **Style** Is your writing too formal or informal for your audience? Have you kept the purpose of your essay in mind? Does your writing "sound like you"? Is the vocabulary too difficult or too informal for the intended audience? Do technical terms need to be defined or explained? Do your sentences have variety?

4. **Word Choice** Have you varied the beginnings, lengths, and structure of your sentences? Would some sentences sound better combined? Can you delete unnecessary words, phrases, or sentences? Look for general, vague words, and replace them with precise ones. If you've used a cliché or an overworked word, such as *very* or *great*, think of a fresh way to express the same idea.

Enriching Your Vocabulary

Narrare, Latin for "to make known or to tell," gives us the noun *narrative* (story or narration). A writer may win critical praise for her exciting *narratives*.

EDITING STRATEGIES

Next, go on to edit your work. When you **edit**, you review your writing in terms of grammar and usage concerns. Look at your paper with the following editing issues in mind.

1. **Sentence Completeness** Are any fragments or run-ons posing as sentences? Does every sentence begin with a capital letter and end with an appropriate punctuation mark? Chapter 5: Parts of a Sentence.

2. **Verbs** Do all present tense verbs agree with their subjects? Are verb tenses consistent and correct? Chapter 9: Subject-Verb Agreement.

3. **Pronouns** Do all the pronouns agree with their antecedents? Are pronoun references clear? Chapter 10: Using Pronouns.

4. **Adjectives and Adverbs** Are adjectives modifying nouns and pronouns? Are adverbs modifying verbs, adjectives, and other adverbs? Are comparisons clear and complete? Do comparisons use *-er/more* and *-est/most* forms correctly?
Chapter 11: Using Modifiers; Lesson 4.4: Adjectives; Lesson 4.5: Adverbs

◖ **Peer editing** involves giving feedback to your classmates and getting help from them on works in progress.

Peer editors make specific suggestions for improving a paper and ask questions about anything that is unclear. They also give positive feedback, telling the writer what they like best about his or her writing.

> ■ **Parts of speech are defined and explained in Grammar Chapter 4.**

> **Some Questions for Peer Editors**
>
> 1. Which parts of the paper do I like best and least?
>
> 2. What is the writer's main idea?
>
> 3. Does the writer give enough details to support his or her main idea?
>
> 4. Are parts of the paper unclear?
>
> 5. Are the beginning and ending effective?
>
> 6. What advice can I give about grammar and usage?

Exercise 7 **Revising and Editing a Letter to the Editor**

Review the revising and editing questions in this lesson before you revise the following letter to the editor. Your audience is the readers of the local newspaper. Your purpose is to persuade. Because there is no single correct way to revise this letter, feel free to make up additional details and to cut sentences that stray from the main idea. Consider adding transitions, combining sentences, and offering examples. Write your revised version on a separate piece of paper. You may do this exercise with a partner or small group. Compare your revised letter to the editor with your classmates' versions. Revised letters will vary.

To the Editor:

Someone has suggested a new law. It's about a curfew. They want us teenagers home by 10 P.M. M–F. They want us kids home by 11 P.M. on weekends. Some kids have to work at night. Most kids don't get into trouble. Why should they be punished? How can you enforce a curfew? What would the punishment be? The word *curfew* comes from the Middle Ages. It means to cover a fire. In those days someone would go around town and ring a bell. That was a signal to cover up the fire in the fireplace and go to bed. I'm against this law. And I have my reasons. It's unfair.

Exercise 8 **Revising and Editing a Paper**

Use the four revising strategies suggested on page 15 to revise any paper you've written for English or for another class. Next, edit the paper by using the editing strategies listed on page 16. Students' writing will vary. Use the assessment rubrics in the teacher pages to evaluate student writing.

Exercise 9 **Peer Editing** *Working Together*

1. Revise and edit the paper you drafted in Lesson 1.2, Exercise 6. Use the revising and editing strategies to improve your draft.

2. Work with a partner to peer edit your paper. Allow your partner to read your paper without your input. Your partner should respond to your writing using the peer editing questions on page 16 as a guide. Encourage your peer editor to make comments directly on your pages.

3. Review the peer editing comments on your paper and incorporate those that you feel will improve your writing. Don't be discouraged if you have to rewrite some passages. Caution peer editors to be positive about the essays they read. Encourage them to suggest possible solutions to problems they find.

Proofreading and Publishing

◖ When you **proofread**, you search for mistakes in spelling, punctuation, and capitalization.

Don't let these errors slip by. Part of the quality of your writing depends on your ability to use the conventions of standard written English. Use the following list as you proofread your work. If you are in doubt, use the index to find rules about specific conventions.

Enriching Your Vocabulary

The verb *transpose* comes from the Latin *transponere*, which means "to change the position of." *Transpose* can also be used in the sense of "to change in nature or form." The director *transposed* the setting of *Romeo and Juliet* from Verona to Civil War America.

Proofreading Symbols		
CORRECTION	SYMBOL	EXAMPLE
Delete (remove).	ℓ	He greated the the onions.
Insert.	∧	We planed the party. (n)
Transpose (switch).	⎡⎤	I only spent a dollar.
Capitalize.	≡	did you visit Walden Pond?
Make lowercase.	/	The irises bloom each Spring.
Start a new paragraph.	¶	¶"No," she said.
Add space.	#	Allegra lives in San Juan. (#)
Close up space.	◡	Pat is a child hood friend.

PROOFREADING QUESTIONS

1. Spelling Are words spelled correctly? (Use a college dictionary or a spell checker on a computer.) Have you used a correctly spelled word that doesn't fit the sentence (*you're* instead of *your*, for example, or *hear* instead of *here*—mix-ups that a computer's spell checker won't catch)? Chapter 16: Spelling.

2. Capitalization Do proper nouns and proper adjectives begin with capital letters? Have you capitalized a word that's supposed to start with a lowercase letter?   Chapter 15: Capitalization.

3. Punctuation Are commas and other punctuation marks used correctly? Is dialogue correctly punctuated? Chapters 13 and 14: Punctuation.

4. Apostrophes Do contractions and possessive nouns have apostrophes in the right place? Do possessive pronouns have *no* apostrophes? Chapter 14: Punctuation; Lesson 14.7: Apostrophes.

◖ A **proofreading log** is a record that shows corrections to your spelling, punctuation, and capitalization mistakes.

■ See, Mechanics, Chapters 13-16 for more on the rules for many of the errors you are looking for as you proofread your work.

Keep a proofreading log in a separate notebook or folder. Review your log occasionally so that you don't keep repeating mistakes.

● **Publishing** means sharing or presenting what you've written.

Your audience can be wider than your classmates, family, and friends. You can read your writing aloud to members of a school club, e-mail an essay to a distant pen pal, videotape a discussion of issues, or leave an anthology of writing models for future ninth-graders.

Publishing Suggestions
WRITTEN WORDS
Magazine of student writing
School or local newspaper
Local or national poetry, story, or essay contest
Class anthology
Writing portfolio
Letters/e-mail
SPOKEN WORDS
Speech
Audiocassette
Oral interpretation
Radio broadcast
Reader's theater
Interview
Debate
MULTIMEDIA
Book with illustrations
Videotape
Performance with music
Bulletin board or library display
Literature festival for the community

Exercise 10 Proofreading a Paragraph

Find and correct every error in the following paragraph.

[1]People who make maps are called cartographers. [2]They ~~carefuly~~ *carefully* draw each country's borders. [3]During the 1930s, cartographers began to draw ~~there~~ *their* maps from photographs taken from airplanes. [4]Now they use ~~satelite~~ *satellite* photographs to create even more accurate maps.

[5]If you look at a map, ~~youll~~ *you'll* find New zealand, two large islands and several smaller islands southeast of australia. [6]According to *The columbia Encyclopedia*, New Zealand contains 103,377 square miles. [7]How can geographers figure out the number of square miles New Zealand contains? [8]They can't possibly multiply ~~it's~~ *its* length by ~~it's~~ *its* width! [9]Modern map makers and geographers use computers to draw maps. [10]They also use computers to measure a country's square ~~miles~~ *mileage*.

Exercise 11 Creating Editing and Proofreading Exercises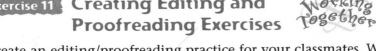

Create an editing/proofreading practice for your classmates. Write one or two paragraphs that have at least ten mistakes (or more if you want) in grammar, usage, spelling, punctuation, and capitalization. Exchange paragraphs with your classmates, and see if you can correct all the errors. Answers will vary.

Writing Effective Paragraphs and Essays

Unity

🔹 A paragraph has **unity** (it is unified) when all of its sentences focus on a single main idea.

🔹 A **topic sentence** directly states the paragraph's main idea.

When a topic sentence is the first or second sentence in a paragraph, it announces what's coming in the rest of the paragraph. When a topic sentence is at the end of a paragraph, it summarizes the main idea that has not been directly stated in the preceding sentences.

Not all paragraphs have directly stated topic sentences. The main idea may be **implied** rather than stated directly. But even without a topic sentence, the main idea should be clear to the reader.

🔹 A paragraph that starts with a topic sentence may end with a **clincher sentence** which restates or summarizes the main idea.

Clincher sentences can be especially effective in persuasive paragraphs, but you should use them sparingly in an essay.

The following annotated model illustrates the principle of unity.

> ■ See Lesson 2.4 for more techniques for writing different types of paragraphs.

Writing Hint

In an essay, a topic sentence that begins a paragraph does double duty: It states the paragraph's main idea, *and* it ties the paragraph to the rest of the essay.

WRITING MODEL

¹Ashe leaves us with a good lesson: There is a place in sports for smart people. ²Intelligence—used well in analysis, study, practice—helps you in anything you try to do, whether it's a backhand lob at a surprising moment or a moral stand on a complex issue. ³He was a very talented tennis player, blessed with extraordinary reach and power and touch, but his victories were victories of the wits. ⁴When he faced Connors on Centre Court in 1975, it certainly seemed like old smarts and old bones against the brashly cruel, indefatigable force and speed of youth. ⁵So it was. ⁶Force and speed never had a chance. ⁷Ashe showed that if you are better at thinking, you can then work hard physically to keep the advantage when you move into the field of action. ⁸Arthur the Man blew Jimbo the Boy away. ⁹Nine years later, Connors gave us the opportunity to see that Ashe's shrewdness was

Topic sentence about intelligence

Background information

Incident that supports main idea

Second incident
that supports
main idea

not just an advantage conferred by age and experience. [10]In the 1984 final, Jimbo—still playing in full force as The Boy, despite his seniority—was utterly destroyed by the much smarter John McEnroe. [11]Like Ashe, McEnroe demonstrated a strategic control (is *that* what manliness is?) that made Jimmy's reckless force and willful cuteness (and is *that* boyishness?) look ridiculous.

—Bruce Brooks, "Arthur Ashe"

SKILLS FOR MAINTAINING UNITY

1. Topic Sentence Keep in mind that there's more than one way a writer can word a topic sentence. Here's another option Brooks could've used.

Ashe proved that the best athletes are smart athletes.

But the following sentences would have been too weak to be topic sentences for Brooks's paragraph.

Everyone thinks all the time. [too broad]

Ashe had a high IQ. [too narrow]

2. Single Main Idea All the sentences in the model paragraph stick to the main idea. Brooks avoids cluttering his paragraph with unnecessary sentences such as the following.

Ashe's intelligence was nurtured by the schools of Richmond, Virginia.

Wit, after all, is what separates humans from animals.

3. Clincher Sentence Brooks could have summed up his paragraph with a clincher sentence such as the following.

So we see in these two incidents that brains can dominate muscles.

Exercise 1 Choosing a Topic Sentence

1. Which of the following sentences would work in place of the topic sentence that Brooks wrote? Give reasons for your choice on a separate piece of paper.
   a. We will remember Ashe for what he taught us about smarts in sports.
   b. Ashe made a positive impression on lots of people.   Students' reasons will vary.

2. Which of the following sentences could more easily be added to Brooks's paragraph without detracting from its unity? Explain your choice on a separate piece of paper.
   a. Ashe spoke intelligently and movingly about AIDS.
   b. We need more athletes with Ashe's intelligence.

   Choice **a** is too specific for the information in the paragraph. Choice **b** adequately identifies the main idea of the paragraph.

Elaborating with Supporting Details

● **Elaboration** is the process of adding details to support a main idea.

Develop, or support, the paragraph's main idea with the following kinds of details: **facts**, **statistics**, **quotations**, **definitions**, **anecdotes** or **incidents**, **examples**, **reasons**, and **comparisons**. It's fine to use more than one kind of supporting detail in a single paragraph. Just make sure that each sentence adds something new.

The writer of the following paragraph realized that the first draft did not contain enough specific details to support the topic sentence. Notice the details she added during revision.

■ **Review Grammar Lessons 6.6 and 7.4 for more about combining sentences by inserting phrases and clauses.**

¹Every spring and summer, the Coast Salish of the

Pacific Northwest moved from their winter villages to

temporary camps near the coast and beside the rivers with

used spears

the goal of gathering food for the winter. ²The men ~~brought~~

and nets to catch salmon, cod, trout, and halibut.

~~in fish.~~ ³They smoked and dried the surplus fish for winter

food for the whole village. ⁴The women and children

shellfish from the beaches and edible wild plants and roots.

collected ~~food too~~.

Exercise 2 ## Improving Unity and Adding Details

Work with a partner or small group to revise the following paragraph. Cross out any words or sentences that destroy the paragraph's unity because they move away from the main idea. Then, from the list below the paragraph, select the details that you think would improve the paragraph. Write the letter of the detail where you think it belongs in the paragraph. Then write your revised paragraph on a separate piece of paper. Some of the details can be inserted as phrases and clauses.

Enriching Your Vocabulary

The origin of the noun *debris*, as used in Exercise 3, can be traced to the French verb *debriser*, which means "to break to pieces." The objects in a mound of *debris* are broken and battered. Archaeologists can learn many things from the *debris* of an ancient civilization.

[1]Blue jeans as we know them go back to 1853. [2]In that year in San Francisco, Levi Strauss, a Bavarian immigrant, made the first pair of jeans. [3]~~Bavaria was a state in the southeastern part of Germany.~~ [4]Strauss used a tough, brown canvas.
Detail A
[5]He sold his durable work pants, called Levi's, to gold miners. [6]~~Gold was discovered at Sutter's Mill in 1848.~~
Details C and D
[7]Soon Strauss switched to denim ~~(the word *denim* comes from the French *de Nimes*).~~

Details
A. ~~The rough, brown canvas was~~ originally meant for the tops of covered wagons.
B. Thousands of miners rushed to California to hunt for gold.
C. Denim originally was a heavy cotton cloth imported from Nimes, France.
D. Strauss dyed the denim indigo blue.

Exercise 3 Improving Unity and Adding Details

Work with a partner or small group to revise the following paragraph. Cross out any words or sentences that destroy the paragraph's unity because they move away from the main idea. Then, from the list at the top of page 25, select the details that you think would improve the paragraph. Write the letter of the detail where you think it belongs in the paragraph. Then write your revised paragraph on a separate piece of paper. Some of the details can be inserted as phrases and clauses.

[1]Several theories have been advanced to explain the disappearance of dinosaurs from Earth. [2]The current favorite theory is that a gigantic asteroid struck Earth some 65 million years ago. [3]The impact created billions of tons of smoke, dust, and debris in Earth's atmosphere.
Detail A
[4]Plants died, then plant-eating dinosaurs, then the dinosaurs that fed on the plant-eating dinosaurs. [5]~~By examining the anatomy of dinosaur fossils, scientists can decide whether dinosaurs ate plants or animals or both.~~ [6]~~Tyrannosaurus rex, a a widely-studied dinosaur, was a flesh-eating dinosaur.~~ [7]There are other theories, too.
Detail C
[8]Some speculate that dinosaurs became extinct because of climate changes. [9]Other scientists think they may have been wiped out by a dinosaur disease; still others believe that mammals might have wiped out all dinosaurs by eating their eggs.

Details

A. The pollution in the atmosphere may have kept sunlight from reaching Earth for six months to a year.

B. Tyrannosaurus rex is also the most easily recognized dinosaur.

C. The climate changes, with extremes of heat and cold, would have been more than the dinosaurs could handle.

Exercise 4 **Writing a Paragraph from Notes**

On a separate piece of paper, write a unified, well-developed paragraph based on the information in the note card below. You do not need to use all of the information. Begin your paragraph with a topic sentence.   Students' paragraphs will vary.

American Sign Language (known as ASL)

Used by deaf and hearing-impaired people

Based on gestures (hand movements), facial expressions, and body movements to represent ideas (concepts)

Examples of ASL signs:

"not"—move thumb forward under chin

"school"—hands held horizontally in front of body; clap hands twice, left palm up

"happy"—with one hand; pat chest several times, using upward motion

"know"—with right hand, tap upper right forehead with four fingers (not thumb) held flat

ASL also uses finger spelling: manual alphabet with different finger/hand position or gesture for each letter

---

Exercise 5 **Elaborating on a Topic Sentence**

Write a paragraph using one of the topic sentences below or one of your own. Support the topic sentence you choose with quotations, anecdotes, examples, or any other details. Reread your paragraph to eliminate any details that do not support the topic sentence.

Students' paragraphs will vary. Use the assessment rubrics in the teacher pages to evaluate student writing.

A. Being a good shopper means watching out for good bargains.

B. The best way to learn about music is to listen to it often.

C. The real heroes in life are those people for whom simple things are difficult.

Coherence

◗ Each of your paragraphs should be **coherent**; that is, its sentences should be sensibly organized so that your reader can follow your thoughts easily.

STRATEGIES FOR WRITING COHERENTLY

1. **Be Clear** Express your thoughts simply and directly.

2. **Guide the Reader** Use signposts that show the reader what lies ahead and how thoughts relate to one another. Some signposts are transitional expressions like those on page 27. Others are pronouns and synonyms (words that mean almost the same thing), which refer to terms you have already used. Repeating key words or terms also improves coherence.

3. **Put Your Thoughts in Order** Arrange information so that "first things come first."

The following list includes four common ways of organizing paragraphs and essays. Unless you have a good reason not to do so, choose one of these orders as a framework.

- **Chronological Order** Organizing your writing chronologically means telling about events in the order in which they occurred. Use chronological order for narrative paragraphs, which may tell a true story or a fictional one; for writing about a historical event; and for describing steps in a process.

- **Spatial Order** Organize your paragraph spatially when you want to describe a person, an animal, a place, or an object. Include details in an orderly way; moving from left to right, top to bottom, near to far, or inside to outside.

- **Order of Importance** Organize your paragraph by degree of importance when trying to persuade your audience. State the least important reasons and other details first, and end with the most important ones—or the reverse.

- **Logical Order** Organize your paragraph logically to give information in the order a reader needs to know it. Usually, logic determines which details you group together or where you provide background information or definitions of terms.

The revisions in the following model show how one writer improved coherence in response to the peer-editor's notes in the margin.

WRITING MODEL

[1]Here's how to throw a boomerang so that it returns to you.

Add transition. [2]*First,* Hold the boomerang vertically, not horizontally. [3]*Because* The boomerang's

Move and make into a complex sentence. wings are unequal. *Then* Throw ~~the boomerang into the air~~ *it* with a quick

snap of the wrist. [5]A right-handed boomerang will lean a little ~~bit of~~

Add transition. ~~the way~~ to the left. [6]~~It will~~ start to fly in ~~the shape of~~ a big circle. *and*

[7]A boomerang keeps leaning to one side more and more as it flies ~~in~~

until gradually it becomes

Eliminate wordiness. ~~the air.~~ [8]~~It will change its position relative to the earth.~~ [9]~~It will~~

rotors

Use precise noun. ~~become~~ horizontal like the ~~blades~~ on ~~the top of~~ a helicopter. [10]If you

correctly,

Eliminate wordiness. have thrown the boomerang ~~in just the right kind of way,~~ it will return

~~and come back~~ to you.

Some Common Transitional Words and Expressions			
To show time	**To show examples**	**To show order of importance**	**To compare**
after — first	for example — namely	above all — second	also — as
afterward — immediately	for instance — that is	finally — then	and — similarly
at last — later	in addition	first — lastly	like — too
before — soon	in other words	most important	likewise
during — then			
finally — when	**To summarize**	**To show cause and effect**	**To contrast**
	all in all — finally	as a result — since	although — but
To show place	as a result — therefore	because — so	however — still
above — inside	in conclusion	consequently — so that	in contrast (to) — yet
across — into	in summary	if . . . then — therefore	nevertheless
among — off		for that reason	on the other hand
behind — outside	**To emphasize**		
below — there	for this reason — again		
between — through	moreover — in fact		
in front of — under	most important		

Exercise 6 ## Revising a Paragraph for Coherence

Work with a partner or small group to improve the coherence of the following paragraph. Try adding transitional words and expressions, reordering information, and combining sentences. Make any other changes you think will improve the paragraph. Write your revised paragraph on a separate piece of paper.

¹In 1810 Mary Ann Anning was eleven years old. ²She and her brother collected fossil seashells. ³They sold the seashells to make money. ⁴~~Their mother was a widow.~~ ⁵~~They needed the money they made from selling seashell fossils to support themselves.~~ ⁶Mary
in Lyme Regis in southwestern England.
Ann uncovered huge bones in the chalk of a cliff ⁷The bones were four flippers, tail,
of an extinct dinosaur.
head, backbone, ribs, and teeth. ⁸Have you heard the tongue twister "She sells seashells down by the seashore"? ⁹It is supposed to be about Mary Ann Anning. ¹⁰Paleontologists came to see Mary Ann's discovery. ¹¹~~Mary Ann discovered the fossilized bones of an~~
They
~~extinct dinosaur.~~ ¹²~~The paleontologists~~ named the ~~extinct~~ dinosaur, whose bones she
, which means "fish lizard"
discovered, Ichthyosaurus. ¹³~~Mary Ann found it on the beach in Lyme Regis in~~
~~southwestern England.~~ ¹⁴~~Ichthyosaurus means "fish lizard."~~

Exercise 7 ## Writing a Paragraph from Notes

Write a coherent, unified paragraph based on the following note card. Include a topic sentence. Students' paragraphs will vary. Use the assessment rubrics in the teacher pages to evaluate students' writing.

> _Langston Hughes (1902–1967)—African American poet. Called Poet Laureate of Harlem._
>
> _How Hughes was "discovered": Working as busboy in Washington, D.C., hotel. Vachel Lindsay; white poet, staying there. Hughes put 3 poems beside Lindsay's plate._
>
> _"The next morning on my way to work, as usual I bought a paper—and there I read that Vachel Lindsay had discovered a Negro busboy poet! At the hotel the reporters were already waiting for me." (autobiography The Big Sea, 1940)_
>
> _1st book of poems, The Weary Blues (1926)_

Types of Paragraphs

Your writing varies not only because of its content but also because of its purpose. In this lesson, you will study four different purposes for writing paragraphs and essays.

DESCRIPTIVE

When your purpose is to describe a person, a place, an object, or an animal, use the following suggestions.

- Use **sensory details** to appeal to the reader's five senses (sight, hearing, smell, touch, and taste) and to create a **main impression,** or **mood**.

- Use **spatial order** to present the sensory details from left to right, top to bottom, or closest to farthest.

WRITING MODEL

[1]From a safe distance, I measured the crocodile with my eye. [2]It was longer than three average basketball players laid out head to foot in a straight line. [3]It lay flat on its belly in the dusty pen, open mouthed. [4]Dozens of pointed teeth edged the huge jaws. [5]I could see two nostrils toward the base of its narrow snout and two glittering eyes set in bumps on its flat head. [6]Large scales of varying size covered its whole body except for what looked like sharp, black claws on the powerful, short legs. [7]Like armor, rows of spikes lined its back down to the end of its powerful tail. [8]Even at rest, the crocodile seemed dangerous and armed.

Context—writer's position and setting

Spatial order: head first

Sight detail

Touch details
Spatial order: tail last

Main impression

NARRATIVE

When your purpose is to tell a story—either a fictional story or a true narrative—or to explain the steps in a process, use the following suggestions. See Lesson 3.1: Narrative Writing: Autobiographical Incident.

- Break the story or process into its most critical events or steps.

- Use **chronological order** (time order) to relate events in the order they occurred. This is also a useful order for explaining a step-by-step process.

Writing Hint

Writers sometimes use a one-sentence paragraph for emphasis. When the surrounding paragraphs are of normal length, a single-sentence paragraph packs a punch.

Event A — *WRITING MODEL*

[1]Through the night, emergency workers piled sandbags along the river banks, and behind them other workers built emergency dikes. [2]But nothing could stop the Red River at Grand Forks, North Dakota. [3]On April 18, the river crested, rushing over sandbags and dikes. [4]As the waters flooded downtown and residential neighborhoods, residents fled, some in motorboats. [5]The next day, Saturday, all of Grand Forks's 50,000 residents were ordered to leave. [6]As they left, a second disaster struck: an electrical fire downtown. [7]With waist-deep water everywhere and fire hydrants underwater, the firefighters couldn't control the blaze.

Event B

Event C

Event D

EXPOSITORY   See Lesson 3.3: Expository Writing: Compare and Contrast Essay

There are several ways to explain and to inform: You can compare and contrast; you can discuss cause and effect; you can define, classify, or analyze. When writing exposition, use the following suggestions.

- State your **main idea** as early and as clearly as possible.

- Use facts, examples, quotations, statistics, and definitions as supporting details to develop the main idea.

- Present the details in a **logical order**—in a way that makes sense to the reader. Transitions help your reader follow your thinking.

Main idea

Facts: date, design — *WRITING MODEL*

[1]The Vietnam Veterans Memorial in Washington, D.C., has a simple, powerful design. [2]But in 1981 when judges chose Maya Lin's V-shaped design from 1,421 entries, controversy erupted. [3]For instance, some people complained that the two black intersecting walls were too plain. [4]There was nothing to see, they said, nothing heroic. [5]Yet in the years since, visitors have often praised two features. [6]First, on the monument's walls, the names of the 58,156 dead or missing Americans are engraved in chronological order of their death or disappearance; people find this order more emotional than alphabetical order. [7]Second, they comment positively on Lin's choice of a highly polished black granite for the two long walls. [8]She wanted, she said, to have visitors, especially veterans, "see their own reflection" in the names.

Transition

Statistic: number of names

Quotation

PERSUASIVE   See Lesson 3.2: Persuasive Writing

When your purpose is either to convince someone that your opinion is right or to persuade someone to take action, use the following suggestions.

- Begin with a sentence that is an **attention grabber**.

- Include an **opinion statement** that clearly expresses your point of view.

- Supply **reasons** and other **evidence** (facts, examples, statistics, anecdotes, quotations) to support your opinion.

- Arrange the supporting details in the **order of importance**—from most to least important, or the reverse.

- Include a **call to action** that tells the reader what to do.

Attention grabber

Statistic

Drastic solutions
to make a point

Opinion
statement
Call to action

¹Something drastic must be done. ²Fewer than half of the eligible voters actually go to the polls to elect a President, and in local elections, the turnout is abysmal. ³Perhaps the government should issue a tax credit to voters, or perhaps nonvoters should pay a fine. ⁴Maybe nonvoters shouldn't be allowed to get or renew their driver's licenses. ⁵Voting isn't just a privilege that half the citizens can ignore; it's a serious responsibility. ⁶Have you registered to vote yet? ⁷Do it now. ⁸If you are registered, go to the polls every chance you get.

Exercise 8   Writing with Different Purposes

Write at least two different types of paragraphs. You may use the suggested topics below or choose a topic of your own. Students' paragraphs will vary. Use the assessment rubrics in the teacher pages to evaluate students' writing.

1. A persuasive paragraph for or against wearing school uniforms or imposing a curfew on teenagers

2. A descriptive paragraph about a favorite place, a piece of clothing, an animal, or a person

3. A narrative paragraph about an accident, a surprise, or an adventure

4. An expository paragraph giving information about your school, your community, an invention, or a sports figure

Writing Essays

● All **essays** (pieces of writing on a limited topic) have three things in common: an introduction, a body, and a conclusion.

INTRODUCTION

The beginning paragraph of an essay accomplishes two things: It makes the reader think, "Hmmmm, I want to read this," and it presents the overall idea of the essay.

Some Ways to Begin an Essay
anecdote
vivid image
example
quotation
question
bit of dialogue
startling statement
or fact

The **thesis statement** of an essay is the overall idea. It can be called a **claim** or a **controlling idea**.

The thesis statement is for the whole essay what the topic sentence is for the paragraph. Each paragraph in the body of your essay should support your thesis statement. For example, the paragraph about blue jeans on page 24 could be part of an essay with the following thesis statement.

> The wardrobe of most Americans consists of three garments with remarkable histories: jeans, T-shirts, and sneakers.

The side column lists ways to begin an essay. Here's what not to write:

> In this paper, I am going to write about . . .
> This paper is about . . .

Enriching Your Vocabulary

The English adjective *nocturnal*, as used in Exercise 11, comes from the Latin adjective, *nocturnus*, which means "of, at, or by night." Many animals are *nocturnal* hunters.

BODY

The body of the essay can go on for many paragraphs. Here is where you say everything you have to say about your thesis. The following three suggestions will help you draft the body of an essay.

1. **Topic Sentences** Think of the body as a series of main ideas, each one expressed in the topic sentence of a paragraph and each one supported by details.

2. **Organization** Arrange your main ideas logically, in the way that's easiest to follow. Begin with background information, and then move through your main ideas in the way your reader needs to know them. When you outline an essay before you write, you are organizing the ideas for the body.

■ For more on outlining see **Composition Lesson 1.2.**

3. **Focus** Avoid repetition, and eliminate wordiness. First ask yourself, "What am I trying to say?" Then say it as clearly as you can.

CONCLUSION

When you've said everything that is important about your topic, stop! The concluding paragraph has only one job to do: It provides a definite ending. It doesn't have to be long; one or two sentences can do. See the side column for ways to end the essay.

Here's what not to write:

I'm sorry I can't tell you more about ...
That is all I know about ...

> **Some Ways to End an Essay**
>
> • summary of main ideas
> • comment on importance of topic
> • thought-provoking question
> • quotation
> • prediction about the future
> • call to action

Exercise 9 Drafting an Introduction

Assume you have to write a narrative essay based on an autobiographical incident and you choose the time you were called to the stage to receive an award. Going up the steps in full view of every student and teacher, you tripped and landed on your face. Draft an introduction that will make your classmates want to read your whole essay. Make up any details that you need. Encourage students to be creative and to begin with an exciting attention grabber. Students' paragraphs will vary.

Exercise 10 Drafting a Conclusion

Draft a concluding paragraph for a persuasive essay about a proposed curfew law for teenagers in your community. (See page 31 for some suggestions for writing persuasively.) In your conclusion, state your opinion and the main reasons for your opinion. Students' paragraphs will vary.

Exercise 11 Writing Body Paragraphs Based on Notes

Use the following notes to write one or more paragraphs for the body of a research paper about bats. Give each paragraph a topic sentence, and support the topic sentence with facts. Your audience should be your high school science class. Students' paragraphs will vary.

Characteristics of bats (background info)

Only mammal that flies   *Nocturnal (awake at night, sleep by day)*

Use echolocation (a kind of sonar) to navigate in dark and locate food

More than 1,000 species; many endangered

impt: all those species can be classified into only 2 kinds of bats:

(1) larger megabats (called "flying foxes") eat fruit, nectar, pollen; pollinate trees and plants in rainforests

(2) smaller microbats mostly eat insects; live in caves

Exercise 12 Revising and Editing an Essay

Revise the following brief essay to strengthen the introduction, body, and conclusion. Eliminate sentences that destroy the unity of the essay, and reorganize the paragraphs so that information is presented in the most logical order. Make any other changes to improve the essay.   Students' revisions will vary. Sample revisions suggested.

[1]~~The main point of this paper is to tell you that~~ stargazing can be ~~pretty~~ easy to start even if you live in a city where there is a lot of light. [2]At no cost to yourself, you can learn about the natural universe from your backyard or rooftop. [3]You'll enjoy fitting the pieces of the night sky together using a simple star map. [4]Even if you live in a place where lights stay on all night, you may have the most access to learning about the stars. [5]~~I learned about the stars from my brother who has a night guard job~~. [6]~~He watches stars a lot~~.

[7]Look for constellations that are particularly bright, such as Orion the Hunter, Cassiopeia's Chair, and The Big Dipper. [8]Next, start identifying the constellations of the zodiac. [9]You'll find that some of them look like their name, such as Taurus the Bull. [10]Others bear no relation to their name, such as Aires the Ram. [11]One of the most rewarding ways to start learning about the stars is to get a copy of a star map from an encyclopedia, from a newspaper, or from a star atlas in your library. [12]A star map will help you locate the most well-known constellations. [13]~~When you go out on a cold night, take warm clothes and a dim light so you can see your map~~.

[14]People who live in cities often feel that only people in the country can get a clear view of the stars. [15]Not true! [16]Cities often have several amateur organizations for observing stars. [17]These groups are filled with people, young and old, who are fascinated by the beauty and mystery of the stars. [18]In addition, cities often have excellent planetariums with weekend and evening programs on the universe, stars, or even the seasons. [19]~~Visiting a planetarium is more interesting than visiting an art museum~~. [20]On a clear night, the brightest constellations are visible even in the most light-polluted areas in the country. [21]Furthermore, unlike rural areas, most large cities are fantastic centers of sky observing.

[22]That's about all I can tell you about looking at stars. [23]I know that if you start going out on clear nights in a city, or if you ever visit the desert where the air is dry and clear, you will be able to pick out dozens of constellations with very little practice.

Students should rewrite conclusion.

Writing Workshops

Narrative Writing: Autobiographical Incident

Everyone has stories to tell. When you write about an autobiographical incident, you tell a true story about something that happened to you.

In his memoir *Days of Grace*, tennis great Arthur Ashe recalls two incidents and what they meant to him. As you read, think about how each incident relates to what Ashe says about character.

Character

from *Days of Grace* by Arthur Ashe

Ashe comments on the incidents he will present.

[1]What others think of me is important, and what I think of others is important. [2]What else do I have to go by? [3]Of course, I cannot make decisions based solely on what other people would think. [4]There are moments when the individual must stand alone. [5]Nevertheless, it is crucial to me that people think of me as honest and principled. [6]In turn, to ensure that they do, I must always act in an honest and principled fashion, no matter the cost.

Presents first incident and its setting

[7]One day, in Dallas, Texas, in 1973, I was playing in the singles final of a World Championship Tennis (WCT) tournament. [8]My opponent was Stan Smith, a brilliant tennis player but an even more impressive human being in his integrity. [9]On one crucial point, I watched Smith storm forward, racing to intercept a ball about to bounce a second time on his side of the net.

Introduces conflict

[10]When the point was over, I was sure the ball had bounced twice before he hit it and that the point was mine. [11]Smith said he had reached the ball in time. [12]The umpire was baffled. [13]The crowd was buzzing.

[14]I called Smith up to the net.

Quotes dialogue

[15]"Stan, did you get to that ball?"

[16]"I did. I got it."

[17]I conceded the point. [18]Later, after the match—which I lost—a reporter approached me. [19]Was I so naive? [20]How could I have taken Smith's word on such an important point?

[21]"Believe me," I assured him, "I am not a fool. [22]I wouldn't take just anybody's word for it. [23]But if Stan Smith says he got to the ball, he got to it. [24]I trust his character."

Presents second incident and its setting

[25]When I was not quite eighteen years old, I played a tournament in Wheeling, West Virginia, the Middle Atlantic Junior Championships. [26]As happened much of the time when I was growing up, I was the only black kid in the tournament, at least in the under-eighteen age section. [27]One night, some of the other kids trashed a cabin; they absolutely destroyed it.

Introduces
conflict

[28]And then they decided to say that I was responsible, although I had nothing to do with it. [29]The incident even got into the papers. [30]As much as I denied and protested, those white boys would not change their story.

States feeling

[31]I rode to Washington from West Virginia with the parents of Dickie Dell, another one of the players. [32]They tried to reassure me, but it was an uncomfortable ride because I was silently worrying about what my father would do and say to me. [33]When I reached Washington where I was to play in another tournament, I telephoned him in Richmond. [34]As I was aware, he already knew about the incident. [35]When he spoke, he was grim. [36]But he had one question only.

Quotes more
dialogue

[37]"Arthur Junior, all I want to know is, were you mixed up in that mess?"

[38]"No, Daddy, I wasn't."

[39]He never asked about it again. [40]He trusted me. [41]With my father, my reputation was solid.

Comments
after
presenting
incidents

[42]I have tried to live so that people would trust my character, as I had trusted Stan Smith's. [43]Sometimes I think it is almost a weakness in me, but I want to be seen as fair and honest, trustworthy, kind, calm, and polite. [44]I want no stain on my character, no blemish on my reputation.

Critical Thinking

After you read the autobiographical incident, answer the questions below.
Use the following questions to lead a class discussion.

1. Suppose you had a chance to talk with Ashe about his views on character. What would you say to him?

2. How does each incident relate to Ashe's comments on character? Which incident do you think has more impact on the reader? Which do you like better? Why?

3. Imagine that both incidents were reported without dialogue. What does the dialogue add?

4. Choose one of the two incidents that Ashe narrates, and pay close attention to *how* he describes it. Analyze (a) the order and (b) the amount of space given to each of the following: background information, setting, dialogue, and report of what happened. What kinds of details does Ashe omit?

5. With a partner, read aloud one of the accounts of the incidents. Then analyze the sentences for variety in length, structure, and beginnings.

6. Build your vocabulary. Underline the words in the selection that you do not know. Use a dictionary to find their meaning and write a brief definition in the margin or in your notebook. The following list may help: *principled* (sentence 5), *integrity* (sentence 8), *intercept* (sentence 9), *naive* (sentence 19), *blemish* (sentence 44).

Writing Strategies The purpose of writing an autobiographical incident is to narrate the series of events that made the incident come about. The audience can be any that you choose. For example, you might write for children, for your peers, or for a far-away friend. Use the following strategies to help.

1. **Select an incident.** An incident is a mini-story. It has a plot (what happens), characters, and a setting (when and where the events occur). You are the "I," the narrator, who is telling your story from the first-person point of view.

2. **Watch time order.** An incident doesn't stretch over a long period of time; it happens all at once or in a few hours or (at most) days. Usually, you can break an incident into several, individual events that happen in chronological order, beginning at the beginning and marching straight through to the end.

3. **Ask questions.** Your readers will want to know *Who? What (happened)? Where? When? Why?* and *How?* (These are the *5-W and How?* questions that newspaper reporters answer at the beginning of a news story. For more about these questions, see page 11.) *Why?* and *How?* are complicated, but make sure you answer as many of the other questions as you can, and provide enough background information for the reader to understand the incident.

4. **Answer, "What's the point?"** You remember an incident for a particular reason. Why? Is it an example of something? What does it show or prove? Once you have determined the whole point of the incident, you will be able to comment on what it means to you. Look back at Arthur Ashe's comments. How well do his comments fit the two incidents?

5. **Include your thoughts and feelings.** Try to remember what you thought and felt at the time the incident happened. Then see if you can figure out what you feel and think about the incident now. Include your thoughts and feelings as you write.

6. **Sprinkle with sensory details.** A few sensory details (sights, sounds, smells, tastes, sensations of touch) will help the reader imagine clearly what you remember. Watch out, however, because too much description dulls and delays the story.

7. **Add some dialogue.** No one remembers exactly what was said long ago, but you probably have a general idea. Take a guess at who said what, and add some dialogue. Look back at the model "Character" to see how and where Ashe uses dialogue.

Exercise 1 Get Started

Use one or two of the prewriting techniques (clustering, writer's notebook, etc.) discussed on pages 9–11 to jot down some incidents you can write about. You might, like Ashe, write about "a moment when you stood alone." Or you might try to think of a "first," for example, a first day on a job, a first date, or a first time alone shopping. As you brainstorm, be sure to include notes on your feelings about the incident.

Remember: (1) The incident must be in some way important to you. (2) You must remember the incident vividly. (3) It must have taken place in a short time period.
You might want to refer to the teacher page "Purposes of Writing" for additional information.

Exercise 2 Plan Your Autobiographical Incident

Use a **story map** to plan your essay. A story map is a graphic device that you can use as you gather details when you write a story or when you report an autobiographical incident. Fill in the right column of the story map below. Answers will vary.

Story Map	
a. What is the **setting**?	
b. Identify the main **characters**, and describe them briefly.	
c. Identify the **conflict**, and briefly summarize the **plot**.	
d. What are your **feelings** about the incident?	

Exercise 3 Draft the Autobiographical Incident

Draft your paper in whatever way feels comfortable to you. Your audience for the incident should be your classmates. Your purpose can be to let them know you better. Like Ashe, you might make a personal comment both before and after the incident(s). Or you might choose to comment only once—either at the beginning or the end. Here are some strategies for drafting the incident.

- **Zero in on what's important**. Ashe probably could have written much more about each incident, but he gets right to the point. His incidents are not bogged down by too much description and detail.

- **Be clear about what the incident means to you**. Ashe says it twice—at the beginning and the end. Summarize your feelings about the incident at least once in your essay.

Exercise 4 Revise Your Autobiographical Incident

Try reading your paper aloud to yourself. Work on getting the sentences to read smoothly. Then—or maybe at the same time—focus on your word choice. See if you can find just the right words to replace vague, general nouns and verbs. Go back over your comment(s) and incident(s) to eliminate padding and unnecessary words. When you are satisfied with your paper, share it with a partner and ask for comments, questions, and suggestions.

See "Step-by-Step Revising and Editing" in the teacher pages for more information.

Exercise 5 Proofread and Publish

Check your revised paper for errors in grammar and usage, spelling, punctuation, and capitalization. You might increase its chances of being error-free by exchanging papers with a partner—or several—to see if you've missed anything.

Share your autobiographical incident with friends and family, especially with anyone who was present when the incident happened. If you have enjoyed this assignment, you might write several more incidents and bind them together as a memoir. You might give the bound book to a relative as a gift, or keep it and add to it as the years go by.

Refer to Chapters 13–16 for punctuation, capitalization, and spelling rules. See teacher pages for "Proofreading Checklist."

Persuasive Writing

When you write to **persuade**, you try to make your reader agree with your opinion. You build an argument based on the **logical appeals** of reasons and evidence. You may also add **emotional appeals** to persuade your reader. The persuasive essay below was written by Al Gore when he served as Vice-President of the United States. As you read the essay, think about *how* Gore tries to persuade you.

Wiring Schools to the Internet Is Essential to the Way Kids Learn
by Al Gore

[1]As *Time* wrote last October, "All kids, not just ones from families that can afford a home computer, should grow up with a mouse in their hand." [2]The President and I could not agree more. [3]Access to the basic tools of the information age is no longer a luxury for our children. [4]It is a necessity.

Grabs reader's attention

States position

[5]Today communications and information technology are transforming our economy and our society, changing the way we live, the way we work, and the way we relate to one another. [6]In recent years, information technology has been responsible for more than one-quarter of real economic growth. [7]Jobs in information technology pay significantly more than nontechnology jobs. [8]By the year 2000, sixty percent of all jobs will require the technology skills that only a fraction of Americans now have.

States reasons for position

[9]But technology skills become important long before people look for jobs. [10]They become important as soon as children begin to learn. [11]In a decade-long series of studies, the Education Department reports that students in classes that use computers outperform their peers on standardized tests of basic skills by an average of thirty percent. [12]And a 1996 study showed that students with access to the Internet not only presented their final projects in more creative ways but also turned in work that was more complete and had better syntheses of different points of view. [13]Numerous other studies show that children in technology-rich learning environments showed more enthusiasm, had higher attendance rates, developed better writing skills, and displayed a greater capacity to communicate effectively about complex problems.

Statistic supports position

[14]Some critics view the new technology as a frivolous tool of education. [15]But more and more, computers are at the very heart of how schools teach and children learn. [16]Other critics are worried about the changes they imagine the new technology may bring. [17]Over the course of history, progress often spurs anxiety. [18]When Greek merchants began importing Egyptian paper into Athens, Socrates condemned it, complaining that the use of paper would, according to writer Nicholas Allard, depersonalize interactions,

Cites opposition to position

Counters opposition with anecdote

disrupt human ties, and "replace public discourse with less desirable and potentially dangerous private communication."

[19]Still other critics say we are diverting needed resources away from other, more pressing educational priorities. [20]But we need not limit ourselves to investing in one or the other. [21]We can do both, and we must.

Restates opinion in conclusion

[22]All parents want to help prepare their children for the future. [23]Today that challenge means helping them grow up in a world in which information and communications technology dominate the economy and shape our society. [24]We must give our children—all our children—the chance to succeed in the information age, and that means giving them access to the tools that are shaping the world in which they live.

Critical Thinking

After you read the persuasive essay, answer the questions below.
Use the following questions to lead a class discussion.

1. Briefly outline how Gore tries to persuade you to believe that his opinion is right.

2. Who do you think the audience is for Gore's persuasive essay?

3. What do you think about the following statement from sentence 1: "[K]ids . . . should grow up with a mouse in their hand"?

4. Identify the three criticisms that oppose Gore's position. Do you think he effectively counters each criticism? Why?

5. Reread sentence 18. Explain how Socrates' condemnation of Egyptian paper relates to the proposal for wiring schools to the Internet.

CONVINCE EMPLOYER YOU ARE BEST FOR JOB.

Writing Strategies — A letter to the editor is brief—perhaps two or three paragraphs long. A persuasive essay, such as Gore's, gives you more room to argue your point. For both types of persuasive writing, however, the same strategies apply.

1. **Present a clear opinion, or position statement.** No one should come away from your letter or essay wondering what you think. State your opinion as clearly as you can in a single sentence or two. In a letter to the editor, the opinion statement usually comes at the beginning. In a persuasive essay, the opinion statement (sometimes called a **thesis statement**) often comes in the essay's introduction—but not always. Gore's opinion is stated in the title and in the first paragraph of the essay.

> **Step by Step**
>
> **Building Your Argument**
> Opinion statement
> • Reason 1 supported by evidence
> • Reason 2 supported by evidence
> • Reason 3 supported by evidence
>
> Conclusion or Restatement of Opinion
>
> Call to Action
>
> (You may add emotional appeals, but you should not rely solely on such appeals.)

2. **State reasons for your opinion.** A **reason** is a statement that tells why you hold your opinion. Usually, you will need two or three strong and distinctly different reasons to support your opinion.

3. **Support reasons with evidence.** To support your reasons, use a variety of evidence, such as facts or expert opinions.

   • A **fact** is a statement that can be proven. Make sure that you get your facts from reliable reference sources.

   • Use **expert** opinions or quotations. Choose someone who knows a great deal about your topic. Be sure to identify the expert and, if quoting, use that person's exact words.

   ■ **For more on punctuating quotations, see Mechanics, Lesson 14.5.**

   • A **definition** is a statement of the meaning of a word or phrase. Definitions are often used for emphasis.

   • **Statistics** are facts expressed in numbers: "Sixty percent of all jobs will require the technology skills that only a fraction of Americans now have." Include statistics when you want to show some scientific support for your opinion.

   • You know what an **example** is—a particular type or instance used as an illustration. Use examples to support your position.

   • An **anecdote** is an incident that actually happened, one that is often based on the writer's personal experiences or observations. Gore tells an anecdote about Greek merchants importing paper.

4. **Support reasons with emotional appeals**. Persuasive writers sometimes appeal to a reader's fears, hopes, wishes, or sense of fairness. **Loaded words**—words carrying either positive or negative connotations—can sway the reader's emotions.

5. **Present and, if possible, demolish counterarguments**. A persuasive writer may acknowledge the opposing point of view and then give reasons and evidence to prove that view wrong.

6. **End with a call to action**. Some persuasive writing ends with a call to action. The writer urges the reader to do something such as write a letter, donate money, vote for a candidate, or buy a product.

Exercise 6 Choose a Topic

Work with a small group to brainstorm at least three topics for a persuasive essay or letter to the editor. Use these hints.   Students' topics will vary. You may wish to propose
one of the topic ideas found in the teacher pages.

• The topics must be arguable, not just a matter of personal taste. They should be something that people disagree about.

• The topics must be something you have a strong opinion about. Be careful! Not every topic is appropriate for school assignments. Check with your teacher if you are unsure about the appropriateness of your topics.

Exercise 7 State Your Opinion

1. Discuss these three opinion statements with your writing group. Decide which is the strongest and tell why.

    (a) In my opinion, I think that wiring high school classrooms to the Internet is probably a good idea.

    (b) Internet access in school is a good idea.

    (c) In order to be accredited by a state, all high schools should be required to be connected to the Internet.

2. Choose one of the topics you brainstormed in Exercise 1. Try to state your opinion clearly, precisely, and forcefully in one or two sentences. You might draft several different versions of your opinion statement, then choose the best one.

Exercise 8 Support Your Opinion

Before you write, think about your audience so that you can choose those reasons, evidence, and emotional appeals that are suited to your readers. You also should give them the background information that they will need to understand your subject. Use the following hints:

- **Be specific**. Provide specific examples, facts, and numbers from reliable sources. Avoid general expressions, such as "most states" or "many people . . . ." Mention your sources; your audience will be impressed that you've done your research.

- **Stay focused**. Keep your argument tight. Don't waste words or wander.

Do some research and jot down specific examples that support your opinion.

Exercise 9 Draft Your Letter or Essay

Write your first draft. Remember these three elements of effective writing:

- **Provide support**. The more support you give for your opinion, the more persuasive you'll be. Just make sure that everything you say is relevant—to the point.

- **Give cues**. As you follow a brief outline like the one called "Building Your Argument," let your readers know where your argument is headed. For example, mention the number of reasons you'll give: "I oppose the proposed curfew for three reasons. . . ." Then, as you mention each reason, alert your reader with transitions, such as *First, Second, Third,* and *Finally.*

- **Aim for clarity**. Concentrate on expressing every thought as clearly as you can.

Exercise 10 Revise, Edit, Proofread, and Publish

Revise your essay by adding, deleting, or moving content. Then edit to eliminate unnecessary words and sentences. Tighten your argument by dropping anything that doesn't directly support your main point. Include loaded words and emotional appeals in your argument. Share your paper with a writing group, or use the following publishing suggestions.

- If you've written a letter to the editor, send it to your local paper. Begin it with "To the Editor:" and end it with your name, address, and phone number.

- If you've written a persuasive essay, send it to a government representative or an official who might act on the issue you've discussed.

- Send any kind of persuasive writing to a local radio or TV station.

Refer to "Step-by-Step Revising and Editing" in the teacher pages for more information. You might want to have the rest of the class be reviewers of students' essays before the essays are submitted to publishers.

Expository Writing: Compare and Contrast Essay

When you **compare**, you identify the way two or more subjects, or topics, are alike. When you **contrast**, you identify differences between subjects. Here are parts of an essay about two Civil War generals.

Grant and Lee: A Study in Contrasts
an excerpt by Bruce Catton

[1]When Ulysses S. Grant and Robert E. Lee met in the parlor of a modest house at Appomattox Court House in Virginia, on April 9, 1865, to work out the terms for the surrender of Lee's Army of Northern Virginia, a great chapter in American life came to a close, and a great new chapter began. . . .

[*Most of Catton's essay analyzes how the two generals differ. Catton discusses Lee first. Lee had an aristocratic Virginia background, he believed in a society ruled by landowners, and he was intensely loyal to the South. Then Catton contrasts the same three features in Grant. Grant had a working-class Western background, he believed in a democratic society where anyone can achieve wealth and power through hard work, and he was fiercely loyal to the Union. Then Catton continues as follows.*]

[2]Yet it was not all contrast, after all. [3]Different as they were—in background, in personality, in underlying aspiration—these two great soldiers had much in common.

[4]Each man had, to begin with, the great virtue of utter tenacity and fidelity. [5]Grant fought his way down the Mississippi Valley in spite of acute personal discouragement and profound military handicaps. [6]Lee hung on in the trenches at Petersburg after hope itself had died. [7]In each man there was an indomitable quality . . . the born fighter's refusal to give up as long as he can still remain on his feet and lift his two fists.

[8]Daring and resourcefulness they had, too, the ability to think faster and move faster than the enemy. [9]These were the qualities which gave Lee the dazzling campaigns of Second Manassas and Chancellorsville and won Vicksburg for Grant.

[10]Lastly, and perhaps greatest of all, there was the ability at the end to turn quickly from war to peace once the fighting was over. [11]Out of the way these two men behaved at Appomattox came the possibility of a peace of reconciliation. [12]It was a possibility which was not wholly realized in the years to come but which did, in the end, help the two sections to become one nation again . . . after a war whose bitterness might have seemed to make such a reunion wholly impossible. [13]No part of either man's life became

---

Enriching Your Vocabulary

To understand the meaning of the adjective *indomitable*, you need to know the meaning of its two root words. The prefix *in-* means "not." The verb *domitare* is Latin for "to tame." Thus, *indomitable* means "incapable of being tamed." We all admire a person who faces a crisis with *indomitable* courage.

Summarizes differences and begins discussion of similarities

Claims both men had tenacity and fidelity and gives examples

Claims both were daring and resourceful and gives examples

States most important similarity

Conclusion: restatement of thesis statement

him more than the part he played in their brief meeting in the McLean house at Appomattox. [14]Their behavior there put all succeeding generations of Americans in their debt. [15]Two great Americans, Grant and Lee were very different, yet under everything very much alike. [16]Their encounter at Appomattox was one of the great moments of American history.

Critical Thinking

After you read the compare and contrast essay, answer the questions below. Use the following questions to lead a class discussion.

1. Reread the introduction and the conclusion of the essay. What do you think the author's purpose is?

2. Name the ways Catton says the two generals are alike. What proof, or support, does he give?

3. The word *yet* at the beginning of the second paragraph is a **transition**; it indicates that an opposite idea will follow. List some other transitions Catton uses to help the reader follow his thinking.

4. Build your vocabulary. Look at the following three words in context, and discuss what each word means: *aspiration* (sentence 3), *tenacity* (sentence 4), and *reconciliation* (sentence 11). If you can't define or aren't sure of a word, check a dictionary, and add the word to your vocabulary notebook.   Encourage students to use these words when they speak and write.

Writing Strategies

The purpose of writing a compare and contrast essay is to inform your readers about a subject or to explain a subject. It is critical, therefore, that you plan your essay carefully and that you organize your thoughts clearly. Use the following suggestions.

1. **Choose your subjects**. If your topic is not assigned, choose one that allows you to compare and contrast two subjects that you know something about—and about which you want to think even more. For example, choose two persons, two places, two events, or two objects.   Refer to "Ideas for Writing" in the teacher pages for additional topics.

2. **List their features**. Think about your subjects in terms of as many features, or categories, as possible. Start with the following categories.

appearances   histories or backgrounds

advantages or disadvantages   costs and benefits

actions or behaviors   effects on you or other people

most special qualities or traits

3. **Use a Venn diagram**. A Venn diagram is a useful prewriting tool for identifying differences and similarities. In the overlapping part of two circles, list features that your two subjects share. In the parts of the circles that do not overlap, list their differences. Use the following model as a guide.

GENERAL LEE

1. Background: aristocratic Virginian

2. Believed in government by landowners

3. Loyal to the South

Similarities

1. Tenacious and loyal

2. Resourceful

3. Ready for peace

GENERAL GRANT

1. Background: working-class, Westerner

2. Believed in government by everyone

3. Loyal to the Union

4. **Organize**. Use one of the two basic formats for organizing a compare and contrast essay listed on the chart on page 49. Choose the one that best makes your points.

In the **block method**, discuss one subject at a time. First, discuss all the features about one subject. Then move on to the second subject, discussing the same features in the same order.

In the **point-by-point method**, first deal with one feature in subject 1 and subject 2. Then present a second feature in subject 1 and subject 2, and continue the same way for the remaining features.

In general, the block method works better for shorter papers; the point-by-point method is better for longer ones.

5. **Use clear transitions**. Transitional expressions help the reader follow your thinking. *Like, also, similarly, both,* and *in the same way* signal similarities. *Yet, but, on the other hand, in contrast,* and *nevertheless* signal differences. Transitions can also highlight each new feature: *first, second, finally, more important,* and *most significant.*

Two Methods for Organizing a Compare and Contrast Essay

Block Method:
One subject at a time

All about Lee

Feature 1: background
Feature 2: government
Feature 3: loyalty to region

All about Grant

Feature 1: background
Feature 2: government
Feature 3: loyalty to nation

Point-by-Point Method:
Contrast one feature at a time

Feature 1: Background

Lee: Southerner
Grant: Westerner

Feature 2: Government

Lee: Government by the few
Grant: Government by the many

Feature 3: Loyalty

Lee: Loyal to the South
Grant: Loyal to the Union

Exercise 11 Choose Subjects

Use one or all of the following suggestions to come up with two things to compare or contrast.

Apples and oranges The subjects you choose may be very different or quite similar, but they *must* have at least one feature in common—as apples and oranges do. The easiest subjects to write about are specific, limited ones which you can observe directly. Try comparing or contrasting two of the following items

people	paintings	movies	singers	food
places	TV shows	animals	sports (teams, players)	

Then/Now You might compare a single subject in the past with the same subject in the present. For example, what was your community like a hundred years ago? How is it different today? Suggest that students research what their community was like a hundred years ago.

An imaginative comparison Use your imagination to find similarities between two situations or actions that seem, at first, to have nothing in common. For example, how is pumping up a bicycle tire like listening to a complaining friend? Encourage students to look for the humor in this comparison.

Exercise 12 Gather Information

Decide which features of your two subjects you will examine as you compare and contrast. As you begin prewriting, use one or more of the following techniques.

- **Observe your subjects**. Take notes as you actually look at and/or listen to your subjects.

- **Do some research**. If you're writing about subjects you don't know a lot about (such as Grant and Lee), use encyclopedias or other reference books to gather facts, examples, and other information. You will need specific details to back up your general statements.

- **Know the difference between fact and opinion**. Don't confuse them. A **fact** is a statement everyone agrees is true; it is something that you can measure or prove. An **opinion** is a person's idea or belief. It cannot be proven true, but it can be supported with reasons and other evidence.

After you have gathered information, choose the features of comparison that you will use in your essay. A Venn diagram may help you sort out your notes (see page 48).

Exercise 13 Organize Your Essay

1. Limit the number of features. From the notes you've made about the features of your subjects, choose only two or three to focus on. List the features you've chosen on the organizer below.

2. Choose the organization that suits your subjects and features better—the block or point-by-point method. Decide which subject you will put first and why, or decide which feature you will mention first and why.

3. On a separate piece of paper, make a rough outline. Your rough outline should look like one of the two methods for organizing an essay shown on page 49.

Organize Your Essay

Feature 1 _____
_____

Feature 2 _____
_____

Feature 3 _____
_____

Exercise 14 Draft Your Essay

Remember the three elements that need to be included in your essay.

1. **Introduction** Your first paragraph should (1) identify your subjects, (2) let your reader know whether you will discuss their similarities or differences or both, and (3) catch your reader's attention. Be sure to draft a **thesis statement** that summarizes the essay's main (or controlling) idea. Refer to Lesson 2.5 to help you draft a thesis statement.

2. **Body** Following the order of your rough outline, begin explaining your information to your readers. Insert transition words to help your reader follow your explanation.

3. **Conclusion** Summarize your findings at the end of your essay. You might point out how the subjects are more alike or more different or how one feature of comparison is more important than all the rest.

> **Writing Hint**
>
> Make sure all your comparisons are complete. If you write, "Killer whales are larger," will your reader know that you mean "larger than dolphins"?

Exercise 15 Revise and Edit

Revise your essay using the four-step revising strategy that was suggested on page 15. Be sure you have given enough support for each general statement. Eliminate wordiness, and add transitions to help the reader follow your thoughts.
Usage, Chapters 9–12 will help students revise their essays.

Refer to "Step-by-Step Revising and Editing" in the teacher pages for more information.

Exercise 16 Proofread and Publish Your Essay

Working Together

Reread your paper and ask a partner to check it, too. Once you have corrected every error in grammar, usage, mechanics, and spelling, find a way to share your paper with an audience. Refer to Chapters 13–16 for punctuation, capitalization, and spelling rules.

Read your paper aloud to classmates. Ask them to take notes as they listen. Can they summarize the controlling idea of your comparison or contrast essay?

Compile separate anthologies of compare and contrast essays on individual topics such as history, biology, or literature. Donate these anthologies to other classes or to the school library for other students to use.

Writing About Literature: Analyzing Fiction

When you write about a story or novel, you usually create one of three kinds of essays. The three serve very different purposes.

1. In a **personal response** essay, you write about how you felt and what you thought as you read, about the passages that seemed particularly meaningful, and about the other works that the story reminded you of.

2. In an **evaluation**, you write about how good or bad the work is. Your evaluation is based on objective **criteria**, or standards, that are used to measure the excellence of a literary form. For example, here are two criteria for measuring a short story:

   • The characters are believable.

   • The plot engages the reader's interest.

3. In a **literary analysis**, you discuss one or more of the **elements of fiction**: characters, plot, setting, point of view, and theme.

The following excerpt is from a long literary analysis of Ernest Hemingway's novel *The Old Man and the Sea.* Here, Carlos Baker discusses the feelings that the main character, Santiago, has for birds and fish while he is battling a marlin.

Hemingway's Ancient Mariner
an excerpt from an essay by Carlos Baker

¹According to the ancient mariner of Coleridge, "[h]e prayeth best who loveth best all things both great and small." ²Along with humility, pride, and piety, Hemingway's ancient mariner [Santiago] is richly endowed with the quality of compassion. ³Of course, he is not so foolish as to love all creatures equally. ⁴He dislikes, for example, the Portuguese men-of-war, whose beautiful "purple, formalized, iridescent, gelatinous" bubbles serve to buoy up the "long deadly purple filaments" which trail a yard behind them in the water and contain a poison which will paralyze the unwary passersby. . . . ⁵He has another set of enemies in the water of the tropic sea. ⁶For he genuinely hates, and gladly destroys, the voracious sharks which attack and disfigure the marlin he has fought so long to win.

⁷But his hatred is more than overbalanced by his simple love and compassion for all those creatures which swim or blindly soar. ⁸His principal friends on the ocean are the flying fish. ⁹He loves the green turtles and the hawksbills "with their elegance and speed." . . . ¹⁰Porpoises delight him. ¹¹"They are good," he says. ¹²"They play and make jokes and love one another.

Enriching Your Vocabulary

Voracious comes from the Latin verb *vorare*, meaning "to swallow up, eat greedily, or devour." This versatile adjective may be used in both a literal [concrete] and a figurative [an abstract] sense. A person who has a *voracious* appetite is likely to eat huge quantities of food. Someone with a hunger for knowledge may be a *voracious* reader.

Reference to the poem "The Rime of the Ancient Mariner" by Coleridge

Thesis statement

Example

Another example

General statement

Many examples

---

¹³They are our brothers like the flying fish." ¹⁴Several times in the course of his struggle he feels pity for the great marlin he has hooked—so "wonderful and strange" in his power to pull the skiff for so many hours, without sustenance, without respite, and with the pain of the hook in his flesh.

General statement ¹⁵For the lesser birds his compassion is greatest, "especially the small delicate dark terns that were always flying and looking and almost never finding." ¹⁶The birds, he reflects, "have a harder life than we do except for **Quotations** the robber birds and the heavy strong ones. ¹⁷Why did they make birds so delicate and fine as those sea swallows when the ocean can be so cruel? ¹⁸She is kind and very beautiful. ¹⁹But she can be so cruel and it comes so suddenly and such birds that fly, dipping and hunting, with their small sad voices are made too delicate for the sea."

General statement ²⁰His grateful sense of brotherhood with the creatures of the water and the air is, though full of love, essentially realistic and unsentimental. ²¹His implied or overt comparisons between subhuman and human brothers often open out, therefore, in as many directions as our imaginations wish to follow. ²²A memorable example of this tendency appears in the incident of the land-bird, a warbler, which comes to rest on Santiago's skiff far out at sea. . . .

²³This gently humorous monologue with its serious undertone of implied commentary on the human condition encourages the old man at this stage of his struggle. ²⁴"Stay at my house if you like, bird," he said. ²⁵"I am sorry I cannot hoist the sail and take you in with the small breeze that is rising. ²⁶But I am with a friend." ²⁷It is just at this point that the marlin gives a sudden lurch, the tautened line jerks, and the warbler flies away—towards whatever it is that awaits him on the long voyage home. ²⁸Hawks or sharks, the predators wait, whether for tired young birds or tired old men. . . .

²⁹To their hazard or their sorrow, Hemingway's heroes sometimes lose touch with nature. . . . ³⁰But Santiago is never out of touch. ³¹The line which ties him to the fish is like a charged wire which guarantees that the circuit will **Comparison with St. Francis** remain unbroken. ³²Saint Francis with his animals and birds is not more closely allied to God's creation than this Santiago with his birds and his fish. **Quotation** ³³These are his brothers, in all their sizes. ³⁴"I am with a friend," he cheerfully tells the warbler. ³⁵When the bird has departed, he is momentarily smitten by a sense of his aloneness on the vast waters. ³⁶Then he looks ahead of his skiff **Reference to incident** to see "a flight of wild ducks etching themselves against the sky over the water, then blurring, then etching again." ³⁷Once more he is convinced of what he has only momentarily forgotten: No man is ever alone on the sea. ³⁸This sense of solidarity with the visible universe and the natural creation is **Conclusion** another of the factors which help to sustain him through his long ordeal.

Writing About Literature:
Analyzing Fiction

Critical Thinking

After you read the analysis above, answer the following questions.
Use the following questions to lead a class discussion.

1. From what you have read of Baker's essay, would you enjoy reading *The Old Man and the Sea*? Explain why or why not.

2. Find two or three general statements that Baker makes. Then find the support Baker gives for each of these general statements.

3. In your own words, summarize the essay's controlling idea.

4. With a partner or small group, focus on the last paragraph of the essay. Read it aloud. How does Baker make his sentences flow smoothly? What connecting words or phrases does he use?

5. Build your vocabulary. Underline the words in the selection that you do not know. Use a dictionary to find their meaning and write a brief definition in the margin or in your notebook. The following list may help: *compassion* (sentence 2), *voracious* (sentence 6), *respite* (sentence 14), *monologue* (sentence 23), *smitten* (sentence 35), and *solidarity* (sentence 38). Encourage students to use these words when they speak and write.

Writing Strategies

The purpose of an essay about a literary work is to explain your interpretation of it. Use the following strategies as you write.

1. **Identify title and author**. In the first paragraph, identify the work you are writing about.

2. **Present a thesis statement**. A **thesis statement** at the end of your introduction clearly summarizes your controlling idea in a sentence or two. (Use the "Questions for a Literary Analysis" beginning on page 55 for help.)

■ See **Composition** Lesson 2.5 for more about writing a thesis statement.

3. **Give a very, very, very brief plot summary**. Here is where many students make a big mistake: Don't get bogged down in details. Spend no more than *a few sentences* summarizing a short story and no more than a *paragraph* summarizing a novel.

4. **Make clear, general statements**. Your main points about your thesis statement form the backbone of your essay.

5. **Use present tense**. When you refer to characters or events in the work, their actions should be stated in the present tense.

EXAMPLE   Santiago **struggles** with the marlin and **battles** the sharks.

6. **Support your statements**. The stronger your support, the better your reader will understand each of your general statements. Use the following hints.

- **Quote from the text**. Enclose a direct quotation in quotation marks that show direct examples of your point. Sentence 34 is a good example of this.

- **Refer to details in the text**. You can refer to an incident or character without quoting from the text. Find at least one example of such a reference in Baker's essay.

- **Make comparisons**. Baker refers to a poem by Coleridge when he quotes, "He prayeth best. . . ." A comparison or contrast with a different text may clarify the point you are making.

- **Summarize an expert**. Do research to discover literary criticism about the work or the writer. If you quote or summarize another critic's ideas, give full credit to that writer.

7. **Watch your tone**. The tone of your essay should be formal and serious. Avoid contractions, sentence fragments, and slang.

> # Writing Hint
>
> When you are quoting from a text:
>
> - check to see that you have quoted exactly.
>
> - enclose single words, phrases, and short sentences in quotation marks.
>
> - make sure that quotations larger than three lines are indented as a block; do not enclose the indented block in quotation marks.
>
> - use ellipsis points (. . .) to indicate omissions in a quoted text. At the end of a sentence, indicate an omission with (. . . .), a period followed by three ellipses points.

■ See
Mechanics
Lessons 14.5
for help with
punctuation
of quotations.

QUESTIONS FOR A LITERARY ANALYSIS

The following questions will help you come up with an idea for writing. Also try clustering or brainstorming. See page 10.

Characters What does the character want or need at the beginning of the story? How does the main character change by the end? What does the main character learn or discover? What is the character's relationship with other characters? How does the writer reveal what the main character is like?

Plot What is the conflict or conflicts? Is the conflict external or internal? How is it resolved? What does the outcome reveal about the theme? Does the writer use foreshadowing or suspense?

Setting Could the story take place in a different setting? How does the setting influence the characters, action, or outcome?

Point of View Who tells the story? Is the narrator a character in the story? How would the story change if the story were told from a different point of view?

Theme Does the work convey a message about life or people? Is this message universal? Which passages most clearly convey the theme? If the theme isn't expressed directly, how can the reader figure it out? (The title, changes in the main character, and the outcome of the conflict often provide clues to the theme.)

Exercise 17 Prewriting: Choose and Limit a Topic

Choose a story you have already read and want to write about. Use the questions above to help you choose one literary element to write about. Of all the elements, character, plot, and theme are the ones that are the most likely to yield suitable topics. After choosing your literary element, narrow your focus further. In his essay Baker focuses by analyzing *one* aspect of Santiago's character: his compassion for animals.

Exercise 18 Prewriting: Major Points and Supporting Details

1. Reread the literary work carefully. Take notes on everything you notice that is relevant to your limited topic.

2. Write your two or three main points—your general statements on the organizer below.

3. From the main points, draft a thesis statement, a single sentence that expresses what you will cover in your essay. Don't agonize about it; you can change it later.

4. List specific details (quotations, incidents, examples) that "prove" each main point, and mark the strongest details with a check. (If you put notes—especially quotations— on a computer, you can add them to your essay when you draft it.)

Organize Your Analysis

General
    Statement 1 _____

_____

General
    Statement 2 _____

_____

General
    Statement 3 _____

_____

Exercise 19 Organize and Draft Your Essay

Before you start writing, review your notes. Choose two or three of your most important points. Then sit down and start writing—anywhere in the essay. Do not worry about perfect sentences. Just get your ideas down in sentences and paragraphs so that you will have something to revise.

- **Introduction, body, conclusion** Make sure you have included everything that belongs in each of the three basic parts.

- **Title** Think of a possible title; try out several. Your title should suggest both the work and your essay's focus.

> **A Literary Analysis**
>
> **INTRODUCTION**
> - Author and title of work
> - Brief plot summary
> - Thesis statement
>
> **BODY**
> - Major point 1
>   Support, support
> - Major point 2
>   Support, support
>
> **CONCLUSION**

Exercise 20 Revise and Edit Your Essay

Let the draft sit awhile. Then use the four revising strategies suggested in Lesson 1.3. Read for accurate content, clear organization, and appropriate style for your purpose and audience. As you and your peer editors revise, ask these questions:

Usage, Chapters 9–12 will help students revise their essays.

- Is the essay coherent, or well-organized?

- Are the general statements clearly expressed but not wordy?

- Have you elaborated enough to support or "prove" each main point?

- Is everything unified, or directly related to, the main point?

Exercise 21 Edit, Proofread, and Publish Your Essay

Double-check each quotation for accuracy and also for punctuation. When you are satisfied that you have corrected all errors in grammar, usage, and mechanics, exchange papers with a partner to check for any you may have missed.

Refer to Chapters 13–16 for punctuation, capitalization, and spelling rules.

You might form two reading-and-discussion groups: one for short stories and one for novels. Take turns reading aloud papers to the appropriate group. If others in the group have read the work you have written about, see if they agree with your analysis and if they have comments or ideas to add. Your group might also name other stories or novels that members might enjoy.

You might also compile a "lit crit" anthology of everyone's essays analyzing literature. Then share the anthology with other English classes.

Refer to "Step-by-Step Revising and Editing" in the teacher pages for more information.

Expository Writing: Research Paper

You may be asked to write a research paper in all of your classes, not just in English. A **research paper** is based on a thorough investigation of a limited topic. There are four types:

1. The most common type of research paper **summarizes** or **explains information** you have gathered from several different sources. You **synthesize** (put together to form a new whole) what other writers have reported.

2. Another type of research paper adds your **evaluation**, or opinion. For example, in a **problem–solution** research report, you might discuss a community problem and evaluate the effectiveness of several proposed solutions.

3. A third type of paper summarizes your **original research**. In social studies, you might draw conclusions and present findings based on surveys, questionnaires, or interviews you have conducted. A science research paper might report a long series of your observations and experiments. Your paper details the hypothesis, or theory, that you began with and the carefully controlled experiments you conducted to test that theory. You also include a survey of the literature, which includes scientific articles related to your investigation.

4. An **I-Search paper** narrates the story of how you wrote your research paper. It not only presents information you discovered about a limited topic but also explains why you chose that topic, how you conducted your research, and what you experienced along the way.

Science research papers follow a format and style of documentation that is different from the Modern Language Association (MLA) style described in this workshop.

On the following pages are excerpts from a high school student's research report that explains and synthesizes what other writers said about a world event that occurred in 1962. The research paper also evaluates the effects of the event. The paper includes parenthetical references to its sources and ends with a Works Cited list, both of which are discussed later in this workshop.

Leslie Porter
Mr. Charles Fass
U.S. History
December 3, 1999

Title and subtitle

**The Cuban Missile Crisis:
Immediate Responses and Lasting Effects**

**Attention-
grabber about
Chinese
character**

**Reference to
book on Works
Cited list**

**Thesis statement
ends introduction**

The Chinese character for the word "crisis" has two very different meanings. The first is the meaning we usually associate with the word in English: "a dangerous event or period." But the same character can also mean "opportunity." The fact that a crisis can actually have beneficial effects or can be the means for reaching a new understanding is often overlooked in international politics (Craig and George 129). Yet by reviewing the press coverage of the Cuban Missile Crisis at the time it was happening and by considering the crisis from our later perspective, we can see that the crisis had important, positive effects in both national and world politics.

A brief summary of the events from October 16 through October 28, 1962, is helpful in order to understand the importance of the crisis. On Tuesday morning, October 16, President John F. Kennedy received word that aerial photographs proved conclusively that the Soviets were building offensive—not defensive—nuclear weapons bases in Cuba. Kennedy and his advisors spent six days deliberating what the best course of action would be. They discarded the notion of an invasion of Cuba and settled on a blockade, which they decided to call a quarantine.

News of the crisis first reached the American public on the evening of October 22, when Kennedy addressed the nation on radio and television. The President detailed the discovery of Cuban missile bases, announced the U.S. quarantine of Cuba, and promised that the U.S. would take further action if necessary. For the next several days, the world breathlessly awaited a direct confrontation that, luckily, never happened. Soviet Premier Nikita Khrushchev ordered Russian ships to turn around or avoid the American blockade. However, work on the missile bases continued. Finally, on October 26, Khrushchev sent Kennedy a letter ordering to withdraw the missiles in return for a U.S. pledge not to invade Cuba. The next day a second letter arrived from Khrushchev, demanding U.S. withdrawal of missiles from Turkey. The U.S. ignored the second letter but responded affirmatively to the first, warning that withdrawal must take place by October 28 or the U.S. would conduct an air strike on Cuba. On October 28 Khrushchev announced the withdrawal of the missiles from Cuba. . . .

**Some
background
information has
been omitted
from these
excerpts.**

Result 1

One result of the Cuban Missile Crisis was a change in the way people and nations viewed President Kennedy. Joseph Grunwald, who lived in Miami at the time, remembers that before the Cuban Missile Crisis, people thought of

Porter 2

Kennedy as "immature, young, and inexperienced" and especially weak on foreign policy (Grunwald). . . . After the crisis, Kennedy's popularity and power increased greatly. . . . *Newsweek* summed it up: "Mr. Kennedy's behavior during the past two weeks has given Americans a sense of deep confidence in the temper of their president" ("Lessons").

Result 2

The crisis was almost uniformly seen as a tremendous victory for the United States in the Cold War. A November 2 editorial in *Life* proudly announced, "The Cuban blockade is a major turning point in the 17-year Cold War. The U.S. has dramatically seized the initiative." ("New"). We had taken a stand, made our position quite clear, and in the game of military chicken, the Russians jumped first. Not only was American public opinion overwhelmingly behind the President, but the U.S. got the support of its allies, including a 19-0 vote of confidence from the OAS (Reston). On the other hand, "the Soviet setback in Cuba clearly diminished Khrushchev's prestige in the Communist world," and Khrushchev was seen as discredited and handicapped ("What"). . . .

The Cuban Missile Crisis made the ever-present fear of nuclear war dramatically apparent. This was nowhere more evident than in South Florida, only 90 miles from Cuba. The Miami airport closed, and the military arrived by planeloads and truckloads. Fearing nuclear attack, people descended on supermarkets for canned foods, water, candles, and batteries (Grunwald). . . .

The crisis showed the necessity of communication and direct negotiations between the superpowers. The whole concept of escalation suggested that events could very easily spiral out of the policymakers' control. In a letter to JFK, Khrushchev wrote that it would be dangerously simple for "matters to slide into the disaster of war" (Kennedy 126). Two weeks after the crisis had ended, a letter writer in *Newsweek* made this hopeful forecast: "The success of the Cuban blockade will truly prove a victory for all mankind if Russia and the U.S. will now sit down to serious and fruitful disarmament talks" (Walker). . . .

Result 3

The Cuban Missile Crisis had acted like a bucket of cold water thrown over the heads of world leaders, who were so frightened by the nuclear danger that they decided that negotiation and communication were of the utmost importance. As a result of the crisis, the following year the United States and the Soviet Union hammered out the Limited Nuclear Test Ban Treaty. Also, a special "hotline" was established for instant communication between the White House and the Kremlin. During the crisis, it had become clear that "seven-hour delays for messages to reach Washington and the reliance on bicycle-riding Western Union messengers were unacceptable means of communication in a nuclear age" (Finklestein 109). These were perhaps the two biggest dividends of the Cuban Missile Crisis.

Porter 3

Concluding paragraph— importance of crisis

Observers at the time recognized that the Cuban Missile Crisis held tremendous significance for the nation and the world. "The ships of the U.S. Navy were steering a course that would be marked boldly on the charts of history," *Life* proclaimed, and "the steel perimeter clamped around Cuba by the U.S. could be the tripwire for World War III" ("Blockade"). *Newsweek* predicted that the crisis "may turn out to have consequences of incalculable importance for this century" ("Showdown"). Things could have turned out very differently

Recalls Chinese character for "crisis"

than they did, but the prudence and caution of both Kennedy and Khrushchev altered this crisis into an opportunity for peace.

Porter 4

Works Cited

unsigned article

"The Blockade: The U.S. Puts It on the Line." *Life* 2 Nov. 1962: 35.

essay found on Internet

Chang, Laurence, and Peter Kornbluh. "The Cuban Missile Crisis, 1962: An Introduction." *The Cuban Missile Crisis, 1962: A National Security Archive Documents Reader.* New York: New Press, 1992. Online. Internet. 18 Sept. 1995 Available www.seas.gwu.edu/nsarchive/nsa/cuba_mis_cri/cmcintro.html/.

book by two authors

Craig, Gordon A., and Alexander L. George. *Force and Statecraft.* New York: Oxford UP, 1990.

book by one author

Finklestein, Norman H. *Thirteen Days/Ninety Miles: The Cuban Missile Crisis.* New York: Julian Messner, 1994.

original interview by student

Grunwald, Joseph. Personal interview. 2 Dec. 1995.

Kennedy, Robert F. *Thirteen Days: A Memoir of the Cuban Missile Crisis.* New York: Norton, 1969.

"The Lessons Learned." *Newsweek* 12 Nov. 1962: 25.

"A New Resolve to Save the Old Freedoms." *Life.* 2 Nov. 1962: 4.

Reston, James. "Khrushchev's Misjudgment on Cuba." *New York Times* 24 Oct. 1962, sec. 1: 38.

"Showdown-Backdown." *Newsweek* 5 Nov. 1962: 28.

Walker, William. Letter. *Newsweek* 12 Nov. 1962: 4.

"What Happened in the Kremlin?" *Newsweek* 12 Nov. 1962: 26.

Writing Strategies

The following specific strategies apply to all four types of research papers. You must also use the writing strategies in Chapter 1 and the general advice for writing essays in Lesson 2.5.

1. **Budget your time**. Don't wait until the last minute. The chart on page 62 suggests a time budget for each step.

2. **Find multiple sources**. Your assignment may require you to use both primary and secondary sources.

A **primary source** is an original text or document, such as a literary work, a diary, letters, a speech, an interview, or a historical document.

A **secondary source** presents the writer's comments on a primary source. Reference books, biographies, literary criticism, and history and science textbooks are secondary sources.

By using a computer, you can find a wealth of primary and secondary information. In many libraries, electronic databases have replaced card catalogues, the *Readers' Guide to Periodical Literature*, and newspaper indexes. For example, when you enter key words to search Infotrac's General Reference Center, you access not only the titles of relevant magazine articles but also the text of the articles. A writer doing a research paper today could enter the key term "Cuban Missile Crisis" in Infotrac and get a listing of encyclopedia excerpts, reference book excerpts, newspaper articles, and periodical articles. By selecting the titles that are listed, the researcher could read and print the articles that seem most useful. In addition, a contemporary researcher can use various Internet search engines to explore the World Wide Web for new information about the Cuban Missile Crisis.

Research Schedule		
STEP	TOTAL TIME	
	6 weeks	8 weeks
Choose and limit topic.	2 days	3 days
Find and evaluate sources; make bibliography cards.	2 days	3 days
Take notes.	1 week	1 ½ weeks
Draft thesis statement and title.	1 day	2 days
Draft outline.	2 days	1 week
Write first draft.	1 week	1 week
Document sources.	1 day	2 days
Revise.	1 ½ weeks	1 ½ weeks
Proofread.	2 days	2 days
Prepare final manuscript.	3 days	3 days

3. **Evaluate possible sources**. All sources are not equal. The secondary sources you consult should be up-to-date, accurate, and relevant.

• **Up-to-date** Which is a better source for information about space stations: a twenty-year-old book or last month's article in *Scientific American*?

• **Accurate** Don't believe everything you read. Reliable sources are both accurate and unbiased. You can trust a *New York Times* article more than the headline in a sensational tabloid. Be careful about Internet sources, too. A government database is a reliable source; someone's personal home page might not be.

• **Relevant** Finally, the information you spend time with must directly relate to your limited topic. Do not start straying into information that is fascinating but unrelated.

4. **Keep track of your sources**. For every source you use, make a **source card** (sometimes called a bibliography source card) containing all essential publishing information. Give each source a number, and write the number in the upper

SAMPLE SOURCE CARD

> *Chang, Laurence, and Peter Kornbluh.*   *1*
> *"The Cuban Missile Crisis, 1962: An Introduction."*
>
> *The Cuban Missile Crisis, 1962: A National*
> *Security Archive Documents Reader. New York:*
> *New Press, 1992.*
>
> *Accessed online via Microsoft Internet Explorer.*
> *18 Sept. 1995*
> *www.seas.gwu.edu/nsarchive/nsa/cuba_mis_cri/*
> *cmcintro.html/.*

**Number of
source**

Some Sources
to Explore

- Periodicals
  (newspapers,
  magazines, journals)
- Books about your topic
- Reference books
  (encyclopedias,
  specialized books
  such as atlases)
- Publications by
  government agencies
- Publications by
  nonprofit
  organizations
- Internet
- Electronic databases
- Other media (movies,
  television, radio,
  CD-ROMs)
- Museums, zoos, and
  other institutions
- Published interviews
  and surveys
- Original interviews
  you conduct

right-hand corner of the source card. Then, when you
take notes, instead of rewriting all this information on
each note card, you can place the source's number in
the upper right-hand corner of your note card.

5. **Take notes.** After you have read a source, you may
   quote it exactly (use quotation marks!), or you may put
   the information into your own words. Do your best to
   use your own words when you can.

   - You can **summarize** the information by giving only
     the most important ideas in your own words.

   - Or you can **paraphrase** the information, restating
     every idea in the same order as in the original—but
     in your own words.

At the top of each note card, write the main idea, and
underline it.

SAMPLE NOTE CARD

> *National Security Archive worked to get documents*   *1*
> *about Cuban Missile Crisis declassified.*
>
> *In 1980s, filed Freedom of Information Act requests*
> *and lawsuit to make State Dept. release files from the*
> *crisis of 1962.   (page 23)*
>
> *By mid-1989: 2,000 docs. were totally or partially*
> *declassified   (page 24)*

Main idea

**Summary in
researcher's
own words**

6. Make an outline. Look for three or four main ideas in your note cards, and follow the outline format at the right. Also, learn the two-point rule. You need at least two points under every heading; you can't have just one point.

7. Draft a thesis statement. It's a toss-up whether you write an outline or draft a thesis statement first. Either way is acceptable. Your **thesis statement**, or statement of your controlling idea, comes at the end of your introduction. The thesis statement tells your readers what you are going to tell them in the rest of your paper.

8. Give credit. A research paper shows where your information comes from. You will need to acknowledge a source whenever you (1) quote a phrase, sentence, or passage directly; or (2) summarize or paraphrase another person's ideas in your own words. The Modern Language Association (MLA) has created a system for giving credit to sources. The research paper model on page 59–61 demonstrates the system:

• The student uses **parenthetical documentation** at the point of citing each source.

• The student gives complete information about each source at the end of the paper in the **Works Cited** list.

For more information about MLA style, consult the *MLA Handbook for Writers of Research Papers*, 4th edition, by Joseph Gibaldi. An online version of Gibaldi's work is accessible at *www.mla.org*. Also be aware that some instructors prefer that students cite each source in a footnote or endnote rather than in parentheses in the paper itself.

9. Don't plagiarize. Using someone else's words or ideas without giving credit is **plagiarism**, which is a serious offense. High-ranking officials have lost their jobs because of plagiarism, and writers have been sued. Do not attempt to borrow or buy someone else's research paper either. Teachers and other readers can detect writing that is not your own.

Sample Outline

Draft of thesis statement: <u>The crisis led to positive developments.</u>

I. First result: better opinions of President Kennedy
  A. Bad views of JFK
    1. Bay of Pigs fiasco
    2. Cold War in general
  B. Improved views
    1. Support from media
    2. Still, ongoing criticism
      a. from Republicans
      b. from conservative citizens
II. Second result: victory for U.S.

■ Use the rules listed in **Mechanics Lesson 14.5 and 14.6** for punctuating quotations and dialogue.

Exercise 22 Prewriting: Choose a Limited Topic

"What can I write about?" Your teacher may specify a general subject (animals and the environment, for instance), or you may have the whole world to choose from. Use the suggestions below to choose a topic and limit it to a manageable size.
Refer to "Ideas for Writing" in the teacher pages.

Inquiry-based The best research topic answers your own questions. Brainstorm a list of statements that begin, "I wonder . . . ." Or jot down a list of questions you are curious about. Try freewriting or looking back at your writer's journal for topic ideas.

Not too big, not too little—just right Your topic should be limited enough for you to handle in the number of pages you are supposed to write. (See Lesson 1.1 for strategies on how to limit topics.)

Exercise 23 Prewriting: Gather Information

Write a **direction statement** about what you are planning to research—for example, "I am going to write about the good effects of the missile crisis."

Use Strategies 2–5 on pages 62–63 to begin your research. As you dig out sources and examine them, keep the following ideas in mind.

• **Purpose** Your purpose is to give information. You may need to provide background information and define technical terms. But also look for new and interesting information; don't give only facts that your readers already know.

• **Audience** Your audience is likely to be your teacher and classmates, but keep in mind that you may publish your research paper more widely.

Exercise 24 Prewriting: Write an Outline

After you have prepared notes from a number of sources, make piles of note cards that deal with the same main idea. Here are three common problems and some advice:

• **Too few main ideas** You will need at least three or four. Can some of your main ideas be divided? If you have too few main ideas, you need to do more research.

• **Not enough supporting information**. Are you sure you need more? If the answer is yes, do more research. Explore new sources.

• **Too much information**. Arrange your note cards with the strongest cards at the top, the weakest at the bottom. You may discard the weakest note cards later.

Once you have fixed any problems, you are ready to create your outline (Strategy 6 on page 64). Your outline will set up a working structure to get you started.

Exercise 25 Write a First Draft with Documentation

Start drafting long before your paper is due so that you will have plenty of time to revise. Apply Skills 7–9 from page 64. Keep the following advice in mind too.

- **Title** As you draft, think about what you might title your research paper.

- **Quotations** Quotations show that you have done your research, but don't overload your paper. It should be mostly your own words.

- **Documentation** Work in your parenthetical citations and complete citations as you draft.

- **Introduction and conclusion** Many writers write these parts last, after they see what they have written.

Exercise 26 Revise and Edit Your Draft

Note that the timetables allow more than a week for revising. Read through your draft many times, focusing on something different each time: content, organization, style, mechanics. Check to see that you've arranged your ideas in the most logical order. Look for places to add transitions within a paragraph as well as at the beginning of a paragraph. Do the best revising job you can, and then ask for input from peer editors.
Usage, Chapters 9–12 will help students revise their essays.

Exercise 27 Proofread Your Paper

Now is the time to check the accuracy and punctuation of all the quotations that you have included. Check the style of the parenthetical citations and of Works Cited list, too. Make sure you have provided publishing information in the right order and punctuated exactly as required. Refer to Chapters 13–16 for punctuation, capitalization, and punctuation rules.

Exercise 28 Prepare the Final Copy and Publish

Congratulations! Your final paper is an enormous accomplishment, so prepare it carefully. Double-space your entire paper including the Works Cited page. Read the final paper again before you turn it in. If you find any last-minute mistakes, correct them neatly in ink. Ideally, your paper should be error-free.
See "Step-by-Step Revising and Editing" in the teacher pages for more information.

Special Writing Tasks: Essay Tests

What is the difference between an **objective test** and an **essay test**? In an objective test, you can guess an answer to a multiple-choice or a sentence-completion question and have a chance of getting it right. But on an essay test, you start with a blank piece of paper. Essay questions measure not only your knowledge of a subject but also how well you can communicate that knowledge. Here is an essay question from a biology test. The sample response that follows was considered excellent by teachers who read it.

Essay Question

Living organisms have different outer (exterior) coverings. From among the animals you have studied this year, identify two that have extremely different exterior coverings. In an essay of 250-300 words, explain how each exterior covering functions, how it meets the animal's needs, and what its limitations are.

RESPONSE

[1]All animals have some kind of barrier between their inner organs and the outside world. [2]Two animals with very different exteriors are lobsters and human beings. [3]Their exterior coverings protect them in various ways but also limit them.

— **Brief introduction**

— **Thesis statement—two sentences**

[4]A lobster's exterior covering, or exoskeleton, resembles the covering of many insects in three ways. [5]The exoskeleton is hard, it is made mainly of lime and a protein called chitin, and it is divided into segments. [6]The lobster's hard covering prevents it from twisting or moving sideways, so a lobster can move only forward and backward. [7]Like a snake, a lobster must shed its covering so that it can grow larger. [8]A lobster's exoskeleton serves as armor, protecting it from predators. [9]When it sheds its exoskeleton, the defenseless lobster hides until its new hard covering grows.

Block method—all about lobsters first

Comparisons with other animals

[10]People are covered with a continuous layer of soft, flexible skin, which does not hinder motion. [11]Human skin has two layers: a thin outer layer (epidermis) and a thicker inner layer (dermis). [12]Skin protects people from bacterial infection and also from the elements. [13]Skin is waterproof and, to some extent, protects against the sun's harmful rays. [14]Sweat, which is excreted through the skin's pores, helps maintain an even body temperature. [15]Nerve cells embedded in the skin enable people to sense dangerous extremes of heat and cold. [16]One advantage human skin has over a lobster's shell is that humans never have to shed their skin to grow. [17]New skin cells continually push to the surface to replace old, dead skin cells that are shed. [18]Unlike the lobster's shell, human skin doesn't do much to protect a person from creatures determined to do harm.

All about humans next

Specific contrasts with lobsters

[19]A lobster's shell and a person's skin look very different, but both serve to protect the animal and keep organs intact.

— **Brief conclusion**

Critical Thinking

After you read the essay on page 67, answer the following questions. Use the following questions to lead a class discussion.

1. Which features of exterior coverings does the writer discuss in comparing and contrasting the two subjects?

2. What grade would you give the sample response? Why?

Writing Strategies

The purpose of writing an answer to an essay question is to clearly explain everything you know about the topic. However, a good essay depends not only on your knowledge of the subject but also on your ability to express your thoughts clearly. The following strategies will help.

1. **Read the question carefully**. Make sure you understand exactly what you are being asked to do. Look for numbers: A question may have two or three parts; you may be asked to provide three or four reasons or to refer to two or more works; you may have to choose one of several questions to answer. The question may also specify how many words or paragraphs you are required to write. Read the question several times and follow the instructions exactly.

2. **Find the key words**. The most important thing to look for in an essay test question is the key word which directs how you approach the topic.

   • **Analyze** When you analyze, you take something apart and consider each part or element of it. If you analyze a poem, for example, you might consider these three elements: figures of speech, sound effects, and imagery. Often, a question doesn't specify the parts of the whole for you to consider. It is up to you to figure out what they are and then discuss them.

   • **Interpret** When you interpret, you describe your idea of what a statement or event means. You support your interpretation by citing examples, facts, or lines from a text.

   • **Compare/contrast** When you compare two or more things, you point out their similarities. When you contrast two things, you show how they differ. When a question asks for a comparison of two things, it is usually understood that you are to identify both their similarities and differences. (For more about comparison/contrast, see pages 46–51.)

   • **Explain** When you explain, you help the reader to understand something. You might give reasons or provide information that it makes clear why something has certain characteristics. Sometimes, you can explain by comparing/contrasting.

   • **Discuss** *Discuss* is the most general of all key words. When you are asked to discuss a topic, you are free to write about it in any way you choose.

3. **Make a plan. Be specific** Spend a minute or less making a simple **outline**. Jot down words and phrases to remind yourself of the main points and supporting details that you will be including in your answer. Then decide in what order you will present the main points. Essay graders look for a logical, step-by-step order. Also, draft a **thesis statement** summarizing your main points.

4. **Include an introduction and a conclusion**. Keep them brief. A successful formula is to say what you're going to say (introduction with thesis statement); say it (body); then say what you said (conclusion).

■ For more about the thesis statement, see page 32.

■ For more about introductions and conclusions, see pages 32–33.

5. **Watch your language**. Avoid difficult vocabulary and convoluted sentences. Strive for sentences that read smoothly and make sense immediately. Transitions will help show how ideas and details are related. (See page 27.)

6. **Watch your time**. If the test has several essay questions that need to be answered, divide your time among them depending on how many points each question is worth.

7. **Use the writing process**. When writing an answer to an essay test, practice everything you have learned about the stages of the writing process.

Exercise 29 **Select an Essay Question**

Choose one of the following essay questions to answer in this workshop.

Literature question Setting—the time and place where the action occurs—is important in some stories or pieces of nonfiction but unimportant in others. From the reading you have done, choose two works in which setting plays an important role. Explain how setting influences the outcome of each work. Write an essay of 250-300 words.

Government question If you had a chance to change or add to the U. S. Constitution's Bill of Rights, what would you change or add? Or would you leave the Bill of Rights unchanged, exactly as it was adopted? In an essay of 250-300 words, state your position persuasively, and give reasons to support it. Be specific.

Exercise 30 **Plan Your Answer**

Before you start writing, figure out—in general terms—what you're going to say.

• **Avoiding panic** Take a minute to brainstorm and to lay out a brief outline. Start with one main point, and below it, jot down details that support it.

- **Two major points** Now write down a second main idea. An essay answer is not sufficiently developed unless it offers two or more main points. Make sure the points are distinct. Also make sure that you can think of supporting details for each one. Jot those points down to help you stay focused.

- **Introduction** Now back up to planning your introduction. Identify for your reader exactly what you will be discussing in your essay answer.

- **Thesis statement** A strong thesis statement is specific and summarizes what your essay answer covers. Usually, the thesis statement belongs in your introduction. A thesis statement may be one or two sentences.

Draft a brief outline and a thesis statement on the topic you chose in Exercise 29.

Exercise 31 Draft Your Answer

While you are putting your thoughts into sentences on paper, keep the following advice in mind.

- **Tone** Try to sound confident, as if you are sure of what you are saying. Do not use hedge words such as *maybe, probably, perhaps*. Avoid slang and sentence fragments.

- **No padding** As you write, concentrate on being clear. In the body of your response, do not keep saying the same thing in different ways; once is enough. Eliminate wordiness.

- **Focus** Do not give in to the temptation to show off everything you know. Write about only what is relevant—directly related—to your thesis statement. In the model response, for example, the comparison of lobsters with insects and snakes works well as *brief* bits of extra knowledge that are directly related to the topic.

Exercise 32 Revise Your Essay

Go back over your writing carefully to eliminate unnecessary words and sentences. Remember to drop anything that doesn't directly support your main points. Also, consider whether you have enough support—or whether you must add more.
Usage, Chapters 9–12 will help students revise their essays.

Exercise 33 Edit and Proofread Your Answer

A day or two before you take an essay test, review both the editing strategies on page 16 and your proofreading log so that you do not repeat mistakes you have made in the past. The conventions of English count. During the test, allow time to reread your essay answer in order to find and correct any errors in usage or any problems in punctuation, capitalization, and mechanics.
Refer to Chapters 13–16 for punctuation, capitalization, and spelling rules.
See "Step-by-Step Revising and Editing" in the teacher pages for more information.

Parts of Speech

STUDENT WRITING
Narrative Essay

One Meal Made a Big Difference
by Sarah Swenson
high school student, The Woodlands, Texas

I fixed the big, rubber glove on my hand as I nervously grabbed the tray I was handed from my right. I took the spoon in my other hand and put a big spoonful of food, if you can even call it that, on the tray. I couldn't even bear to look up as I passed the tray over the counter. I feared that I would totally break down if I looked into their eyes.

After a while, I switched spots with someone and started handing out trays. All of a sudden, this lady walked out of the line and over to the piano. She played for a minute before she scurried back into line. As she moved toward me, I looked up into her eyes. They were a gentle brown.

I quickly swallowed the lump in my throat and pushed the tears from my eyes as I tried to put on my brightest smile.

"That was beautiful," I managed to get out.

"Thank you," she said as the line moved forward. "How has your day been?" she asked me as we were now standing almost face-to-face.

"Good," I replied, "and yours?"

"Mine has been pretty good," she responded as she reached to take her tray. "I'm alive, so it's good."

I don't know her name and it doesn't matter. That day, that one person changed my whole life. After that, I couldn't resist watching the smiles on people's faces as we gave them food.

When I first looked at what we were told to serve, I was disgusted. I never would have touched it. But then, I'm not really sure what happened. Everything just changed. I realized that for once in my adolescent life, I was making a difference. It may not seem like a big deal, but it was to me.

I was feeding people who needed to be fed—not because they had had a small breakfast, but because this was the only meal that they would have all day.

In fact, that one meal which I helped serve would have to tide them over for two days.

Ever since Sunday, I have tried so hard to go back to my peaceful, simple teen-aged life, but my mind keeps wandering back to those people.

I wonder, 'Why are they out there? How do they manage to live on the street?' I just can't get those people out of my mind.

And now, instead of being afraid of going and serving them food, I find that I can't wait until I get to go again.

The events in Sarah's autobiographical essay take place in a short period of time. She also includes dialogue to make the events seem more real. Most important, in the last two paragraphs, she explains why the incident is important to her.

As you complete the writing exercises in this chapter and then write your own autobiographical incident, you will become aware of the parts of speech of each word you write. Allow time for students to discuss the student writing. Suggest that they identify its strengths and propose possible improvements. Use the model to introduce the concepts in the chapter.

Nouns

Everything that you can see and touch and many things that are invisible are named by a noun.

🖋 **Nouns** are words that name persons, places, things, or ideas.

PERSONS   grandfather, Serena, player, friend, Tiger Woods
PLACES   home, bridge, Chicago, Washington Monument
THINGS   computer, Internet, parade, refrigerator, mailbox
IDEAS   love, democracy, justice, fear, happiness

🖋 Nouns that name ideas, such as the ones listed above, are called **abstract nouns**. You use abstract nouns when writing or speaking about feelings, characteristics, or qualities. In contrast, **concrete nouns** name things that you can see, hear, smell, taste, or touch.

ABSTRACT   courage, intelligence, vitality, theme, cost
CONCRETE   lemon, snow, sand, telephone, puppy

🖋 **Proper nouns** name particular persons, places, things, or ideas. Always capitalize proper nouns. Some proper nouns contain two or more words. Because **common nouns** are general, not particular, they are not capitalized.

PROPER   Texas, Empire State Building, Mexico, Justice Ginsburg
COMMON   state, building, country, judge

🖋 **Collective nouns** name a group of people or things. How many groups named by collective nouns are you part of?

family, team, group, troop, committee, herd

🖋 **Compound nouns** consist of two or more words. Use a dictionary to find out if a compound noun is hyphenated or written as one word or two words.

great-uncle, one-third, paperweight,
fire fighter, high school, New Mexico

P.S. Don't feel overwhelmed by the names for these different types of nouns. The whole point of learning the names and functions of the eight parts of speech is so that you can use them effectively—and correctly—when you write and speak.

Enriching Your Vocabulary

Vitality stems from the Latin *vita*, which means "life." The word *vitality* may be used to mean not only physical but intellectual energy as well. The English philosopher Alfred North Whitehead, for example, observed that "the vitality of thought is in adventure."

Writing Hint

Use nouns that are as specific as possible.
   terrier
The ~~dog~~ barked at the *letter carrier* ~~man~~.
    bride
The ~~woman getting married~~ *roses and baby's breath* wore ~~flowers~~ in her hair.

Exercise 1 **Identifying Nouns**

Underline all the nouns in the following passage. Look for common nouns, proper nouns, abstract nouns, concrete nouns, compound nouns, and collective nouns.

¹At the start of the twentieth century, students usually carried their own chalkboards or pads to school. ²As the twenty-first century gets underway, many students still use paper in class and for homework. ³Some of them prefer loose-leaf notebooks, and others favor spiral-bound ones. ⁴At the same time, a small but growing percentage of students come to classrooms, studios, labs, and libraries without paper notebooks but with computerized notebooks, also known as laptops.

⁵Why do young people use laptops (which weigh less than some textbooks)? ⁶Here are three reasons to start with. First, they use the machines to take notes, to copy down assignments, to write stories and essays, and to create art. ⁷Second, they load a CD-ROM or similar collection of data onto their machines and find huge amounts of organized information at their fingertips. ⁸Third, they use the laptops to communicate and to tap into up-to-the-minute text, sound, and pictures. Do not penalize students who identify *leaf* and *spiral* in sentence 3 as nouns. Explain that these function as adjectives.

Exercise 2 **Revising and Editing a Paragraph**

The paragraph below is weak because it contains so many vague words. With a partner, improve it by replacing the italicized words with specific, concrete nouns or proper nouns. Also, add details, drop or add words, and combine sentences. Compare your responses with those made by other pairs.

¹One *day* at *a certain time, a person* was picking *fruit*. ²She was in *a place* that was owned by *a relative*. ³She listened to the *sounds* around her. ⁴She enjoyed the *smells*. ⁵She especially liked the *sights*. ⁶After *time* had passed, she could see and feel the coming *weather*. ⁷She dropped her *container* half filled with *fruit* and hurried toward a *building*. ⁸*The person's pet* ran beside her. ⁹When they reached *the building, the person* and *her pet* waited *a long time* for the *weather* to stop.
Paragraphs will vary. Caution students to avoid singsongy descriptions.

Pronouns

🔖 **Pronouns** are words that take the place of a noun or other pronouns.

Most—but not all—pronouns clearly refer to another word in the sentence or in a preceding sentence. The word the pronoun replaces is called its **antecedent**. In the following sentences, arrows point to the antecedents of the pronouns.

Terra and **her** sister are disc jockeys. **They** have a radio program on

Saturday morning. **It** is on WZZZ.

The list at the right shows different types of pronouns.

🔖 The pronouns you use the most are the **personal pronouns** and their **possessive forms**.

PERSONAL **I** went with **him** to the movies.

POSSESSIVE **My** cat licks **her** chops at **their** parakeet.

🔖 **Indefinite pronouns** express an amount or refer to an unspecified person or thing.

Most of us studied.   **Somebody** sneezed.

Anything you can do, I can do better.

🔖 **Demonstrative pronouns** point to specific people or things.

That is Ivan's cousin.   **Those** are mine.

This will go down in history.

🔖 **Interrogative pronouns** begin a question.

Who has the key?   **What** is the problem?

🔖 **Reflexive pronouns** end in -*self* or -*selves* and refer to an earlier noun or pronoun in the sentence. **Intensive pronouns** add emphasis.

Tricia cut **herself** slicing a bagel.

I **myself** don't believe the story.

For information about **relative pronouns** and **adjective clauses**, see Lesson 7.2.

Editing Tip

Possessive pronouns never take an apostrophe.

The dog wagged ~~it's~~ *its* tail.

That backpack is ~~her's~~ *hers*.

Personal Pronouns

I	me	we	us
you	he	him	she

Possessive Pronouns

my	her
mine	hers
your	his
yours	their
our	theirs
ours	its

Some Indefinite Pronouns

all	another
any	anybody
anyone	anything
both	each
either	everybody
everyone	everything
few	most
many	neither
nobody	none
no one	one
several	some
somebody	someone

Demonstrative Pronouns

this	these
that	those

Some Interrogative Pronouns

Who?	Whom?
Whose?	What?
Which?	

Reflexive and Intensive Pronouns

myself	yourself
himself	herself
itself	ourselves
yourselves	themselves

Exercise 3 Identifying Pronouns

Underline all the pronouns in this paragraph, including possessive pronouns that come before nouns. **Hint:** You'll find 21 pronouns.

¹A while ago Wynton Marsalis played some of his music on television. ²Then he talked to students in the audience. ³They hoped to become musicians themselves. ⁴This is part of his advice to them: ⁵Write out a practice schedule, and set goals to chart your development. ⁶Concentrate when you practice. ⁷Relax and practice slowly; invest yourself. ⁸Play everything as if you were singing. ⁹Don't be too hard on yourself when you make a mistake. ¹⁰Remember, it is not the end of the world. ¹¹Just make sure you learn from your mistakes. ¹²Think for yourself and be optimistic. ¹³How you feel about living in the world determines your success.

Exercise 4 Writing with Pronouns

Write ten interesting, complete sentences about yourself—about your family, friends, hobbies, hopes, and memories. Try to use each kind of pronoun from the preceding page at least once. Underline all of the pronouns in your sentences. Look for sentence variety and accurate use of pronouns.

Exercise 5 Write What You Think

The principal of your school has asked you to write a letter to a student named Anja. She has always lived in Finland, but her family is moving, and Anja will attend your school next year. She is worried that she won't fit in at your school. On a separate piece of paper, write her a letter in which you give her advice on how to be a successful ninth-grader in your school. You might cover such topics as friends, clothing, classes, studying, tests, sports, clubs, and so on. When you've finished writing your letter, underline all of the pronouns that you've used. See teacher pages for assessment rubrics.

Verbs

For many reasons, verbs are the heart of a sentence. You can't make a statement about a noun or pronoun unless you use a verb, too.

● **Verbs** are words that express an action or a state of being. Every sentence has at least one action verb or one linking verb.

Some action verbs express an action you can observe: *slide, giggle, carry.* Other action verbs express an action you usually can't see: *worry, dislike, love, appreciate.*

> George Lucas **wrote** and **directed** *Star Wars*. His ideas for the plot **came** from Hollywood Westerns and the myths of many cultures.

Verbs change form to indicate time. (For more about verb tenses, see Lesson 8.5.)

> The bear **roared**. The bear **roars**. The bear **has been roaring**.

Some action verbs (V) take direct objects (DO). (For more about direct objects, see Lesson 5.8.)

>   V   DO
> The boys **ate sushi** for dinner.

● **Linking verbs** join—or link—the subject of a sentence with a word that identifies or describes it. (For more about subjects and predicates, see Lesson 5.2.)

> For 123 years Mt. St. Helens **remained** dormant.

Some verbs can be both linking and action verbs—but not at the same time. They are linking verbs only when they are followed by a word that identifies or describes the subject.

> LINKING VERB The milk **tastes** sour. He **grew** quiet.
> ACTION VERB Jill **tasted** the milk. The farmer **grew** corn.

● A **verb phrase** contains a main verb plus one or more **helping verbs** (HV).

>   HV   V
> They **may have gone** home.
> HV   V
> **Does**n't anyone here **speak** Spanish?

Not (*n't* in a contraction) is never part of a verb phrase.

Linking Verbs: Some Forms of *Be*

am	are	is
was	were being	
can be	have been	
will be	should be	
would have been		

Some Other Linking Verbs

appear	become
feel	grow
look	remain
seem	smell
sound	taste

Some Helping Verbs

be (is, am, are, was, were, be, been, being)
have (has, have, had)
do (does, do, did)

can	could	may
might	must	shall
should	will	would

Using forms of the verb *to be* makes a sentence passive. Refer to Lesson 8.6 on the active voice.

Writing Hint

Use vivid action verbs to help readers imagine an action clearly.
      roared
"Aha!" she ~~said~~.
 gripped
She ~~held~~ the doorknob.

Exercise 6 Identifying Verbs

Underline every verb and verb phrase in the following sentences. **Hint:** Two sentences have more than one verb.

1. The Anasazi Indians <u>built</u> a community on steep cliffs.

2. Their stone dwellings <u>contain</u> hundreds of rooms.

3. When Spanish explorers <u>found</u> these cliff dwellings, they <u>called</u> the area Mesa Verde, which <u>means</u> "green table."

4. The Anasazi <u>grew</u> corn, squash, beans, and cotton.

5. They <u>made</u> cloth, turquoise jewelry, pottery, and baskets.

6. Sometime around 1300 the Anasazi <u>abandoned</u> Mesa Verde.

7. Archaeologists <u>guess</u> that they <u>left</u> because of a drought, an epidemic, or enemy raids.

8. For hundreds of years, Mesa Verde <u>remained</u> empty.

9. Ranchers <u>rediscovered</u> the dwellings in the 1800s.

10. In 1906, the federal government <u>declared</u> Mesa Verde a national park.

Exercise 7 Revising and Editing a Paragraph

The following paragraph is weak because it contains imprecise verbs and nouns. With a partner, strengthen the paragraph by adding vivid verbs and precise nouns. You can make up details and add, drop, or combine sentences. Compare your revision with that of other pairs.

¹One summer a boy wanted a job. ²He went to places and talked to people and asked people for a job, but no one gave him one. ³The boy thought about what he could do. ⁴He was good at sports. ⁵He played a musical instrument, and he could fix things that broke. ⁶Sometimes he took care of his young relatives. ⁷The boy went to a place that took care of children. ⁸He talked to a person there. ⁹She gave him a job. ¹⁰He helped with children. ¹¹He showed them how to play sports. ¹²He liked his summer job.

Paragraphs should correctly use a variety of verbs. Suggest that students read the paragraph aloud to hear the awkward choppy sound.

Mid-Chapter Review

Exercise A Identifying Nouns and Pronouns

On a separate sheet of paper, list all the nouns in the following quotations in one column. In another column list all the pronouns. Pronouns are circled, nouns are underlined. Student lists should appear in two columns.

1. When I look into the future, it's so bright it burns my eyes.
   —*Oprah Winfrey*

2. Without feelings of respect, what is there to distinguish men from beasts? —*Confucius*

3. Children have never been very good at listening to their elders, but they have never failed to imitate them. —*James Baldwin*

4. If I feel physically as if the top of my head were taken off, I know that is poetry. —*Emily Dickinson*

5. When I step onto the court, I don't have to think about anything. . . . It's like therapy. It relaxes me and allows me to solve problems.
   —*Michael Jordan*

6. When you cannot get a compliment in any other way, pay yourself one.
   —*Mark Twain*

7. Nothing is more difficult, and therefore more precious, than to be able to decide. —*Napoleon*

8. We do not inherit the land from our ancestors; we borrow it from our children. —*Native American Proverb*

9. Don't count your chickens before they are hatched. —*Aesop*

10. Don't cross the bridge until you come to it. —*Proverb*

Exercise B Reviewing Verbs

Underline all the verbs and verb phrases in the paragraph below.

¹A shy fourteen-year-old approached a classmate. ²The two teenagers were standing in front of school. ³Classes had ended, and many students were waiting for their school buses. ⁴The shy fourteen-year-old asked his classmate for the homework assignment in math. ⁵The classmate had had a bad day and ignored the boy's request. ⁶When the boy repeated his question, the classmate yelled at him angrily. ⁷"Can't you take no for an answer?" ⁸The boy edged away nervously. ⁹Everyone stared, but no one moved or spoke. ¹⁰What would you have done or said if you had been there?

Exercise C **Revising a Report**

Make changes to improve the following report. Use vivid verbs and specific nouns. Consider using pronouns to avoid repeating nouns. **Hint:** There is no single correct way to revise the report, and not every sentence needs revision.

[1]Frederick Douglass was a great African American person who led other people. [2]In 1817, Frederick Douglass was born into slavery in Maryland. [3]As a child, Frederick Douglass was constantly hungry and often cold. [4]When Frederick Douglass was ten, the person who owned the boy sent the boy to a new family, the Aulds. [5]The boy asked the wife of Mr. Auld to help him read, and Mrs. Auld did. [6]But Mrs. Auld didn't any more when Mr. Auld said people who were slaves were not allowed to learn to read or write, and there were laws saying so.

[7]Frederick Douglass ran away from the person who owned him as a slave in 1838. [8]At an antislavery meeting in Nantucket, he told about the past years of his life. [9]Douglass was a powerful speaker and person who wrote things. [10]He went across the northern states talking against slavery. [11]Douglass put on paper into book form his true life story called *Narrative of the Life of Frederick Douglass*. [12]Frederick Douglass started a newspaper that worked to stop slavery.

[13]During the Civil War, Frederick Douglass put together two regiments of army fighters who were African Americans. [14]Frederick Douglass went to the White House and strongly asked the person who was President, Abraham Lincoln, for equal treatment for these soldiers. [15]After the war ended, Frederick Douglass worked to have freed slaves made citizens. [16]At the end of his time of being alive, he worked for women's being able to cast a ballot in an election. [17]Frederick Douglass died in 1895.

Students may wish to expand this report by doing independent research.

Adjectives

Whenever you describe a thing, a person, or a place, you use adjectives.

● **Adjectives** are modifiers. They give information about the nouns and pronouns they modify.

WHAT KIND?	**gray** clouds, **irreverent** humor, **crisp** apple, **quiet** pond
HOW MANY?	**three** weeks, **several** mistakes
HOW MUCH?	**less** noise, **more** dessert
WHICH ONE?	**first** answer, **this** jacket, **next** year, **best** poster

Give students a hint for when to use a comma with two or more adjectives. If you can reverse the last two adjectives before a noun, use a comma. If you can't, then the last adjective is part of the noun.

the white, fluffy cloud
the fat mother hen

Two or more adjectives may modify the same noun.

Five funny, clumsy ducklings waddled after their mother.

Picasso's ceramics are **colorful** and **humorous**.

● The adjectives *a* and *an* are called **indefinite articles**. They refer to any one member of a group and so are indefinite. The adjective *the* is called a **definite article**. It points out a particular noun and so is definite.

INDEFINITE	**A** puppy makes a good pet.
DEFINITE	**The** puppy chewed her shoe.

● **Proper adjectives**, which come from proper nouns, always begin with a capital letter.

Shakespearean sonnet	**Mexican** fiesta
African mask	**Democratic** candidate

● Many adjectives come right before the noun they modify, but **predicate adjectives** follow a linking verb to modify the subject of a sentence. (For more about subjects, see Lesson 5.2.)

The tulips are **purple**.

The ocean looks **blue** and **clear**.

When a noun modifies another noun, it functions as an adjective.

kitchen table	**church** music
Romeo's sword	Back **porch** swing

Enriching Your Vocabulary

The prefix *ir-*, like *in-*, usually serves to form a word opposite in meaning to the root word to which it is joined. *Irreverent*, for example, means lacking reverence or respect. Other examples of such *ir-* words are *irregular*, *irrational*, and *irreversible*.

Writing Hint

Replace general, all-purpose adjectives with adjectives that make your writing sharper.

The candidate gave a ~~good~~ **concise but persuasive** speech.

Identifying Adjectives

Underline the adjectives and proper adjectives in the following paragraph. Do not underline definite and indefinite articles.

¹<u>Regional</u> and <u>ethnic</u> music in America has <u>many</u> roots. ²<u>Traditional</u> <u>American</u> <u>Indian</u> music uses <u>male</u> voices and sometimes drums and rattles. ³During the 1890s, jazz developed from <u>two</u> <u>African</u> <u>American</u> traditions: ragtime and blues. ⁴<u>Gospel</u> music dates back to the 1930s. ⁵Thomas A. Dorsey wrote the <u>first</u> <u>gospel</u> songs, based on <u>African</u> <u>American</u> spirituals and <u>jazz</u> rhythms. ⁶<u>One</u> source of <u>Appalachian</u> music is <u>Irish</u> <u>folk</u> tunes. ⁷<u>Tex-Mex</u> music blends the sounds of <u>Mexican</u> bands with the <u>polka</u> rhythms of <u>German</u>, <u>Polish</u>, and <u>Czech</u> immigrants. ⁸<u>Cajun</u> music in Louisiana, led by the accordion and fiddle, has <u>French</u> and <u>Creole</u> roots. ⁹<u>Jewish</u> <u>klezmer</u> bands, traditionally made up of violins and clarinets, first played in <u>Eastern</u> <u>European</u> cities and towns. ¹⁰Hawaiians developed a <u>unique</u> sound with the <u>steel</u> guitar.

Exercise 9 **Revising Sentences to Add Information**

Revise the sentences below to give the reader more information and to create more interesting sentences. You may add or change words and make up details. Underline all of the adjectives in your revised sentences. Do not underline definite and indefinite articles.

EXAMPLE A man served the food.
The <u>elderly</u> owner of the <u>Polish</u> restaurant served us a <u>delicious</u> casserole with potatoes and kielbasa.

1. Clouds filled the sky.

2. The woman lives in a house on a street.

■ See Composition Lesson 2.4 for more about details in descriptive paragraphs.

3. The dog wore a sweater.

4. The girl grabbed the ball.

5. Students are doing projects in class.

6. Boats crowded the harbor.

7. The child played with a ball.

8. A car was parked in the lot.

9. A man stood on the beach.

10. Friends ate pizza.

Encourage students to use several types of adjectives and to be creative with their sentences. Students may wish to read their favorite sentences aloud to the class.

Adverbs

● **Adverbs** modify—or tell more about—verbs, adjectives, and other adverbs. They answer the questions *when, where, how,* and *to what extent.*

MODIFIES VERB	We **happily** visited Adam.
MODIFIES ADJECTIVE	The **extremely** graceful swan swims.
MODIFIES ADVERB	Jackie ran **very** quickly.

Many adverbs can come either before or after the verbs they modify.

Suddenly the light went out.

The light went out **suddenly**.

The light **suddenly** went out.

Many adverbs end with the suffix *-ly* (*quickly, easily, carefully,* for example). However, many frequently used adverbs do not end in *-ly* (*soon, never, quite,* for example).

● **Intensifiers** are adverbs that answer the question to what extent?

I feel **rather** tired today.

The movie was **too** long.

Mozart was an **extraordinarily** gifted child.

No one was **more** surprised than I!

It's a **really** good book.

Exercise 10 **Identifying Adverbs**

Underline the adverbs in each sentence below.
Hint: One sentence contains more than one adverb.

1. Jeff did <u>not</u> spear the line drive to right field.

2. Tanisha <u>easily</u> won the girls' triple jump with her 39-foot jump.

3. <u>Yesterday</u> our team squandered a 3-run lead and lost in the final inning.

4. Kim <u>also</u> ran the 400-meter hurdles in 52.97 seconds.

5. Richard bowled <u>well</u> though he missed five spares in the final game.

6. The tournament was delayed <u>again</u> by <u>exceptionally</u> heavy rains.

7. Benjie lost control of his model plane and wrecked it <u>completely</u>.

8. Marie has <u>just</u> won her fifth track-and-field trophy.

Some Common Adverbs That Do Not End in -ly

almost	already	also
always	fast	here
just	late	more
much	not (n't)	never
seldom	still	then
there	today	too
well	tomorrow	
yet	yesterday	

Some Common Intensifiers

exceptionally		less
extraordinarily		least
more	most	nearly
only	quite	rather
really	so	very
truly	too	
somewhat		

Step by Step

Adjective or Adverb?

To decide whether you need to use an adjective or an adverb, decide which word you need to modify.

1. If you need to modify a noun or pronoun, use an adjective.

   The drill was **quick**.

2. If you need to modify a verb, adjective, or another adverb, use an adverb.

   The towel dries **quickly**.

Exercise 11 — Choosing the Correct Modifier

When you write and speak in school and in business, you need to use the modifier—adjective or adverb—that correctly fits the sentence. Underline the correct modifier in the sentences below.

1. Tai-chi movements are (real, <u>really</u>) (<u>graceful</u>, gracefully).

2. A tornado can touch down (quick, <u>quickly</u>) and then move on.

3. Residents of Quebec, Canada, speak French (regular, <u>regularly</u>).

4. Harry Houdini could escape (easy, <u>easily</u>) from locks and chains.

5. Being overweight makes a health problem more (<u>serious</u>, seriously).

6. Pizza tastes quite (different, <u>differently</u>) with pineapple.

7. Mangoes and papayas can't survive in a (real, <u>really</u>) cold climate.

8. Hiawatha was (extreme, <u>extremely</u>) successful in ending feuds.

9. The beetle has an (unbelievable, <u>unbelievably</u>) large number of species—350,000.

10. In a parallelogram, opposite sides are parallel and (<u>equal</u>, equally).

Exercise 12 — Adding Adjectives and Adverbs

Give the reader a clearer picture by adding adjectives and adverbs to the following sentences. Replace general nouns and verbs, and add details.

EXAMPLE   The child picked up the toy.
            Jimmy, a wiry toddler, quickly grabbed the dump truck.

1. The animal moved.

2. A box lay on the table.

Answers will vary. Students may wish to read their revised sentences aloud to the class.

3. The girl heard a series of sounds.

4. The wind damaged the car.

5. A line of people waited outside the building.

6. His pet was frightened.

7. The woman jogged around the lake.

8. The man served dessert to his guests.

9. The bird dove into the water for a fish.

10. The girl knit a sweater.

Combining Sentences: Inserting Single Words

Effective writers can come up with alternatives to a long series of short, choppy sentences. They combine sentences by inserting key words from one sentence into another sentence.

ORIGINAL   The trees swayed in the wind. The trees were palms. The trees swayed wildly. The wind was fierce.

COMBINED   The **palm** trees swayed **wildly** in the **fierce** wind.

The combined sentence sounds smoother because it avoids unnecessary repetition. Notice that the single words inserted into the sentence work as modifiers—adjectives and adverbs.

ORIGINAL   A museum opened in Rapid City, South Dakota. The museum is new. It opened recently.

COMBINED   A **new** museum opened **recently** in Rapid City, South Dakota.

Sometimes the key words change form when you combine sentences (in the first example above, *palms* becomes *palm*).

ORIGINAL   The museum combines stories about the Black Hills with exhibits. The exhibits are by geologists. The stories belong to the Lakota Indians.

COMBINED   The museum combines **Lakota Indian** stories about the Black Hills with **geological** exhibits.

ORIGINAL   Mt. Rushmore is part of the Black Hills. The Black Hills are mountains.

COMBINED   Mt. Rushmore is part of the **mountainous** Black Hills.

Step by Step

Combining Sentences

To combine a series of short sentences:

1. Find the sentence that gives the most information.

2. In the other sentences, look for single words that can be picked up and inserted into the sentence you picked in Step 1.

3. Insert the single words where they make sense. You may need to change the word forms.

4. Re-read the combined sentence to see if it sounds natural.

Exercise 13 Combining Sentences

With a partner, on a separate piece of paper combine the following groups of sentences into single sentences. Drop some words, and change the form of others. For the last two numbered items, follow the hints in parentheses. Compare your combined sentences with those of other pairs.

EXAMPLE   Frank Lloyd Wright was an architect. He was famous. He was born in America.

Frank Lloyd Wright was a famous American architect.

> Combined sentences should not omit any information from the given sentences.

1. Mercury is an element used in dental fillings. The element is metallic.

2. The novelist Mary Renault wrote about Greece. The Greece she wrote about is ancient. Mary Renault was English.

3. Pierre-Auguste Renoir was a painter known for his style. Renoir was French. His style was colorful.

4. James Naismith invented basketball in 1891 as a sport. The sport was played indoors. (Change *indoors* to an adjective form.)

5. Romans founded London in A.D. 43 as a city. The Romans were ancient. The city had walls. (Change *walls* to an adjective form with an *-ed* ending.)

Exercise 14 Revising and Editing a Paragraph

With a partner, improve the following paragraph. Look for opportunities to combine sentences. Compare your revised paragraph with those of other pairs.

¹"Share a Smile Becky" is a friend of Barbie's. ²Like all Barbie dolls, Becky has outfits. ³Her outfits are many and different. ⁴She is an 11½-inch blond. ⁵Her blond hair is a strawberry color. ⁶What's important about Becky is her wheelchair. ⁷That's really important. ⁸Becky's wheelchair is hot pink. ⁹Becky's legs have joints so she can sit. ¹⁰The joints are bendable. ¹¹The company that produces the toys tries to acknowledge children with disabilities. ¹²Other companies produce toy buses and schoolhouses with ramps. ¹³The ramps are for wheelchairs. ¹⁴Kids play with the toys. ¹⁵Kids learn about disabilities. ¹⁶Some kids have their own physical disabilities. ¹⁷Some kids do not have physical disabilities. ¹⁸Kids who play with Becky might understand disabilities better.

¹⁹The company hopes that Becky will help.

Paragraphs will vary. Look for sentence variety and correct grammar.

■ See **Composition** Lesson 1.3 for more on combining sentences to improve style when you revise.

Prepositions

◖ Prepositions connect another word in a sentence to a noun or pronoun (and its modifiers, if any) to form a prepositional phrase. A preposition never stands alone. (For more about prepositional phrases, see Lesson 6.1.)

> Will we travel **beyond** the Milky Way?
> What do you see **over** the rainbow?

Some prepositions are **compound** (made up of more than one word).

> His health improved **on account of** new research.
> Who will attend **in addition to** us?

Words that are prepositions in one sentence may be adverbs in another sentence. Look to see if the word is part of a prepositional phrase. If it is not part of a prepositional phrase, it is an adverb.

ADVERBS
> Please put the package **down** carefully.
> We had seen her **before** at the football game.

PREPOSITIONS
> Alice fell **down** a rabbit hole.
> She stood **before** the Red Queen.

Exercise 15 **Expanding Sentences**

On a separate sheet of paper, expand the sentences below by adding prepositional phrases. Avoid adding more than four to each sentence. (More than four can make a sentence sing-songy.) Make up all the details you need in order to create interesting sentences. Underline all of the prepositions you add to the sentences.

EXAMPLE
Carla found her notes.
Yesterday <u>after</u> dinner Carla found her missing notes <u>for</u> her research paper <u>under</u> the front seat <u>in</u> her older brother's car.

1. Jenna slipped and fell.

2. Cary threw the ball.

3. The cat leaped.

4. We heard a sound.

5. No one noticed.

6. We go.

7. Can you tell?

8. Nobody was home.

9. It's dark.

10. We were alone.

Sentences will vary. Students may wish to read their favorite sentences aloud to the class.

Some Commonly Used Prepositions

about	above	across
against	along	around
at	before	below
beside	between	beyond
but (meaning "except")		
by	during	except
for	from	inside
into	like	near
of	off	on
out	outside	over
since	through	to
toward	under	until
up	upon	
with	without	

Some Common Compound Prepositions

according to	along with
apart from	aside from
as to	due to
instead of	in front of
in place of	in spite of
because of	out of
in addition to	

Writing Hint

In the past, students were taught never to end a sentence with a preposition. British Prime Minister Winston Churchill is said to have challenged this rule by saying: "This is the sort of [English] up with which I will not put." Today, ending a sentence with a preposition is usually acceptable.

What are you looking **for**? Here's the pen I spoke **about**.

Exercise 16 Choosing Prepositions

Some prepositions help pinpoint location and time. In the parentheses in each sentence below, underline every preposition that makes sense in the sentence. Notice how the meaning changes, depending on which preposition you use.

1. (<u>Before</u>, Until, <u>After</u>, <u>During</u>, In spite of) dinner Lisa noticed a dark blob (in, <u>on</u>, <u>under</u>, <u>in front of</u>, between, <u>above</u>) the front door.

2. A giant spider was crawling (<u>up</u>, <u>down</u>, <u>around</u>, through) the front door.

3. When she saw the spider, Lisa ran (<u>toward</u>, <u>out</u>, <u>in front of</u>, over, on, under, <u>near</u>) the door.

4. Her brother hid (<u>under</u>, <u>behind</u>, inside, above, <u>beneath</u>, <u>next to</u>, <u>near</u>, with, between) the couch.

5. "Boy, these kids are scary!" the spider thought (within, inside, toward, <u>to</u>, upon, before) himself.

Exercise 17 Distinguishing Prepositions from Adverbs

Fill in the blank with *PREP* if the underlined word is functioning as a preposition or with *ADV* if the underlined word is functioning as an adverb.

<u>PREP</u>   1. In this state, you can turn right <u>on</u> a red light.

<u>ADV</u>   2. Turn the light <u>on</u>, please.

<u>ADV</u>   3. "Look <u>up</u>!" shouted the child watching the fireworks.

<u>PREP</u>   4. Go <u>up</u> the stairs quietly so that you don't wake anyone.

<u>ADV</u>   5. Are you going <u>out</u> tonight?

<u>PREP</u>   6. Look <u>out</u> the window to see when the taxi comes.

<u>PREP</u>   7. The spilled milk soaked <u>through</u> the tablecloth.

<u>ADV</u>   8. I want to be the first student <u>through</u> with the test.

<u>PREP</u>   9. The mouse ran <u>down</u> the clock.

<u>ADV</u> 10. When the battery ran <u>down</u>, the clock stopped.

Enriching Your Vocabulary

An extreme and illogical fear (as, for example, of spiders) is called a *phobia*. The word stems from the Greek word *phobus*, which means "fear." You are probably familiar with the word *claustrophobia*, but what of *agoraphobia* (fear of open spaces) or *xenophobia* (fear of strangers)?

Conjunctions and Interjections

● **Conjunctions** join words or groups of words.

● **Coordinating conjunctions** join words or groups of words that are equal in importance.

> *Darren* **and** *she* have finished their science projects.
> *They are done,* **but** *I am not.*

● **Correlative conjunctions** are always used in pairs.

> **Either** *Elisha* **or** *I* will call you. **Both** *Karen* **and** *Jules* are nurses.

It is important to place the correlative conjuction correctly. The words or phrases joined by a correlative conjuction should play the same role in a sentence, for example, it might join two subjects or two clauses.

INCORRECT	Either the girls like or dislike the movie.
CORRECT	The girls either like or dislike the movie.
CORRECT	Either the girls like the movie, or they dislike it.

● **Subordinating conjunctions** connect adverb clauses to main clauses. (For more about adverb clauses and a list of subordinating conjunctions, see Lesson 7.3.)

> Kabuo bought a fishing rod **because** *he had always wanted one.*
> **When** *an underwater earthquake takes place,* tidal waves form.

● **Interjections** express mild or strong emotion.

Interjections have no grammatical connection to the rest of the sentence. They are set off by a comma or by an exclamation point.

> **Hey**! Watch where you're going!   **Well**, I certainly am surprised!

Exercise 18 **Adding Interjections to a Dialogue**

Insert interjections where they seem natural in the following dialogue.

1. LEAH: David, what do you say?
2. DAVID: I was just thinking about you.
3. LEAH: What were you thinking?
4. DAVID: I was wondering if maybe you'd like to go to a movie.
5. LEAH: What's playing?
6. DAVID: Have you seen *E.T.*?

Coordinating Conjunctions

and	but	or
nor	so	yet

Some Correlative Conjunctions

both . . . and
either . . . or
neither . . . nor
not only . . . but also
whether . . . or

Some Common Interjections

aha	cool	oh
yo	hooray	ouch
well	wow	ugh
hey		

Enriching Your Vocabulary

Mediate, used in Exercise 19, comes from the Latin *mediare,* which means "to be in the middle." The verb form stems from the Latin *medius,* or "middle," which is the root of many other English words (for example, *media, median, mediocre,* and *medieval*).

Have pairs of students read the dialogue aloud to help them find the interjections that sound most natural to their ears.

7. LEAH: I hate that movie.

8. DAVID: What about *Return of the Jedi*?

9. LEAH: I'd love to.

10. DAVID: I'll see you Saturday.

Exercise 19 Identifying Conjunctions

Underline all of the conjunctions in the paragraph below. **Hint:** Not every sentence contains a conjunction.

¹Peer-mediation centers are spreading to elementary, middle, <u>and</u> high schools throughout the country. ²As peer mediators, student volunteers receive special training. ³They practice how to get students in conflict to sit down <u>and</u> listen to each other. ⁴In one middle school in Cleveland, mediators most often deal with disputes caused by name-calling, rumors, teasing, <u>or</u> gossip. ⁵Each student presents his <u>or</u> her side of the dispute, <u>and</u> the other student must listen without interrupting. ⁶Conflicts are defused <u>either</u> with an apology <u>and</u> a handshake <u>or</u> a promise to stay away from each other. ⁷In a dispute, students say they are more likely to listen to their peers than to a teacher <u>or</u> guidance counselor. ⁸<u>Both</u> students <u>and</u> school officials praise peer-mediation programs.

Exercise 20 Write What You Think

Here are the steps in peer mediation:

• Any student involved in a conflict can ask for a mediation hearing.
• Peer mediators track down the other student or students involved in the dispute and bring the parties together.
• Each student must listen to the other side without interrupting.
• Peer mediators help students find ways of ending the dispute.

What kinds of disputes do you see among students in your school? Do you think that all—or most—of these arguments can be settled with peer mediation? On a separate piece of paper, write a paragraph on this topic. Support your opinions with facts and examples. See teacher pages for assessment rubrics.

Combining Sentences: Using Coordinating Conjunctions

● You can combine a series of short, related sentences by using the coordinating conjunctions *and, but,* and *or.*

ORIGINAL   Kerri is looking for a summer job. Jeff is looking for a summer job. I am looking for a summer job.

COMBINED   Kerri, Jeff, **and** I are looking for summer jobs.

When you combine related sentences, some words will drop out, and some may change. For example, in the combined sentence above, the verb has changed from the singular (is looking and am looking) to the plural form (are looking). Notice also that commas come after the names Kerri and Jeff because they are part of a series. (For more about commas in a series, see Lesson 13.2.) Here are some more examples.

ORIGINAL   Summer jobs give students the chance to earn money. A summer job also gives them the opportunity to gain work experience.

COMBINED   Summer jobs give students the opportunity to earn money **and** gain work experience.

ORIGINAL   Money from a paycheck can be saved for a long-term goal. The long-term goal might be college. The long-term goal might be a car.

COMBINED   Money from a paycheck can be saved for a long-term goal, such as college **or** a car.

Exercise 21 Using Coordinating Conjunctions

Combine the sentences in each numbered item by using a coordinating conjunction (*and, but,* or *or*).   Combined sentences should eliminate repetition.

1. Most high school students want summer jobs. Most high school students have trouble finding them.

2. Job applicants should be on time for an interview. Job applicants should dress neatly. Job applicants should answer questions truthfully.

3. Teens want to work to help their families. They want to work to buy clothes. They want to work to buy cars.

4. When the summer ends, many teenagers continue to work weekends. Many teenagers continue to work after school.

5. Some nonprofit agencies help students fill out applications. Some nonprofit agencies help students look for jobs.

■ Eliminating wordiness is part of the revising process. For additonal information see **Composition** Lesson 1.3.

Exercise 22 **Revising and Editing a Paragraph**

With a partner or small group, make any changes you think will improve Wilma's flyer, below, which she will hang in her local grocery store. Look for opportunities to combine sentences. Compare your revision with that of other pairs or groups.

Babysitting Jobs Wanted

¹Do you need a babysitter during the week? ²Do you need a babysitter on the weekend? ³I will take your child to the library. ⁴I will take your child to the playground. ⁵I will take your child to the park. ⁶If it rains, we will read books. ⁷We will paint. ⁸We will draw. ⁹We will sing songs. ¹⁰I am very experienced. ¹¹I am very reliable. ¹²I have many satisfied customers. ¹³You can ask the parents. ¹⁴You can ask the children. ¹⁵Please call me during the day. ¹⁶You can call me in the evening. ¹⁷My number is 555-7809. ¹⁸You can also reach me at 555-7728. ¹⁹My e-mail address is *wilmaj@cosmic.com.*

Wilma Jeffers

Check that coordinating conjunctions are used correctly. Students may wish to use this as a model to write their own flyers.

Exercise 23 **Writing a Paragraph**

Using the notes below write a paragraph describing the summer jobs of Dino and his friends. You don't have to use all of the information. You can add new details and change wording. Write in complete sentences. As you write, see if you can combine related ideas by using coordinating conjunctions.

Hint

You will have to drop repeated words, and you may also have to add commas for a series of three or more.

> *Dino—dog-walking business; $3 a day per dog; walk three times a day*
>
> *Maria, Shira—pet vacation care (walking & feeding): Dogs, cats, birds, other creatures*
>
> *Sam, Harriet, Adam—gardening: planting, weeding, cutting grass*
>
> *Annie—swimming lessons to adults; swimming lessons to children; Red Cross certification as lifesaver & swimming instructor; 2 years' experience at day camp*

Paragraphs will vary. Extend this exercise by asking students to write a paragraph describing their summer or year-round jobs.

Determining a Word's Part of Speech

Some words can function as more than one part of speech. For example, if you look up the word *light* in a dictionary, you will find that it can be a noun, a verb, an adjective, or an adverb.

◗ A word's part of speech is determined by how the word is used in the sentence.

NOUN	A prism separates **light** into a rainbow of colors.
VERB	Two paper lanterns **light** the path to the party.
ADJECTIVE	They played two innings in a **light** rain.
ADVERB	To mix a **light** pink color, add a bit of red to white.

Exercise 24   Identifying Parts of Speech

Fill in the blank to identify the part of speech of each underlined word as it is used in the sentence. You can use these abbreviations:

N=noun   ADV=adverb
PRON=pronoun   PREP=preposition
V=verb   CONJ=conjunction
ADJ=adjective   INTER=interjection

_____N_____ 1. Word histories, or <u>etymologies</u>, show how meanings change.

_____V_____ 2. Sometimes a word's meaning <u>changes</u> gradually.

_____ADV_____ 3. *Nice* <u>originally</u> meant "frivolous" or "ignorant."

_____N_____ 4. In the thirteenth century *nice* <u>meant</u> "foolish."

_____ADJ_____ 5. Later, a <u>shy</u> person was called nice.

_____PREP_____ 6. <u>During</u> the 1700s, the word *nice* started to mean "agreeable."

_____ADJ_____ 7. "<u>Nice</u> guys finish last," claimed baseball manager Leo Durocher.

_____PRON_____ 8. Would you be pleased or insulted if <u>someone</u> called you nice?

_____N_____ 9. *Nice, wonderful,* and *great* are used so often that they are tired <u>words</u>.

_____V_____10. You <u>should try</u> to avoid tired words when you write.

Enriching Your Vocabulary

Frivolous here means "lacking in seriousness" or "silly." It can also mean "of little importance" or "without basis" as, for example, in describing a lawsuit or claim.

Revising and Editing Worksheet

Revise the following draft of a report. Consider:

• adding more specific nouns
• using vivid action verbs rather than forms of *to be* or other weak verbs
• adding some adjectives and adverbs
• introducing the best conjunctions and clearest prepositions

You may combine sentences, add or leave out details, and replace words. When you finish revising and editing, proofread the draft, and fix spelling, capitalization, and punctuation problems.

¹Elephants are the largest land mammals. ²There are two species of elephants. ³There are african elephants. ⁴There are Indian elephants. ⁵The african elephant is bigger. ⁶The african elephant has larger ears. ⁷The african elephant has a longer trunk. ⁸A male african elephant may be 13 feet tall. ⁹A male african elephant may be as much as 6 to 8 tons heavy on a scale. ¹⁰A male Indian elephant may be 9 feet tall. ¹¹It may measure 3.5 tons on a scale.

¹²An elephant's nose and upper lip form a trunk. ¹³An elephant uses it's trunk to gather food. ¹⁴They use their trunks for picking up objects. ¹⁵They use their trunks for sucking up water. ¹⁶They also suck up dust. ¹⁷They spray the water into they're mouths. ¹⁸They spray the dust on their bodies.

¹⁹Elephants in the wild have no homes. ²⁰They travel in a herd. ²¹They travel to find food. ²²The herd is large—100 elephants. ²³They travel at about 4 miles an hour. ²⁴They can run faster. ²⁵They run quick at 30 miles an hour. ²⁶They do this when they are angry, threatened.

²⁷Elephants can live for 60–70 years. ²⁸They are an animal in danger from extinction. ²⁹Hunters kill elephants for the ivory in their long tusks. ³⁰Ivery is carved into nice art objects. ³¹To protect elephants, many countries have banned trade in ivory.

Revised and edited report should use parts of speech correctly. Students may wish to use this report as a model for writing a short report on their favorite animals.

Chapter Review

Exercise A Identifying Parts of Speech

In the space provided, identify the part of speech of the underlined word in each quotation. Use these abbreviations:

N=noun   ADV=adverb
PRON=pronoun   PREP=preposition
V=verb   CONJ=conjunction
ADJ=adjective   INTER=interjection

<u>ADJ</u>   1. If a man does not keep pace with his companions, perhaps it is because he hears a <u>different</u> drummer. —*Henry David Thoreau, Walden*

<u>ADV</u>   2. <u>Always</u> do right. This will gratify some people and astonish the rest. —*Mark Twain, from a speech*

<u>V</u>   3. If I read a book and it makes my whole body so cold no fire can ever <u>warm</u> me, I know that is poetry. —*Emily Dickinson, Letters*

<u>PRON</u>   4. <u>We</u> all live with the object of being happy; our lives are different and yet the same. —*Anne Frank, The Diary of a Young Girl*

<u>PRON</u>   5. Everything happens to <u>everybody</u> sooner or later if there is only time enough. —*George Bernard Shaw, As Far As Thought Can Reach*

<u>PREP</u>   6. No one can make you feel inferior <u>without</u> your consent. —*Anna Eleanor Roosevelt, This Is My Story*

<u>INTER</u>   7. <u>Oh</u>, beat the drum slowly, and play the fife lowly. . . . —*The Cowboy's Lament*

<u>CONJ</u>   8. History knows no resting places <u>and</u> no plateaus. —*Henry Kissinger, White House Years*

<u>N</u>   9. We must build a new world, a far better world—one in which the eternal <u>dignity</u> of man is respected.—*Harry S Truman, from a speech*

<u>ADJ</u>   10. The ballot is <u>stronger</u> than the bullet.—*Abraham Lincoln, from a speech*

Exercise B **Revising and Editing a Story Beginning**

Improve the draft of the opening paragraphs of a short story. Feel free to make any changes that will make these paragraphs stronger and more interesting. Replace words, add specific details, add dialogue, combine sentences, and cut words or sentences. After improving the beginning of the story, you may want to write the rest of it on a separate sheet of paper.

[1]Ruth woke up. [2]She felt nervous. [3]Today was Friday. [4]It was the day it would happen. [5]Maybe her wishes would come true. [6]Maybe they would not.

[7]Ruth and Pat had been best friends. [8]They had been best friends since kindergarten. [9]Both of them had been nominated for the same office. [10]They were both running for president of the student council. [11]For a long time, they tried to get enough votes to win the election. [12]They had to make campaign posters. [13]They had to make campaign speeches. [14]Things were not the same between them.

[15]Right after it happened, Ruth told Pat that she hoped they could stay best friends. [16]Pat told her that she was sure they would remain best friends. [17]But things just did not seem to be the same between them any more. [18]Pat had been eating lunch with other friends. [19]She had been doing that for weeks. [20]And they did not talk to each other every night any more. Revised and edited draft should use parts of speech correctly. Remind students who finish the story to save it in their Writing Notebooks.

Exercise C **Write What You Think**

Think of an issue in your community or school. Write a persuasive speech about how the issue might be settled. Remember to state your opinion clearly and support it with facts and statistics. Be sure to answer the following questions in your speech.

What is the issue?
How is the issue affecting the listener?
What should the listener do the help settle the issue?

Answers will vary. Give students full credit if they have stated an opinion on an issue and attempted to support the opinion. They should also have written grammatically complete sentences that begin with a capital letter and end with an appropriate end punctuation mark.

CHAPTER 5

Parts of a Sentence

STUDENT WRITING
Book Review

Atlas Shrugged by Ayn Rand
Review by Peter Tanpitukpong
high school student, Wilmington, Delaware

Ayn Rand's most notable, as well as most controversial novel, is spellbinding excitement. From the beginning, *Atlas Shrugged* includes suspense, deceit, and a pedagogical analysis of her philosophy, Objectivism. What distinguishes this novel from other classic best-sellers is that Ayn Rand "writes for all ages."

Ayn Rand lived in Soviet Russia under the flag of Communism. Her philosophy, Objectivism, portrays the antithesis of this ideology. Her dealings and life experiences behind the harsh "Iron Curtain," where bread for the poor was a rarity but caviar for the leaders was abundant, tremendously influenced her book.

The novel follows the mind of the main character, Dagny Taggart, who is the epitome of the industrialist: ambitious, knowledgeable, greedy. But the negative connotation of "greedy" is suddenly reversed in a purely ironic fashion. To [Taggart], money is not just a stamp collection [in which] the accumulation of more stamps for the sake of impressing others is the goal; rather, it would be solely for the enjoyment and pleasure of the philatelist. Monetary gain is a form of enjoyment for Dagny Taggart because it reflects what matters most to her: her work.

The suspense of this book stems from the unending subplots. There are no dull moments; in the beginning, Dagny tells of her preoccupation with her biggest project; she later suffers mercilessly at the hands of a stifling directive; later, she goes on a futile search for John Galt, [a media mystery figure].

The most impressive feature of this book to me is its intellectual content. *Atlas Shrugged* has different outlooks and the way it was written impresses me. I recommend this book as a timeless classic of literature even if you don't agree with Rand's philosophy.

This book review contains a brief opinion statement, a short plot synopsis, and a concluding paragraph. The writer also includes some background on the author of the book, a sketch of the main character, and a description of the most impressive feature of the book.

The sentences have a good tempo because the writer has seamlessly combined short sentences into long ones. The lessons in this chapter will help you become more aware of the parts of sentences as you write.

Allow time for students to discuss the student writing. Suggest that they identify its strengths and propose possible improvements. Use the model to introduce the concepts in the chapter.

Using Complete Sentences

◖ A **sentence** is a grammatically complete group of words that expresses a thought.

A sentence must tell you two things: (1) the person, animal, or thing that the sentence is about and (2) what that person, animal, or thing does or is.

Every sentence begins with a capital letter and ends with an end punctuation mark—a period, a question mark, or an exclamation point.

◖ A **sentence fragment** is a group of words that is not grammatically complete. Avoid sentence fragments when you write.

Fragments may look like sentences because they start with a capital letter and end with an end punctuation mark, but don't let them fool you.

FRAGMENT	Sketched the lions. [Who sketched the lions?]
FRAGMENT	Jerri and I. [This doesn't tell what Jerri and I do.]
SENTENCE	Jerri and I sketched the lions.
FRAGMENT	While Jerri and I sketched the lions. [The word *while* turns the words into an incomplete thought.]
SENTENCE	While Jerri and I sketched the lions, they slept.

◖ A sentence always has one of four purposes:

1. **Declarative sentences** make a statement. They end with a period.

   The parade starts at three o'clock.

2. **Imperative sentences** make a command or a request. They end with either a period or (if the command shows strong feeling) an exclamation point.

   Come to the parade with us. Hurry up, you guys!

3. **Interrogative sentences** ask a question. They end with a question mark.

   Isn't that elephant heading straight toward us?

4. **Exclamatory sentences** express strong feeling. They end with an exclamation point.

   Run for your life! Oh, the elephant's loose!

> **Writing Hint**
>
> Even though sentence fragments are not acceptable in standard written English, you often use them when you talk and when you write dialogue.
>
> If you say so. Right. OK. Not!

Identifying Sentences and Sentence Fragments

For each numbered item, circle the letter before the words that form a complete sentence.

1. a. Ellis Island in New York harbor, where millions of immigrants entered United States from 1892 to 1943.
   b. Millions of immigrants entered the United States from 1892 to 1943 at Ellis Island in New York harbor.

2. a. In the United States, women won the right to vote in 1920.
   b. In the United States, the right to vote in 1920.

3. a. Although glaciers cover Greenland and Antarctica.
   b. Glaciers cover Greenland and Antarctica.

4. a. Almost half of the 206 bones in the human skeleton are in the hands and feet.
   b. Almost half of the 206 bones in the human skeleton.

5. a. Because the greenhouse effect raises temperatures on Earth.
   b. The greenhouse effect raises temperatures on Earth.

Exercise 2 **Writing Complete Sentences**

On a separate piece of paper rewrite the following notes (which are fragments) as complete sentences. Work with a partner or small group. Be sure to begin each sentence with a capital letter and to add the appropriate end punctuation mark. Compare your sentences with those of other pairs or groups.

Helicopter = type of aircraft.

Vertical (straight up and down) take-off and landing. Can hover (stay in one place without moving).

Lifts by means of horizontal rotor (like airplane's propeller). Rotor powered by engine.

Leonardo da Vinci (16th-century Italian inventor & artist) = first to imagine helicopter but no engines then.

1st successful helicopter flight: 1907.

Igor Sikorsky, U.S. engineer—1939: designed 1st practical single-rotor helicopter; 1941: designed 1st commercial helicopter.

Helicopter from Greek: helico = "spiral"; ptero = "wing."

Sentences will vary. Check that none are fragments. You may wish to have students combine the sentences into a paragraph.

Subject and Predicate

Every sentence has two essential parts: a subject and a predicate. The subject is the part of the sentence that names the person, thing, or idea that the sentence is about. The predicate is the part of the sentence that tells what the subject does, what it is, or what happens to it.

SUBJECT	PREDICATE
The eagle on the Great Seal	holds a motto in its beak.

A subject and a predicate may be a single word or a group of words.

🔹 The **simple subject** is the key word or words in the subject. When a proper noun is the simple subject, it may be more than one word. The complete subject is made up of the simple subject and all of its modifiers such as adjectives and prepositional phrases.

🔹 The **simple predicate** is always a verb or verb phrase that tells something about the subject. The complete predicate contains the verb and all its modifiers, objects, and complements.

You'll review objects and complements in Lessons 5.8 and 5.9.

Throughout the rest of this book, the term *subject* refers to the simple subject, and the term *verb* refers to the simple predicate. The verb may be a single verb or a verb phrase. In the examples below, the highlighted words are the simple subject and the simple predicate.

COMPLETE SUBJECT	COMPLETE PREDICATE
The **eagle** on the Great Seal	**holds** a motto in its beak.
E Pluribus Unum	**has been** the motto of the United States for a long time.
The **motto**	**means** "out of many, one."
Many other **symbols**	**are** also **included** on the Great Seal.

 No one outside the world of school will ever ask you to identify subjects and predicates when you write or speak. You're learning how to identify subjects so that you will know how to choose verbs that agree with their subjects. You'll learn more about subject-verb agreement in Chapter 9.

Enriching Your Vocabulary

From the Latin adjective *unus* (*una, unum*), which means "one," comes the stem for many English words. *Unison*, for example, means "agreement" or "a sounding together as one." Other common words formed from *unus* are *unity, union, unit, unite, universe,* and *uniform*.

In each sentence, underline the subject (the simple subject) once and the verb (the simple predicate) twice. **Remember:** When the subject is a proper noun, underline the entire proper noun.

EXAMPLE   Alfred Nobel was a nineteenth-century Swedish chemist and inventor.

1. He made a great deal of money as the inventor of dynamite.

2. Nobel created a fund for prizes for outstanding achievement.

3. Since 1917, committees of Swedish experts have been awarding annual prizes in chemistry, physics, medicine, literature, and peace.

4. Each prize carries a cash award, a medal, and worldwide recognition.

5. Nobel Prize winners are called Nobel laureates.

6. Sometimes two or more persons share an award.

7. In some years, no award is given in a field.

8. Winners in literature have included Wole Soyinka from Nigeria and Octavio Paz from Mexico.

9. Dr. Martin Luther King, Jr., won the Nobel Peace Prize in 1964.

10. The Dalai Lama has also won the Peace Prize.

Exercise 4 **Writing Complete Sentences**

On a separate piece of paper, rewrite the following notes (which are fragments) as complete sentences. Work with a partner or small group. Be sure to begin each sentence with a capital letter and to add the appropriate end punctuation mark. Compare your sentences with those of other pairs or groups.

> *Nitrogen cycle—essential to all living things.*
>
> *Nitrogen = colorless gas; makes up 78% of Earth's atmosphere.*
>
> *Nitrogen from soil to plants, which manufacture necessary proteins (nitrogen compounds) for the plants.*
>
> *Waste products from plants & animals. Plants/animals: die, decay.*
>
> *Bacteria in soil: they act on decaying matter (to release nitrogen compounds).*
>
> *Resulting nitrogen gas goes back to atmosphere and soil.*
>
> *Nitrogen cycle: on and on and on.*

Sentences will vary. Students may wish to combine the sentences into a paragraph and store it in their Writing Notebook.

Correcting Sentence Fragments

Use these three strategies to correct sentence fragments.

1. **Attach it**. Join the fragment to a complete sentence before or after it.

   FRAGMENT   When you were in elementary school. Did you ever know a bully?

   REVISED   When you were in elementary school, did you ever know a bully?

2. **Add some words**. Add the missing subject or verb or whatever other words are necessary to make the group of words grammatically complete.

   FRAGMENT   Two major problems. How to change a bully's behavior and to protect a bully's victims.

   REVISED   Two major problems are how to change a bully's behavior and how to protect the bully's victims.

3. **Drop some words**. Drop the subordinating conjunction that creates a fragment.

   FRAGMENT   Because children need to learn strategies for coping with a bully.

   REVISED   Children need to learn strategies for coping with a bully.

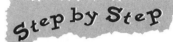

The Sentence Test

To determine whether a group of words is a sentence, ask these three questions:

1. Does it have a subject?

2. Does it have a verb?

3. Does it express a complete thought?

If you can't answer yes to all three questions, you have a fragment. Fix it.

Exercise 5   Editing Sentence Fragments

On a separate piece of paper, edit each numbered item to correct all sentence fragments. Use the three strategies just presented.

1. Bullies are usually older and bigger. Than their victims.
   Bullies are usually older and bigger than their victims.
2. Because a typical victim blames himself or herself for being

   pushed around.   A typical victim blames himself or herself for being pushed around.
3. When a child becomes a bully. A child becomes a bully.

4. Schools coping with the problem of dealing with bullies.
   Schools cope with the problem of dealing with bullies.
5. One strategy that may work for young children. Ignoring a
   One strategy that may work for young children is to ignore a bully's threats.
   bully's threats.

Exercise 6 Editing Sentence Fragments

Read the paragraph below carefully. If the numbered group is not a sentence, add words or omit words to make it a sentence.

[1]Have you ever read *Black Boy*? [2]Richard Wright's autobiography first published in 1937. [3]One episode called "The Streets of Memphis." [4]Often appears in literature anthologies. [5]In this episode, Wright, who is very young, and his brother and mother are living in Memphis, Tennessee. [6]One day Wright's mother sends him to the grocery store. [7]With a basket, some money, and a shopping list. [8]Before he gets to the store. [9]A gang of boys attack him. [10]They knock him down. [11]And take his money and basket. [12]That same evening when his mother sends him to the store again. [13]The boys take his money and hit him. [14]When Wright comes home crying a second time. [15]His mother gives him more money and a heavy stick. [16]Tells him that she will beat him. [17]If he comes home without the groceries. [18]Terrified and furious. [19]Wright goes back to the street and fights the whole gang. [20]When they try to steal his money a third time. [21]He uses the stick and chases them. [22]"That night," the author writes, "I won the right to the streets of Memphis."   Paragraphs will vary. Students should use complete sentences with correct end punctuation.

Exercise 7 Write What You Think

On a separate piece of paper, write what you think about one of the questions below. When you've finished writing, check each sentence to make sure it has a subject, a verb, and expresses a complete thought.

■ Additional tips for writing a persuasive paragraph are in **Composition** Lesson 2.4.

1. What do you think causes someone to become a bully?

2. What do you think schools and students can do to prevent bullies from threatening and hurting other students?

3. What do you think parents should teach their children about how to deal with bullies?

Answers will vary. Give students full credit if they have stated an opinion on one of the issues and attempted to support the opinion. They should also have written grammatically complete sentences that begin with a capital letter and end with an appropriate end punctuation mark.

Combining Sentences: Compound Subjects and Compound Verbs

The repetition in the following sentences not only wastes space but also sounds boring.

ORIGINAL   Emma is on the All-Star soccer team. Liz is on the All-Star soccer team. Jody is on the All-Star soccer team.

A writer can say the same thing more efficiently and gracefully in a single sentence with a compound subject.

REVISED   Emma, Liz, and Jody are on the All-Star soccer team.

The word *compound* means "two or more of something." Any sentence part can be compound.

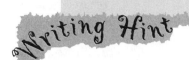
Writing Hint

Use these conjunctions to create a compound subject or a compound verb.

COORDINATING CONJUNCTIONS
and or but nor yet

CORRELATIVE CONJUNCTIONS
either . . . or
neither . . . nor
not only . . . but also
both . . . and

◗ A sentence with a **compound subject** has two or more subjects sharing the same verb. Use a conjunction to join the separate subjects.

SEPARATE SUBJECTS	Coal is a fossil fuel. Natural gas is a fossil fuel. Petroleum is a fossil fuel.
COMPOUND SUBJECTS	Coal, natural gas, and petroleum are fossil fuels.
SEPARATE SUBJECTS	Alaska has large deposits of oil. Texas has large deposits of oil.
COMPOUND SUBJECTS	Both Alaska and Texas have large deposits of oil.

Refer to Lessons 13.2 to 13.5 for rules about using commas.

◗ A sentence with a **compound verb** has two or more verbs sharing the same subject. Use a conjunction to join the separate verbs.

SEPARATE VERBS	People can heat their homes with fossil fuels. People can drive their cars with fossil fuels.
COMPOUND VERB	People can not only **heat** their homes but also **drive** their cars with fossil fuels.
SEPARATE VERBS	Many people waste fuel. Many people complain about the high cost of fuel.
COMPOUND VERB	Many people **waste** fuel yet **complain** about the high cost of fuel.

P.S. If you've spoken English all your life, you already know how to combine sentences when you talk. Think of sentence combining as a useful tool to help you vary sentence lengths and create smoother-sounding sentences when you write.

Enriching Your Vocabulary

The verb *convey* used in Exercise 9 came into English from the French *conveier*, which means "to go with" or "escort." The French word is formed from the Latin *con*, which means "with," and *via*, meaning "way." The sense of the Latin roots is *conveyed* to this day in the modern English meaning "to transport" or "to communicate."

Combining Sentences

On a separate piece of paper, combine the sentences in each numbered item into a single sentence with a compound subject or a compound verb. In your revised sentences, underline the subject(s) once and the verb(s) twice. Do not underline the conjunction as part of the compound. See Answer Key.

1. Photography developed in the 1820s. Photography became a new art form.

2. The scenes in photographs can be both moving and powerful. The faces in photographs can be both moving and powerful.

3. During the Civil War, Mathew Brady photographed soldiers and battle scenes. Mathew Brady's assistants also photographed soldiers and battle scenes during the Civil War.

4. In 1888, George Eastman's box camera made photography easy for everyone. That year George Eastman's roll film made photography easy for everyone.

5. Margaret Bourke-White photographed Americans during the Great Depression of the 1930s. Walker Evans photographed Americans during the Great Depression of the 1930s. Dorothea Lange photographed Americans during the Great Depression of the 1930s.

Exercise 9 ## Revising and Editing a Report

With a partner or small group, improve the following passage from a report. Look for ways to combine sentences, using compound subjects and compound verbs. Compare your revised passage with those of other pairs or groups.

Hint

Not every sentence in the passage needs to be changed.

[1]In 1955, Edward Steichen created a special photography exhibit. [2]Steichen called it *The Family of Man*. [3]Photographs from sixty-eight countries appeared in the exhibit. [4]Quotations from all over the world appeared in the exhibit. [5]Steichen grouped the photos according to themes. [6]Steichen hung the photos in the Museum of Modern Art in New York City. [7]He was curator of photography there. [8]Children are the subjects in the photos. [9]Families are the subjects in the photos. [10]Workers are the subjects in the photos. [11]The photographs show activities common to all people. [12]The photographs convey a simple message: We are all part of one family—the human family.

Answers will vary but should show correct use of compound subjects and verbs.

Finding the Subject

In every sentence you write, you need to be able to identify the subject so that you can choose the right verb to go with it. In some cases, however, finding the subject in a sentence takes a careful read.

● In an **inverted sentence**, the verb (v) comes before the subject (s).

           V   S   S

At the end of the tunnel are a green **door** and a red **one**.

           V   S

Behind one of the doors is a mysterious **prize**.

● The words *here* and *there* are never the subject of a sentence. In a sentence beginning with *here* or *there*, look for the subject after the verb.

     V   S

Here are the missing golden **apples**.

     V   S

There can be only one **reason** for their disappearance.

● The subject of a sentence is never part of a prepositional phrase.

          S   V

Different **areas** on the tongue register sweet, salty, sour, and bitter tastes. [The subject is not *tongue* because *on the tongue* is a prepositional phrase modifying *areas*, the subject.]

          S   V

The two **functions** of the human ear are balance and hearing.

● To find the subject of a question, turn the question into a statement.

     V   S

How long is your Works Cited **list**? [Your Works Cited list is _____ long?]

● In a command or request (an imperative sentence), the subject is always *you* (the person being spoken to).

The word *you* is called the **understood subject** because it does not appear in the sentence.

  S   V   V

[You] Please turn off the lights, and lock the door.

Even when the name of the person being spoken to is mentioned, the subject is still understood to be *you*.

    S   V   V

Tony, **[you]** please turn off the lights and lock the door. [*You* is the understood subject of the verbs *turn* and *lock*.]

Step by Step

Finding the Subject

1. Find the verb or verb phrase.
2. Ask "Who?" or "What?" before the verb.
   The girl in the red sweater plays second base.
   VERB plays
   WHO PLAYS? girl
3. **Remember**: *There* and *here* are never subjects, and prepositional phrases never contain the subject.

In each sentence, underline the simple subject once and the verb twice.
If the subject is understood to be *you*, write the word *you* after the sentence.
Remember: When the subject is a proper noun, underline the entire
proper noun.

1. During the Middle Ages, there were many popular stories about King
   Arthur and his knights of the Round Table.

2. The legendary King Arthur may have been based on a Celtic war chief of
   the fifth and sixth centuries.

3. At first, there was only the oral tradition of the storytellers, bards, and
   minstrels.

4. Among the earliest written stories about King Arthur were those by the
   twelfth-century writer Wace.

5. Toward the end of the Middle Ages, Sir Thomas Malory wrote *Morte
   d'Arthur*.

6. Did Malory write *Morte d'Arthur* during his last twenty years in prison?

7. Can you name any of the knights of the Round Table?

8. There were Sir Gawain, Sir Launcelot, Sir Galahad, and many others.

9. Here is a copy of *Sir Gawain and the Green Knight*.

10. Carey, please tell us about Tennyson's *The Idylls of the King*.   you

11. Have you read T. H. White's *The Once and Future King*?

12. Don't miss this exciting, easy-to-read retelling.   you

13. In White's retelling of the Arthur story, Merlin changes young Arthur into
    different animals.

14. From each experience as an animal, Arthur learns some wisdom.

15. The young Arthur in Malory's version pulls a sword from a marble block.

16. All of the English nobles had tried but failed.

17. After pulling out the sword, Arthur is crowned king of all Britain.

18. There have been several movies about Arthur and a successful musical.

19. In the starring roles on Broadway were Richard Burton as Arthur and Julie
    Andrews as Guinevere.

20. Have you seen the movie version of Lerner and Lowe's *Camelot*?

Mid-Chapter Review

Exercise A Identifying Subjects and Verbs

In each numbered item, underline the simple subject once. Underline the verb twice. If the subject is understood to be *you*, write the word *you* after the sentence. **Hint:** Look for compound subjects and verbs.

EXAMPLE   Jodi and Maria are washing Maria's car.

1. Did you find a copy of your report?
2. Someone in the athletic office called Josh and left a message.
3. Behind the cereal boxes in the cupboard is a small bag of flour.
4. Come with us to the concert on Saturday. you
5. Under the tree lay a sleeping dog and two kittens.
6. There are at least three good reasons for my decision.
7. What did you think of the updated version of Romeo and Juliet?
8. Jewell and her older sister are working at a day-care center after school.
9. Two of the winners in the photo contest are Hakim and JoEllen.
10. Here is a photo of me as a three-month-old baby.

Exercise B Combining Sentences

On a separate piece of paper, combine the sentences in each numbered item into a single sentence with a compound subject or a compound verb. You may need to change or omit words. In your revised sentences, underline the subject(s) once and the verb(s) twice. Do not underline the conjunction as part of the compound. Combined sentences should eliminate repetition.

1. Arteries are blood vessels. Veins are blood vessels.
2. The lungs transport oxygen from the air to the blood. The lungs remove carbon dioxide from the blood.
3. The brain is part of the nervous system. The spinal cord is part of the nervous system. The nervous system also contains nerves themselves.
4. Nerves in every part of the body receive messages from the brain. Nerves in every part of the body also transmit messages to the brain.
5. Regular exercise is essential to a person's health. A balanced diet is essential to a person's health.

1. Arteries and veins are blood vessels.
2. The lungs transport oxygen from the air to the blood and remove carbon dioxide from the blood.
3. The brain, spinal cord, and nerves are part of the nervous system.
4. Nerves in every part of the body receive messages from the brain and also transmit messages to the brain.
5. Regular exercise and a balanced diet are essential to a person's health.

Exercise C **Writing Complete Sentences**

On a separate piece of paper, rewrite the paragraphs below to correct any sentence fragments and to combine sentences where appropriate. Check to see that every sentence has a subject and a verb and expresses a complete thought.

¹Twins are either fraternal or identical. ²Identical twins grow from a single egg. ³Always the same sex, look very much alike. ⁴Have the same blood type and share other characteristics, too. ⁵Fraternal twins grow from two different eggs. ⁶They can be different sexes. ⁷They can look nothing alike. ⁸They can be totally different in personality.

⁹Identical twins claim they have a special relationship. ¹⁰Even before they are born. ¹¹Often extremely close and consider each other best friends. ¹²But needs to have his or her own identity, too. ¹³When you have identical twins who dress alike. ¹⁴How do you tell them apart?

Revised paragraphs will vary. Students may wish to extend this exercise by writing a narrative paragraph about twins they have known.

Exercise D **Write What You Think**

In a paragraph, answer one of the following questions. When you finish writing, check to see that your paragraph contains only complete sentences, not fragments.

1. Would you like to be an identical twin? Give several reasons explaining your answer. (If you are an identical twin, tell about a humorous incident involving you and your twin.)

2. If you were the parent of twins (or triplets or quadruplets), how would you raise them? Would you dress them alike? What do you think would be important to teach them?

Answers will vary. Give students full credit if they have stated an opinion on one of the issues and attempted to support the opinion. They should also have written grammatically complete sentences that begin with a capital letter and end with an appropriate end punctuation mark.

Compound Sentences

◖ A **compound sentence** combines two or more simple sentences into a single sentence.

ORIGINAL   A penguin is a bird. It doesn't fly.

COMPOUND SENTENCE   A penguin is a bird, but it doesn't fly.

Don't confuse a compound sentence with a simple sentence that contains a compound subject (S) or compound verb (V).

    S   S   V   V

Eitan and **Ron collect** snakes and **know** a lot about them. [simple sentence with compound subject and compound verb]

In a compound sentence, each simple sentence has at least one subject and one verb.

    S   V   S   V

Eitan has a pet boa constrictor, and **Ron has** two coral snakes. [compound sentence made up of two simple sentences]

          S   S   V

Both **Eitan** and **Ron volunteer** at the Delta Snake Museum, and

    S   V   V

they have lectured and **handled** snakes in schools. [The first simple sentence has a compound subject, and the second has a compound verb.]

Use these three strategies to combine sentences into a compound sentence.

1. Use a **comma** and a **conjunction** to combine the sentences.

    About 2,700 species of snakes live on the earth, **but** only one fifth of them are poisonous. **Either** I have to get over my fear of snakes, **or** the camping trip won't be fun.

2. Use a **semicolon** alone to combine the sentences.

    About 2,700 species of snakes live on the earth; one-fifth of them are poisonous.

3. Use a **semicolon** followed by a **conjunctive adverb** to combine two sentences. A comma always follows the conjunctive adverb.

    About 2,700 species of snakes live on the earth; **however,** only one-fifth of them are poisonous.

Some Common Conjunctive Adverbs

accordingly	meanwhile
also	moreover
besides	nevertheless
consequently	otherwise
finally	similarly
furthermore	still
however	therefore
indeed	thus
instead	

P.S. You don't need to memorize the list of conjunctive adverbs or even learn their "name." Just be aware that you can use these words to combine sentences and show the relationship between ideas.

Identifying Subjects and Verbs in Compound Sentences

In each of the compound sentences, underline each simple subject once. Underline each verb twice. Remember to watch out for compound subjects and compound verbs in each simple sentence.

1. Snakes appear in myths around the world, and not all of them are evil.

2. In the mythology of India, Nagas are a race of snakes; they are powerful and sometimes dangerous.

3. Nagas are usually ordinary snakes, but sometimes they appear in human form.

4. The Nagas live in a splendid underworld kingdom; similarly, in Incan myth, snakes guard the treasures of the underworld.

5. The ancient Egyptian snake-goddess is shown as a snake with a human head, or sometimes she is a three-headed snake.

Exercise 12 **Writing Compound Sentences**

Insert words and punctuation marks, and make any other changes that are needed to combine each group of sentences into a compound sentence. Use more than one strategy for combining the sentences. Answers will vary.

EXAMPLE   You know about the snake in the Garden of Eden. Do you know other stories about snakes?
You know about the snake in the Garden of Eden, but do you know other stories about snakes?

1. Mertseger was worshiped as a kindly goddess. She also punished wrongdoers.
   Mertseger was worshiped as a kindly goddess, yet she also punished wrongdoers.
2. In West Africa, a snake in the shape of a circle is a powerful symbol.
   In West Africa, a snake in the shape of a circle is a powerful symbol; it stands for life,
   It stands for life, continuity, and eternity.
   continuity, and eternity.
3. In ancient Japan, the god of thunder was a snake. In Dahomey (now Benin),
   In ancient Japan, the god of thunder was a snake; also, in Dahomey (now Benin), thunder's
   thunder's servant is the Rainbow Snake.
   servant is the Rainbow Snake.
4. The ancient Toltecs of Mexico worshiped the snake-bird Quetzalcoatl.
   The ancient Toltecs of Mexico worshiped the snake-bird Quetzalcoatl, for he was the Morning
   He was the Morning Star and Breath of Life.
   Star and Breath of Life.
5. Quetzalcoatl sailed away to the East. He promised to return one day.
   Quetzalcoatl sailed away to the East, but he promised to return one day.

Run-on Sentences

A **run-on** sentence is made up of two or more sentences that are incorrectly run together as a single sentence.

Use these five strategies for correcting a run-on sentence.

1. **Separate them**. Add end punctuation and a capital letter to separate the sentences.

   RUN-ON   In 1921, Franklin Delano Roosevelt was stricken by polio, seven years later, he was elected governor of New York.

   CORRECTED   In 1921, Franklin Delano Roosevelt was stricken by polio. Seven years later, he was elected governor of New York.

2. **Use a conjunction**. Use a word like *and*, *but*, *or*, *yet*, or *so* preceded by a comma.

   RUN-ON   "Life was meant to be lived curiosity must be kept alive."

   CORRECTED   "Life was meant to be lived, and curiosity must be kept alive." —*Eleanor Roosevelt*

3. **Try a semicolon**. Use a semicolon to separate the two sentences.

   RUN-ON   "Speak softly and carry a big stick, you will go far."

   CORRECTED   "Speak softly and carry a big stick; you will go far." —*Theodore Roosevelt*

4. **Add a conjunctive adverb**. Use a semicolon together with a conjunctive adverb (*however, therefore, nevertheless, still, also, instead,* etc.). Be sure to put a comma after the conjunctive adverb.

   RUN-ON   On November 19, 1863, Edward Everett spoke for two hours, President Lincoln's speech, The Gettysburg Address, lasted only three minutes.

   CORRECTED   On November 19, 1863, Edward Everett spoke for two hours; **however**, President Lincoln's speech, The Gettysburg Address, lasted only three minutes.

5. **Create a clause**. Turn one of the sentences into a subordinate clause. (See Chapter 7 for more on subordinate clauses.)

   RUN-ON   Lincoln's speech lasted only three minutes it is one of the most famous speeches in American history.

   CORRECTED   **Although Lincoln's speech lasted only three minutes**, it is one of the most famous speeches in American history.

Editing Tip

A run-on with only a comma separating its sentences is called a **comma splice**.

COMMA SPLICE
John Adams was the second president, his oldest son was the sixth president.

CORRECTION
John Adams was the second president, and his oldest son was the sixth president.

Exercise 13 Editing Run-on Sentences

On a separate piece of paper, correct and rewrite the run-on sentences by adding words and punctuation marks. Use a variety of strategies. See Answer Key.

1. Freedom Riders rode buses in the South their goal was to end racial segregation on public buses.

2. Alaska became the forty-ninth state in 1959, Hawaii became the fiftieth state in that same year.

3. Anthropology is the scientific study of human beings archaeology is the scientific study of ancient societies.

4. Lewis Carroll wrote *Alice in Wonderland*, in real life he was Charles Lutwidge Dodgson, a mathematics lecturer at Oxford.

5. Butterflies, cockroaches, and fleas are insects scientists have identified more than a million species of insects.

Exercise 14 Revising and Editing a Report

Work with a partner or small group to correct all of the run-on sentences and fragments in this report. Use a variety of strategies. Compare your revision with those of other pairs or groups.

[1]George Orwell is the pseudonym, or pen name, of Eric Blair he was a twentieth-century English essayist and novelist, Orwell's best-known works are the novels *Animal Farm* (1945) and *Nineteen Eighty-Four* (1948).

■ **Find a list of strategies for writing your own report about literature in Composition Lesson 3.4.**

[2]*Animal Farm* is a political satire it is also a fable, complete with talking animals. [3]In this novel, the animals of Manor Farm rebel against the cruelty of Farmer Jones, at first the animals in Orwell's novel work fairly well together soon the pigs usurp power over all the other animals. [4]"All animals are equal but some animals are more equal than others" the pigs post this proclamation on the barn, it's the most famous quotation from *Animal Farm*.

[5]Orwell's *Nineteen Eighty-Four* presents a frightening picture of a future society. [6]With no individual freedom. [7]Its citizens are controlled by government from birth to death "Big Brother is watching you." Is the slogan on posters all over the society.

Answers will vary. You may wish to extend this exercise by having students use this as a model for writing a brief report on their favorite books.

Direct and Indirect Objects

In this lesson, you'll review two kinds of objects: direct objects and indirect objects.

🖊 A **direct object** (DO) is a noun or pronoun that receives the action of an action verb. A direct object answers the question *whom* or *what* following the verb.

         DO
Jenny takes advanced **algebra**. [Takes—*what?*—algebra. *Algebra* is the direct object.]

      DO
Rob tested the **twins** in math. [Tested—*whom?*—the twins. *Twins* is the direct object.]

Do you remember the two kinds of verbs—action verbs and linking verbs? Only action verbs (see Lesson 4.3) can have objects. Not all action verbs have objects, but when they do, they're called **transitive verbs**.

🖊 An **indirect object** (IO) is a noun or pronoun that answers the question *to whom* or *for whom* or *to what* or *for what* following an action verb.

Indirect objects never stand alone. You can have a direct object without an indirect object, but you can't have an indirect object without a direct object. The indirect object always comes before the direct object.

         IO   DO
Their mother gives **them** piano **lessons**. [Gives lessons to—*whom?*—them. *Them* is the indirect object; *lessons* is the direct object.]

           IO   DO
Jenny gave the calculus **problem** one more **try**. [Gave one more try to—*what?*—to the calculus problem. *Problem* is the indirect object; *try* is the direct object.]

Like subjects, direct objects and indirect objects never appear within a prepositional phrase. Even though the following two sentences mean the same thing, only the first one has an indirect object.

       IO   DO
Please tell **Jim** the **answer**.

          DO
Please tell the **answer** to Jim. [*To Jim* is a prepositional phrase.]

Step by Step

Finding Direct and Indirect Objects

To find a direct object:

1. Find the action verb.

2. Ask the question *whom?* or *what?* after the action verb.

To find an indirect object:

1. Find the action verb.

2. Find the direct object.

3. Ask the question *to* or *for whom?* or *to* or *for what?* after the action verb.

Exercise 15 Identifying Direct and Indirect Objects

Underline every direct object and indirect object. Label them *DO* for direct object and *IO* for indirect oject.

EXAMPLE Democrats gave John F. Kennedy [IO] the presidential nomination [DO] in 1960.

1. Kennedy's charm won the loyalty [DO] of many supporters.

2. However, many Democratic leaders doubted his ability [DO] to win the election.

3. Some questioned Kennedy's experience [DO] since he was just forty-three years old.

4. Others gave him [IO] high marks [DO] for the hope and energy he inspired among Americans.

5. Kennedy's calm confidence on televised debates earned him [IO] votes [DO] in a close election.

Hint

Like every sentence part, objects may be compound, and a compound sentence may have objects after each subject and verb.

Exercise 16 Identifying Direct and Indirect Objects

Underline every direct object once and indirect object twice in the paragraphs below. **Hint:** Not every sentence has an object.

[1]In 1960, televised debates impacted the outcome of a presidential election for the first time. [2]In these debates, Democratic candidate John F. Kennedy argued his case against his opponent, Republican Richard Nixon. [3]Kennedy understood the power of his television appearance. [4]He practiced his speeches carefully. [5]His aides gave him test questions. [6]They anticipated the questions of the debate panel. [7]Finally, they gave Kennedy make-up to wear that would help him look healthy and calm.

[8]Nixon did not practice his speeches. [9]He also did not wear make-up. [10]During the debate, Nixon mopped his brow. [11]Nixon answered questions easily, but he gave television viewers an impression of strained nervousness. [12]Voters who watched the debate gave Kennedy their support, and in November, he won the closest presidential race in history.

Exercise 17 Write What You Think

On a separate piece of paper, write a paragraph in answer to the question below. Support your opinion with facts and examples.

Given the powerful impact of the media on Americans, how can you be sure you are getting a fair and accurate portrayal of national public events?
See teacher pages for writing assessment rubrics.

Predicate Nominatives and Predicate Adjectives

What's wrong with the following groups of words, punctuated as sentences?

The tall young man next to Sally is. He seems.

The verbs *is* and *seems* are linking verbs, and neither "sentence" expresses a complete thought.

🍃 A **linking verb** needs a noun or an adjective after it in order to express a complete thought. That noun (N) or adjective is (ADJ) called a **subject complement**.

                                            N
The tall young man next to Sally is my **cousin**.

      ADJ
He seems **happy**.

There are two kinds of subject complements: predicate nominatives and predicate adjectives.

🍃 A **predicate nominative** (PN) is a noun or pronoun that follows a linking verb (LV) and renames or identifies the subject (S).

      S LV   PN
Nina's **aunt is** a police **officer**. [*Officer* is a noun that renames the subject *aunt*.]

      S   LV PN
The **person** in charge of the investigation **is she**. [*She* is a pronoun that identifies the subject *person*.]

🍃 A **predicate adjective** (PA) is an adjective that follows a linking verb and modifies, or describes, the subject.

      S   LV   PA
Old **Justin seems angry** about something. [*Angry* is an adjective that modifies the subject *Justin*.]

   LV S   S   PA
Are Luis and **she upset**, too? [The adjective *upset* modifies the subjects *Luis* and *she*.]

Linking Verbs

All the forms of *be* are linking verbs.
These other verbs can also be linking verbs:

appear	remain
become	seem
feel	smell
grow	sound
look	taste

For more about linking verbs, see Lesson 4.3.

Editing Tip

In formal usage, a pronoun used as a predicate nominative must be in the subject form. (See Lessons 10.1 and 10.2.) The correct answer to the question "Is Rosa there?" is: "This is *she*."

Identifying Predicate Nominatives and Predicate Adjectives

Underline every predicate nominative and predicate adjective in the sentences below. In the space provided, write *PN* for predicate nominative or *PA* for predicate adjective.

_PN_ 1. For Todd, the most difficult test questions are word <u>analogies</u>.

_PA_ 2. Those little green peppers on the pizza certainly taste <u>fiery</u>.

_PN_ 3. Rachel became the youngest <u>member</u> of the jazz band.

_PA_ 4. Jed feels extremely <u>uncomfortable</u> in airplanes, so he doesn't fly.

_PA_ 5. Does this quart of milk smell <u>sour</u> to you?

Exercise 19 **Writing a Description**

A movie director is looking for a place to film her new movie. Work with a partner to write a letter describing your community or neighborhood as the possible location for the movie. When you've finished writing, underline and label every predicate adjective and predicate nominative in your sentences. Use the worksheet below to help you start.

■ Additional tips for writing a descriptive paragraph are in **Composition** Lesson 2.4.

> ## A Great Place to Make a Movie
>
> Type of community (city, small town, farm, suburb)
>
> Type of land (hilly, desert, seashore, etc.)
>
> What my community looks like
>
> What the main street looks like
>
> What the building I live in looks like
>
> What my street looks like
>
> What my school looks like

Community descriptions will vary. Students may wish to store this community description in their Writing Notebooks.

Eliminating Wordiness

Here are techniques for writing what you mean as clearly as possible.

● **Get Rid of Padding and Unnecessary Repetition**. Don't say the same thing twice in different words. When you revise, look for unnecessary words and get rid of them.

ORIGINAL   In my opinion, I think that having all students who are in ninth grade take a class in debate should be a requirement.

REVISED   I think debate should be required for all ninth-graders.

REVISED   Debate should be required for all ninth-graders.

● **Write in Your Own Voice**. Don't try to impress your reader with fancy words and complicated sentences. Say what you mean simply and directly.

ORIGINAL   The practice of acquiring skills in how to debate and in presenting arguments aids and encourages students in their development of logical skills in thinking.

REVISED   Debating helps develop logical thinking.

Writing Hint

When you write an essay, you may sometimes restate your main idea or main points in a concluding paragraph. Repetition there is fine. In general, though, avoid repeating or restating the same idea in sentences that follow each other. That's padding.

Exercise 20   **Editing Sentences**

On a separate piece of paper, edit the following wordy sentences.
Answers will vary from samples given.

1. Those who are debaters embark on a learning experience in supporting their opinions and what they think about the issues. Debaters learn to express their opinions clearly.

2. They mention and cite factual evidence with facts and examples to back up and support their ideas and main points. They support their ideas by citing facts and examples.

3. In addition, debaters also acquire the development of the skill and the ability to argue both sides and positions of any issue that they debate. Debaters also develop the ability to argue both sides of an issue.

4. Frequently, debaters often discover and come to see that there are no easy, simple solutions to complex problems that are complicated. Debaters often discover that there are no simple solutions to complex problems.

5. By reading recent newspapers and magazines, debaters gather evidence about the issues being debated and discussed through their reading of current periodicals, including magazine articles and newspaper articles. By reading newspapers and magazines, debaters gather evidence about current issues.

Revising and Editing Worksheet

Improve the following paragraphs to correct sentence fragments and run-on sentences and to eliminate wordiness. Make any other changes you think will improve the paragraphs. Work with a partner or small group to revise these paragraphs. Write your report on a separate piece of paper and compare your response with those made by other pairs or groups. When you are finished revising and editing, proofread the draft and fix spelling, capitalization, and punctuation problems.   Revised and edited report should be free of fragments and run-on sentences.

[1]Every September in Coos Bay, Oregon, a race called the Prefontaine Memorial Run occurs the race is held in honor of a track athlete from Coos Bay named Steve Prefontaine. [2]Steve Prefontaine did not win any Olympic gold medals, but Steve Prefontaine is considered to be one of the greatest distance runners who ever lived. [3]In his senior year of high school, Steve Prefontaine, nicknamed Pre, broke the U.S. high school record for running two miles by nearly seven seconds. [4]He ran two miles in eight minutes, forty-one and a half seconds. [5]Pre was not tall and lanky like some great runners. [6]But Pre had determination. [7]And confidence that he could run faster and longer than anyone else. [8]His high school track coach Walt McClure said, "His talent was his ability to control his fatigue and his pain. [9]His threshold for pain was higher than that of most people."

[10]Steve Prefontaine held every American outdoor track record from the 2000 meters through the 10,000 meters. [11]In all, he set fourteen American records and broke the four-minute-mile barrier nine times. [12]A remarkable feat among distance runners.

[13]At age 21, Pre competed in the 5,000 meter race at the 1972 Olympic Games. [14]A dramatic race. [15]Pre finished fourth against the fastest runners of his day? [16]He trained for two years after that year, and many thought that Pre would win the 1976 Olympic race.

[17]Pre never competed in the 1976 Olympic Games on May 30, 1975, Pre died in a car accident. [18]The world would never know if Pre had the stamina to be the fastest man in the world.

Chapter Review

Exercise A Identifying Subjects and Verbs

In each sentence, underline the simple subject once and the verb twice. If the subject is understood to be *you*, write *you* following the sentence.

1. During the famine of the 1840s, many Irish <u>people</u> <u><u>emigrated</u></u> to America.

2. <u><u>Have</u></u> <u>you</u> <u><u>seen</u></u> photos of the 1500-mile-long Great Wall of China?

3. Please <u><u>explain</u></u> this reference to the Trojan horse.   you

4. High in the Himalayas, north of India, <u><u>is</u></u> <u>Nepal</u>.

5. According to the Boy Scout Law, <u>scouts</u> <u><u>should be</u></u> trustworthy and kind.

6. <u>Ben Franklin</u> <u><u>wrote</u></u> *Poor Richard's Almanack* and a famous autobiography.

7. In an eclipse of the sun, the sun's <u>light</u> <u><u>is blocked</u></u> by the moon.

8. <u>Romeo</u> and <u>Juliet</u> <u><u>fall</u></u> in love and <u><u>marry</u></u> but <u><u>do</u></u> not <u><u>live</u></u> happily after.

9. In what year did the <u>Berlin Wall</u> <u><u>come</u></u> down?

10. <u>Cesar Chávez</u> <u><u>organized</u></u> the United Farm Workers union.

Exercise B Identifying Complements

In each sentence, identify the italicized word(s). Above each word, write *DO* (direct object), *IO* (indirect object), *PA* (predicate adjective), or *PN* (predicate nominative).

1. "The Secret Life of Walter Mitty" is a popular *story*[PN] by James Thurber.

2. Harriet Tubman led *hundreds*[DO] of former slaves to freedom via the Underground Railroad.

3. Carbon dioxide is a *compound*[PN] with one atom of carbon and two of oxygen.

4. Utah's Great Salt Lake is *large*[PA], *shallow*[PA], and *salty*[PA].

5. The government gives *applicants*[IO] for citizenship a written *test*[DO].

6. Margaret Mead became a leading *anthropologist*[PN].

7. Thousands of meteorites strike the *earth*[DO] each year with great force.

8. Before the storm, the sky became *yellow-green*[PA].

9. Old Mother Hubbard did not give her *dog*[IO] a bone.

10. Clara Barton founded the *American Red Cross*[DO] in 1881.

Exercise C Combining Sentences

On a separate piece of paper, combine the sentences in each numbered item into one sentence. You may change or omit words and insert punctuation. See Answer Key.

1. Ellen left at 5 A.M. for a bike ride at Shark Valley. Ellen's sister left at 5 A.M. for a bike ride at Shark Valley.

2. The baseball stadium holds fifty thousand people. Every seat was sold.

3. Li Jian finished playing Beethoven's *Moonlight Sonata*. The audience applauded enthusiastically.

4. Joe is a counselor at a summer camp. Amy is a counselor at a summer camp. Columbus is a counselor at a summer camp.

5. Lori lost her driver's license. She applied for a new one.

6. Either Jed will return the library book and pay the fine. Or his brother will return the library book and pay the fine.

7. The speed limit near a school is 15 miles an hour. The speed limit is strictly enforced.

8. Weekends Jo goes to the mall. Weekends Jo's friends go to the mall.

9. The meeting was scheduled for 9 A.M. By 8:30 every seat was taken.

10. Lee wants to attend the U.S. Military Academy at West Point. She has written to her senator.

Exercise D Write What You Think

On a separate piece of paper, write two paragraphs stating what you think about both of these questions.

1. Should everyone be required to take three years of a foreign language in high school? Why or why not?

2. Which language would you most like to learn? Explain why.

Check your paragraphs to make sure that every group of words marked as a sentence is indeed a complete sentence. Check also to make sure you have expressed your thoughts as clearly and directly as possible.

Answers will vary. Give students full credit if they have stated an opinion on one of the issues and attempted to support the opinion. They should also have written grammatically complete sentences that begin with a capital letter and end with an appropriate end punctuation mark.

Phrases

Direct students to chapter-specific portfolio projects on Sadlier-Oxford's website.

STUDENT WRITING
Expository Essay

Help the Environment by Recycling
by Dorothy Schardt
high school student, Darien, Illinois

The students of Hinsdale South are committed to many organizations and ideals. Sports, academics, service, drug-free life styles—these and many others are an integral part of our everyday lives. However, there is one important area in which our school is lacking, and that is in our commitment to the planet.

One hundred and sixty million tons of garbage per year enters our country's landfills. On an individual level, that is approximately three and a half pounds of trash per person every day. Our cafeteria certainly produces a share of that waste.

Communities both large and small, in this country and others, have been swept up in the wave of recycling. In many European countries, for example, fines are given for throwing out recyclables, which include a variety of things such as multicolored glass or cork. Numerous school communities, from around the country and this area, have followed these models and started up school recycling programs. . . .

While we already recycle white office paper and aluminum cans, it is possible to implement a far more extensive program to encompass all parts of our lives. At a nominal charge, one that would appear to balance the cost of renewable waste disposal, [a private collector] would pick up our recyclable waste on a weekly basis. On our part, we would be required to collect recyclables in sorted bins. Styrofoam, plastics, glass, paper, and aluminum, generated at lunch time, could all be collected. The Environmental Concerns Club would be willing to help pay for the bins, and it has been suggested that the community-based students in the deaf and hard-of-hearing program would be interested in clearing the containers. If the school does not want to start such an extensive program, certainly it would be a good idea to start with just some of the materials previously mentioned. As a last resort, we could even simply switch from styrofoam to recycled paper plates.

While people can certainly think of many excuses as to why any recycling program would be impractical, expensive, and time-consuming, we must look at these reasons for what they are—excuses.

The future of our planet rests on how we care for it today, and no excuse can be good enough to justify our continued and blatant destruction of the earth that sustains us. We cannot keep taking from the earth. While recycling does not constitute giving anything new to the earth, it does allow us to give back what we have taken. While some people may be against this plan because it necessitates more time and energy than does merely throwing all waste into one place, recycling is the right thing to do, not only for us, but for the people of the future.

Allow time for students to discuss the student writing. Suggest that they identify its strengths and propose possible improvements. Use the model to introduce the concepts in the chapter.

Dorothy's expository essay identifies a problem and offers a solution. She lists statistics that give evidence of the problem and a detailed explanation of a solution. Her essay ends with an emotional appeal for support.

As you study phrases in this chapter, you will recognize the many types that Dorothy uses in her essay. Phrases add variety to the sentences in an essay and help a writer combine short sentences into longer, more interesting ones.

Prepositional Phrases: Adjective and Adverb Phrases

🖎 A **prepositional phrase** always begins with a preposition and ends with an object (a noun or pronoun). A prepositional phrase may have a compound object. All modifiers of the object(s) are part of the prepositional phrase.

PREP	ADJ	OBJ	PREP	OBJ	OBJ	PREP	ADJ	OBJ
under	the green	couch	to	her and	me	in	three	hours

🖎 A prepositional phrase adds information to a sentence by modifying another word in the sentence.

The gorilla ran. [Which gorilla? Where did it run?]

The gorilla **near the fence** ran **to the zookeeper with food**.

Sometimes, as in the sentence above, a prepositional phrase modifies the object in a preceding prepositional phrase. Also, more than one prepositional phrase may modify the same word.

For several minutes the gorilla stared **at me**. [Both phrases modify the verb *stared*.]

🖎 An **adjective phrase** is a prepositional phrase that modifies a noun or pronoun in the sentence. Adjective phrases (like adjectives) answer the questions "Which one?" or "What kind?"

The gorilla **in the tree** is named Sam. [The adjective phrase modifies the noun *gorilla*.]

Sam is one **of the gorillas** born last spring. [The adjective phrase modifies the pronoun *one*.]

🖎 An **adverb phrase** is a prepositional phrase that modifies a verb, an adjective, or another adverb.

The gorilla laughed **at me**. [The adverb phrase modifies the verb *laughed*.]

He was the largest **of all the gorillas**. [The adverb phrase modifies the adjective *largest*.]

Remember: Some words function as either an adverb or a preposition, depending on the sentence. Prepositions never stand alone. They are always part of a prepositional phrase. If the word is alone, it's an adverb for sure.

ADV	PREP
Lee Ann fell **down**.	Lee Ann fell **down** the steps.

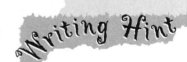

Writing Hint

Help readers visualize objects, people, and actions by using prepositional phrases to add specific details.

NO DETAILS
The man beckoned.

DETAILS
The man in **the black hat** beckoned **to me**.

Exercise 1 **Identifying Adjective and Adverb Phrases**

Underline every prepositional phrase in the sentences below, and draw an arrow to the word each phrase modifies. Label the phrase *ADJ* for an adjective phrase or *ADV* for an adverb phrase.

ADV

EXAMPLE Mumps is caused **by a virus**.

1. Mumps is common <u>during childhood</u> but may also strike adults. *ADV*

2. Infants are given shots <u>for measles, mumps, and rubella</u>. *ADJ*

3. Distant objects look blurry <u>to people</u> *ADV* <u>with myopia</u>. *ADJ*

4. Nearsighted people can see distant objects <u>with eyeglasses or contact lenses</u>. *ADV*

5. Iron is a mineral <u>for red blood cells</u>. *ADJ*

6. Foods rich <u>in iron</u> include spinach, liver, lima beans, and green peas. *ADV*

7. Calcium <u>for bones and teeth</u> *ADJ* is found <u>in all dairy products</u>. *ADV*

8. Most vegetarians eat all types <u>of vegetables, fruits, and beans</u>. *ADJ*

9. A diet <u>without any meat</u> *ADJ* can still provide plenty <u>of protein</u>. *ADJ*

10. What do you eat <u>on a typical day</u> *ADV* <u>for breakfast, lunch, and dinner</u>? *ADV*

Working Together

Exercise 2 **Revising and Editing a Paragraph**

Work with a partner or small group to revise the following draft of a newspaper story for your local paper. Newspaper stories are supposed to answer the questions "Who?" "What?" "When?" "Where?" "Why?" and "How?" Make up details for the story; and on a separate piece of paper, see how many prepositional phrases you can add. Be on the lookout for sentence fragments and run-on sentences. Correct them. When you have finished improving the paragraph, underline every prepositional phrase. Compare your improved news story with those of your classmates. See teacher pages for assessment rubrics.

Hint

Some sentences have more than one prepositional phrase.

■ See **Composition Lesson 1.1** for more on the 5 W and H strategy.

¹There was a car accident. ²One driver was driving a van. ³The second driver was driving a car. ⁴Both cars were damaged. ⁵A passenger was injured. ⁶A police car arrived. ⁷Then an ambulance, then two tow trucks. ⁸The police officer ticketed the driver. ⁹Traffic stopped. ¹⁰The street was blocked.

Participles and Participial Phrases

A **verbal** is a verb form that functions as a different part of speech. Three kinds of verbals that you will learn are participles, gerunds, and infinitives. (See Lessons 6.4 and 6.5.)

• A **participle** is a verb form that acts as an adjective, modifying a noun or a pronoun. There are two kinds of participles: present and past. **Present participles** always have an *-ing* ending; **past participles** usually end in *-d* or *-ed*. The past participles of irregular verbs have different endings. (See Lessons 8.2 and 8.3.)

When you put a helping verb before a participle, you have a verb phrase. When you use a participle alone, you have a modifier that functions as an adjective.

VERB PHRASE	Laurie **is winning** the race.
PARTICIPLE	Who has the **winning** ticket?
VERB PHRASE	**Have** you ever **broken** a bone?
PARTICIPLE	The X ray showed a **broken** bone.

• A **participial phrase** is made up of a participle and all of its modifiers. A participial phrase may contain objects, modifiers, and prepositional phrases. The whole phrase acts as an adjective.

Looking intently at the map, Jerry found New Hope.

Larry made the crown **worn by Queen Esther.**
See Lesson 13.4 for a discussion
of punctuating phrases.

Writing Hint

Place a participial phrase close to the word it modifies. Otherwise, you may say something you do not mean.

I watched a TV show about a wild elephant sitting in my living room.

Lesson 11.4 covers misplaced and dangling modifiers more thoroughly.

Exercise 3 Identifying Participles

Underline every participle or participial phrase in each sentence. Draw an arrow to the word each participle or participial phrase modifies.

EXAMPLE   The doctor showed Jim the X ray of his leg broken in two places.

1. Have you ever had an X ray taken by a doctor or a dentist?

2. X rays made in hospital emergency rooms reveal broken bones.

3. Reading X rays of internal organs, doctors can diagnose diseases.

4. Dental X rays show cavities and teeth growing below the gum line.

5. Superman, famed for his X-ray vision, can see through buildings.

6. A German physicist named Wilhelm Roentgen discovered X rays in 1895.

7. Patients <u>admitted to a hospital</u> often have a routine chest X ray.

8. <u>Penetrating</u> light rays travel through solid bodies and register images on a photographic plate.

9. X rays can destroy living tissue in patients <u>exposed for too long</u>.

10. Earth's atmosphere protects us from X rays <u>emanating from the sun</u>.

Exercise 4 Writing Sentences with Participial Phrases

For each of the following participial phrases, write a complete sentence on a separate piece of paper. Place the participial phrase close to the word it modifies.

EXAMPLE   taken at the beach
This photograph, taken at the beach, shows Grandma as a girl.

1. written on a tiny scrap of paper
2. celebrated on July 4th
3. floating just offshore
4. run by volunteers
5. quoting from a famous speech

6. visiting from Mars
7. surprised by the news
8. warning of danger
9. seen up close
10. sliding into first

Answers will vary. Check that phrases are not used as verbs.

Exercise 5 Identifying Participles

Underline any participles and participial phrases in the following paragraph.

¹The workers <u>struggling to build the Panama Canal</u> were at grave risk of getting yellow fever. ²The disease <u>carried by mosquitoes</u> killed thousands of canal workers. ³<u>Charged with improving the sanitary conditions of the canal zone</u>, Colonel William C. Gorgas borrowed techniques from <u>respected</u> Cuban and American scientists. ⁴Gorgas drained swamps, cleared the land <u>infested with mosquitoes</u>, and killed rats <u>carrying the plague</u>. ⁵The canal, <u>completed in 1914</u>, took ten years to build. ⁶<u>Dedicated</u> workers dug through mountains and swamps to make an <u>easily navigated</u> passageway for ships. ⁷It continues to be a <u>frequently used</u> shipping lane between the Atlantic and the Pacific oceans.

Exercise 6 Write What You Think

On a separate piece of paper, write five sentences on any topic that contain participles and participial phrases. Exchange papers with a partner to check your work. Student sentences will vary.

Effective Paragraphs: Varying Sentence Beginnings

When every sentence in a paragraph starts with its subject, the rhythm of the sentences becomes quite monotonous.

■ See **Composition** Lesson 1.3 for more on revising your writing for content and style.

◗ For variety, begin some of your sentences with a phrase.

ORIGINAL	Katie threw a Frisbee to her dog for fifteen minutes.
REVISED	**For fifteen minutes**, Katie threw a Frisbee to her dog. [prepositional phrase placed first]
ORIGINAL	Jed swam through the underwater tunnel, holding his breath.
REVISED	**Holding his breath**, Jed swam through the underwater tunnel. [participial phrase placed first]
ORIGINAL	The old house, battered by gale-force winds, remained undamaged.
REVISED	**Battered by gale-force winds**, the old house remained undamaged. [participial phrase placed first]

Watch your punctuation. Insert a comma following a participial phrase at the beginning of a sentence.

Exercise 7 Rewording Sentences

Underline every prepositional and participial phrase in each sentence, and write *PREP* for a prepositional phrase or *PART* for a participial phrase. On a separate piece of paper, rewrite the sentence so that it begins with one or more phrases.

EXAMPLE   Jiro paused <u>for a moment</u> <u>at the top</u> <u>of the stairs</u>.
           At the top of the stairs, Jiro paused for a moment.

1. Mike changed his mind <u>at the last minute</u>.
       PREP

2. Cinderella lost one <u>of her glass slippers</u> <u>rushing down the steps</u>.
       PREP   *PART*

3. Bev's mom, <u>standing at the top of the ladder</u>, still couldn't reach the kitten.
       PART

4. Grandpa Max recalled his childhood, <u>speaking into the tape recorder</u>.
       PART

5. The winding road, <u>covered by a heavy fog</u>, was impassable.
       PART

It's never wrong to use a comma after one or a series of introductory prepositional phrases, but it's not always necessary to do so.

COMMA OR NO COMMA OK
To me you look great.
To me, you look great.

COMMA NECESSARY TO PREVENT MISREADING
After dinner, time flies.
In German, nouns are capitalized.

6. He received news of the art contest winners <u>after more than a month</u>.
   PREP

7. Lobster Shack has been serving its famous clam chowder <u>in this same spot</u>
   PREP
   <u>since 1935</u>.
   PREP

8. Sean, <u>exploring the World Wide Web</u>, found many sites <u>about Ireland</u>.
   PART   *PREP*

9. Lionfish, <u>protected by a deadly poison on their fins</u>, aren't bothered <u>by</u>
   PART
   <u>predators</u>.
   PREP

10. The Greek goddess Athena, <u>known for her wisdom</u>, has an owl as <u>her</u>
    PART
    <u>symbol</u>.   Reworded sentences should begin with a phrase.
    PREP

Working Together

Exercise 8   Writing a Paragraph

Use the following notes to write a paragraph on a separate piece of paper. Vary your sentence beginnings. Start at least one sentence with a prepositional phrase or phrases and begin at least one sentence with a participial phrase. Work with a partner or small group and compare your finished paragraphs.

Antigone

Ancient Greek mythology: Antigone (daughter of Oedipus), a heroine

<u>Antigone</u>, tragedy by Sophocles, ancient Greek dramatist—written about 411 B.C.

Theme of play: conflict between society's law vs. higher moral law (individual's conscience)

Creon, king of Thebes, orders people not to bury Antigone's brother's body (his enemy)

Antigone refuses to obey uncle's order ; she twice performs burial ritual for her brother

Conflict mounts: Antigone discovered as the one disobeying Creon's order; Creon refuses to change his mind.

End of play, Antigone & Haimon (Creon's son)—both dead

See teacher pages for assessment rubrics.
You may wish to extend this exercise by having students read *Antigone* and write a brief report on the play.

Mid-Chapter Review

Exercise A Identifying Adjective and Adverb Phrases

Underline every prepositional phrase in the sentences below. Write *ADJ* for a prepositional phrase acting as an adjective phrase or *ADV* for a prepositional phrase acting an an adverb phrase. **Hint:** Some sentences have more than one phrase.

EXAMPLE Remains of prehistoric animals [ADJ] are preserved in fossils [ADV].

1. Most fossils are found in sedimentary rocks [ADV].

2. Prehistoric insects have been preserved in amber [ADV].

3. In the novel [ADV] *Jurassic Park*, DNA from a dinosaur [ADJ] was retrieved from blood [ADV] in a prehistoric mosquito [ADJ].

4. Fossilized bones of a saber-toothed tiger [ADJ] were found in the La Brea [ADV] tar pits.

5. The science of collecting fossils [ADJ] is called paleontology.

Exercise B Identifying Participles and Participial Phrases

Underline every participle and participial phrase in the sentences below. Remember that a participial phrase may contain one or more prepositional phrases. Count these as part of the participial phrase. **Hint:** Some sentences have more than one participle or participial phrase.

1. The Spanish artist Francisco de Goya did a series of etchings showing the horrors of war.

2. Goya also painted portraits commissioned by Spanish nobles.

3. Working on his back on a scaffold high above the floor, Michelangelo painted the ceiling of the Sistine Chapel.

4. The colors in the recently restored ceiling frescoes are extremely bright.

5. Georgia O'Keeffe is a modern American artist known for her huge close-ups of flowers.

Exercise C **Editing Sentence Beginnings**

Reword each sentence so that it begins with one or more phrases. You may move a phrase from within the sentence or add a new phrase of your own. Identify the type of phrase you have placed at the beginning. Be sure to use a comma after an introductory participial phrase. To be safe, also use a comma after one or a series of prepositional phrases at the beginning of a sentence. See Answer Key.

1. Harvey hiccupped for hours on Thursday and all through his algebra final.

2. Mrs. Gittleson handed out the achievement awards at the graduation assembly.

3. The child wailed and sobbed, refusing to leave the toy department.

4. The elderly couple, kneeling in the hot sun, weeded the vegetable garden behind their house.

5. Josie boarded the train, turning once for a last look and a wave.

Exercise D **Revising and Editing a Paragraph**

Improve the following paragraph. Try to combine sentences, vary sentence beginnings, and add specific details that you make up. Use at least one prepositional phrase and one participial phrase in your revision.

¹Dave was driving his car. ²He was talking on a cell phone at the same time. ³He was talking to Miriam. ⁴She is his girlfriend. ⁵It was six o'clock on a winter night. ⁶Icy rain made the streets slippery. ⁷Traffic is always bad at six o'clock. ⁸The rain made it worse. ⁹The car in front of Dave stopped suddenly. ¹⁰Dave wasn't watching. ¹¹He was laughing at Miriam's joke. ¹²Dave stopped laughing. ¹³He saw the stopped car right in front of him. ¹⁴He was frightened. ¹⁵Dave slammed on his brakes. ¹⁶It was too late.

¹⁷His car screeched and skidded. ¹⁸His car crashed into the other car.
Paragraphs will vary. Check for correct use of prepositional and participial phrases.

Exercise E **Write What You Think**

Write a paragraph expressing your view on both of the following questions. Support your opinion with reasons and examples.

1. Should a law be passed prohibiting drivers from talking on the phone?

2. If such a law were passed, how might it be enforced?
See teacher pages for assessment rubrics.

Gerunds and Gerund Phrases

The present participle of a verb (the *-ing* form) sometimes functions as an adjective (see Lesson 6.2). This lesson shows what else *-ing* words can do.

● A **gerund**, ending in *-ing*, is a verb form that acts as a noun. Gerunds in a sentence can do anything that nouns can do.

Skiing is her favorite sport. [subject]
Her favorite sport is **skiing.** [predicate nominative]
Have you ever tried **skiing?** [direct object]
Give **skiing** a chance. [indirect object]
Sue borrowed a book about **skiing.** [object of the preposition]

● A **gerund phrase** is a phrase made up of a gerund and all of its modifiers and complements. The entire phrase functions as a noun. A gerund's modifiers include adjectives, adverbs, and prepositional phrases.

Waiting a long time in a restaurant annoys him. [subject]
His pet peeve is **waiting in a restaurant.** [predicate nominative]
Anna tried **taking tennis lessons.** [direct object]
Jason left for school without **taking his backpack.** [object of the preposition]

Note: Check the spelling of gerunds formed from verbs that end in *e*. See Lesson 16.3 for more about spelling words when you add *-ing*.

Nouns and pronouns that modify a gerund should be in the possessive form.

'*s*
The **baby** ∧ crying didn't stop.
his
We admired ~~him~~ dancing.

Exercise 9   Identifying Gerunds and Gerund Phrases

Underline every gerund and gerund phrase in the sentences below. A gerund phrase may contain one or more prepositional phrases. Count these as part of the gerund phrase.

1. Karla's ambition is hitting two home runs in one game.

2. Laughing, Jeff says he would be happy with scoring a run or two.

3. Lenny admits his pitching is sometimes erratic.

4. The home team's fans went wild at Ken's stealing third base.

5. Patrick left the dugout without telling anyone.

6. The umpire stopped play because of fans' throwing things onto the field.

7. The manager protested the umpire's ruling on a close play at second.

Enriching Your Vocabulary

The adjective *erratic*, like its verb and noun relations *err* and *error*, stems from the Latin *errare*, "to wander." Erratic has come to mean "lacking consistency." Its close relative *errant* has among other meanings that of "straying from a proper path." From an *erratic* pitcher, therefore, you might see thrown an *errant* pitch.

8. The pitcher's batting average is .074, so the cheering fans were astonished at his <u>hitting a double</u>.

9. In the bottom of the eighth, Kirk's team tied the game by <u>scoring two runs</u>.

10. The game ended at 7–6 with Marla's <u>hitting a home run</u>.

Exercise 10 Writing Sentences with Gerunds and Gerund Phrases

■ This exercise is a good addition to the Writing Notebook described in **Composition Lesson 1.1.**

On a separate piece of paper, answer each question below in a complete sentence that contains one or more gerunds or gerund phrases. In brackets following each question, you'll find a suggested sentence starter or sentence ending for your answer. Underline each gerund or gerund phrase in your sentences. Exchange papers with a partner or small group to compare your answers. A sample response is given.

Questionnaire

1. What are your hobbies? [. . . are my hobbies.] <u>Painting, reading, and watching TV</u> are my hobbies.

2. If there were one extra day in the week, how would you spend it? [I would spend it . . .]

3. Do you have chores or responsibilities at home? If so, what are they? [Some of my jobs are . . .]

4. What jobs or careers are you considering? [I am considering . . .]

5. Name at least two skills that are important in the careers you are considering. [. . . are important skills in the careers I am considering.]

6. What would you consider a perfect vacation? [. . . are my ideas of a perfect vacation.]

7. What do you do when you have a cold and fever? [I treat a cold and fever by . . .]

8. If you could choose six courses you really wanted to study, what would you take next semester? [I would spend next semester . . .]

9. What do you think are the most important responsibilities of a parent? [A parent's most important responsibilities are . . .]

10. How do you think a good friend behaves? [A good friend shows his or her friendship by . . .]

Hint

Not every *-ing* word is a gerund. A gerund functions as a noun in sentences.

Infinitives and Infinitive Phrases

🖌 An **infinitive** is a verb form that is almost always preceded by the word *to*. In a sentence, an infinitive can act as a noun, an adjective, or an adverb.

Anne-Marie likes **to paint**. [infinitive as noun]
We were among the first people **to leave**. [infinitive as adjective]
He is quick **to anger**. [infinitive as adverb]

The word *to* is called the sign, or marker, of the infinitive. But remember that *to* can also be a preposition. *To* is part of an infinitive if it is followed by a verb; *to* is a preposition if it's the start of a prepositional phrase.

INFINITIVE   PREPOSITIONAL PHRASE
The toddler likes **to sing**.   The toddler hands the doll **to her father**.

🖌 An **infinitive phrase** is a phrase made up of an infinitive and all of its modifiers and complements. It may contain one or more prepositional phrases.

To become an electrical engineer is David's ambition.
It is easy **to paint a room with a roller**.

Sometimes the *to* of an infinitive or an infinitive phrase is left out; it is understood.

Hal helped **[to] wash the car**.
Please let me **[to] finish this mystery**.

P.S. Knowing about infinitives and infinitive phrases gives you another tool for expressing your ideas. When you write and speak, you don't have to know whether the infinitives you use are functioning as nouns, adjectives, or adverbs as long as you use them correctly.

Exercise 11 Identifying Infinitives and Infinitive Phrases

Perhaps the most famous infinitives are Hamlet's in Act III:

"To be, or not to be, that is the question. . . ."

Underline every infinitive and infinitive phrase in the following quotations from William Shakespeare's works. Remember to include in an infinitive phrase all its modifiers (including prepositional phrases) and complements.

1. "If you have tears, prepare to shed them now." —*Julius Caesar*

2. "To weep is to make less the depth of grief." —*Henry VI, Part III*

3. "I had rather have a fool <u>to make me merry</u> than experience <u>to make me sad</u>." —*As You Like It*

4. "Conscience is but a word that cowards use, / Devised at first <u>to keep the strong in awe</u>." —*Richard III*

5. "These words are razors to my wounded heart." —*Titus Andronicus*

6. "Who buys a minute's mirth <u>to wail a week</u>? / Or sells eternity <u>to get a toy</u>?" —*The Rape of Lucrece*

7. "He was not born to shame; / Upon his brow shame is ashamed <u>to sit</u>." —*Romeo and Juliet*

8. "See what a scourge is laid upon your hate, / That heaven finds means <u>to kill your joys with love</u>." —*Romeo and Juliet*

9. "Things sweet <u>to taste</u> prove in digestion sour." —*Richard II*

10. "He was wont [inclined] <u>to speak plain</u> and to the purpose." —*Much Ado About Nothing*

Exercise 12 Revising and Editing a Biography

Underline the infinitives and infinitive phrases in this draft of a brief biography of Shakespeare. Then work with a partner to correct sentence fragments and to make any other changes you think will improve the biography. (Review in Lesson 5.3 the strategies for correcting sentence fragments.)

¹William Shakespeare is generally acknowledged. ²<u>To be the greatest playwright of all time</u>. ³Born in Stratford-upon-Avon in 1564. ⁴He attended Stratford Grammar School for seven years. ⁵Learning Latin, English composition, and the Bible. ⁶At the age of eighteen Shakespeare married Anne Hathaway, who was eight years older than he. ⁷The couple had a daughter and then twins, a boy and a girl. ⁸About 1587 or 1588, Shakespeare left his family and went to London. ⁹<u>To become an actor and a playwright</u>. ¹⁰By 1592, he had written several plays. ¹¹He soon achieved great fame and prospered. ¹²He managed. ¹³<u>To write more than 36 plays and 150 poems</u>. ¹⁴Shakespeare left London in 1612 or 1613. ¹⁵<u>To retire to his home in Stratford, where he lived quite comfortably</u>. ¹⁶Continued <u>to manage his London acting company and their two theaters</u>. ¹⁷<u>To write plays until his death in 1616</u>.

Combining Sentences: Inserting Phrases

Besides combining sentences using compound subjects and verbs and compound sentences (see Lessons 5.4 and 5.6), writers combine sentences with phrases.

◗ Combine related sentences by inserting a phrase from one sentence into another sentence. Sometimes the phrase you move from one sentence to another requires a slight change. Sometimes you can just pick up a phrase from one sentence and drop it into another. Usually there is more than one way to combine two sentences.

ORIGINAL	Danny was practicing his trumpet. He hit a wrong note.
COMBINED	**Practicing his trumpet,** Danny hit a wrong note. [participial phrase]
ORIGINAL	John set up his tent. He set up his tent near a pile of rocks. The rocks were on the beach.
COMBINED	John set up his tent **near a pile of rocks on the beach.** [prepositional phrases]
ORIGINAL	Mia has a goal tonight. She wants to finish her first draft.
COMBINED	**Finishing her first draft** is Mia's goal tonight. [gerund phrase]
COMBINED	**To finish her first draft** is Mia's goal tonight. [infinitive phrase]

Exercise 13 Combining Sentences

On a separate piece of paper use phrases to combine the sentences in each numbered item. Don't forget to add commas where they belong.

EXAMPLE   Many college students receive letters. The letters urge them to apply for credit cards. The credit cards are already approved.
Many college students receive letters urging them to apply for already approved credit cards.

1. Credit-card companies charge very high interest. The interest is charged on all unpaid balances. Credit-card companies charge very high interest on all unpaid balances.

2. Every month the finance charge increases the debt. The debt increases even with no new purchases. Every month the finance charge increases the debt even with no new purchases.

3. A thirty-year-old woman is struggling. She is named Carol. She struggles to pay her $16,000 credit-card bill.
A thirty-year-old woman named Carol is struggling to pay her $16,000 credit-card bill.

4. Carol wishes she had never used a credit card. Carol works two jobs. She works hard to pay off her debt. [**Hint:** Use an introductory participial phrase.]
Wishing she had never used a credit card, Carol works hard at two jobs to pay off her debt.

5. It will take her five years. By then, she will pay off her debt. The debt is overwhelming. It will take her five years to pay off her overwhelming debt.

6. The average debt for young people is $2,400. The young people are in their twenties. The average debt for young people in their twenties is $2,400.

7. They pay $75 a month. At that rate, it will take three and a half years to pay off the debt. At the rate of $75 a month, it will take three and a half years to pay off the debt.

8. Experts advise these young people. They say young people should not incur more debt. They should destroy their credit cards. Experts advise these young people to destroy their credit cards.

Exercise 14 **Writing Paragraphs**

Use the information in the charts and graph below to write one or more paragraphs about credit-card debt. Exchange papers with a partner, and make suggestions for improving each other's paragraphs. Try combining related sentences by inserting phrases. See teacher pages for assessment rubrics.

Consumer Credit Counseling Services

AVERAGE DEBT ON MAJOR CREDIT CARDS

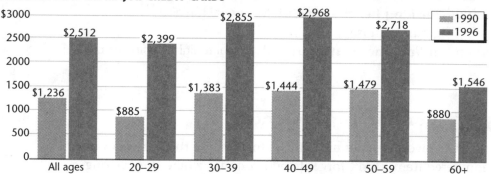

CLIENT OVERVIEW

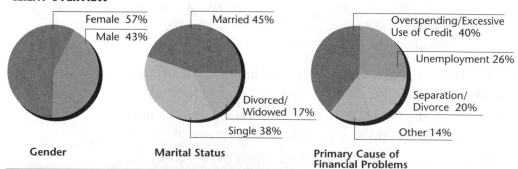

Gender   Marital Status   Primary Cause of Financial Problems

Typical Client Age: 34   Monthly gross income: $2,600
Average debt: $15,100   Average number of creditors: 8.4

Source: Claritas, Inc.

Appositives and Appositive Phrases

◀ An **appositive** is a noun or pronoun that identifies or explains the noun or pronoun that precedes it. An **appositive phrase** is a phrase made up of an appositive and all of its modifiers.

Using appositives and appositive phrases helps you to combine sentences and avoid unnecessary repetition. In the following examples, the appositive phrases are set off from the rest of the sentence with commas.

ORIGINAL   Bryan is moving to Colorado. He is our next-door neighbor.

COMBINED   Bryan, **our next-door neighbor**, is moving to Colorado.

Do not use commas if an appositive is essential to understand the sentence.

NO COMMAS   Then explorers **Lewis and Clark** traveled though the Northwest Territory. [Since there were many explorers the appositive is essential. Do not use commas.]

COMMAS   The capital of Colorado, **Denver**, is one mile above sea level. [The appositive adds extra information but is not essential since there is only one capital.]

Exercise 15   Combining Sentences with Appositives

On a separate piece of paper, combine the sentences in each numbered item with an appositive or appositive phrase. **Hint:** Clues tell you if the appositive is essential.   See Answer Key.

1. Geronimo attended Teddy Roosevelt's inauguration. Geronimo is an Apache leader.

2. The reformer worked to obtain the vote for women. The reformer is Susan B. Anthony.

3. This ancient Greek statue is famous for its beauty. *Venus de Milo* is famous.

4. Portuguese is spoken in Brazil. The largest South American country is Brazil.

5. World War II ended in Europe on V-E Day. May 8, 1945 is V-E Day.

6. Sean's dog is named Sniffles. Sniffles disappeared three days ago. [Sean has three other dogs.]

7. I play my favorite CD loudly. Vivaldi's *The Four Seasons* is my favorite.

8. Diana got an *A* on Friday's test. Friday's test was her algebra final.

9. This postcard is from my friend in London. Jerrie sent me this postcard. [I have four friends in London.]

10. Ben's job starts today after school. His job is working in a bookstore.

Revising and Editing Worksheet

Improve the following report to make it sound less choppy and to eliminate unnecessary repetition. Combine some sentences and vary some sentence beginnings. You may rearrange sentences, change or omit words, and add new details. Work with a partner or small group to improve these paragraphs. Write your improved report on a separate sheet of paper, and compare your changes with those made by your classmates. See teacher pages for assessment rubrics.

[1]Hercules is the greatest figure in ancient Greek mythology. [2]Known for his great strength. [3]The Greeks called him Heracles. [4]Hercules is his Roman name. [5]Hercules was the son of Zeus and a mortal woman. [6]His mother was named Alcmena. [7]She was princess of ancient Thebes. [8]Zeus was the chief god.

[9]Hercules is legendary for performing twelve labors. [10]As punishment for a terrible deed. [11]Hercules had to serve the king of Mycenae for twelve years. [12]He had to do what the king commanded. [13]His labor the first year. [14]To kill the Nemean lion a ferocious lion no weapon could wound. [15]The second labor was. [16]To kill a monster called Hydra. [17]Hydra was a water snake. [18]Her nine heads grew back every time Hercules cut them off.

[19]Hercules's fifth labor is his most famous. [20]Cleaning the Augean stables in a single day. [21]For many years, no one had ever cleaned the stables, where thousands of cattle lived. [22]Hercules accomplished the deed by doing something. [23]He diverted two rivers. [24]He made them flow through the stable.

[25]The eleventh and twelfth labors were the most difficult. [26]In the eleventh year, Hercules had to find the Golden Apples of the Hesperides. [27]And in the twelfth, he journeyed to the Underworld. [28]To bring the three-headed dog Cerberus up from the Underworld. [29]The twelfth labor was Hercules's last.

[30]In the northern skies, you can see a large constellation. [31]It is named after this Greek hero. [32]Hercules's name is also remembered. [33]The name appears in two English expressions. [34]A *herculean task* is one that requires enormous effort. [35]To accomplish. [36]A *herculean effort* is what it takes. [37]To complete a herculean task.

Chapter Review

Visit us at
www.sadlier-oxford.com

Exercise A Matching Definitions

Match the term in Column 1 with its definition in Column 2. Write the letter of the definition in the space provided.

COLUMN 1

<u>e</u> 1. gerund

<u>c</u> 2. preposition

<u>b</u> 3. infinitive

<u>a</u> 4. participle

<u>d</u> 5. appositive

COLUMN 2

a. The *-ing* verb form that functions as an adjective

b. A verb form that is almost always preceded by the word *to*

c. A word used to show the relationship between two words in a sentence, such as *in*, *with*, or *over*.

d. A noun or pronoun that identifies or explains the noun or pronoun preceding it

e. The *-ing* verb form that functions as a noun

Exercise B Identifying Phrases

Identify each underlined phrase by writing one of these abbreviations above the phrase:

PREP = prepositional phrase
PART = participial phrase
GER = gerund phrase

INF = infinitive phrase
APP = appositive phrase

Remember: When a prepositional phrase is part of another kind of phrase, you don't have to label the prepositional phrase separately. For example, the sentence below shows *published in 1884* labeled as a participial phrase but does not identify *in 1884* as a prepositional phrase.

EXAMPLE   *The Adventures of Huckleberry Finn* by Mark Twain, <u>published in 1884</u>, [PART] has been called "the first American novel."

1. The novel is a masterpiece of realism, <u>portraying life on and around the Mississippi River about 1845.</u> [PART]

2. Twain drew <u>from his boyhood</u> memories of Hannibal, Missouri. [PREP]

3. Huck is the novel's narrator, <u>observing the events around him.</u> [PART]

4. Twain excelled at <u>writing dialect</u>, the way people talk in a certain region. [GER]

5. <u>At the beginning</u> of the novel, Huck lives with Widow Douglas. [PREP]

CHAPTER REVIEW

6. Huck's brutal father appears one night and forces him <u>to leave the</u> ^{INF} widow's home.

7. <u>Locked in a cabin by his father</u>, Huck escapes and runs away. ^{PART}

8. After a few days alone, he finds Jim, <u>a runaway slave from his</u> ^{APP} <u>hometown</u>.

9. The two drift <u>down the beautiful Mississippi River</u> on a raft. ^{PREP}

10. By the novel's end, Huck has learned a great deal <u>about life and loyalty</u>. ^{PREP}

Exercise C Combining Sentences

Use phrases to combine the sentences in each numbered item. Write your combined sentences on a separate piece of paper. Add commas where they belong. **Hint:** A suggestion is given for a type of phrase that you can use to combine them. See Answer Key.

1. Many people prefer something. They prefer reading the original novel to watching a movie version. [gerund phrases]

2. *The Adventures of Huckleberry Finn* has been made into a movie and a musical. It is Mark Twain's greatest novel. [appositive phrase]

3. Songs were written. They were written for a 1974 movie version of *The Adventures of Huckleberry Finn.* [prepositional phrases]

4. Ron Howard starred in a TV adaptation. Ron Howard played the role of Huckleberry Finn. [participial phrase]

5. *Big River* was unsuccessful on Broadway. *Big River* was another musical version of *The Adventures of Huckleberry Finn.* [appositive phrase]

6. *Les Misérables* was a very successful musical. It was based on a long novel by the French novelist Victor Hugo. [participial phrase]

7. The musical's writers decided something. They decided to cut the novel to the bare bones of its plot. [infinitive phrase]

8. *Cats* is one of the longest-running musicals. *Cats* was adapted from poems by T. S. Eliot. [participial phrase]

9. You can meet the original cats. You can find them in T. S. Eliot's *Old Possum's Book of Practical Cats.* [prepositional phrase]

10. Many movies have been unsuccessful. These unsuccessful movies have been adapted from great novels. [participial phrase]

Clauses

STUDENT WRITING
Research Paper

Biedermeier Vienna and the
Music of Franz Schubert
by Emma Sheanshang
high school student, New York, New York

At the close of the eighteenth century, the only true capital in the German–speaking countries was Vienna. Vienna had—and still retains—the reputation of being the most enchanting city in Europe, famous for coffee houses, a beautiful historic district, and above all, music. In the past, many people have based their impressions of the city exclusively on these pleasant elements. This romanticized image of Vienna does not encompass other equally important aspects of its rich culture and history. At the beginning of the nineteenth century, during the time Beethoven and Schubert lived and worked in Vienna, Europe was beginning to emerge from a period of almost constant warfare. In 1815, the year in which many believe the modern world began, war ended and the populace grew excited at the promise of peace. But while the resulting period of stability benefited the empire, it came at the expense of the people and, in particular, the new middle class that was emerging in Vienna. In the early nineteenth century, the Viennese found themselves occupying a city that simultaneously illuminated and endangered their lives. Various conflicts and paradoxes complicated every aspect of daily life, causing profound confusion throughout the populace. An understanding of these paradoxes is essential [if one is] to penetrate the seductive facade of tranquillity and gain a real sense of the spirit and culture of the city.

The first paragraph of a research paper should carefully set up the rest of the paper. Here, the writer begins with general statements that grab a reader's attention. Next, she provides some background information to give a context for her thesis. She ends with a three-sentence thesis statement.

The writer has used clauses to improve sentence variety and to help achieve a lively writing style. In this chapter you will practice using clauses in your own writing.

Allow time for students to discuss the student writing. Suggest that they identify its strengths and propose possible improvements. Use the model to introduce the concepts in the chapter.

Independent Clauses and Subordinate Clauses

Every clause is either independent or subordinate.

🔹 **An independent** (or **main**) **clause** has a subject and a verb and expresses a complete thought.

Does this definition sound familiar? It should. It's also the definition for a sentence. An independent clause can stand alone as a sentence; that's why it's called independent.

                   S   S   V

INDEPENDENT CLAUSE   Karen and Jon are late as usual.

A **compound sentence** is made up of two or more independent clauses joined by a conjunction.

                                   CONJ

We finished the jigsaw puzzle, but two pieces were missing.

🔹 **A subordinate** (or **dependent**) **clause** has a subject and a verb but doesn't express a complete thought.

  S V   S V

that I told you about   because she is trying to save money

A subordinate clause can't stand alone. It must be attached to or inserted into an independent clause, or the word that makes it a subordinate clause must drop out.

           SUBORDINATE CLAUSE   INDEPENDENT CLAUSE
          S   V   S   V

Because she is trying to save money, Sheila has been packing her lunch. [The subordinate clause has been attached to an independent clause.]

             SUBORDINATE CLAUSE
     S   S   V   V

The person **who called this morning** didn't leave a message. [The subordinate clause has been inserted into the independent clause.]

Editing Tip

Remember that a subordinate clause can't stand alone. When it does, it's a **clause fragment** and needs to be corrected.
~~Because~~ helium is lighter than air.

        OR

Because helium is lighter than air, *it is used in balloons*.

Exercise 1 Identifying Clauses

On the blank for each numbered item, write *I* for an independent clause or *S* for a subordinate clause. On a separate sheet of paper, revise every subordinate clause to make it a complete sentence.

_____ 1. Responsibly written articles and research papers are factual and well documented.

    __S__   2. Because you can't always tell whether the articles and stories you read are true.

    __I__   3. Statistics interpreted carelessly weaken a paper.

    __S__   4. Avoiding the risk of angry readers and objections.

    __S__   5. When you write a research paper, carefully documented sources.

    __S__   6. That your documentation is important to prove that you did not make up your facts.

    __I__   7. Reliable sources are academic journals, reference books, and articles or books written by experts in a field.

    __S__   8. Being proud of your accuracy.
Revised sentences will vary.

Exercise 2 Revising and Editing Paragraphs

Review the following paragraphs, correcting all fragments. When you are finished revising and editing, proofread the paragraph for spelling and punctuation mistakes.   See teacher pages for revising and editing suggestions.

[1]Establishing political rights for, citizens in the American colonies was sometimes a rocky process. [2]In 1735, John Peter Zenger helped establish the right of freedom of the press. [3]Zenger was a German immigrant. [4]Who went to work for newspaper called; *The New York Weekly Journal*. [5]Zenger and the newspaper attacked corrupt officials in New York. [6]Printing articles that told the truth about the actions of the officials. [7]Zenger's articles printed in the newspaper. [8]Soldiers were ordered to burn the newspaper in the public square. [9]John Peter Zenger was arrested and charged with libel. [10]Or making a false, statement in writing to injure a person's reputation! [11]Zenger's trial forced the jury to answer this question: Should the press be permitted to criticize the acts of public officials? [12]After only ten minutes of deliberation. [13]The jury found Zenger not guilty. [14]A decision that helped paved the way for freedom of the press.

Exercise 3 Write What You Think

Write a paragraph in response to the following statement, and give reasons to support your opinions.

> Among the many political rights of American citizens, the right to freedom of the press has the most impact on our lives.

When you finish writing, check your work to make sure you have written complete sentences. At least two of your sentences should include subordinate clauses.

Answers will vary. Students should use independent and subordinate clauses correctly.

Adjective Clauses

You will learn about three kinds of subordinate clauses: adjective clauses, adverb clauses, and noun clauses.

🖢 An **adjective clause** is a subordinate clause that functions as an adjective. It modifies a noun or pronoun.

An adjective clause follows the word it modifies.

Dave, **who is six feet tall**, is Elaine's boyfriend.
He is the person **whom I told you about in my letter**.
San Diego is the city **where he grew up**.

Look for the introductory words listed on the right. Often (but not always), they signal the beginning of an adjective clause. These words are generally called **relative pronouns** and **relative adverbs**. Most of these words also function as other parts of speech.

An introductory relative pronoun may be omitted from the sentence. Read aloud the sentences below. You'll see that they make sense without the bracketed words.

Where is the CD [**that**] **I lent you**?
Sara is the person [**whom**] **you should see**.

When an adjective clause is **essential** to the meaning of a sentence, it should not be set off from the rest of the sentence with commas. But when an adjective clause is **nonessential**, it is set off with commas. An essential clause adds information that is necessary to understand the sentence. A nonessential clause adds information that is not necessary.

Some Words that Introduce Adjective Clauses

Relative Pronouns
that   whom
which   whose
who

Relative Adverbs
than   where
when

WHO OR WHOM?
Who serves as the subject of a clause, and *whom* serves as the object of a clause. If *he* or *she* would make sense in the sentence, use *who*; if *him* or *her* would make sense in the sentence, use *whom*.

[**Who** or **He**] wants to eat dinner.

The dinner is served to [**him**. or **whom**?]

ESSENTIAL (no commas)	NONESSENTIAL (set off with commas)
Every player **who hits a home run** receives a trophy.	The players, **who vary in age from eight to twelve**, wear blue uniforms.
Jeff is looking for the dog **that bit his sister yesterday**.	The dog, **which no one recognized**, is a black poodle.

P.S. You learned about essential and nonessential clauses when you studied appositives in Lesson 6.7. The same rules about commas apply to adjective clauses. In other textbooks, you may see the term *nonrestrictive* used for *nonessential* and *restrictive* used for *essential*. These termes are synonyms.

Identifying Adjective Clauses

Underline the adjective clauses in the sentences below. **Hint:** Not every sentence has an adjective clause. Write *None* if the sentence does not have an adjective clause.

1. Tai chi is an exercise that is more than five thousand years old.

2. Tai chi, which is one of the martial arts, developed in ancient China.

3. In China, you can visit parks where hundreds of people do tai chi.

4. Tai chi is a low-impact exercise that a person can do alone.

5. Do you know anyone who practices tai chi?

6. Tai chi, which is a continuous series of gentle movements, is said to relieve stress.

7. According to tai chi teachers, tai chi improves balance, strengthens leg muscles, and creates energy. None.

8. An exerciser balances his or her chi, or internal energy, during a tai chi workout. None

9. Each series of tai chi movements has a name that sounds like poetry.

10. "The White Crane Spreads Its Wings" is a series of moves that involves the entire body.

Exercise 5 Writing Sentences with Adjective Clauses

Your class is planning a yearbook with a photograph and brief biographical information for every student. Underline the adjective clauses in the biography below. Then, on a separate piece of paper, write a paragraph about yourself that you would feel comfortable including in the yearbook. In your paragraph, use at least three adjective clauses and underline them.

■ See
Composition
Lesson 3.1 for
strategies for
writing an
autobio-
graphical
essay.

[1]Last year my family moved here from Chicago, where I was born and grew up. [2]We lived in Hyde Park on the South Side, and I knew everyone who lived in my neighborhood. [3]It was really hard for me to move. [4]When I first came to this school, everyone seemed so unfriendly. [5]But after a couple of weeks, I became friends with some students who are in my classes, and now I like it here. [6]I'm a long-distance runner on the track team, which I really like a lot. [7]One of my friends taught me to play chess, and I joined the chess club. [8]Mrs. Caleb, who is the adviser, wants me to join the chess team. [9]The class that I enjoy most is debate. [10]I've learned debating techniques that I use on my older brother.

See teacher pages for writing rubrics. Students should use adjective clauses correctly in their paragraphs.

Adverb Clauses

🔹 **An adverb clause** is a subordinate clause that functions as an adverb. It modifies a verb, an adjective, or another adverb.

Because the school bus broke down, Jeff missed first period.
[modifies the verb *missed*]
I am three years older **than she is**.
[modifies the adjective *older*]
Tamiko left for work ten minutes earlier **than she usually does**.
[modifies the adverb *earlier*]

Look for the introductory words listed at the right. Often (but not always), they signal the beginning of an adverb clause and at such times they are called **subordinating conjunctions**.

In an **elliptical adverb clause,** some words are omitted. In the following examples, the bracketed words are understood.

Julio is older **than Sheila [is]**.
I'm more worried about the math test than you are **[worried about the math test]**.
Have you ever met anyone as confident as **Andrew [is]**?

Subordinating Conjunctions

after	so that
although	than
as	though
as long as	unless
as soon as	when
as though	whenever
because	where
before	wherever
even though	whether
if	while
since	

Exercise 6 ## Identifying Adverb Clauses

Underline each adverb clause in the following sentences.
Hint: Not every sentence contains an adverb clause, and some have more than one.

1. Whenever lightning strikes, it is always accompanied by thunder.

2. Thunder occurs when lightning heats the air and causes it to expand rapidly.

3. Even though thunder sounds scary, it poses no danger.

4. A person who is struck by lightning receives a severe electric shock.

5. Because light travels much faster than sound, you can see lightning before you hear the thunder.

6. If you count the seconds in the interim between the lightning and thunder, you can judge the distance of the source of the lightning.

7. When you see lightning and hear thunder at the same time, watch out because the lightning is very close.

Writing Hint

When you use an adverb clause at the beginning of a sentence, follow it with a comma. If you use an adverb clause at the end of a sentence, you do not need to use a comma before it.

If you're outdoors in a thunderstorm, find shelter right away.

Find shelter right away **if you're outdoors in a thunderstorm**.

Enriching Your Vocabulary

Interim comes to us unchanged in form from the Latin adverb meaning "meanwhile." In English the noun means "the time between." The word is also an adjective meaning "temporary" or "coming between two points in time."

8. If you are caught outside in an electrical storm, stay away from water because water is a good conductor of electricity.

9. Don't stand under a tree during an electrical storm because lightning hits the tallest objects.

10. Talking on a telephone is dangerous, too, since lightning can travel through the wires.

Exercise 7 **Writing Sentences with Adverb Clauses**

Work with a partner or small group to write (and perhaps illustrate) a small pamphlet about lightning safety. Your audience is children in the third and fourth grades, so make your sentences easy to read. Use the following notes as an outline for topics to cover in your pamphlet. When you have finished writing a first draft of your pamphlet, underline all of the adverb clauses you have used. You may wish to extend this exercise by having students write pamphlets for a school event or on a subject of their choice.

What to Do During an Electrical Storm

Stay off the phone. [Explain why.]

Stay out of water. [Explain why.]

Don't stand under a tall tree. [Explain why.]

Stay indoors, and stay away from open windows. [Explain why.]

Exercise 8 **Revising and Editing a Story**

■ Look for revising strategies in **Composition Lesson 1.3.**

On a separate piece of paper, rewrite this story beginning to make it more interesting. Work with a partner or small group to add specific details and information about how and where and why the events happened. Make any other changes that you think will improve the paragraph. When you're finished revising and editing, underline any adverb clauses you may have added.

^{1}The power went out. ^{2}The streets were totally dark. ^{3}The traffic signals didn't work. ^{4}Volunteers controlled traffic in each intersection. ^{5}People were stuck for hours in elevators. ^{6}People were stuck in crowded subways. ^{7}A spirit of patience and cooperation prevailed. ^{8}No one was hurt. ^{9}There was no TV. ^{10}People talked to each other.

See teacher pages for revising and editing suggestions. Students may wish to complete the story for extra credit.

Combining Sentences: Using Subordinate Clauses

◖ You can combine two sentences by turning one sentence into an adjective clause.

Begin the adjective clause with *who, which, that,* or another word from the list on page 147. Then insert the adjective clause to modify a noun or pronoun in the remaining sentence. Don't forget the commas to set off nonessential adjective clauses.

ORIGINAL   Jack won first prize in the art contest. Jack is Peggy's brother.

COMBINED   Jack, **who is Peggy's brother**, won first prize in the art contest.

COMBINED   Jack, **who won first prize in the art contest**, is Peggy's brother.

ORIGINAL   He won it for an oil self-portrait. He painted his self-portrait in art class.

COMBINED   He won it for an oil self-portrait, **which he painted in art class**.

◖ You can combine two sentences by turning one sentence into an adverb clause.

Use a subordinating conjunction to create an adverb clause out of one sentence. Then attach the adverb clause to the remaining sentence. Choose a subordinating conjunction that shows how the ideas in the two sentences are related. For example, *because* and *since* show a cause-effect relationship; *while, when, whenever, before, after,* and *until* show a time relationship.

■ Transition words are critical for essays in chronological or step-by-step order. See **Composition** Lesson 3.3 for more on using transition words.

ORIGINAL   The blizzard dumped thirty inches of snow on the city. Schools will be closed tomorrow.

COMBINED   Schools will be closed tomorrow **because the blizzard dumped thirty inches of snow on the city**.

ORIGINAL   A few main streets are plowed. Schools and businesses will remain closed.

COMBINED   **Although a few main streets are plowed**, schools and businesses will remain closed.

Exercise 9 Sentences with Adjective Clauses

Even though the directions ask students to turn the second sentence into an adjective clause, many can be combined by turning the first sentence into a clause.

Work with a partner to combine each pair of sentences into a single sentence by changing the second sentence into an adjective clause. An introductory word is suggested in parentheses. Write your responses on a separate piece of paper and underline the adjective clause. **Remember:** Set off nonessential adjective clauses with commas. See Answer Key for sample answers.

EXAMPLE   The Zuni are known for their jewelry. The Zuni are a Pueblo people. (who)
The Zuni, who are a Pueblo people, are known for their jewelry.

1. Blood plasma is a colorless liquid. Blood plasma contains red blood cells, white blood cells, and blood platelets. (which)

2. George Washington Carver developed hundreds of uses for the peanut. He was a chemist and a botanist. (who)

3. Mary Cassatt is an American Impressionist painter. Mary Cassatt's paintings often portray mothers with children. (whose)

4. In 1947 an observer coined the term flying saucer. The observer saw strange objects in the sky near Mt. Rainier. (who)

5. Nitrogen is a chemical element. Nitrogen makes up almost 80 percent of Earth's atmosphere. (which)

Exercise 10 Sentences with Adverb Clauses

Combine each pair of sentences into a single sentence with an adverb clause. Use the subordinating conjunction suggested in parentheses—or one of your choice. Write your responses on a separate piece of paper, and underline the adverb clause. See Answer Key for sample answers.

EXAMPLE   Germans rejoiced. The Berlin Wall came down in 1989. (when)
Germans rejoiced when the Berlin Wall came down in 1989.

1. The Beast turns into a handsome prince. Beauty agrees to marry him. (when)

2. Don Quixote attacks a windmill. He thinks it is a giant. (because)

3. Dorothy clicks her ruby-red shoes together. She finds herself back in Kansas. (as soon as)

4. According to Aesop's fable, the ever-plodding tortoise won the race. The sleeping hare could run much faster. (even though)

5. The giant chased Jack down the beanstalk. Jack stole the goose that laid golden eggs. (after)

Accept any combined sentence that contains an adverb clause.

Mid-Chapter Review

Exercise A **Identifying Independent and Subordinate Clauses**

On the blank before each numbered item, write *I* for an independent clause or *S* for a subordinate clause. On a separate piece of paper, revise every subordinate clause to make it a complete sentence. **Hint:** You may combine subordinate clauses with sentences from this exercise.

Sample answers are suggested to correct subordinate clauses.

_____I_____ 1. Puerto Rico is an island in the West Indies.

_____I_____ 2. Its name means "rich port" in Spanish.

_____S_____ 3. ~~Which~~ Puerto Rico is the name Ponce de León gave to San Juan in 1508.

_____S_____ 4. ~~When~~ Columbus landed in Puerto Rico in 1493.

_____I_____ 5. Columbus found the Arawak people living there.

_____I_____ 6. Spain ruled Puerto Rico from the 1500s to 1898.

_____S_____ 7. ~~After the~~ The Spanish-American War ended in 1898.

_____I_____ 8. Puerto Rico became a U.S. territory and then a U.S. commonwealth.

_____S_____ 9. ~~Which~~ It governs itself by electing a governor and a legislature.

_____S_____ 10. ~~Whose~~ Its main agricultural products are sugar, coffee, and cattle.

Exercise B **Identifying Adjective and Adverb Clauses**

Underline each subordinate clause in the sentences below. On the blank before each numbered item, write *ADJ* for an adjective clause or *ADV* for an adverb clause.

EXAMPLE _____ADJ_____ The ancient Greeks had a myth that <u>explains the origin of seasons</u>.

_____ADJ_____ 1. Demeter, <u>who was the goddess of grain and fertility</u>, had a beautiful daughter named Persephone.

_____ADV_____ 2. <u>When Persephone was picking flowers one day</u>, the earth opened up and Pluto kidnapped her.

_____ADJ_____ 3. Pluto, <u>who was god of the Underworld</u>, was madly in love with Persephone.

_____ADV_____ 4. <u>After Persephone disappeared</u>, Demeter searched all over the earth.

____ADV____ 5. Pluto was so important <u>that Demeter couldn't simply take Persephone home again</u>.

____ADV____ 6. Demeter was so unhappy <u>that she quit working</u>.

____ADJ____ 7. Her strike, <u>which caused all crops and cattle to die</u>, endangered the earth's existence.

____ADJ____ 8. Zeus, <u>who was the chief Greek god</u>, became alarmed, and they agreed to a compromise.

____ADV____ 9. <u>Whenever it was winter</u>, Persephone stayed in the Underworld.

____ADV____ 10. In the spring, <u>when all the earth breaks into blossom</u>, Persephone returned to her mother.

Exercise C ## Combining Sentences: Using Subordinate Clauses

On a separate piece of paper, combine each pair of sentences by changing one sentence into a subordinate clause. Use the word in parentheses to introduce the subordinate clause. Underline the subordinate clause in your combined sentence, and be sure to add commas where they are needed. Begin at least two of your sentences with a subordinate clause.

Hint: One combined sentence may have two subordinate clauses.
See Answer Key for sample answers.

1. Laura volunteers at a nursing home. Laura's mother works at the nursing home. (where)

2. Howie coaches a Little League team. Howie is my older brother. (who)

3. Julie's poem will appear in the literary magazine. Julie wrote her poem in Mr. Li's class. (which)

4. I have a great idea. You will like my great idea. (that)

5. Nora and Ben send each other e-mail every night. Nora lives in Hawaii. Ben lives in California. (who)

6. The Spraggs have to leave their house for two days. Their street was flooded. (while *or* because)

7. We'll leave for the beach at eight o'clock. It's pouring. (unless)

8. Kris and Jenny are best friends. They don't like the same movies. (although)

9. George didn't have many friends. He met Gwen. (until)

10. Ralph takes his dog for a long walk every day. Ralph gets home from work. (after)
    Answers will vary somewhat. Make sure students have put a comma after an introductory adverb clause.

Noun Clauses

◆ A **noun clause** is a subordinate clause that functions as a noun.

A noun clause can do any job a noun can do. It can function as a subject, predicate nominative, direct object, indirect object, or object of a preposition. In the following examples, notice that noun clauses can have modifiers and complements. They can come at the beginning, middle, or end of a sentence.

Which of the twins is older is not important. [subject]

The big question is **whether she will finish the marathon**. [predicate nominative]

I could see **that you were annoyed**. [direct object]

Please give **whoever calls** this message. [indirect object]

Neeley is ready for **whatever she encounters**. [object of preposition]

See at the right a list of words that can introduce a noun clause. Sometimes a noun clause's introductory word is not stated but understood.

We hope [that] **the rain delay ends soon**.

All of the fans know [that] **this game is crucial**.

Exercise 11 Writing Sentences with Noun Clauses

On a separate piece of paper, write a sentence using each group of words as a noun clause. Check your work to be sure that you have written a noun clause, not an adjective or adverb clause.
See sample answers.

1. that many children are afraid of the dark

2. how to change a flat tire

3. whether it will rain tomorrow

4. whoever attends the concert

5. why birds fly south in fall

6. that you're my best friend

7. what we need most

8. whoever crosses the finish line first

9. what you have learned

10. that the worst of the storm is over

how	which
if	who
that	whoever
what	whom
whatever	whomever
when	whose
where	why
whether	

Writing Hint

Too many noun clauses make your writing sound wordy and overly formal, especially when they are used as subjects.

ORIGINAL
That Ollie runs at least a mile every day is something that everyone knows.

BETTER
Everyone knows **that Ollie runs at least a mile every day**.

1. Everyone knows that many children are afraid of the dark.
2. Our driving instructor showed us how to change a flat tire.
3. Whether it will rain tomorrow is anybody's guess.
4. Whoever attends the concert will receive a free ticket to next week's concert.
5. Can you tell me why birds fly south in fall?
6. Have I ever told you that you're my best friend?
7. She asked us to think about what we need most.
8. Whoever crosses the finish line first will win the gold medal.
9. Please tell me what you have learned so far.
10. I suspect that the worst of the storm is over.

Exercise 12 Create Your Own Exercise

With a partner, make up ten sentences that have noun clauses. Your sentences can be about any topic. Exchange sentences with another team, and see if you can identify all of the noun clauses.

Exercise 13 Revising and Editing a Biology Report

When Jeff wrote the biology report below, he tried to make his writing sound very intelligent. Jeff's teacher returned the report to him with this note: "Please say what you mean more clearly." First, underline all of the noun clauses in Jeff's report. Then work with a partner or small group to revise the report, expressing the ideas as clearly and as directly as possible. Eliminate wordiness and repetition, and make any other changes you think will improve the report.

[1]That all green plants require air to manufacture food has been known by scientists for a long period of time. [2]Who first determined this fact is Jan Ingenhousz, an eighteenth-century Dutch scientist. [3]Biology textbooks tell whoever studies biology that the process by which plants manufacture food is called *photosynthesis*. [4]"Putting together by light" is what the word *photosynthesis* means. [5]No one doubts that the essential ingredients for a plant to manufacture glucose are sunlight, water, and carbon dioxide. [6]What has been determined is that the cells of green leaves contain chlorophyll and that the chlorophyll in the cells of green leaves collects energy from sunlight. [7]Furthermore, scientists know that the energy from sunlight provides the power for a chemical reaction within the green leaves. [8]Carbon dioxide from the air and water from the soil react chemically to produce glucose and oxygen. [9]Whoever studies biology should recognize this formula:

$$6CO_2 + 6H_2O \rightarrow C_6H_{12}O_6 + 6O_2.$$

[10]What this formula is is the chemical formula for the process of photosynthesis.

Look for clarity in students' revisions. Students should eliminate wordiness and repetition.

Four Types of Sentence Structures

All sentences can be classified according to their structure. You need to be able to think about the variety of sentence structures so that you can vary your sentences when you write a paragraph or a longer paper.

🖋 A **simple sentence** has one independent clause and no subordinate clauses.

You may be surprised to find that simple sentences can be quite long and complicated. A simple sentence may have a compound subject, a compound verb, and many different kinds of phrases.

>   S   V
> Unlike many other languages, the English alphabet has twenty-six letters to represent the sounds of its words.

🖋 A **compound sentence** has two or more independent clauses and no subordinate clauses.

> S   V   S   V
> *Alphabet* comes from *alpha* and *bet*; these are the names of the first two letters in the Greek alphabet.

🖋 A **complex sentence** has one independent clause and at least one subordinate clause.

>   S   S V   V
> The Cyrillic alphabet, which is the writing system for Russian, has thirty-one characters. [subordinate clause within independent clause]

🖋 A **compound-complex** sentence has two or more independent clauses and at least one subordinate clause.

> S   S   V   V
> Sequoyah, who lived from 1766 to 1843, created a writing system,
> S   V
> and he taught it to other Cherokee.

Exercise 14 **Identifying Sentence Structure**

Identify the sentence structure of each sentence in the paragraph below. On the blank before each numbered sentence, write *S* for simple; *CD* for compound; *CX* for complex; and *CD-CX* for compound-complex.

¹ __CD__ Every language has different rules, and there are many different writing systems. ² __S__ For example, Hebrew is written from right to left on horizontal lines. ³ __CX__ A Hebrew book begins at what English

speakers would consider the back of the book. ⁴ _S_ The traditional Chinese writing system doesn't use letters. ⁵ CD-CX Instead, the Chinese writing system, which dates back to the fourteenth century B.C., uses ideograms, and each ideogram stands for a syllable or a whole word. ⁶ _CX_ Although the languages differ, the Japanese borrowed Chinese ideograms for their writing system. ⁷ _CX_ Both Chinese and Japanese are traditionally written in vertical columns, which are read from top to bottom and right to left. ⁸ _S_ Learning to read and write Japanese requires knowing several thousand ideograms. ⁹ _CX_ Modern Chinese and Japanese governments have tried to simplify the writing system so that more people can read and write.

Exercise 15 Editing Sentences

Expand each of the following simple sentences by making up interesting details. On a separate piece of paper, identify the type of sentence you have written. Write at least one example for each type of sentence structure. Compare your expanded sentences with a partner or small group.

EXAMPLE   Andie is in first grade.
Although Andie is in first grade, she is learning to speak French, English, and Korean.
COMPLEX

1. Andie likes to read.

2. She is only six.

3. She is learning to write.

4. Spelling is a problem.

Expanded sentences will vary. Students should identify the sentence structures correctly.

5. Andie uses her imagination.

6. Mrs. Warner tells the class.

7. Everyone writes books.

8. Kyle and Andie draw pictures.

9. They listen to each other's stories.

10. Their families enjoy the books.

Varying Sentence Beginnings and Structure

◖ For variety, begin some of your sentences with a subordinate clause.

Lesson 6.3 provides practice in beginning sentences with one or more phrases. Subordinate clauses give you another tool for varying sentence beginnings. Here is the same idea expressed in a number of ways.

ORIGINAL	Giacomo Puccini died in 1924 before he finished the last act of his opera *Turandot*.
PREPOSITIONAL PHRASE	**In 1924,** Giacomo Puccini died before he finished the last act of his opera *Turandot*.
PARTICIPIAL PHRASE	**Not yet finished with the last act of his opera *Turandot*,** Giacomo Puccini died in 1924.
ADVERB CLAUSE	**Before he finished the last act of his opera *Turandot*,** Giacomo Puccini died in 1924.
NOUN CLAUSE	**That Giacomo Puccini died in 1924, before finishing the last act of his opera *Turandot*,** meant that another composer had to finish it.

Too much of anything becomes monotonous, so don't make your sentences all simple or all compound or all complex. An experienced writer, which is what you are becoming, is able to express ideas by using a variety of sentence structures.

Exercise 16 Editing Sentence Beginnings

On a separate piece of paper, rewrite each sentence to change the way it begins. You may reword the sentences if necessary.

1. Hank Aaron broke Babe Ruth's home-run record when Aaron hit 755 home runs during his major league career.

2. Cuban exiles tried to invade Cuba during the Bay of Pigs invasion in 1961, but their attempt failed.

3. Harry S Truman won the election in 1948 despite the fact that newspapers and commentators predicted his defeat.

4. Two hundred Sioux men, women, and children were killed by army troops in 1890 at Wounded Knee Creek in South Dakota.

5. New Zealand gave women the right to vote in 1893, more than twenty years before American women could vote.

1. When Hank Aaron hit 755 home runs during his major league career, he broke Babe Ruth's home-run record.
2. In 1961, Cuban exiles tried to invade Cuba during the Bay of Pigs invasion, but their attempt failed.
3. In 1948, Harry S Truman won the election despite the fact that newspapers and commentators predicted his defeat.
4. In 1890 at Wounded Knee Creek in South Dakota, army troops killed two hundred Sioux men, women, and children.
5. In 1893, more than twenty years before American women could vote, New Zealand gave women the right to vote.

Exercise 17 Revising and Editing a Press Release

Work with a partner or small group to revise the following press release. Your audience is the readers of your local newspaper. In your revision, try to vary some sentence beginnings and structures. Combine sentences, and find other ways to eliminate unnecessary repetition. See teacher pages for revising and editing suggestions.

¹Tarquin is the Shaw High School drama club. ²Tarquin will present *Kiss Me, Kate*. ³*Kiss Me, Kate* will be presented November 6, 7, 8. ⁴Performances are in the Shaw High School auditorium. ⁵Performances begin at eight o'clock. ⁶Tickets are $8.00. ⁷Jim Austin and Nancy Magnusson play the leading roles. ⁸Jim Austin plays Petruchio, and Nancy Magnusson plays Kate.

⁹*Kiss Me, Kate* is a musical by Cole Porter. ¹⁰It opened in 1948. ¹¹Some popular songs from *Kiss Me, Kate* are "So in Love" and "We Open in Venice." ¹²Cole Porter based *Kiss Me, Kate* on *The Taming of the Shrew*. ¹³*The Taming of the Shrew* is a play by William Shakespeare.

Exercise 18 Writing a Paragraph

Use the notes below to write a paragraph on a separate piece of paper. Try to vary your sentence beginnings and structures. See teacher pages for writing assessment suggestions.

■ See Lesson 2.4 for more on writing an expository paragraph.

> *U.S. flag—also called Stars and Stripes, Old Glory*
>
> *Betsy Ross (seamstress in Philadelphia) sewed & designed first American flag—no proof of this story; a legend?*
>
> *Congress adopted official flag, June 14, 1777: 13 (1 for ea. colony) red/white stripes; 13 stars on blue field—representing a "new constellation"*
>
> *Flag Day celebrated June 14, anniversary of date*
>
> *Flag changed many times—new stars added for new states; stripes remain @ 13*

Students may wish to extend the exercise by writing a brief report on the American flag. Remind students to save their paragraphs in their writing notebooks.

Revising and Editing Worksheet 1

Improve the following story beginning. Correct sentence fragments and try to vary sentence structures and beginnings. You may combine sentences, add or leave out details, and replace or drop words. When you are finished revising and editing, proofread your story for spelling and punctuation mistakes. See teacher pages for revising and editing suggestions.

[1]As soon as the lights went out. [2]Sally heard a tiny sound. [3]The sound came from the closet. [4]The closet was next to her bed. [5]It was a faint sound. [6]She lay there hardly breatheing. [7]So that she could hear the faint sound. [8]Listening.

[9]What could the faint sound be? [10]She had never heard the noise before. [11]What on Earth could it be? [12]Sally decided something. [13]Something alive was in her closet.

[14]Sally knew something. [15]She was alone in the house. [16]Her parents were out. [17]Her parents wouldnt be back for hours.

[18]Sam wasn't home. [19]Sam was Sally's brother. [20]Sam was eight years older than Sally. [21]Sam was spending the weekend with Jerry. [22]Jerry was Sam's best freind. [23]Jerry, Sam, and Jerry's father were camping at Lake Nelly.

[24]Even Maggie was away. [25]Maggie was the family dog. [26]She was staying overnight in the kennel. [27]Maggie had had majory surgery. [28]The vet wanted to keep her overnight. [29]He would let her come home. [30]He knew that she was all right.

[31]Sally listened. [32]She was intent. [33]All her being was focused on the sound. [34]The sound happened several times a minute. [35]Seemed to be getting louder. [36]And maybe faster. [37]What could she do?

Suggest that students complete the story in their own way.

Revising and Editing Worksheet 2

Working
Together

In a small group, improve the following report on recycling. Correct sentence fragments and try to vary sentence structures and beginnings. You may combine sentences, add or leave out details, and replace words. When you are finished revising and editing, proofread your report for spelling and punctuation mistakes.

See teacher pages for revising and editing suggestions.

[1]Recycling is important. [2]Because it reduces solid wastes. [3]Landfills are filling up. [4]Landfills are where governments dump solid wastes. [5]Recycling reduces pollution. [6]And saves natural resources, too.

[7]Many American cities started recycling during the 1970s. [8]During the 1970s the ecology movement became populer. [9]In some states, charged nickel or dime deposits to customers. [10]These were the customers who bought food or drinks in glass and plastic containers. [11]Container deposits also helped reduce litter. [12]Many cities have recycling programs today. [13]They recycle glass. [14]They recycle paper. [15]They recycle plastics. [16]They recycle metals.

[17]Recycled glass is used in makeing new glass. [18]First, the recycled glass is sorted into colors. [19]Then it is crushed. [20]Crushed glass is called *cullet*. [21]Because cullet melts at a lower temperature then the raw materials used in making glass. [22]When cullet is used to make glass. [23]Less energy is needed.

[24]Aluminum companies pay people by the pound. [25]For recycled aluminum. [26]Because aluminum is very light. [27]It takes many soft drink cans to weigh a pound. [28]About 65,000 soft drink cans are recycled every minute in the United States. [29]Recycled aluminum is used to make ships, planes, aluminum foil, and more soft drink cans.

[30]California and Connecticut were the first states with recycleing laws. [31]Now many other states require. [32]That manufacturers use recycled materials. [33]For example, by the year 2005, 65 percent of glass containers in California will be made of recycled glass. [34]Some states require that phonebooks and newsprint be made of 50 percent recycled material. [35]Recycling paper and cardboard saves trees. [36]And helps reduce pollution, to.

Chapter Review

Exercise A **Identifying Independent and Subordinate Clauses**

On the blank before each numbered item, write *I* for an independent clause or *S* for a subordinate clause.

EXAMPLE   __S__   Who was an important American painter.

_____I_____   1. Henry O. Tanner decided to be a painter.

_____S_____   2. When he was thirteen years old.

_____I_____   3. His father was a bishop in the African Methodist Episcopal Church in Pittsburgh.

_____S_____   4. Before Tanner was a student at Philadelphia's Academy of Fine Arts.

_____I_____   5. He studied with the American painter Thomas Eakins.

_____I_____   6. Tanner left the United States to study art in Paris.

_____I_____   7. His greatest successes were paintings of biblical scenes.

_____S_____   8. Which are naturalistic and at the same time filled with emotion.

_____I_____   9. For the rest of his life, Tanner remained in Paris.

_____S_____ 10. When the French government made him a Chevalier of the Legion of Honor.

Exercise B **Identifying Types of Clauses**

On the blank before each numbered item, identify the underlined clause in each sentence by writing *ADJ,* for an adjective clause, *ADV* for an adverb clause, or *N* for a noun clause.

EXAMPLE   __N__   If you have to ask <u>what jazz is</u>, you'll never know.
                         — *Louis Armstrong*

___ADJ___   1. These are the times <u>that try men's souls.</u> —*Thomas Paine*

___ADJ___   2. No one will ever get at my verses <u>who insists on viewing them as a literary performance</u>. —*Walt Whitman*

___ADV___   3. <u>When I think of our condition</u>, my heart is heavy.
              —*Chief Joseph of the Nez Percé*

___N___   4. I know <u>why the caged bird sings. . . .</u> —*Paul Laurence Dunbar*

___ADJ___   5. "Music is the thing of the world <u>that I love most</u>."
              —*Samuel Pepys*

_____ADV_____ 6. No question is ever settled / <u>Until it is settled right</u>.
—*Ella Wheeler Wilcox*

_____ADJ_____ 7. A truth <u>that's told with bad intent</u> / Beats all the lies you can invent. —*William Blake*

_____N_____ 8. <u>What's virtue in man</u> can't be vice in a cat.
—*Mary Abigail Dodge*

_____ADV_____ 9. The game isn't over <u>till it's over</u>. —*Yogi Berra*

_____ADV_____ 10. There are only two or three human stories, and they go on repeating themselves as fiercely <u>as if they had never happened before.</u> —*Willa Cather*

Exercise C Identifying Sentence Structure

Underline every subordinate clause in the sentences below. Then on the blank before each numbered item, identify the sentence structure by writing *S* for simple, *CD* for compound, *CX* for complex, and *CD-CX* for compound-complex.

_____S_____ 1. In 1927, Charles Lindbergh flew nonstop and alone across the Atlantic.

_____CD-CX_____ 2. The Nile River, <u>which is more than four thousand miles long</u>, flows north from central Africa through Egypt; it is the world's longest river.

_____S_____ 3. Two stars in the bowl of the Big Dipper point to Polaris, the North Star.

_____CX_____ 4. The pull of gravity is so great in a black hole <u>that not even light can pass through it.</u>

_____CX_____ 5. Veterans Day is observed on November 11, <u>which is the day the fighting stopped in World War I.</u>

_____CX_____ 6. DNA molecules contain information <u>that controls hereditary features.</u>

_____CX_____ 7. <u>After Johan Gutenberg printed the first Bible in 1455,</u> books became available to ordinary people.

_____CD_____ 8. The Mercalli scale measures an earthquake's intensity; the Richter scale measures its magnitude.

_____CX_____ 9. Did you know <u>that a judo expert wears a black belt?</u>

_____CX_____ 10. Dr. Seuss is the pen name of Theodor Geisel, <u>who wrote *The Cat in the Hat.*</u>

Cumulative Review

Exercise A **Identifying Parts of Speech**

In the space above each numbered item, identify the part of speech of each underlined word in the sentences below. Use these abbreviations:

N = noun   ADJ = adjective   CONJ = conjunction
PRON = pronoun   ADV = adverb   INTER = interjection
V = verb   PREP = preposition

EXAMPLE   *INTER*
           Alas, this is the last day of vacation.

1. She found an <u>old</u> letter <u>between</u> the pages of the photo album.
    ADJ   PREP

2. <u>Look</u>, here is the list of e-mail <u>addresses</u> you asked for.
  INTER   N

3. Has <u>anyone</u> been looking for me?
    PRON

4. The restaurants <u>usually</u> close <u>for</u> the summer.
         ADV   PREP

5. Neither Scott <u>nor</u> Tomás <u>wants</u> the job.
        CONJ   V

Exercise B **Writing Complete Sentences**

Revise the following paragraph to correct sentence fragments and run-on sentences and to eliminate wordiness. Revised paragraphs will vary.

[1]Old Faithful is a geyser in Yosemite National Park in Wyoming, it erupts regularly. [2]Usually about every sixty-five minutes. [3]Like other geysers, Old Faithful is a hot spring. [4]A geyser is a fissure, or crack, in the earth's surface. [5]Connected to a water supply far below the surface. [6]Geysers shoot steam and boiling water high into the air. [7]Old Faithful, about 150 feet into the air. [8]And about eleven thousand gallons of water each time. [9]The word *geyser* comes from the name of a specific geyser in Iceland, it means "gusher." [10]Geysers are found in Iceland, New Zealand, and the western United States.

Exercise C **Identifying Phrases**

On the blank before each numbered item, identify each underlined phrase by writing one of these abbreviations in the space provided:

PREP = prepositional phrase   INF = infinitive phrase
PART = participial phrase   APP = appositive phrase
GER = gerund phrase

EXAMPLE   *APP*   Mr. Haas, <u>the band teacher</u>, plays the cello and bass.

  PREP   1. You'll find the hammer <u>in the bottom drawer</u> of the desk.

___INF___ 2. Jonas is ready <u>to leave for school</u> by 7 A.M.

___GER___ 3. The twins enjoy <u>playing table tennis</u> and are really good at it.

___PREP___ 4. Amanda sent a thank-you note <u>to her grandmother</u>.

___INF___ 5. <u>To raise money</u>, Key Club members are collecting aluminum.

___APP___ 6. Elliot cooked French toast, <u>his favorite breakfast</u>.

___GER___ 7. Whose responsibility is <u>washing the car</u>?

___PART___ 8. Tree branches <u>broken during the ice storm</u> lay across the road.

___PREP___ 9. This year classes begin the week <u>before Labor Day</u>.

___PART___ 10. Anya was able to grab the kitten <u>hiding under the bed</u>.

Exercise D Identifying Clauses

Underline every subordinate clause in the sentences below. Then identify each clause by writing *ADJ* for an adjective clause, *ADV* for an adverb clause, or *N* for a noun clause in the space before each sentence.

___ADJ___ ¹The word *volcano* comes from Vulcan, <u>who was the Roman god of fire and destruction</u>. ___ADV___ ²<u>When most people think of volcanoes</u>, they visualize cone-shaped mountains with fire and lava exploding from the top. ___ADJ___ ³Volcanoes are actually vents—or cracks—in the earth's surface <u>that connect directly to the molten rock deep below the surface</u>.

___ADV___ ⁴<u>When a volcano is active</u>, it belches forth molten lava, hot gases, and ash. ___ADV___ ⁵Some volcanoes are called dormant (sleeping) <u>because they have been inactive for a very long time</u>. ___N___ ⁶Scientists know <u>that a dormant volcano can become active without any warning</u>. ___ADJ___ ⁷In 1980, Mount St. Helens, <u>which had been dormant for more than 120 years</u>, erupted violently. ___N___ ⁸Scientists expect <u>that an extinct volcano will never erupt again</u>. ___ADV___ ⁹There are volcanoes underwater too, and <u>when they erupt</u>, they can form islands. ___ADJ___ ¹⁰Hawaii, <u>which is made up of twenty volcanic islands</u>, has an active volcano, Mauna Loa, and a dormant one, Mauna Kea.

Grammar Test

Identifying Errors

Directions: Each numbered item either is totally correct or contains an error in one of the underlined word(s) or punctuation. In the answer section to the right of each item, circle the letter of the underlined word(s) or punctuation mark that contains the error. If the sentence is correct, circle *D* for NO ERROR.

EXAMPLE   One of the <u>real</u> difficult problems all people must <u>deal with</u> is
              A   B

preserving <u>their</u> food supply.   <u>NO ERROR</u>
              C   D

Ⓐ B C D

1. Four basic methods of <u>preserving</u> food are drying<u>,</u>
                          A   B

   heating, refrigerating, and using chemicals<u>.</u>   <u>NO ERROR</u>
                                            C   D

1. A B C Ⓓ

2. The earliest <u>of these methods</u> is probably drying<u>,</u> fish, meat, fruits, grains,
                     A   B

   and vegetables can be <u>successfully</u> dried.   <u>NO ERROR</u>
                              C   D

2. A Ⓑ C D

3. Early people placed food in the sun<u>, and</u> the <u>sun's</u> rays
                                       A   B

   removed <u>it's</u> moisture.   <u>NO ERROR</u>
              C   D

3. A B Ⓒ D

4. Manufacturers today use <u>extremely</u> complex machinery and chemicals
                              A

   <u>to dry</u> a variety of foods. <u>Including beef, tomatoes, and grapes.</u> <u>NO ERROR</u>
      B   C   D

4. A B Ⓒ D

5. Freeze-drying is a <u>fairly recent</u> development<u>;</u> freeze-dried foods are
                          A   B

   lightweight and <u>especially</u> useful on camping trips.   <u>NO ERROR</u>
                       C   D

5. A B C Ⓓ

6. Native Americans dried ears of corn for winter food. <u>Just</u> as people
                                                          A

   <u>living in Scotland</u> dried oats <u>for oatmeal.</u>   <u>NO ERROR</u>
        B   C   D

6. Ⓐ B C D

7. Smoking, a drying method <u>used for meat and fish,</u> keeps food from spoiling
                               A

   and adds a pleasant<u>,</u> smoky flavor that many people <u>like</u>   <u>NO ERROR</u>
                       B   C   D

7. A B Ⓒ D

8. Refrigerators and freezers <u>greatly</u> reduce food spoilage, which is a <u>really</u>
                                 A   B

   serious problem <u>when the electricity goes off.</u>   <u>NO ERROR</u>
                       C   D

8. A B C Ⓓ

9. Vinegar is used <u>for pickling vegetables</u> and meats<u>; sugar</u> preserves fruit

                       A   B

    in jams and jellies<u>, which are sometimes called preserves.</u>   <u>NO ERROR</u>

                                     C   D

9. A B C Ⓓ

10. Irradiation <u>destroys harmful bacteria in food</u> and is <u>gradual</u> becoming

                            A   B

    more common<u>, but</u> the public has been resisting it.   <u>NO ERROR</u>

                       C   D

10. A Ⓑ C D

Exercise 2 Correcting Errors

Directions: Each numbered item either is totally correct or contains one or more errors. If the numbered item is correct, circle *D* for NO ERROR. If the numbered item contains errors, circle the letter of the correctly written revision.

EXAMPLE   Larry plays chess good. He learned quick.

                A. Larry plays chess good. He learned real quick.

                B. Larry plays chess well. He learned quick.

                C. Larry plays chess well. He learned quickly.

                D. NO ERROR

A B Ⓒ D

1. Laura read the directions quick. Jeff took more time.
   A. Laura read the directions quick, Jeff took more time.
   B. Laura read the directions quickly. Jeff took more time.
   C. Laura read the directions quickly, Jeff took more time.
   D. NO ERROR

1. A Ⓑ C D

2. The turtle laid it's eggs on the beach. And covered them with sand.
   A. The turtle laid its eggs on the beach. And covered them with sand.
   B. The turtle laid its eggs on the beach and covered them with sand.
   C. The turtle laid its' eggs on the beach and covered them with sand.
   D. NO ERROR

2. A Ⓑ C D

3. Brianna likes folk dancing her brother likes line dancing.
   A. Brianna likes folk dancing; her brother likes line dancing.
   B. Brianna likes folk dancing, her brother likes line dancing.
   C. Brianna likes, folk dancing; her brother, likes line dancing.
   D. NO ERROR

3. Ⓐ B C D

4. Crossing the street, a car just missed the speeding dachshund.
   A. Crossing the street, a speeding car just missed the dachshund.
   B. A speeding car just missed the dachshund crossing the street.
   C. A speeding car, just missed the dachshund, crossing the street.
   D. NO ERROR

4. A Ⓑ C D

5. Before anyone had time to object. The committee voted.
   A. Before anyone had time to object the committee voted.
   B. Before anyone had time, to object the committee voted.
   C. Before anyone had time to object, the committee voted.
   D. NO ERROR

5. A B (C) D

6. Is this calculator your's, or does it belong to Tuoyo.
   A. Is this calculator your's. Or does it belong to Tuoyo?
   B. Is this calculator yours, or does it belong to Tuoyo.
   C. Is this calculator yours, or does it belong to Tuoyo?
   D. NO ERROR

6. A B (C) D

7. When you were two hours late, we were all real worried.
   A. When you were two hours late we were all real worried.
   B. When you were two hours late, we were all really worried.
   C. When you were two hours late we were all really worried.
   D. NO ERROR

7. A (B) C D

8. In front of the building is an unbelievably tall tree.
   A. In front of the building is an unbelievable tall tree.
   B. In front of the building, is an unbelievably tall tree.
   C. In front of the building, is an unbelievable tall tree
   D. NO ERROR

8. A B C (D)

9. The doors opened sudden. And the crowd rushed to find bargains?
   A. The doors opened sudden. And the crowd rushed to find bargains.
   B. The doors opened suddenly, and the crowd rushed to find bargains.
   C. The doors opened suddenly and the crowd rushed to find bargains.
   D. NO ERROR

9. A (B) C D

10. Leslie wrote the song lyrics. Who wrote the music.
   A. Leslie wrote the song lyrics, who wrote the music.
   B. Leslie wrote the song lyrics; who wrote the music.
   C. Leslie wrote the song lyrics. Who wrote the music?
   D. NO ERROR

10. A B (C) D

Exercise 3　Combining Sentences

Directions: On a separate piece of paper, combine the sentences in each item into a single sentence. There is more than one way to combine most sentences.

EXAMPLE   Harriet Beecher Stowe was a writer. She was an important writer.
               She was American.
               Harriet Beecher Stowe was an important American writer.
               See Answer Key.

1. She was born on June 14. She was born in 1811. She was born in Litchfield, Connecticut.

2. Have you read her novel? Her novel is famous. *Uncle Tom's Cabin* is Harriet Beecher Stowe's novel.

3. *Uncle Tom's Cabin* was first published serially. It appeared in 1851 to 1852. It was published in an abolitionist newspaper.

4. Stowe was violently opposed to slavery. In her novel, she powerfully portrays the sufferings of slaves.

5. Stowe's novel increased antislavery sentiments in the North. Her novel was extremely popular. It sold more than 300,000 copies in a single year.

Exercise 4 Identifying Parts of a Sentence

Directions: Answer each numbered question by circling the letter of the sentence that contains the named sentence structure. If no sentence contains that structure, circle *D* for NONE OF THE SENTENCES.

1. Which sentence contains a **direct object**?
   A. Are you finished with your test?
   B. The doorbell rang, and a second later the phone rang.
   C. Nina rolled the clay into a long coil.
   D. NONE OF THE SENTENCES

   1. A B Ⓒ D

2. Which sentence contains a **compound verb**?
   A. Todd's fly ball smashed the window, and everybody ran.
   B. We were wet and cold but didn't turn back.
   C. These books are due tomorrow; please don't forget them.
   D. NONE OF THE SENTENCES

   2. A Ⓑ C D

3. Which sentence contains a **gerund phrase**?
   A. The planes were flying directly over our heads.
   B. Taking care of people is what Gloria does best.
   C. Floating on her back, she felt calm and happy.
   D. NONE OF THE SENTENCES

   3. A Ⓑ C D

4. Which sentence contains an **adjective clause**?
   A. Who is in charge of selling tickets?
   B. Aunt Myrtle is the relative whom I most admire.
   C. I'm interested in hearing your opinion on that issue.
   D. NONE OF THE SENTENCES

   4. A Ⓑ C D

5. Which sentence contains a **predicate nominative**?
   A. Helena usually wins every argument with her brother.
   B. After reading the letter, he seemed terribly upset.
   C. Lori and Mark are clowns in the circus.
   D. NONE OF THE SENTENCES

   5. A B Ⓒ D

Using Verbs

Direct students to
chapter-specific
portfolio projects
on Sadlier-Oxford's
website.

STUDENT WRITING
Narrative Essay

Dancing
by Joshua Vinitz
high school student, Queens, New York

I go to parties and dances a lot. The problem is that until recently, I hated to dance. I disliked the music, and I still do. I used to go to the dances because all of my friends did. Now I go to them for the "right" reason—to dance.

For many years, I would just sit in the back and talk with my friends as our girlfriends danced the night away. None of us really liked to dance, and it would usually take an act of Congress to get us on the floor. The girls would constantly try to get us to dance while we tried to get them to sit down with us and talk. Both sides' attempts were futile. We weren't about to lose our seats and they weren't about to stop partying.

Not too long ago, however, all of this changed for me. I don't know what came over me, but one of the girls just connected. She just plucked me out of my chair; I had no choice in the matter. I started dancing, and I liked it!

I won't say that I'm good at it or anything. As one of my friends commented, "You dance worse than you parallel park." But I have discovered something. Dancing is a lot more fun than sitting on the side and complaining to my friends about how bad the music is. Time goes so much faster when you're out there dancing.

Joshua wrote the narrative above to explain how he changed his mind about dancing. He starts his narrative essay using present-tense verbs. He tells the anecdote in the past tense; then he summarizes his new opinion of dancing in the present tense again. Joshua uses verbs to lead his reader through his experience. The lessons in this chapter will help you notice the verb tenses you use in your own writing.

Allow time for students to discuss the student writing. Suggest that they identify its strengths and propose possible improvements. Use the model to introduce the concepts in the chapter.

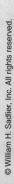

Regular Verbs

🔵 All verbs have four basic forms, or **principal parts**. They are the present, the present participle, the past, and the past participle.

Verbs are classified as either regular or irregular, depending on the way they form their past and past participle.

🔵 Regular verbs add -*d* or -*ed* to the present to form the past tense and past participle.

Principal Parts of Regular Verbs			
PRESENT	PRESENT PARTICIPLE (Use with *am, is, are, was, were.*)	PAST	PAST PARTICIPLE (Use with *has, had, have.*)
join	(is) joining	joined	(had) joined
carry	(is) carrying	carried	(had) carried
hike	(is) hiking	hiked	(had) hiked

The **present participle** of regular verbs ends in -*ing*. It works with the verb *be* (*am, is, are, was,* or *were*), to make a verb phrase.

  I **am waiting** for a bus.   Joey **was waiting** at home.

The **past participle** of regular verbs ends in -*d* or -*ed*. It works with the helping verb *have* (*has, have,* or *had*), to make a verb phrase.

  I **have asked** for help.   Joey **had** also **asked** for help.

When you add -*ing* and -*ed* to the present form of a verb, you have to apply spelling rules about dropping the final -*e*, changing -*y* to *i*, and doubling consonants: *hope, hoping, hoped; carry, carried; shop, shopping, shopped.* (For more about spelling rules, see Lesson 16.2.)

P.S. Don't get too worried about the labels for all the verb forms. It's the correct *use* of verb forms that is important in writing.

Enriching Your Vocabulary

The noun *migration* comes from the Latin verb *migrare*, which means "to change one's home." It is one of many English words used in connection with the movement of people or animals from place to place. A related word, *migrant*, is used in Exercise 1. The discovery of gold in California triggered a great westward *migration*.

Editing Tip

Both present and past participles work alone as adjectives (see Lesson 6.2), but they always need a helping verb to function as a verb.

PARTICIPLE
Lee is wearing **hiking** shoes.

INCOMPLETE VERB
She hiking on the Appalachian Trail.

VERB PHRASE
She **is hiking** on the Appalachian Trail.

Exercise 1   Using the Principal Parts of Regular Verbs

Complete each sentence by writing the correct past form or past participle form of the verb in parentheses. Some sentences have more than one verb in parentheses.

   EXAMPLE   All but the grin of the Cheshire cat (fade) ___faded___.

1. During the Great Depression, many banks (fail) ___failed___.

2. In 1955, Rosa Parks (refuse) __refused__ to give up her seat on a bus.

3. The Texans who (defend) __defended__ the Alamo (die) __died__ in the massacre of 1836.

4. The nineteenth-century writer Ralph Waldo Emerson (advise) __advised__ his readers, "Hitch your wagon to a star."

5. Before she (marry) __married__, Charlotte Brontë had (live) __lived__ at the parsonage with her father.

6. By l962, César Chávez had (organize) __organized__ migrant farmers into a union.

7. William the Conqueror (defeat) __defeated__ the English in 1066.

8. More than seventy-five thousand people (listen) __listened__ to Marian Anderson sing at the Lincoln Memorial.

9. John James Audubon (travel) __traveled__ (or travelled) across America and (paint) __painted__ birds.

10. A wall built by the Roman emperor Hadrian (stretch) __stretched__ across Britain.

Exercise 2 **Revising a Story Beginning**

Revise the story beginning so that it describes an event that happened in the past. Use the past form or past participle form of the italicized verbs. Compare the original version and your version. Does the story sound better to you in the present tense or in the past tense? Work with a partner or small group to finish the story.

■ For more information about writing a narrative, see **Compostion**, Lesson 2.4.

¹A mysterious figure *approaches* (approached) the old house. ²The person *walks* (walked) carefully up the broken steps and *knocks* (knocked) on the cracked door. ³From inside the old house, the knock *echoes* (echoed) through the empty rooms. ⁴No one *lives* (lived) there anymore. ⁵Outside the house, the dark trees and grasses *look* (looked) wild and overgrown. ⁶The garden *disappears* (had disappeared or disappeared) under a tangle of weeds. ⁷Patiently, the stranger *waits* (waited) before the door. ⁸In an instant, clouds *appear* (appeared), *darken* (darkened) the sky, and *spatter* (spattered) the visitor with huge drops of rain. ⁹Who *answers* (answered) the door when it *creaks* (creaked) open on rusty hinges? ¹⁰And what *happens* (happened) next? Challenge students to use words that connote a humorous, frightful, or surprising ending.

Irregular Verbs 1

All languages have irregular verbs, and English has a lot of them.
Irregular verbs do not form their past or past participle in a predictable
pattern. That is, they don't add -ed to the present form the way regular
verbs do. In fact, because they form their principal parts in various ways,
there's no single rule to help you learn them.

Use the principal parts of these common irregular verbs correctly
when you write and speak. The verb *to be* is used to form the present
and past participles. The forms are listed at the right.

Forms of *to be*

Present

I am	we are
you are	you are
he is	they are

Past

I was	we were
you were	you were
he was	they were

Principal Parts of Common Irregular Verbs			
PRESENT	PRESENT PARTICIPLE (Use with am, is, are, was, were.)	PAST	PAST PARTICIPLE (Use with has, had, have.)
[be] is, are	(is) being	was, were	(had) been
begin	(is) beginning	began	(had) begun
blow	(is) blowing	blew	(had) blown
break	(is) breaking	broke	(had) broken
bring	(is) bringing	brought	(had) brought
burst	(is) bursting	burst	(had) burst
catch	(is) catching	caught	(had) caught
choose	(is) choosing	chose	(had) chosen
come	(is) coming	came	(had) come
do	(is) doing	did	(had) done
drink	(is) drinking	drank	(had) drunk
drive	(is) driving	drove	(had) driven
eat	(is) eating	ate	(had) eaten
fall	(is) falling	fell	(had) fallen
find	(is) finding	found	(had) found
freeze	(is) freezing	froze	(had) frozen
give	(is) giving	gave	(had) given
go	(is) going	went	(had) gone
grow	(is) growing	grew	(had) grown
know	(is) knowing	knew	(had) known
lead	(is) leading	led	(had) led
lie [to fib]	(is) lying	lied	(had) lied
lose	(is) losing	lost	(had) lost
make	(is) making	made	(had) made
put	(is) putting	put	(had) put

The verb *lie* (to fib) is
different from the verbs
lay (to place or put) and
lie (to rest or recline).
Watch out! Their principal
parts are similar and they
are easy to confuse. See
Lesson 8.4 to practice
using these verbs.

 When you aren't sure about a verb form, check a dictionary. All
dictionaries list the principal parts of irregular verbs. The entry
word is the present form. The past, past participle, and present
participle forms are listed after the pronunciation:

break (brāk) **broke, broken, breaking**

If no verb forms are listed following the entry word, you can be
sure that the verb is regular.

Exercise 3 **Using Irregular Verbs**

Rewrite each sentence on a separate piece of paper. Use the past form or past participle form of the verb in parentheses. **Remember:** With a form of the helping verb *have,* use the past participle.

EXAMPLE   Owen and his bride have (choose) their new dishes.
Owen and his bride have chosen their new dishes.

1. Have you (bring) your binoculars with you?   brought

2. Has anyone (be) in touch with Vanessa lately?   been

3. When the temperature was below zero last week, the water pipes (freeze) and (burst).   froze   burst

4. Takeo has (lose) ten pounds by exercising.   lost

5. During the game, players (drink) a lot of water.   drank

6. Ilene (catch) the high pop fly at last week's game.   caught

7. Trees (fall) when winds (blow) sixty miles an hour.   fell   blew

8. When I (go) to the video store last night, I (choose) an Alfred Hitchcock movie.   went   chose

9. Last year, Sam (drive) from Maine to Oregon.   drove

10. Have you ever (eat) one of Guillermo's burritos?   eaten

11. The pencil marks on the door show how Benjy has (grow) since he (be) six.   grown   was

12. Amelia has (put) her name on all her books.   put

13. When he (lead) the hike, Mike (break) a trail through the sawgrass.   led   broke

14. Have you (come) to any conclusion in your research?   come

15. Ed and Gene have (be) in a workshop all day.   been

16. The contest (begin) last week, but Madeline has not yet (begin) her entry.   began   begun

17. Oscar was upset when he (lose) the watch his grandfather had (give) him.   lost   given

18. Jeanetta and her sister (make) the dresses they (be) wearing.   made   were

19. I had (do) the best I could but did not finish.   done

20. Kathy and Marion have (know) each other and have (be) friends since they (be) six.   known   been   were

Irregular Verbs 2

The verbs in this lesson and the previous lesson are not the only irregular verbs, but they are ones that you use most often.

🔷 Use the principal parts of these common irregular verbs correctly when you write and speak.

Principal Parts of Common Irregular Verbs			
PRESENT	**PRESENT PARTICIPLE** (Use with *am, is, are, was, were.*)	**PAST**	**PAST PARTICIPLE** (Use with *has, had, have.*)
ride	(is) riding	rode	(had) ridden
ring	(is) ringing	rang	(had) rung
rise	(is) rising	rose	(had) risen
run	(is) running	ran	(had) run
see	(is) seeing	saw	(had) seen
shake	(is) shaking	shook	(had) shaken
shrink	(is) shrinking	shrank	(had) shrunk
sing	(is) singing	sang	(had) sung
sink	(is) sinking	sank	(had) sunk
sit	(is) sitting	sat	(had) sat
speak	(is) speaking	spoke	(had) spoken
spend	(is) spending	spent	(had) spent
steal	(is) stealing	stole	(had) stolen
sting	(is) stinging	stung	(had) stung
strike	(is) striking	struck	(had) struck
swear	(is) swearing	swore	(had) sworn
swim	(is) swimming	swam	(had) swum
take	(is) taking	took	(had) taken
teach	(is) teaching	taught	(had) taught
throw	(is) throwing	threw	(had) thrown
wear	(is) wearing	wore	(had) worn
write	(is) writing	wrote	(had) written

Ring meaning "to surround" takes the past form *ringed*.

Enriching Your Vocabulary

Both the adjective *requisite* and the past participle *required* as used in Exercise 5, come from the Latin verb *requirere*, which means "to need." A course that is *requisite* or *required* for graduation is one that you need to take.

Exercise 4 Using Irregular Verbs

Rewrite each sentence on a separate piece of paper. Use the past form or past participle form of the verb in parentheses.

1. Paul Revere (ride) a horse to warn the colonists. rode

2. The jack of hearts had (steal) the tarts. stolen

3. As the *Titanic* (sink), passengers (sing) hymns. sank sang

4. The Liberty Bell cracked when it (ring) in 1835. rang

5. In 1954, Roger Bannister (run) a sub-four-minute mile. ran

6. Native Americans (teach) the Pilgrims how to grow corn. taught

Writing Hint

American English has many different **dialects**, or ways of speaking, in certain regions or among certain groups. When you write in school and at work, use standard English verb endings for the irregular verbs.

7. Have you (take) a close look at M. C. Escher's drawings? taken

8. Alex Haley (write) a family history, called *Roots,* that became a best-seller. wrote

9. Miss Havisham had (wear) her wedding dress for years. worn

10. Mark Antony (speak) the words "Brutus is an honorable man." spoke

11. Who was frightened when a spider (sit) down beside her? sat

12. When two bees (sting) Lynn, she had an allergic reaction. stung

13. Lightning (strike) the kite that Benjamin Franklin flew. struck

14. Every president has (swear) to uphold the Constitution. sworn

15. Robinson Crusoe had (swim) to the shipwreck to get supplies. swum

Exercise 5 Editing a Paragraph

Cross out each incorrect verb, and write the correct verb above it. Make any other changes you think will improve the letter.

To the Editor:

¹This is the first time I have ~~wrote~~ written a letter to the editor. ²Our community has ~~saw~~ seen too many people who have drowned. ³A friend of mine ~~swum~~ swam way out. ⁴When she got caught in a riptide, a lifeguard ~~swimmed~~ swam out and ~~bringed~~ brought her back to shore. ⁵No one has ~~teached~~ taught us students swimming safety. ⁶Not all parents have ~~teached~~ taught their youngsters to swim. ⁷Young people have ~~took~~ taken too many chances. ⁸I think the people who ~~have ran~~ run the schools are making a mistake. ⁹They have ~~shrinked~~ shrunk from making swimming required. ¹⁰Too many swimming disasters have already ~~striked~~ struck this community.

Exercise 6 Write What You Think

■ For more information about writing persuasive essays, see **Composition,** Lesson 3.2.

On a separate piece of paper, write a paragraph giving your opinion about the statement below. Do you agree or disagree with it? Support your opinion with reasons and examples. When you finish writing, look back to see if your verb forms are correct.

Before students can graduate from high school, they must pass swimming and lifesaving tests.

Answers will vary. Give students full credit if they have stated an opinion and attempted to support their opinions. Look for grammatically complete sentences that begin with a capital letter and end with an appropriate end punctuation mark.

Mid-Chapter Review

Exercise A Using Regular Verbs

On a separate piece of paper, rewrite each sentence using the past form or past participle form of the verb in parentheses.

1. Have you ever (look) up *John Chapman* in a reference book ? looked

2. He was an American who (live) from 1774 to 1875. lived

3. For forty years, Chapman (travel) across the Midwest. traveled or travelled

4. He (plant) apple seeds and saplings in Pennsylvania, Ohio, and Indiana. planted

5. He (encourage) settlers moving west to plant apple orchards. encouraged

6. The settlers (call) him Johnny Appleseed. called

7. Some of the orchards that he (start) still stand today. started

8. During the War of 1812, he (help) save Mansfield, Ohio. helped

9. He (prevent) a raid on the town when he (travel) thirty miles to get troops. prevented
traveled or
travelled

10. After Johnny Appleseed (die), he became a folk hero. died

Exercise B Using Irregular Verbs

Complete the chart below by filling in the missing principal parts. When you've finished the chart, write two sentences for each verb. Use the past form in one sentence and the past participle form in the other.

Present	Present Participle	Past	Past Participle
1. is	2. (is) being	was, were	3. (had) been
4. bring	(is) bringing	5. brought	6. (had) brought
7. break	8. (is) breaking	broke	9. (had) broken
come	10. (is) coming	11. came	(had) come
12. eat	(is) eating	13. ate	14. (had) eaten
give	15. (is) giving	16. gave	17. (had) given
18. go	(is) going	19. went	20. (had) gone
21. grow	(is) growing	22. grew	23. (had) grown
know	24. (is) knowing	25. knew	26. (had) known
see	27. (is) seeing	28. saw	29. (had) seen
30. sit	(is) sitting	31. sat	32. (had) sat
speak	(is) speaking	33. spoke	34. (had) spoken

Present	Present Participle	Past	Past Participle
swim	35. (is) swimming	36. swam	37. (had) swum
38. take	39. (is) taking	took	40. (had) taken
41. teach	42. (is) teaching	taught	43. (had) taught
throw	44. (is) throwing	45. threw	46. (had) thrown
wear	47. (is) wearing	48. wore	(had) worn
49. write	(is) writing	50. wrote	(had) written

Exercise C **Editing a Paragraph**

In each sentence, correct any mistakes you find in the use of verb forms. Use the past or past participle tense.

¹People who live near a big river always ~~knowed~~ *know or have known* that spring thaws and heavy rains have been a serious problem. ²In one North Dakota city, twelve inches of rain has ~~falled~~ *fallen* in two days. ³The river has risen alarmingly. ⁴In previous years, much of the city ~~been~~ *has been* flooded. ⁵Businesses and houses have been ~~ruin~~ *ruined*, and lives ~~be~~ *have been* lost. ⁶Along the Mississippi River, floods have ~~cause~~ *caused* serious damage when levees, or embankments, ~~bursted~~ *burst*. ⁷People from far away have ~~came~~ *come* to help pile sandbags on top of the levees. ⁸If you watch TV news, you probably ~~seen~~ *have seen* pictures of people sitting on roofs while floodwaters lapped at their ankles. ⁹Rescuers have ~~drived~~ *driven* boats and have ~~maked~~ *made* helicopter flights to help stranded people. ¹⁰Despite the recurring danger of floods, people from flooded cities have ~~speaked~~ *spoken* about their eagerness to go home and start rebuilding.

Answers may vary. Accept either the past or past perfect; in some sentences, such as 1, the present tense is also acceptable. Sample answers have been given.

Exercise D **Write What You Think**

Write a paragraph to answer each of the questions below. Check your sentences for correct verb forms.

1. Have you ever experienced a natural disaster like an earthquake, flood, hurricane, tornado, forest fire, or blizzard? Write about what happened and how you felt while it was happening.

2. Of all the kinds of natural disasters mentioned above, which would you *least* like to experience? Explain why. Answers will vary. Give students full credit if they have expressed themselves clearly. Look for grammatically complete sentences that begin with a capital letter and end with an appropriate end punctuation mark.

Lie, Lay; Sit, Set; Raise, Rise

These pairs of verbs are often confused because their principal parts are similar.

◖ Use correctly the principal parts of the commonly confused verbs **lie** and **lay**, **sit** and **set**, and **rise** and **raise**.

Principal Parts of *Lie, Lay, Rise, Raise, Sit, Set*			
PRESENT	**PRESENT PARTICIPLE** (Use with *am, is, are, was, were.*)	**PAST**	**PAST PARTICIPLE** (Use with *has, had, have.*)
lie (to rest or recline)	(is) lying	lay	(had) lain
lay (to place or put)	(is) laying	laid	(had) laid
rise (to stand up)	(is) rising	rose	(had) risen
raise (to lift or bring up)	(is) raising	raised	(had) raised
sit (to rest oneself on a chair)	(is) sitting	sat	(had) sat
set (to put)	(is) setting	set	(had) set

LIE   Justin **lay** on the couch and fell asleep.

LIE   The newspaper **had lain** in a puddle and was soaked. [*Lie* is also used for objects and animals, not just people.]

                          DO

LAY   She **laid** the heavy package on the table. [*Lay* almost always takes a direct object.]

RISE   Mrs. Kaplan **rose** to speak at the board meeting.

                          DO

RAISE   She **raised** two important questions. [*Raise* almost always takes a direct object.]

SIT   We **sat** on the beach and watched the fireworks.

                          DO

SET   Jim **set** the table and cooked dinner. [*Set* almost always takes a direct object.]

P.S. Lots of English speakers have problems with these verbs. Make a habit of checking yourself against a book such as this one before you hand in a piece of writing. There's nothing wrong with using a reference tool when you write.

Writing Hint

Here's a memory trick to help you distinguish *lay*, *raise*, and *set* from *lie*, *rise*, and *sit*. Remember that the first three take direct objects.

YOU CAN:

lay an egg if you are a chicken.

set an egg down on a counter.

raise an egg over your head before you throw it.

BUT YOU CANNOT:

lie an egg,

sit an egg, or

rise an egg.

Exercise 7 Using Correct Verb Forms

On a separate piece of paper, rewrite each sentence using the past form or past participle form of the verb in parentheses.

1. The sun (rise) on the morning of September 17, 1787. rose
2. The fifty-five delegates to the Constitutional Convention still (lie) in bed.   lay
3. All summer long, they had (sit) in Philadelphia's State House.   sat
4. On May 29, Edmund Randolph had (rise) from his chair to introduce the Virginia Plan. risen
5. In mid-June, New Jersey had (lay) its plan before the delegates. laid
6. The delegates had (raise) important issues and debated them.   raised
7. On September 17, each delegate (rise) from his chair to sign the Constitution. rose
8. It (set) down lasting principles and organized the nation's government. set
9. The power to elect representatives (lie) in the hands of the people. lay
10. Nine justices have always (sit) on the Supreme Court. sat

Exercise 8 Writing Sentences

Write two sentences for each of the verbs below. In one sentence use the past form correctly. In the second, use the past participle form correctly.

1. rise
2. sit
3. lay
4. lie (to rest or recline)
5. set
6. raise

Students' sentences will vary. Encourage students to be creative. You might suggest that they write using a theme similar to that of Exercise 7.

Exercise 9 Choosing the Correct Verb Form

Underline the verb in parentheses that correctly completes each sentence.

1. The kitten (laid, lay) curled up on the bed.
2. Please (set, sit) your heavy suitcase down.
3. Justin (set, sat) in front of the TV, channel surfing.
4. Her hopes (raised, rose) when she saw the fat envelope.
5. Bread dough (raises, rises) if the yeast is active.
6. Phyllis is (laying, lying) tile on the front stoop.
7. Sharon has been (laying, lying) on the couch all evening.
8. In his essay Kiyo (raises, rises) three important points.
9. The love letters had (lain, laid) in the attic for years.
10. Can you stay and (set, sit) awhile?

Verb Tense

◖ A **verb tense** expresses the time an action was performed.

Every English verb has three **simple tenses** (present, past, and future) and three **perfect tenses** (present perfect, past perfect, and future perfect).

The Six Verb Tenses		
TENSE	**WHAT IT SHOWS**	**EXAMPLE**
present	action happening in the present; action that happens repeatedly	I **finish**. The sun **rises** and **sets**.
past	action completed in the past	I **finished**.
future	action that will happen in the future	You and he **will finish**.
present perfect	action completed recently or in indefinite past	I **have finished**. He **has finished**.
past perfect	action that happened before another action	I **had** already **finished** when the rain started.
future perfect	action that will happen before a future action or time	By tomorrow, he **will have finished**.

Each tense also has a **progressive form**, which is made up of a helping verb and the present participle (the *-ing* form). The progressive forms show ongoing action.

The Progressive Forms for the Six Tenses	
PROGRESSIVE FORM	**EXAMPLE**
present progressive	(am, is, are) finishing
past progressive	(was, were) finishing
future progressive	(will, shall) be finishing
present perfect progressive	(has, have) been finishing
past perfect progressive	had been finishing
future perfect progressive	will have been finishing

◖ Don't switch verb tenses needlessly. Keep tenses consistent whenever possible.

ORIGINAL   Scott **gets** out of the car and **looked** around him. He **had** no idea where he **is**.

CONSISTENT   Scott **got** out of the car and **looked** around him. He **had** no idea where he **was**.

A shift in verb tense is sometimes necessary because the meaning requires it. Use verb tenses that make sense in the sentence.

Scott **left** home yesterday; he **is taking** an overnight bus. He **will arrive** here tomorrow.

Everyone **wants** to meet Sara, whom no one **has seen** yet.

Editing Tip

When you write about literature, use the **literary present tense** (see page 54). Talk about the writer and the characters as if they exist in the present.

In "The Most Dangerous Game," Connell **writes** about a strange kind of hunting. As the story **begins**, Rainsford **falls** off a yacht and **swims** to an island.

Writing Hint

There is yet another verb form that's helpful for showing emphasis in writing—the **emphatic form**.

I *do* **drink** juice every day.
He *does* **drink** juice every day.
They *did* **drink** juice every day.

Exercise 10 Using Verb Tenses

Replace the italicized verbs in sentences 1–6 to show actions completed in the past.

¹In 1947, India and Pakistan *become* [became] independent nations. ²Great Britain's control of India *dates* [dated] back to 1857. ³The Empress of India *is* [was] none other than Britain's Queen Victoria. ⁴Mohandas K. Gandhi *has led* [led] India's struggle for independence. ⁵Followers *call* [called] him "Mahatma" Gandhi, which means "great soul." ⁶Gandhi *believe* [believed] in nonviolent resistance.

Replace the italicized verbs in sentences 7–10 with a progressive form to show ongoing action.

⁷Gandhi's nonviolent strategies *continued* [are continuing] to influence us today. (present progressive) ⁸When Dr. Martin Luther King, Jr., organized civil-rights protests in the 1960s, he *thought* [was thinking] of Gandhi. (past progressive) ⁹He also *modeled* [was modeling] his protests on Thoreau's essay called "On Civil Disobedience." (past progressive) ¹⁰We *honor* [will be honoring] Gandhi, Thoreau, and King long into the future. (future progressive)

Exercise 11 Making Verb Tenses Consistent

On a separate piece of paper, revise any of the following sentences in which you find unnecessary shifts in verb tense. If a sentence doesn't need revising, write *No change.* Students may make sentences consistent by changing either verb. Sample answers given.

1. Larry sings whenever he ~~arrived~~ [arrives] home from work.
2. Everyone cheered when the last bell of the school year ~~sounds~~ [sounded].
3. Tomorrow will be Dan's picnic; ~~we've~~ [we will] certainly ~~enjoyed~~ [enjoy] it.
4. Karim tripped on a tree root and ~~breaks~~ [broke] his toe.
5. The heat was awful, so no one left their air-conditioned rooms. No change
6. More registered voters ~~stayed~~ [stay] home than come to vote.
7. Joy scalded two fingers when she ~~pours~~ [poured] water for tea.
8. We announce the winners only when the results ~~had been~~ [are] official.
9. Gary ~~is glancing~~ [glanced] at his watch every few minutes as he waited.
10. A strange package ~~arrives~~ [arrived], but no one knew what it was.

Hint

Most of the sentences that need revising can be fixed in more than one way.

Using the Active Voice

🔹 When a verb is in the **active voice**, the subject of the sentence performs an action. When a verb is in the **passive voice**, the subject receives an action.

A verb in the passive voice always uses some form of the helping verb *be*.

ACTIVE   Jonah **built** the birdhouse.

PASSIVE   The birdhouse **was built** by Jonah.

ACTIVE   Emily **has seen** hummingbirds at the feeder.

PASSIVE   Hummingbirds **have been seen** by Emily.

🔹 Use the active voice when you write because it is stronger and more direct. The passive voice is acceptable when you do not know the performer of the action or when you want to emphasize the receiver of the action, not the performer.

The car **was stolen** from the parking lot. [The performer of the action is unknown.]

Mickey Mouse **was created** by Walt Disney. [The receiver of the action, not the performer, is being emphasized.]

Writing Hint

As you edit your writing, check your sentences for passive voice. Change to the active voice whenever possible, especially if the change saves words.

PASSIVE
The ball had been hit by Guy. (7 words)

ACTIVE
Guy hit the ball. (4 words)

Exercise 12 **Using the Active Voice**

Rewrite the sentences below to use the active voice whenever possible. If the passive voice is acceptable, explain why.

EXAMPLE   A ship's speed is measured in knots.

Keep the passive voice. The sentence has no "performer" of the action.

See Answer Key.

1. The Camp David agreements were signed in 1978 by Sadat and Begin.

2. The ancient city of Rome was built on seven hills.

3. Sixty-three of his sixty-six professional fights were won by Joe Louis.

4. "The Raven" was written in 1845 by Edgar Allan Poe.

5. The koala bear is found only in eastern Australia.

6. Both the Nobel Prize for chemistry and the Nobel Peace Prize were won by Linus Pauling.

7. The city of Machu Picchu was built by the Incas about 1500 A.D.

8. The border between Mexico and the United States is formed by the Rio Grande.

9. Nearly 8,500 species of birds have been identified.

10. *Gulliver's Travels*, a satire, was written by Jonathan Swift.

The object of the preposition *by* can often be made into the subject to change a passive sentence into an active sentence.

Revising and Editing Worksheet

Work with a partner or small group to improve the following report. First, revise the report by combining sentences, changing or omitting words, and rearranging sentences. Then, focus your edits especially on verb usage but make any other changes you think will improve the report. Write your revised report on a separate piece of paper and compare your response with those made by other pairs or groups of classmates. **Hint:** The word *plankton* is plural; it takes a plural verb.

[1]Plankton are tiny organisms. [2]Plankton have varied in size. [3]Some plankton be microscopic. [4]You can only seen these plankton with a microscope. [5]Other plankton are bigger and reached one to two inches long in length. [6]Plankton can be finded in oceans and lakes all over the world. [7]They are finded mostly in coastal waters. [8]Especially in polar and cold waters.

[9]There are two different kinds and types of plankton: plant and animal. [10]Plant plankton had only one cell. [11]Algae and diatoms are examples of plant plankton. [12]Plant plankton form the basis of the food chain.

[13]Animal plankton eaten plant plankton. [14]Then small marine animals eat the animal plankton. [15]These small marine animals included mollusks, snails, shrimp, and mussels. [16]Larger marine animals feed on these small animals. [17]Including seals and porpoises. [18]These animals are ate in turn by some whales and sharks.

[19]Plankton are of extreme importance to life on Earth. [20]First, plant plankton produce 70 percent of Earth's oxygen. [21]Second, plankton played a crucial part in the world's food chain.

[22]Plankton are so tiny that they cannot move on their own. [23]Instead, drifting in the ocean's currents. [24]Plankton float on the water's surface at night and have sank below the surface during the day. [25]At night they raise again to the surface.

Revisions will vary. See teacher pages for writing rubrics.

Enriching Your Vocabulary

The adjective *crucial* is based on the Latin *cruc*, or "cross." Thus, a *crucial* matter is one that requires a final decision such as the one that you need to make if you reach a crossroad.

Chapter Review

Exercise A Using Irregular Verbs

Write the form of the verb in parentheses that correctly completes each
sentence. In some cases, there may be more than one correct answer.

> EXAMPLE   The newspaper has been (lie) in the rain. *lying*

1. How long have you (know) Giorgio? known
2. Harriet (be) tired from working late five nights a week. is
3. No one found the diary, which (lie) right on the desk. lay
4. When she went to her son's apartment, Mrs. O'Keeffe (bring) dinner. brought
5. Has Idria (go) to the bank yet? gone
6. Who (teach) Raphael how to play the flute? taught
7. Yesterday, Shira (swim) fifty-two laps in the pool. swam
8. Justin has (write) a science fiction short story. written
9. Last night we (see) a really good movie. saw
10. I didn't finish the test because my time (run) out. ran
11. I hope you've (take) careful notes. taken
12. For dinner, Ricardo (make) roast beef and mashed potatoes. made
13. Mrs. Chan (throw) out the old magazines she had been saving. threw
14. Since the year began, Larry has (wear) cowboy boots to school. worn
15. Have you ever (ride) on a monorail? ridden

Exercise B *Lie* and *Lay*; *Sit* and *Set*; *Rise* and *Raise*

Underline the verb in parentheses that correctly completes each sentence.

1. Dirty laundry (lay, laid) all over the bedroom floor.
2. Kristy's cat had been (lying, laying) on her homework.
3. Carefully, he (lay, laid) the sweater on a towel to dry.
4. Susie (laid, lay) in the sun too long without sunscreen.
5. Pete and Robin (set, sat) on the fire escape to cool off.
6. She has (set, sat) the table for six for dinner.
7. Please (sit, set) down and talk to me.
8. Julie (rose, raised) to ask a question.
9. You have (risen, raised) several important issues.
10. Tomorrow the sun will (rise, raise) at 6:52 A.M.

Exercise C **Using Verb Tenses**

Change the italicized verbs to the verb tense specified in parentheses. You may look back at the charts on page 183. Write your answers on a separate piece of paper.

1. The twins always *wear* different outfits. (past) wore
2. Nora *make* lasagna at least once a week. (present perfect) has made
3. Next year, everyone *sing* the school song before assemblies. (future) will sing
4. A committee *plan* the picnic. (past perfect progressive) had been planning
5. I *hope* you would call. (past progressive) was hoping
6. Jason *put* out the candles before he *go* to sleep. (past; past) put; went
7. Blanca *catch* the pass. (past) caught
8. Everyone *eat*, so no one *be* hungry. (present perfect; present) has eaten; is
9. Sondra *grow* more spinach next year. (future progressive) will be growing
10. Leslie *worry* about her algebra final. (present perfect progressive) has been worrying

Exercise D **Editing a Paragraph**

Edit the paragraph below for correct verb usage. Use the active voice whenever possible. Decide whether the paragraph should be past or present tense, and make verb tenses consistent. Make any other changes that you think will improve the paragraph.

[1]Homes of all different shapes, materials, and kinds are built by birds. [2]A shallow scrape, or nest in the dirt, is built by pressing their bodies into the earth by Arctic terns. [3]Their eggs were sat on constantly by Arctic terns. [4]Burrows were built below the ground by burrowing owls, bee-eaters, penguins, and puffins. [5]Holes in trees have been made by woodpeckers and flickers to serve as their hidden homes. [6]At the top of very tall poles or trees, large nests are constructed by ospreys. [7]Tiny cup nests are created by hummingbirds. [8]Bits of plants and moss are being woven into the cup nest by hummingbirds. [9]Mud is shaped into nests by flamingos and cliff swallows. [10]Large mud mounds on the ground are built by flamingos, but cliff swallow nests look like an apartment house under a cliff ledge.   Revisions will vary. See teacher pages for writing rubrics.

Subject-Verb Agreement

CHAPTER 9

我們真正學讀英文

i, estamos aprendiendo a leer.

es, we are learning to read.

189

Direct students to chapter-specific portfolio projects on Sadlier-Oxford's website.

STUDENT WRITING
Expository Essay

A Language Plan for Success
by Hugh Field
high school student, San Diego, California

What do you call someone who speaks three languages? Trilingual. What do you call someone who speaks two languages? Bilingual. What do you call someone who speaks one language? American. This old joke has for too long been a sad reality in the schools of San Diego, a city that should be one of the most multicultural in America.

Given our proximity to Mexico, one might expect San Diego residents to have a passing knowledge of the Spanish language.

San Diego Unified School District Superintendent Alan Bersin is finally doing something to increase Spanish knowledge around San Diego. Bersin has proposed a plan in which, if passed, students will be taught both Spanish and English starting in elementary school, in a program designed to benefit both children who have been speaking English all their lives as well as those who may have grown up speaking Spanish only, or a combination of the two.

With the recent implementation of Proposition 227, Spanish speaking children are discouraged from preserving their native language skills. With [Bersin's] new measure, Spanish speaking children would learn grammar skills as well as literacy, allowing many more high school students to take AP Spanish classes. The plan would require all graduates to be academically competent in both English and Spanish.

The strong points of this initiative outweigh any downsides, making it a sensible plan for the future. However, the pilot program only covers the grades before middle school, a time when students are offered other electives that many students find more attractive than Spanish.

Such a situation arose in Miami when a similar pilot program was started. One solution is to require Spanish, in some form, in high school.

While some students may balk at the idea of not being allowed to study the foreign language of their choice, overall, teaching in Spanish and English will help schools graduate well-rounded students and ensure that these students get into college.

Last, this plan will increase the quality of life for all students who go through it. Those with special language skills are guaranteed better and higher–paying jobs, as well as better opportunities for advancement. For as the proverb goes, "He who speaks two languages is worth two."

Allow time for students to discuss the student writing. Suggest that they identify its strengths and propose possible improvements. Use the model to introduce the concepts in the chapter.

Hugh's expository essay begins with an attention grabber. He explains the issue he plans to address; then he details the solution to the problem. Hugh even identifies opposition to the solution—and then counterattacks. His final paragraph has three convincing sentences that sum up his position.

As you reread the essay, notice that Hugh uses complex sentences with clauses and phrases. Complicated sentences require a careful watch on subject-verb agreement, which you'll study in this chapter.

Indefinite Pronouns, Subjects Following Verbs

🔹 An **indefinite pronoun** expresses an amount or refers to an unspecified person or thing. Some indefinite pronouns are always singular and take singular verbs. Others are always plural and take plural verbs.

SINGULAR	**Everyone** in Mrs. Rivera's algebra classes **works** hard.
SINGULAR	**Neither** of the movies **is** a mystery.
PLURAL	**Both** of Kim's uncles **make** custom-designed furniture.

Always Singular

anybody	neither
anyone	nobody
each	no one
either	one
everybody	somebody
everyone	someone

Always Plural

both	many
few	several

🔹 The indefinite pronouns *all, any, most,* and *some* can be either singular or plural. Depending on the word they refer to, these pronouns take either a singular or plural verb.

Lesson 10.5 explains that singular indefinite pronouns take singular possessive pronouns.

	S V
SINGULAR	**All** of your work **is** excellent.
	S V
PLURAL	**All** of the farmers **are planting** winter wheat.
	S V
SINGULAR	**Any** of the food **is** delicious.
	S V
PLURAL	**Any** of these packages **look** interesting.
	S V
SINGULAR	The report is extensive. **Most** of it **is** correct.
	S V
PLURAL	Where are those cats? **Most sleep** during the day.
	S V
SINGULAR	**Some** of the cake **is** frozen.
	S V
PLURAL	**Some** of the cookies **are** broken.

> ### Editing Tip
>
> The pronoun *none* is especially tricky. Use a singular verb only when you can think of the subject as "none of it." Use a plural verb when you can substitute "none of them."
>
> **None** of the test **is** easy. [None of *it* is easy.]
>
> **None** of your answers **are** right. [None of *them* are right.]

🔹 A verb must agree with the subject even when the subject follows the verb.

In a wooden box at the top of the closet **are** all our old **photographs**.

Where **are** your **copies** of the reports?

Here **is** a **book** I really liked.

🔹 A verb agrees with the subject, not with the predicate nominative (PN).

Don't be confused by a predicate nominative following a linking verb. Find the subject, and then make the verb agree.

S   V   PN
Karin's favorite **dessert is** strawberries.

S   V PN
The **subject** of his report **is** solutions to combat crime.

Exercise 3 **Choosing the Correct Verb**

Underline the subject of each sentence and the verb in parentheses that agrees in number with the subject. Then, with a partner write five more sentences that practice subject-verb agreement. Give a choice of two present-tense verbs in parenthesis and exchange sentences with another team. Students' additional answers will vary.

1. One of the nicknames for an American (is, are) Yankee.

2. None of our other national parks (has, have) as many geysers as Yellowstone.

3. Few (is, are) as beautiful as Yosemite in California.

4. Which part of Niagara Falls (is, are) in Canada?

5. Several of the popular sights in Washington, D.C., (is, are) the Vietnam Memorial, the Washington Monument, and the White House.

6. Anyone in Death Valley (knows, know) how dry deserts are.

7. In Denver, everybody (lives, live) a mile above sea level.

8. Some of the land in the Black Hills (is, are) sacred to the Sioux.

9. The street names in New York City (has, have) fascinating histories.

10. None of the Great Lakes (borders, border) an ocean.

Exercise 4 **Editing Sentences**

Extend Exercise 4 by asking students to write a paragraph describing a place where they would like to live and why.

Edit the sentences below. Correct any errors you find in subject-verb agreement.

1. ~~Does~~ Do you know where you would like to live someday?

2. What type of land ~~appeal~~ appeals to you most?

3. There ~~is~~ are magazines that list the ten best places to live.

4. Perhaps one of these cities ~~are~~ is already your home.

5. The best type of scenery ~~are~~ is mountainous.

6. When I ~~thinks~~ think about the place I'd most like to live, I ~~chooses~~ choose a dairy farm in northern Wisconsin.

7. Most of my friends ~~likes~~ like to watch the seasons pass.

8. Among my friends ~~is~~ are many in northern California.

9. My mother's cousins ~~has~~ have a dairy farm.

10. I ~~visits~~ visit them every summer.

Mid-Chapter Review

Exercise A Writing Complete Sentences

On a separate piece of paper, write a complete sentence for each numbered item, using the group of words as the subject of the sentence.

Students' sentences will vary. Sample sentences are given. See Answer Key.

EXAMPLE   Several of my friends
Several of my friends have their driver's licenses.

1. Nobody in the room
2. One of my favorite movies
3. A few of my best CDs
4. All of my teachers
5. None of my friends
6. Few of the people

Exercise B Editing a Paragraph

Edit the following paragraph. Correct any errors you find in subject-verb agreement. Make any other revisions that you think will improve the paragraph. **Hint:** One of the sentences contains no errors; some sentences may have more than one error. Look for subject-verb agreement in subordinate clauses also. Students may make changes other than subject-verb corrections.

Memories Lost and Found

¹What is (are) your most vivid memories? ²Does (Do) you remember your first day of school or the day you turned six? ³For more than a hundred years, scientists all over the world has (have) studied memory and learning. ⁴Nobody know (knows) for sure how memory works or how and why certain experiences is (are) stored and others is (are) forgotten. ⁵There has (have) been many theories about memory. ⁶Some scientists believes (believe) that memory is controlled by the hippocampus. ⁷That structure lie (lies) deep inside the temporal lobe. ⁸When the hippocampus is directly stimulated during surgery, patients recall vivid memories long forgotten. ⁹Is (Are) all the memories you can't recall lost forever? ¹⁰Or is (are) they somehow "asleep" until something awaken (awakens) them again?

Exercise C Writing About a Memory

Think of something that happened when you were very young, something you remember vividly—maybe a favorite game, a trip, an accident, or a party. Write a description of your memory for a friend. Use present-tense verbs as if the scene you recall were happening right now. Describe what you are seeing, smelling, feeling, and thinking. Describe who is with you and what happens. Read your written memory aloud and listen for correct use of subject-verb agreement. Refer to the model below.

Students' paragraphs will vary. Use the model as a sample answer.

> *It is a summer night, and I am four years old. My brother Larry, who is ten, and his friends are collecting fireflies in empty mayonnaise jars with a little grass in the bottom of each jar and holes punched in the lids. They run across lawns, shouting at each other, and swoop up the tiny blinking lights. Larry teases me because I can't catch any fireflies. He orders me to go inside. "No," I yell at him, "they're my fireflies, too!"*

Exercise D **Choosing the Correct Verb**

Underline the verb in parentheses that agrees with the subject.

1. Many of Diego Rivera's murals (shows, <u>show</u>) workers and farmers.

2. Will Rogers said, "Everything (<u>is</u>, are) funny as long as it is happening to somebody else."

3. Nobody (<u>knows</u>, know) the identity of Leonardo da Vinci's *Mona Lisa*.

4. Michelangelo's paintings on the ceiling of the Sistine Chapel in the Vatican (is, <u>are</u>) a great work of art.

5. The American painter Horace Pippin (<u>was</u>, were) self-taught.

6. The Leaning Tower of Pisa (tilt, <u>tilts</u>) because its foundation sank.

7. (Doesn't, <u>Don't</u>) you know who wrote "The Star-Spangled Banner"?

8. A mother with her child (<u>is</u>, are) often the subject of Mary Cassatt's paintings.

9. The purpose of Stonehenge's circle of stones (<u>remains</u>, remain) a mystery.

10. In Egyptian hieroglyphics, pictures (stands, <u>stand</u>) for words and sounds.

Agreement with Compound Subjects

A sentence has a **compound subject** when two or more subjects share the same verb. In the present tense, use the following rules to select the correct verb form.

■ For more about agreement with compound subjects, see **Usage** **Lesson 9.4.**

🔹 When two or more singular subjects are joined by *and*, they take a plural verb.

> Jupiter, Saturn, **and** Neptune **have** many moons.
> Lién **and** Shira **know** a lot about astronomy.

🔹 When two or more singular subjects are joined by *or* or *nor*, they take a singular verb.

> Neither Mercury **nor** Venus **has** a moon.
> Either Martin **or** Pat **takes** the dog out after school.

🔹 When a singular subject and a plural subject are joined by *or* or *nor*, the verb agrees with the subject closer to it.

> Neither the stars **nor** the moon **is** visible tonight.
> Neither the moon **nor** the stars **are** visible tonight.
> **Is** the moon or the stars visible tonight?
> **Are** the stars or the moon visible tonight?

A compound subject that names only one thing or person takes a singular verb.

Chutes and Ladders is a board game.

Fresh berries and yogurt is Melanie's favorite snack.

My friend and adviser always offers her opinion.

Exercise 5 Choosing the Correct Verb

Underline the subject of each sentence and the verb in parentheses that agrees with the subject. **Hint:** Not every sentence has a compound subject.

Step by Step

Agreement with Compound Subjects

1. Identify the compound subjects. Watch out for prepositional phrases!

2. Find the conjunction connecting the subjects: *and*, *or*, or *nor*.

3. When *or* or *nor* connects the subjects, use a singular verb only if the subject nearer the verb is third-person singular.

1. The <u>United States</u> and <u>Russia</u> (has, <u>have</u>) cooperated in space.

2. Snack <u>foods</u> and her <u>family</u> (is, <u>are</u>) what Shannon Lucid missed most during her six months in space.

3. <u>Mood</u> and <u>body</u> (is, <u>are</u>) affected by long space missions.

4. A <u>mother and pilot</u> (<u>is</u>, are) the first woman space commander.

5. Weak <u>muscles</u> or bone <u>loss</u> (<u>concerns</u>, concern) scientists.

6. Either a vacuum <u>treadmill</u> or another <u>piece</u> of exercise equipment (helps, help) to overcome these problems.

7. In space, an <u>accident</u> or <u>emergency</u> (<u>is</u>, are) always a danger.

8. <u>Mission Control</u> or <u>reporters</u> (updates, <u>update</u>) the public.

9. (<u>Is</u>, Are) a space <u>colony</u> or a temporary <u>settlement</u> likely?

10. Neither <u>Mars</u> nor the <u>Moon</u> (<u>has</u>, have) breathable air.

Exercise 6 **Create Your Own Exercise**

With a partner or group, make up five sentences like the ones in Exercise 5. You may write about any topic. Use compound subjects. Exchange sentences with another team, and see if you agree on the correct answers. Students' sentences will vary.

Exercise 7 **Writing a Paragraph**

Write a paragraph based on the following notes. Use present-tense verbs. Then get together in a small group to read your paragraphs aloud and check subject-verb agreement.   Students' paragraphs will vary.

Mercury, Venus, Mars, Jupiter & Saturn = planets known to ancient Greeks

<u>*Planet*</u>*, from Greek for "wanderer" (because planets move in sky)*

Mercury, Venus, Earth, Mars, Jupiter, Saturn, Uranus, Neptune, Pluto = 9 planets we know revolve around sun

Jupiter & Saturn = 2 largest planets; Mercury, Pluto, Mars = smallest planets

Mercury & Venus = 2 closest to sun   Neptune & Pluto = 2 most distant

Earth = third planet from the sun

Answers will vary. Give students full credit if they have stated an opinion and attempted to support their opinion. Look for grammatically complete sentences that begin with a capital letter and end with an appropriate end punctuation mark.

Exercise 8 **Write What You Think**

On a separate piece of paper, write a paragraph about one of the following questions. Check for complete sentences and for subject-verb agreement.

1. You have been invited to spend five years in the first U.S. colony on Mars. What questions will you ask before you decide whether to go or not? What do you think you will decide? Tell why.

2. Some people say that the money spent on our space program should go instead to solving problems on Earth. Do you agree or disagree with this opinion? Give reasons.

Agreement with Special Nouns

🔹 **Collective nouns**, such as the examples on the right, name a group of people or things.

Use a singular verb when you think of a collective noun as one single unit. Use a plural verb when you think of a collective noun as multiple members.

Neely's **family is planning** a summer reunion. [*Family* refers to a single unit and takes a singular verb.]

Neely's **family live** in forty different states. [*Family* refers to multiple members in the group and takes a plural verb.]

Deciding whether a collective noun is acting as a single unit or as multiple members isn't always easy. If you are not sure, use the verb form (singular or plural) that you think sounds better.

🔹 Some nouns ending in *-s* function as singular subjects and take a singular verb. Some function as plural subjects and take a plural verb. A few may be either singular or plural.

The nouns that are always plural are usually a pair of something or an object made up of parts working together. See the examples on the right.

Measles is a serious disease for children and adults.
Your **eyeglasses are** on the bookshelf next to the dictionary.
These **statistics come** from the Centers for Disease Control.
Statistics is a required course for psychology majors.

🔹 The title of a work of art (painting, literature, or music) is always a singular subject and takes a singular verb.

Van Gogh's ***First Steps* is** a copy of a drawing by Millet.

🔹 Use a singular verb with a third-person subject that names a single amount or time. Use a plural verb with a third-person subject that refers to multiple items.

Two **dollars is** the value of that old coin. [a single amount]
These two **dollars are** badly torn. [multiple dollar bills]
Three **months makes** a quarter of a year. [a single time period]
These three **months are** passing very slowly. [multiple items]

🔹 Use a singular verb when *many a, every,* or *each* comes before a compound subject.

Every ninth-grader **and** tenth-grader **takes** math and English.

Some Collective Nouns

audience	flock
class	group
club	herd
committee	(the) press
crowd	(the) public
family	team

Singular

mathematics	news
measles	physics
mumps	

Plural

binoculars	scissors
eyeglasses	slacks
pants	

Singular or Plural

acoustics	statistics
politics	

The words *media* and *data* are technically plural but are often used with singular verbs.

Enriching Your Vocabulary

Around the world, people celebrated the new *millennium*. This word used in Exercise 9 comes from the Latin *mille*, or "thousand," and *ennium* (from *annus*), or "year." So a *millennium* is a period of a thousand years. More generally, the word means a period of happiness and freedom from life's ills.

Exercise 9 **Choosing the Correct Verb**

Underline the verb in parentheses that agrees with the subject.

1. *The Trojan Women* (<u>is</u>, are) a play by Euripedes, an ancient Greek dramatist.

2. A thousand years (<u>is</u>, are) called a millennium.

3. Every chimpanzee, ape, and gorilla (<u>has</u>, have) flexible hands and feet.

4. Statistics (<u>is</u>, are) the branch of mathematics that deals with collecting, classifying, and organizing data.

5. Many a poet and novelist (<u>writes</u>, write) all night.

6. The herd of goats (<u>spends</u>, spend) all summer in the mountains.

7. Sometimes election news (<u>reaches</u>, reach) the public before polls close.

8. A committee of congressional representatives (<u>takes</u>, take) up pressing issues.

9. Four hundred thousand dollars (was, <u>were</u>) destroyed in the fire at the bank.

10. Mumps (<u>causes</u>, cause) fever and painful swelling of the salivary glands.

Exercise 10 **Writing Complete Sentences**

On a separate piece of paper, write a complete sentence for each numbered item, using the word or phrase as the subject of the sentence. Use present-tense verbs and check your sentences for correct subject-verb agreement. Read your sentences aloud to yourself for extra practice in hearing the sound of correct agreement. Students' sentences will vary.

EXAMPLE   team

The team has only one game left in the season.

1. committee
2. audience
3. every man and woman
4. ten minutes
5. *Cats!* (by Andrew Lloyd Webber)
6. mathematics
7. three months
8. scissors
9. team
10. *Grimm's Fairy Tales*

Challenge students to write a fun paragraph using all ten words or phrases. Allow time in class for students to read their paragraphs aloud.

Revising and Editing Worksheet 1

Read the following paragraphs carefully. Correct errors in subject-verb agreement. Make any other changes that you think will improve the paragraphs. **Hint:** Watch out for sentence fragments, spelling mistakes, and punctuation errors.

¹*Great Expectations* are one of Charles Dickens's most popular novels. ²It's main character is named Pip. ³Pip's parents is dead, and the boy lives with his bad-tempered sister and her kindly husband Joe, the village blacksmith. ⁴The family live on the edge of a marsh. ⁵The novel open when Pip find an escaped convict in a graveyard. ⁶The convict orders Pip to bring him food and a file to remove his chains. ⁷Later, there is two escaped convicts fighting, and the police arrests them both.

⁸Soon the wealthy Miss Havisham commands Pip to play with Estella. ⁹A girl who live with her. ¹⁰Pip falls in love with Estella, who treats him cruelly. ¹¹Many years goes by. ¹²Young Pip become an apprentice blacksmith. ¹³Suddenly, a lawyer announces that Pip has received a great deal of money from an anonymous benefactor. ¹⁴Pip go to London—with great expectations—to become a gentleman.

¹⁵Many an adventure and misfortune befall Pip in London. ¹⁶Pip abandons Joe, but Joe is ever faithful. ¹⁷News of Pip's illness reach Joe. ¹⁸Joe hurries to London to nurse the penniless Pip.

¹⁹*Great Expectations* were published in weekly installments from 1860 to 1861 in a magazine that Dickens edited. ²⁰To keep readers interested, there are a great deal of suspense and mystery in the novel. ²¹When Dickens's friends complained that the novel's original ending were to unhappy. ²²Dickens rewrote the ending. ²³In the revised version. ²⁴Pip and Estella meets again. ²⁵They lives happily ever after.

Students' revisions will vary. See teacher pages for assessment rubrics. Students who have read *Great Expectations* may wish to expand this worksheet into an essay for extra credit.

Revising and Editing Worksheet 2

Read the following paragraphs carefully. Correct errors in subject-verb agreement. Make any other changes that you think will improve the paragraphs. **Hint:** Watch out for sentence fragments, spelling mistakes, and punctuation errors. Work with a partner or small group to revise these paragraphs. Write your revised report on a separate piece of paper and compare your response with those made by other pairs or groups of classmates.

¹In *The Odyssey*, the ancient Greek poet Homer tell a tail about Odysseus, the king of Ithaca. ²(*Ulysses* is the ancient Roman name for *Odysseus*.) ³Odysseus with his men head home to Ithaca when the Trojan War ends. ⁴They has spent ten years fighting the Trojans. ⁵They are eager to return to Ithaca. ⁶There journey home takes ten years. ⁷Because of their many adventures. ⁸In the end only Odysseus remain alive. ⁹The one-eyed monster Cyclops, the Sirens, and Scylla and Charybdis is just a few of the obstacles Odysseus and his men faces on their journey home.

¹⁰For twenty years, Odysseus's wife and son wait for his return. ¹¹Telemachus, who is just a baby when his father leaves, is all ready a young man. ¹²No one know if Odysseus is dead or alive. ¹³Many doubts that he is alive and urges his wife, Penelope, to remarry. ¹⁴Many a young man and old man camps out in Odysseus's castle. ¹⁵They argues and eats a lot. ¹⁶While waiting for Penelope to choose one of them for her new husband.

¹⁷But Penelope plays a clever trick. ¹⁸She say that before she remarries, she must finish weaving a burial cloth (a shroud) for her father-in-law. ¹⁹Penelope spends every day at her loom weaving the shroud. ²⁰Every night she undoes what she has woven. ²¹Penelope wait loyally for her husband's return.

²²The climax of *The Odyssey* comes when Odysseus finally returns to Ithaca. ²³He is disguised as a beggar, but his faithful dog and his old nurse recognizes him. ²⁴He reveals his true identity to Telemachus. ²⁵Together they plans revenge on the noisy, boastful suitors. Students' revisions will vary. See, teacher pages for assessment rubrics. Students who have read *The Odyssey* may wish to share their favorite episode with the class.

Chapter Review

Exercise A Choosing the Correct Verb

Choose the verb in parentheses that agrees with the subject.

1. The military (uses, use) camouflage to disguise and protect troops, ships, and weapons.

2. Soldiers in the jungle (wears, wear) mottled green and brown and sometimes (covers, cover) their helmets with foliage.

3. Colors and patterns (helps, help) animals hide from enemies.

4. Some moths or butterflies (looks, look) like damaged leaves.

5. The Indian leaf butterfly (becomes, become) almost invisible on a pile of leaves.

6. Every chameleon (has, have) the ability to change its color.

7. Many a snake and insect also (has, have) patterns and colors that (acts, act) as a disguise.

8. Some creatures (imitates, imitate) the color and pattern of a poisonous species.

9. Knowing that one black-and-white butterfly (tastes, taste) bad, hungry birds (avoid, avoids) the look-alike species.

10. (Is, Are) there ever times when you (wish, wishes) you had camouflage?

Exercise B Editing a Paragraph

For each mistake in subject-verb agreement in the following paragraph, cross out the incorrect verb, and write the correct verb above it. **Hint:** Not every sentence contains an error; some sentences have more than one error.

¹Every year, many new students from other countries ~~arrives~~ [arrive] in our school. ²Jorge and his family ~~comes~~ [come] from Cuba. ³Jorge and his father, who was a political prisoner in Cuba, both ~~works~~ [work] in the same restaurant. ⁴Jorge ~~work~~ [works] after school, and both his father and he ~~works~~ [work] on the weekends. ⁵Marta and her cousin Isabel ~~is~~ [are] from the Dominican Republic. ⁶They are looking for after-school jobs. ⁷Marta ~~live~~ [lives] with her family in an apartment across the street from the drugstore where Marta's mother works. ⁸Marta ~~study~~ [studies] hard and gets good grades. ⁹She ~~say~~ [says] that she wants to become a doctor some day, especially to help children. ¹⁰Francia ~~comes~~ [comes] from

El Salvador, and Van and his family ~~is~~ [are] from Vietnam. [11]I ~~likes~~ [like] learning about all of these countries from my new friends. [12]I especially ~~likes~~ [like] sampling the foods they ~~brings~~ [bring] for us to taste.

Exercise C Writing Complete Sentences

On a separate piece of paper, write a complete sentence for each numbered item. Begin your sentence with the given word or group of words. Use present-tense verbs and check your sentences for correct subject-verb agreement. Students' sentences will vary. See sample sentence given below.

1. One of the essential ingredients in. . . salsa is hot peppers.
2. Pickles and ice cream. . .
3. Neither Luisa nor her little sister. . .
4. Twenty-four dollars and ninety-six cents. . .
5. Alex, Pat, and I. . .
6. Many an argument and a disagreement. . .
7. A group of students. . .
8. Where. . . ?
9. There are. . .
10. Carla or her brothers. . .
11. On top of the bookcase. . .
12. Either Jeff or his two sisters. . .
13. Everyone in all my classes. . .
14. Few of the questions. . .
15. Mathematics or statistics. . .
16. *Romeo and Juliet* by Shakespeare. . .
17. Today's bad news about the weather
18. Both she and I. . .
19. Among my favorite movies. . .
20. Every man, woman, and child. . .

Exercise D Writing a Description

Imagine that you are standing in the doorway of a room. You might choose your favorite room in your home or a room in a museum. Using present-tense verbs, write a paragraph describing what you see for a friend who has never been in the room. Include specific details of colors and objects such as furniture, decorations, and clothing. Make some notes before you start writing, and plan your description. You might begin by considering these questions.

• What is the main impression you get from the room?
• What do you see first? What is the biggest object in the room?
• Which objects are most important to you? Why?
• Is the room brightly lit or in shadows?

Students' paragraphs will vary. Encourage students to write creatively so their descriptions will make someone want to visit their room. You may wish to have students describe their ideal room.

Using Pronouns

Direct students to chapter-specific portfolio projects on Sadlier-Oxford's website.

STUDENT WRITING
Persuasive Essay

Security Guards' Training Beneficial to Students
by Damian Acosta
high school student, Coral Gables, Florida

They like to roam around campus and monitor your every move. When you're in the midst of a conversation among a herd of friends, they'll weave their way around bodies, break up the weekly gossip session, and tell you to get to class.

Those are just the smallest of tasks for the Coral Gables security guards.

You probably ask yourself: Are these guys a group of ex-convicts, terrorists, or car-jackers? [In fact, they're] not. In the long, bothersome process of becoming a security guard, they must first be approved by Miami-Dade County Public Schools and meet certain requirements before administrators even grant them a job interview.

First, the county researches the applicants' private lives and compiles background information on their pasts. If all goes well, [the applicants] advance to Round Two: the urine sample. The slightest trace of the margarita they may have drunk last month could cost them the job. Now school administrators are able to draft them.

At this point, security guards basically undergo training and attend workshops just like regular teachers do. They learn to deal with situations or emergencies that may occur in school and also how to treat students. Recognizing potential suspects or intruders who may cause a threat to campus life is also part of their training.

Violence and forms of vandalism on campus have noticeably diminished, say the guards. People scrapping, sword-fighting, or even thumb-wrestling have become unheard of.

In addition, car break-ins have declined since last year's covert operation on the notorious "strip." The plan involved a security guard who was parked on the strip in an unmarked car. [As he was] scanning the lot, [he] witnessed a break-in. He notified the police, and a car chase ensued. Unfortunately, the police never captured the suspects, but the incident decreased the frequency of car vandalism.

Instead of us nagging, whining, and complaining about the constant hassles we put up with, we should be more appreciative of their effort.

The thesis statement of this persuasive essay is contained in the title. The writer begins with a buildup of negative impressions of his school's security guards and then demolishes those impressions with background information, details, evidence, and an example to support his thesis. He ends the essay with a call to action.

In this chapter you'll learn about pronouns. As you reread the essay above, notice how the writer avoids repetition by using pronouns effectively.

Allow time for students to discuss the student writing. Suggest that they identify its strengths and propose possible improvements. Use the model to introduce the concepts in the chapter.

Using Subject Pronouns

Subject Pronouns	
SINGULAR	PLURAL
I, you, he, she, it	we, you, they

◗ Use one of these subject pronouns when the pronoun functions as the subject (s) of a sentence or a clause.

     S   S
Mitsuko and **I** are designing a time capsule.

    S
We will present our design to the student council.

◗ Use a subject pronoun when the pronoun functions as the predicate nominative of a sentence or clause.

Remember: A **predicate nominative** (PN) is a noun or pronoun that follows a form of *be* and renames or identifies the subject.

                      PN   PN   PN
The committee members are Mitsuko, Howard, and **I**.

                                      PN   PN
The persons in charge of the project are Kevin and **she**.

 You probably use subject pronouns correctly when the pronoun is alone. Watch out for compound subjects, as in the first example above.

Exercise 1 **Choosing the Correct Pronoun**

Underline the pronoun in parentheses that correctly completes each sentence.

EXAMPLE   The persons who thought of a time capsule are Soia and (him, <u>he</u>).

1. Julio and (her, <u>she</u>) wrote to the International Time Capsule Society (ITCS).

2. (Them, <u>They</u>) sent us information about time capsules.

3. (Him and me, <u>He and I</u>) will find a place to bury the capsule.

4. The ones who register our capsule with the ITCS are (us, <u>we</u>).

5. Noam, Helena, and (him, <u>he</u>) are in charge of publicity.

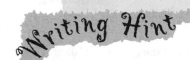

Writing Hint

If someone asks, "Who's there?" you probably answer, "It's me," not "It's I." But in speeches, in essays, and on grammar tests, be sure to use a subject pronoun when the pronoun comes after a form of *be*: "It is **I**." "It is **we**."

Step by Step

To decide which pronoun to use:

Laura and (me, I) want to borrow a CD.

1. Say the sentence with just the pronoun.

   Me want to borrow a CD. [sounds wrong]

   I want to borrow a CD. [sounds right]

2. Use the pronoun that sounds right in the compound subject.

   Laura and **I** want to borrow a CD.

6. Terra and (them, <u>they</u>) are picking objects for the capsule.

7. Our advisors for the project are Mr. Mendez and (<u>she</u>, her).

8. (Us, <u>We</u>) will direct that the capsule be sealed until the year 3500.

9. The student who will write the sealing ceremony is (<u>he</u>, him).

10. Delores and (him, <u>he</u>) are in charge of our reunion in twenty-five years.

Exercise 2 **Editing a Paragraph**

Edit the following paragraph to correct all errors in pronoun usage.

¹Husan, Luisa, and ~~me~~ [I] presented a report about time capsules. ²~~Her~~ [She] and Husan talked about Dr. Thornwell Jacobs, the president of Oglethorpe University in Atlanta. ³The person who built the Crypt of Civilization was he. ⁴On May 28, 1940, ~~him~~ [he] and others sealed the crypt, an underground room the size of a swimming pool, at Oglethorpe University in Atlanta. ⁵The other scientists and ~~him~~ [he] left instructions not to open the crypt until May 28, 8113. ⁶In their report, Luisa and ~~him~~ [he] described some of the objects sealed in the crypt. ⁷Dr. Jacobs and ~~them~~ [they] placed newsreels, records, newspaper articles, a Donald Duck doll, a set of Lincoln logs, and many other objects in the crypt to reveal American life in the 1940s. ⁸Husan and ~~her~~ [she] said that probably ten thousand time capsules have been buried, but most have been lost. ⁹The students who talked about other time capsules were Luisa and ~~me~~ [I]. ¹⁰~~Her~~ [She] and ~~me~~ [I] described the 1947 Notre Dame capsule filled with bacteria, insects, and viruses.

Exercise 3 **Write What You Think**

Get together with a small group of classmates to discuss the tasks involved with creating your own time capsule. Write a paragraph answering the questions below. Include details about who will do which jobs and what you plan to put in the capsule. When you finish writing, check to see that you have used subject pronouns correctly.

1. What objects will you put in the time capsule?
2. Where will you bury the capsule?
3. When will you want it to be opened?

Paragraphs will vary. Give students full credit if they have expressed themselves clearly. They should also have written grammatically complete sentences that begin with a capital letter and end with an appropriate end punctuation mark.

Using Object Pronouns

Object Pronouns	
SINGULAR	**PLURAL**
me, you, him, her, it	us, you, them

● Use an object pronoun when the pronoun functions as the direct object (DO) or indirect object (IO) of a sentence or a clause.

DO   DO

Jana told Derek and **me** about her homing pigeons.

IO   DO

She showed **us** several of her favorite pigeons.

● Use an object pronoun (OP) when the pronoun functions as the object of a preposition in a sentence.

OP

One of her pigeons delivered a message to Ana and **me**.

OP

For Jana and **us**, the pigeons arrive faster than mail.

When an object is compound, use the Step-by-Step approach you learned on page 207. Test each pronoun alone, and say the sentence aloud to yourself. Your ear will tell you which pronoun to use.

Exercise 4 Editing Sentences

Edit the following sentences for the use of subject and object pronouns. Cross out a pronoun that is used incorrectly, and write the correct one above it. If a sentence is correct, write *C*. **Hint:** First, check to see what function the pronoun performs in the sentence.

EXAMPLE   Zeeshan and ~~her~~ [*she*] showed him and ~~we~~ [*us*] the list of birds they've seen.

Their very long list of birds amazed him and us. *C*

1. Brian and ~~me~~ [I] saw Kathy and ~~she~~ [her] at the Audubon Christmas Count.
2. Al gave Issa and ~~she~~ [her] a copy of *Field Guide to Birds*.
3. Elaine and he gave an Audubon field card to Jim and ~~I~~ [me].
4. Jenny showed ~~she~~ [her] and ~~I~~ [me] three different species of heron.

Editing Tip

Be sure to use an object pronoun when the pronoun functions as the object of a preposition. Avoid these common errors:

RIGHT between you and **me**

WRONG between you and I

RIGHT for Carla and **him**

WRONG for Carla and he

Step by Step

To decide whether to use a subject or an object pronoun:

1. Decide what function the pronoun performs in the sentence.

2. If the pronoun is a subject or a predicate nominative, choose the subject pronoun.

3. If the pronoun is a direct object, an indirect object, or the object of a preposition, choose the object pronoun.

5. She told ~~he~~ and ~~I~~ about the fieldfare, a bird that breeds in Greenland.
   him   me

6. The fieldfare is an "accidental" sighting here, according to him and her. C

7. Christy sent Paolo and ~~I~~ some sketches of sandpipers.
   me

8. ~~Her~~ and her aunt drew them and other shorebirds.
   She

9. I asked Myrza and ~~he~~ about their sightings of penguins.
   him

10. "We saw two species of ~~they~~ and other Antarctic birds," she said.
    them

11. We joined a group of amateur bird watchers with Roger and ~~he~~.
    him

12. The leader of our group and ~~them~~ count birds in this area every year.
    they

13. The group will count each species of birds ~~them~~ see.
    they

14. This year, we saw more species of birds than ~~them~~ saw.
    they

15. Our bird count will help ~~she~~ and the Audubon Society keep track of migrations from one year to the next.
    her

Exercise 5 Choosing the Correct Pronoun

Underline the pronoun in parentheses that correctly completes each sentence.

EXAMPLE   The foul ball was heading right toward Rachel and (I, <u>me</u>).

1. Neither Leah nor (<u>he</u>, him) brought a poncho to the game.

2. The coach gave (they and we, <u>them and us</u>) team T-shirts.

3. Without Brenda and (she, <u>her</u>), we wouldn't have a water polo team.

4. Ms. Juringus coached Ash and (he, <u>him</u>) every day.

5. Just between you and (I, <u>me</u>), Owen is the best discus thrower in the state.

6. Nishan and his brother beat Tom and (she, <u>her</u>) in table tennis.

7. (<u>He and I</u>, him and me) cheered Brandon and (they, <u>them</u>) after every goal.

8. Joey threw the ball toward (he and I, <u>him and me</u>), but (<u>we</u>, us) both missed it.

9. Did you watch Brett and (she, <u>her</u>) in the semifinals?

10. According to Karla and (they, <u>them</u>), Tom's backhand is weak.

11. When the match was over the coach took (<u>them and us</u>, they and we) back to school.

12. The extra tickets are for Fiona and (I, <u>me</u>).

13. At the seventh inning, (us, <u>we</u>) stretched.

14. The stadium was crowded so Tony and (<u>he</u>, him) had trouble finding their seat.

15. Bette and (me, <u>I</u>) have plans to go to the playoffs next week.

Who or Whom?

Subject Form
who

Object Form
whom

🔹 Use the subject pronoun *who* when the pronoun functions as a subject or as a predicate nominative in a sentence or in a clause.

 Who was chosen as the Most Valuable Player?

 [*Who* is the subject of the sentence.]

 The player **who** was chosen as the MVP is the Bulls' forward.

 [*Who* is the subject of the adjective clause.]

You can check your choice of pronoun by replacing *who/whom* with *he/him* or *she/her*. If *he* sounds right in the sentence, use the subject pronoun *who*. If *him* sounds right, choose the object pronoun *whom*. You'll need to change a question into a statement to test for the right pronoun.

 (Who, Whom) did you call?

 [Change the question into a statement.]

 You did call (who, whom).

 [Substitute *he, him* for *who, whom*.]

 You did call (he, him).

 [When you try out each pronoun, you will hear that *him* sounds right. Therefore, the sentence requires an object pronoun.]

 Whom did you call? [*Whom* is the object pronoun.]

🔹 Use the object pronoun *whom* when the pronoun functions as the direct object, indirect object, or object of a preposition in a sentence or in a clause.

 Please give this note to the first person **whom** you see.

 [*Whom* is the direct object of the adjective clause *you see whom*.]

When you are choosing *who* or *whom*, ignore parenthetical expressions (such as *I think* and *I hope*) that interrupt a subordinate clause.

 He is the scientist (who, whom), I think, won the Nobel Peace Prize.

 [*Who* is the subject of the clause *who won the Nobel Peace Prize*.]

P.S. Most people don't use *whom* when they talk. In formal writing and speaking, however, and on grammar tests, use *whom* whenever the pronoun functions as an object.

Step by Step

When you need to choose between *who* and *whom:*

1. Decide what function the pronoun performs.

2. Use *who* if the pronoun functions as a subject or a predicate nominative.

3. Use *whom* if the pronoun functions as a direct object, an indirect object, or the object of a preposition.

Enriching Your Vocabulary

The Latin noun *artificium* gives us the English noun *artifice*, meaning "a clever skill" or "trickery." A painter uses *artifice* to create the illusion of a three-dimensional scene on a flat canvas. And, as used in Exercise 6, only an expert may be able to tell the difference between an *artificial* diamond and the real thing.

Choosing the Correct Pronoun

Underline the pronoun in parentheses that correctly completes each sentence.

EXAMPLE   Harry Harlow was a psychologist (<u>who</u>, whom) did research on baby monkeys.

1. He and his wife, (who, <u>whom</u>) he worked with, raised monkeys for experiments.
2. Newborn monkeys (<u>who</u>, whom) were alone in cages clung to cloth diapers.
3. The Harlows, (<u>who</u>, whom) studied infant love, created artificial wire "mothers."
4. (<u>Who</u>, Whom) can guess whether the newborns clung to a cloth-covered "mother" or a bare wire one?
5. The Harlows are only two of the scientists (<u>who</u>, whom) have studied animal behavior.
6. Do you know anyone (<u>who</u>, whom) objects to using animals in experiments?
7. The Harlows, (who, <u>whom</u>) psychologists praised for their experiments, applied their findings to human babies.
8. Human newborns, (<u>who</u>, whom) are more helpless than monkeys, need warmth and contact.
9. (Who, <u>Whom</u>) would you consult for advice on raising children?
10. Would you ask a relative (who, <u>whom</u>) you trust or read a book?

Editing a Paragraph

Edit the following paragraph to correct all errors in pronoun usage.

[1]Elaine's friend Gwen objects to scientists who use animals as research subjects. [2]She and her friends, ~~who~~ whom you may have met, are animal rights activists. [3]They have written to government representatives ~~whom~~ who, they believe, should pass laws protecting animals. [4]They especially oppose researchers ~~whom~~ who, for whatever reason, work with dogs and cats. [5]They have also demonstrated against research scientists who, they say, treat monkeys cruelly. [6]Gwen and her friends, many of ~~who~~ whom are vegetarians, oppose killing animals for fur. [7]Doctors who test medical procedures on animals disagree. [8]Laboratory animals benefit people ~~who~~ whom, they say, are desperately ill. [9]Doctors apply what they learn from animal experiments to save the lives of people who need treatment. [10]~~Who~~ Whom do you agree with on animal rights issues?

Extend this lesson by having motivated students write a letter to their senators explaining their views on using animals for research.

Hint

When *who* or *whom* appears in a subordinate clause, focus on how the word functions within the clause only.

Hint

Some sentences contain no errors.

Appositives and Incomplete Constructions

Remember that an **appositive** identifies or explains the noun or pronoun that comes right before it.

🔹 For a pronoun appositive, use a subject pronoun if the word that the appositive refers to is a subject or a predicate nominative. Use an object pronoun if the word that the appositive refers to is a direct or indirect object or the object of a preposition.

The strongest singers, Evan and **she,** have solos.
[The pronoun *she* refers to *singers,* the subject of the sentence.]
The soloists are the strongest singers, Evan and **she.**
[The pronoun *she* refers to *singers,* the predicate nominative in this sentence.]
The director gave the solos to the strongest singers, Evan and **her.**
[The pronoun *her* refers to *singers,* which now is the object of the preposition *to.*]
The director gave the strongest singers, Evan and **her,** the solos.
[The pronoun *her* refers to *singers,* which this time is the indirect object of the sentence.]

🔹 When the pronoun *we* or *us* is followed by a noun appositive, choose the pronoun form you would use if the pronoun were alone in the sentence.

We girls challenged the boys to a chess match.
[You would say, "*We* challenged the boys. . . ."]
The news of the strike shocked **us** baseball fans.
[You would say, "The news . . . shocked *us.*"]
Ms. Grunwald gave **us** students another chance.
[You would say, "Ms. Grunwald gave *us* another chance."]

🔹 In an incomplete construction, choose the pronoun form you would use if the sentence were completed.

An **incomplete construction** omits some words, which are understood. Usually, an incomplete construction is a comparison. It comes at the end of a sentence and starts with the word *than* or *as.* In the following incomplete constructions, the omitted words appear in brackets.

Sara is two years older <u>than</u> **he** [is].
She is not nearly as tall <u>as</u> **I** [am].
Carlos likes to dance more <u>than</u> **she** [likes to dance].

Editing Tip

Make sure that an appositive is necessary and that it identifies or explains the noun before it. Don't use a double subject.

My sister ~~she~~ won the prize.

Writing Hint

Some incomplete constructions have two very different meanings, depending on the pronoun you choose.

Tammy likes Dave more than [she likes] **me.**
Tammy likes Dave more than **I** [like Dave].

Exercise 8 Choosing the Correct Pronoun

Underline the pronoun in parentheses that correctly completes each sentence.

EXAMPLE   Len, an identical twin, is four minutes older than (he, <u>him</u>).

1. Tuoyo does not write as legibly as (<u>she</u>, her).

2. Aunt Bernice and (him, <u>he</u>) recall a time before television.

3. We petitioned our representatives, Ms. Watts and (he, <u>him</u>).

4. A collie waited with the crossing guards, Lenora and (he, <u>him</u>).

5. The crowd applauded the dancers, Fiona and (she, <u>her</u>).

6. Perry exercises more than either John or (<u>I</u>, me).

7. No one else is as funny as my friends Stacy and (<u>he</u>, him).

8. Awards were given to two students, (he and I, <u>him and me</u>).

9. Nora is a much stronger swimmer than (<u>he</u>, him).

10. Are you as unhappy about moving as (<u>I</u>, me)?

Exercise 9 Editing Sentences

Edit the following sentences for errors with pronouns. Cross out a pronoun that is incorrect, and write the correct pronoun above it. If a sentence is correct, write *C* after it.

EXAMPLE   Hilary has painted more portraits than ~~me~~. (I)

1. Please give ~~we~~ students more information about the contest. (us)

2. The two winners, ~~him~~ (he) and ~~me~~ (I), will play in the finals.

3. Joey and Theresa have been dating longer than ~~us~~ (we).

4. The new rules apply to all of us students. C

5. No one else plays the guitar as well as ~~him~~ (he).

6. The last ones to leave, Theo and ~~me~~ (I), locked the gate.

7. Our best players, Ryan and ~~him~~ (he), each scored twenty points.

8. Melissa has always read more books than ~~me~~ (I).

9. I wrote to my favorite cousins, Leslie and ~~she~~ (her).

10. The first three rows are reserved for ~~we~~ (us) family members.

Agreement with Antecedent

A pronoun must agree with its **antecedent,** the word that the pronoun refers to.

🔹 Use a plural pronoun to refer to two or more antecedents joined by *and.*

> Priya, Lisa, and Frank are celebrating **their** birthdays today.

🔹 Use a singular pronoun to refer to two or more singular antecedents joined by *or* or *nor.*

> Either Paul or Danny has left **his** backpack under the table.

🔹 Use a singular pronoun when the sentence has a compound subject but refers to only one person.

> My teacher and mentor began **her** career at Princeton University.

🔹 Use a singular pronoun when the antecedent is one of the singular indefinite pronouns at right:

> Each of the girls interviewed **her** grandmother.

When a singular indefinite pronouns refers to both males and females, use *his or her.*

> Everyone must turn in **his or her** paper on Friday.
> Some texts allow the use of *their* in this case.

Singular Indefinite Pronouns

anybody	anyone
each	either
everybody	everyone
neither	nobody
no one	one
somebody	someone

Refer to Lesson 9.2 for more on agreement with such indefinite pronouns as *none* and *any.*

Writing Hint

Sometimes *his or her* sounds awkward. You can avoid this construction by making the subject plural or by rephrasing the sentence.

Students must turn in **their** papers on Friday.

Papers are due on Friday.

Exercise 10 Choosing the Correct Pronoun

Underline the pronoun in parentheses that agrees with its antecedent.

> EXAMPLE   Cara and Jim packed (his or her, <u>their</u>) lunches.

1. One of the girls will read (<u>her</u>, their) poem at the assembly.
2. Neither of the boys brought (<u>his</u>, their) flashlight.
3. Jeff's mother and father congratulated (his, <u>their</u>) son.
4. Either Hannah or Dot rides (<u>her</u>, their) bike to school.
5. Someone has left (<u>his or her</u>, their) keys in the door.
6. Did Alex or Dominic use (<u>his</u>, their) calculator on the test?
7. Each of the girls wore (<u>her</u>, their) new school uniform.
8. Jeannie, Bethany, and she wrote (her, <u>their</u>) résumés.
9. Neither Noel nor Matt has finished (<u>his</u>, their) research yet.
10. Bryan and Annette practiced (his or her, <u>their</u>) speeches.

Enriching Your Vocabulary

The English noun *résumé* means "a summary," and comes from the past participle of the French verb *résumer,* which means "to sum up or recapitulate." When you look for a job, you need a written *résumé* of your work experience.

Revising and Editing Worksheet

Work with a partner or small group to improve the following report. Correct errors with pronouns, and make any other changes you think will improve the report. Write your revised report on a separate piece of paper, and compare your response with those made by other pairs or groups of classmates.

[1]The four youngest Brontë children, whom were destined to become famous, grew up in a gloomy parsonage. [2]It was on the windy moors. [3]The moors were in northern England. [4]Their father was a minister, their house was next to a cemetery and his church.

■ For a list of revising strategies, look in Composition Lesson 1.3.

[5]Branwell was the only son. [6]Him and his three younger sisters, whom were Charlotte, Emily, and Anne, did not go to school. [7]They studied at home, and they entertained themselves by making up stories. [8]About soldiers and an imaginary kingdom. [9]Branwell and them wrote the stories in tiny handwriting on little pieces of paper. [10]Branwell, whom drew well, illustrated the stories.

[11]When all of they grew up, Branwell, who, in the sisters' opinion, was the most talented, drank too much and lost his jobs. [12]Each of the sisters tried their hand at writing. [13]The sisters' first book, a collection of poems, was published in 1846. [14]They used the pen names of three men—Currer, Ellis, and Acton Bell. [15]Because it was hard for women to get her writings published.

[16]Charlotte wrote *Jane Eyre* in the dining room at the parsonage the novel is about a poor young governess, or teacher, whom wins the love of her wealthy employer. [17]Emily wrote only one novel, a passionate love story called *Wuthering Heights*. [18]Anne also published a novel, but her was less successful than them.

[19]Us readers are lucky that the Brontë sisters wrote their novels. [20]Charlotte and them died almost 150 years ago, but her novels are still popular among we readers today. Students' revisions will vary. See teacher pages for revising and editing suggestions. Encourage students to investigate the Brontë novels and poems.

Chapter Review

Exercise A Using Subject and Object Pronouns

Fill in each blank with the correct form of a pronoun that makes sense in the sentence. Make sure that the word you add is a pronoun, not a noun.

¹Next week, Ilan, Merry, and __I__ will present our multimedia report on the Underground Railroad. ²__We__ students narrowed our topic to Harriet Tubman, __who__ was a conductor on the Underground Railroad. ³Ilan has written a script, which the three of __us__ will perform. ⁴__We__ will act out scenes from the life of Tubman, beginning when __she__ was a child. ⁵It was then that an overseer, or supervisor, struck __her__ in the forehead with a two-pound weight. ⁶Because of this injury, a sudden deep sleep sometimes overcame __her__, even when __she__ was leading slaves to freedom. ⁷Tubman escaped from slavery in 1849, but __she__ returned to the South nineteen times in ten years to lead more than three hundred slaves to freedom. ⁸__She__ and Sojourner Truth, __who__ also had been a slave, gave speeches about abolishing slavery. ⁹Merry, __who__ has made a costume, will read from Sojourner Truth's autobiography. ¹⁰Then the three of __us__ will talk about some Internet sites, where Ilan and __I__ found information about Tubman.

Exercise B Choosing the Correct Pronoun

Underline the pronoun that correctly completes each sentence.

1. A Greek myth tells of Arachne, (<u>who</u>, whom) challenged Athena.

2. Athena, (who, <u>whom</u>) the Greeks worshiped, was the goddess of weaving.

3. Arachne, a mortal, boasted that she was a better weaver than (<u>she</u>, her).

4. The goddess warned Arachne about (she, <u>her</u>) boasting.

5. They held a contest to see (<u>who</u>, whom) could weave the more beautiful cloth.

6. Athena's tapestry showed the gods punishing mortals (<u>who</u>, whom) angered them.

7. Arachne's cloth showed mortals (who, <u>whom</u>) the gods had fallen in love with.

8. Arachne's tapestry was so perfect that jealous Athena hit (she, <u>her</u>).

9. The goddess turned Arachne into a spider, (<u>who</u>, whom) kept on weaving.

10. Scientists named spiders *arachnids* after (<u>her</u>, she).

Exercise C **Correcting Pronoun Errors**

Correct all pronoun errors in the following sentences. If a sentence is correct, write *C*. **Hint:** A sentence may have more than one mistake.

1. Ms. Li coached Justin and ~~she~~ [her] for a state math contest.

2. The sponsors, Caleb and ~~her~~ [she], presented their proposal to ~~we~~ [us] drama club members.

3. Bethany's band plays reggae music better than ~~them~~ [they].

4. Jack has more work experience than either ~~her~~ [she] or ~~me~~ [I].

5. Please tell the judges, Alexsa and me, about your project. C

6. Megan and ~~her~~ [she] were telling Jenna and ~~I~~ [me] about that movie.

7. The bus left without the trip leaders, Charlie and me. C

8. No one else in our gym class can jump as high as ~~her~~ [she].

9. ~~Us~~ [We] writers for the school paper work more hours than ~~them~~ [they].

10. Everyone ~~who~~ [whom] we students elect serves on the council for a semester.

Exercise D **Agreement with Antecedents**

Fill in each blank with a pronoun that agrees with its antecedent(s).

1. Neither Sheila nor Abby has finished __her__ weekly chores.

2. Uncle Wei and Chen have __their__ own very different opinions.

3. One of the girls lent us __her__ compass for the hike.

4. Everyone in the camera club has __his or her__ own camera.

5. Does anyone in your class have __his or her__ driver's license yet?

6. Either Mike or David needs some help fixing __his__ computer.

7. Oleg, Jessica, and Kyle spend a lot of time in __their__ garden.

8. Anyone in the group can express __his or her__ opinion.

9. Someone left __his or her__ address book in the telephone booth.

10. Alan or Marc left __his__ homework on the bus.

Using Modifiers

STUDENT WRITING
Expository Essay

Driving Home the Point
by Anna Markee
high school student, Tacoma, Washington

The glass shattered as the hammer exploded off the car's windshield. Cheers went up from the crowd. Another blow left a crater in the car's front fender, and onlookers waved their hands to be next.

After months of planning, our celebration of "World No Tobacco Day" was off the ground. Many businesses in town had rejected my request to donate a car for the event, but perseverance paid off. With a little paint and some creativity, our donated vehicle closely resembled a tobacco-branded racecar.

The best thing about this event was the attention it generated from the media and the community. It really helped drive home the message that kids were tired of being targeted by the marketing ploys of big tobacco.

As an active antitobacco advocate, I have long understood the danger of the deceptive advertising techniques used by the tobacco industry. Several years ago, I worked with the Board of Health in my town to pass a "Truth in Tobacco Advertising" resolution to restrict all forms of outdoor advertising. I talked to many local policymakers about the impact this advertising has on kids, especially [about the fact] that kids I knew decided to try a cigarette because they were impressed by slick tobacco ads showing fun, exciting times.

I think it's really important to take a stand against tobacco. That's why I joined SMOOTH (Students Mobilizing Others Out of Tobacco Habits). We've done a lot of great projects and told a lot of kids about the dangers of tobacco. Now, if we could only break the chains of tobacco addiction as easily as we broke the windshield on our donated car.

The purpose of Anna's essay is to explain the reasons for World No Tobacco Day. The beginning of her essay is an attention grabber. She follows her opening with background information about the event, then she explains her own convictions about the tobacco industry. Her final sentence helps explain the link between smashing a car and smoking.

The adjectives and modifiers Anna uses help her communicate the commitment she has to her cause. In this chapter you'll learn more about how to use modifiers correctly to emphasize your own convictions.

Allow time for students to discuss the student writing. Suggest that they identify its strengths and propose possible improvements. Use the model to introduce the concepts in the chapter.

Degrees of Comparison

Suppose you want to compare the hotness of three mustards—one on a sandwich, one on a hot dog, and one on an egg roll. To express yourself, you'll need the three **degrees of comparison**: **positive**, **comparative**, and **superlative**.

POSITIVE   The mustard on my sandwich is **hot**.

COMPARATIVE The mustard on this hot dog is even **hotter**.

SUPERLATIVE The **hottest** mustard I ever tasted was in a Chinese restaurant.

Here are some rules for forming the comparative and superlative degrees.

🌶 **One-Syllable Modifiers** Add *-er* and *-est* to one-syllable modifiers. Sometimes it is necessary to double the final consonant first.

young, young**er**, young**est**   big, big**ger**, big**gest**

slow, slow**er**, slow**est**   tight, tight**er**, tight**est**

🌶 **Two-Syllable Modifiers** Add *-er* and *-est* to most two-syllable modifiers.

yellow**,** yellow**er**, yellow**est**   quiet, quiet**er**, quiet**est**

Sometimes an *-er* or *-est* modifier sounds clumsy. In these cases, use *more* and *most* to form the comparative and superlative degrees.

awkward**,** **more** awkward, **most** awkward

🌶 **-ly Adverbs** Use *more* and *most* for adverbs that end in *-ly.*

quickly, **more** quickly, **most** quickly

Watch out for adjectives that end in *-ly* like *ugly* or *lively.* Add *-er* and *-est* to form their comparisons.

🌶 **More Than Two Syllables** For modifiers of three syllables or more, use *more* and *most* to form the comparative and superlative degrees.

beautiful, **more** beautiful, **most** beautiful

responsible, **more** responsible, **most** responsible

🌶 **Decreasing Degrees** For all modifiers, use *less* and *least* for decreasing degrees of comparison regardless of number of syllables.

sturdy, **less** sturdy, **least** sturdy

🌶 **Irregular Modifiers** The modifiers shown at the top right form their degrees of comparison irregularly.

Irregular Degrees of Comparison

good well	better	best
bad badly ill	worse	worst
many much	more	most
little	less *or* lesser	least
far	farther	farthest

Enriching Your Vocabulary

Not every English word has its roots in another language. The origin of the verb *plod,* used in Exercise 1, is unknown. Some experts think the word is an example of onomatopoeia, that is, a word that imitates a sound, such as that of slow, weary footsteps. At the end of a marathon, many exhausted runners *plod* their way to the finish line.

Step by Step

To form the comparative and superlative degree of modifiers:

1. Count the number of syllables.

2. Apply the appropriate rule:
   one syllable = *-er* and *-est*
   two syllables = personal taste
   three syllables = *more* and *most*
   -ly adverbs = *more* and *most*

3. Memorize the irregular degrees of comparison.

Exercise 1 · Editing a Paragraph

Cross out any incorrect modifiers and write the correct form in the space above it. Make any other changes that are needed to improve the paragraph.

¹Fable writers around the world teach us lessons by telling stories. ²The ~~most~~ [oldest]

~~old~~ fables are found in *The Panchatantra* from India. ³Aesop, an ancient Greek,
wrote many of our ~~familiarest~~ [most familiar] fables. ⁴My ~~favoritest~~ [most favorite or favorite] Aesop fable tells of a race

between a tortoise and a hare. ⁵The tortoise moves so much more ~~slow~~ [slowly] than the

hare that the hare takes a nap in the middle of the race. ⁶But the tortoise plods

on without stopping and finishes more speedily than the hare. ⁷"The opinion of
the ~~most strong~~ [strongest] is always the ~~most good~~ [best]" is the moral, or lesson, of a fable by

Jean de La Fontaine, a seventeenth-century Frenchman. ⁸A ~~recenter~~ [more recent] fable writer

is the American James Thurber. ⁹One of Thurber's ~~entertainingest~~ [most entertaining] fables is about

a princess who must choose a husband. ¹⁰She chooses neither the ~~most kind~~ [kindest]
prince nor the ~~attractivest~~ [most attractive] but the one who gives her the ~~valuablest~~ [most valuable] gift.

Exercise 2 · Forming the Comparative and the Superlative

On a separate piece of paper, write the comparative and superlative degrees for each modifier.

1. comfortable
   more comfortable   most comfortable
2. good
   better   best
3. softly
   more softly   most softly
4. straight
   straighter   straightest
5. dangerous
   more dangerous   most dangerous

6. tensely
   more tensely   most tensely
7. unusual
   more unusual   most unusual
8. bad
   worse   worst
9. happy
   happier   happiest
10. ugly
    uglier   ugliest

Exercise 3 · Writing an Advertisement

Suppose you are the copywriter for an advertising agency. Make up a name for a new cereal, car, soap, toothpaste, soda, or movie. On a separate piece of paper, write an advertisement to persuade readers that this new product is better than any other of its kind. Use at least five comparative and superlative forms in your ad.   Students' ads will vary. Encourage creativity. You might allow time to have students videotape their advertisements and then present them to the class.

Using the Degrees of Comparison

◗ Use the comparative degree to compare two things. Use the superlative degree to compare three or more things.

COMPARATIVE   Ray is three days **older** than Allyson.

SUPERLATIVE   Ray is the **oldest** of four brothers.

◗ **Avoid Double Comparisons** Use either *more* (or *most*) or *-er* (or *-est*), but never use the word *more* (or *most*) and the suffix together.

INCORRECT   We tried to move more closer to see more better.

CORRECT   We tried to move **closer** to see **better**.

INCORRECT   Jed is the more younger of the two brothers.

CORRECT   Jed is the **younger** of the two brothers.

◗ **Avoid Illogical Comparisons** Use the word *other* or *else* to compare something with others in its group.

ILLOGICAL   Tony plays chess better than anyone in his family. [Tony is a member of his family. He cannot play chess better than himself.]

LOGICAL   Tony plays chess better than anyone **else** in his family.

ILLOGICAL   Chicago is larger than any city in Illinois.

LOGICAL   Chicago is larger than any **other** city in Illinois.

◗ **Avoid Unclear Comparisons** Add whatever words are necessary to make a comparison clear.

UNCLEAR   Jenny is more interested in sports than Duane.

CLEAR   Jenny is more interested in sports than Duane is.

   or Jenny is more interested in sports than she is in Duane.

Writing Hint

In conversation, you may hear someone use the superlative form when only two things are being compared:

Of the two restaurants, the one by the river is the **best**.

When you write standard English, however, use the comparative:

Of the two restaurants, the one by the river is **better**.

Exercise 4   **Editing Sentences**

Edit these sentences for the correct use of modifiers. If you find an error, rewrite the sentence correctly on a separate piece of paper. If a sentence is correct, write *C*. Hint: Some sentences have more than one error.

EXAMPLE   Teenagers have more accidents than any group of drivers.
   Teenagers have more accidents than any other group of drivers.

1. The most ~~likeliest~~ ^{likely} time for teenage accidents is after 11 P.M.

2. For drivers under twenty-five, car insurance is more ~~expensiver~~ ^{expensive} than

   for ~~more~~ older drivers.

3. Some teenagers say that insurance costs even more than car repairs. C

4. Jason, my ~~bestest~~ best friend, is the ~~older~~ oldest of three children.

5. At sixteen, he is a safer driver than anyone else in his family.

6. Jason likes driving more than his brother does.

7. Recently, some states have made their rules more difficult for their ~~most~~ youngest drivers.

8. My friend Stephanie, who is fifteen, is more ~~unhappier~~ unhappy than Jason about the state rules.

9. Stephanie, the ~~safer~~ safest person I know, must be at swim practice by 4:30 A.M.

10. She feels ~~worser~~ worse than her mother, who gets up at 4 A.M. to drive her.

Exercise 5 Write What You Think

Write what you think about these two laws, and give reasons to support your opinions.

• No one under seventeen can get a learner's permit for a driver's license. There are no exceptions.

• Drivers under eighteen cannot drive from 11 P.M. until 6 A.M. unless accompanied by a person over twenty-one years of age.

When you finish writing, check each sentence to make sure you've used modifiers correctly. Answers will vary. Give students full credit if they have stated an opinion and attempted to support their opinion.

Exercise 6 Writing a Paragraph

Exercises 5 & 6:
Students should
have written gra-
matically com-
plete sentences
that begin with a
capital letter and
end with an ap-
propriate end
punctuation mark.

Write a paragraph in which you compare two or more objects, people, animals, or places. Here are some possible topics: Students' paragraphs will vary.

two dogs or cats	three TV shows	three cars
two buildings	three movies	three friends

Include at least four comparative or superlative forms in your paragraph, and underline them.

Double Negatives

English has many words that express a negative meaning.

no	not (-n't)	none	nothing	never
no one	nobody	scarcely	hardly	

🖝 Avoid using two negative words together. Only one negative word is necessary to express a negative idea. Count the contraction *-n't* (for *not*) as a negative word.

INCORRECT	I couldn't never have finished without your help.
CORRECT	I could never have finished without your help.
CORRECT	I couldn't have finished without your help.

INCORRECT	Didn't nobody volunteer to do nothing?
CORRECT	Didn't anybody volunteer to do anything?
CORRECT	Did nobody volunteer to do anything?

INCORRECT	I haven't got no time for nothing except writing.
CORRECT	I have no time for anything but writing.
CORRECT	I haven't got time for anything but writing.
CORRECT	I have time for nothing but writing.

Note that in correcting a double negative you may need to change some words.

CHANGE	TO
nobody	anybody
never	ever
no one	anyone
nothing	anything
none	any

Note also that a double negative can usually be corrected in more than one way. Choose the way that sounds best to you.

Editing Tip

In colloquial speech, some people say *ain't* as a contraction for *am not*, *is not*, and *are not*. In formal writing, *ain't* is widely considered inappropriate.

Exercise 7 **Editing Misquoted Sayings**

You don't have to be familiar with the original sayings to fix all of the double negatives in these misquoted sayings. Eliminate or change words as necessary.   Corrected sentences will vary. Samples given.

EXAMPLE	Little Bo-Peep has lost her sheep, / And cannot ~~scarcely~~ tell where to find them. . . — Nursery rhyme

1. Don't ~~never~~ sell America short. —American saying, 1920s

2. There ~~ain't never~~ no such animal. —Cartoon caption, 1907, of a farmer looking at a circus camel

3. Don't ~~never~~ count ~~none of~~ your chickens before they're hatched.
   —Moral from an Aesop fable

4. The cunning seldom gain their ends; / The wise ~~aren't~~ ^{are} never without friends. —Moral from *The Fox and the Hen*

5. Jack Sprat ~~couldn't never~~ ^{could} eat no fat, / His wife ~~couldn't hardly~~ ^{could} eat no lean. . . —Nursery rhyme

6. Indeed your dancing days are done / Oh, Johnny, I ~~didn't never~~ hardly knew ye. —Irish folk song

7. Old soldiers ~~don't~~ never die; / They only fade away! —British World War I song

8. Fifty million Frenchmen can't ~~hardly~~ be wrong. —American saying during World War I

9. . . . All the king's horses / And all the king's men / Couldn't ~~never~~ put Humpty Dumpty back together again. —Nursery rhyme

10. A rolling stone ~~hardly~~ gathers no moss. —Folk saying

Exercise 8 **Editing a Paragraph**

Correct all errors involving negatives in the paragraph below. Read the paragraph aloud to help you find errors.

¹The exaggerated heros of tall tales ~~ain't~~ ^{are} nothing like ordinary human beings. ²For example, nobody ~~couldn't~~ ^{could} really be as strong or as tall as Paul Bunyan. ³Paul, the loggers' hero, didn't go ~~nowhere~~ ^{anywhere} without his giant blue ox, Babe. ⁴He ~~didn't think~~ ^{thought} nothing of cutting down twenty-three trees with a single swing of his ax. ⁵Pecos Bill, the cowboys' hero, didn't ~~scarcely~~ mind being raised by coyotes, for he learned to speak the languages of all the animals. ⁶It was Pecos Bill, the cowboys say, who ~~didn't have~~ ^{had} no problem lassoing a cyclone. ⁷He rode the bucking cyclone to Texas, which hadn't ~~hardly~~ gotten any rain for ages. ⁸People say there ~~wouldn't~~ ^{would} have been no Grand Canyon without Pecos Bill, for the cyclone's rain washed out the canyon. ⁹John Henry ~~wasn't~~ ^{was} no ordinary steel driver, ~~neither~~ ^{either}. ¹⁰He raced against a steam drill machine to see who could crush more rock. ¹¹He ~~hadn't~~ ^{had} scarcely won the race when he keeled right over and died.   Corrected paragraphs will vary but should eliminate double negatives. Accept all correct revisions. Sample answers are given.

Misplaced and Dangling Modifiers

◖ A **misplaced modifier** is a word, phrase, or clause that's in the wrong place. It modifies a different word than the one it's meant to modify.

Correct a misplaced modifier by moving it as close as possible to the word it is meant to modify.

MISPLACED	One morning I shot an elephant in my pyjamas.
CORRECT	In my pyjamas one morning, I shot an elephant.
MISPLACED	He wrote about the Loch Ness monster in his bedroom.
CORRECT	In his bedroom, he wrote about the Loch Ness monster.

◖ A **dangling modifier** is a word, phrase, or clause that doesn't logically modify any word in the sentence.

Correct a dangling modifier by rewording the sentence. Add a word or words that the phrase or clause can modify.

DANGLING	Upon turning ten, my family moved to Florida.
CORRECT	When I was ten, my family moved to Florida.
DANGLING	Hot and thirsty, the lemonade was refreshing.
CORRECT	Because I was hot and thirsty, the lemonade was refreshing.

Exercise 9 **Editing Sentences**

On a separate piece of paper, rewrite each sentence to correct all dangling and misplaced modifiers. If a sentence is correct, write *C.*

EXAMPLE   Walking toward the subway, the restaurant was closed.
Walking toward the subway, I saw that the restaurant was closed.
See Answer Key for sample answers.

1. We could see the mountains in the distance driving toward Colorado.

2. Scrambling wildly up the drapes, Jim tried to stop the kitten.

3. To arrive at the airport in plenty of time, the alarm was set for 6 A.M.

4. Before leaving for the movies, pictures of the wedding were shown.

5. While eating dinner, the power went off.

6. Surrounding the moon, Shelley could see a faint light during the eclipse.

7. A tern plunged into the water and came up with a fish flying just above the canal.

8. Forgetting the combination to her locker, the dream kept recurring.

Enriching Your Vocabulary

Recur comes from *recurrere,* a Latin verb that means "to return or run back." The conflict between love and duty is a theme that *recurs* in many plays and novels.

9. At the far reaches of the solar system, Reiko read about a new star.

10. Although well prepared, the algebra test was difficult.

11. The little girl held a garter snake who was wearing jeans and a red-striped T-shirt.

12. To change a flat tire, a jack is in the trunk.

13. Hoping for the best, the application was mailed.

14. Annoyed by the constant interruptions, the phone was turned off.

15. Jacques is the tall forward sitting on the bench wearing the number 27.

Exercise 10 Editing an Anecdote

Work with a partner to correct misplaced and dangling modifiers in this anecdote. Compare your changes with those made by other teams. Some sentences may be correct.   See teacher pages for assessment rubrics. Answers will vary.

■ Look for additional editing strategies in **Composition** Lesson 1.3.

¹Walking into the crowded room, the faces were unfamiliar. ²She walked onto the terrace and stood awhile, next to a grapevine breathing in the fresh air. ³Standing near the edge, the Brooklyn Bridge glowed in the moonlight. ⁴Traffic swirled in the streets looking down from the twentieth floor. ⁵At last, someone opened the door whom she had gone to school with. ⁶Glad to see a familiar face, the terrace was abandoned.

⁷"It's you!" she shouted above the noise, extending her hand, made by the crowd of laughing people.

⁸"It is," the young man agreed, "but we've never met before," wearing a black T-shirt and jeans. ⁹Grasping her hand, his smile was warm.

¹⁰She laughed and murmured, "I'm glad to meet you now," blushing and embarrassed.

Exercise 11 Creating Your Own Exercise

Dangling and misplaced modifiers can be funny. Work with a partner or small group to make up at least five sentences or a paragraph with dangling and misplaced modifiers. Then exchange sentences with another team or group, and correct each other's sentences.   Students' sentences will vary.

Revising and Editing Worksheet 1

Read the following comparison/contrast essay carefully. Correct errors in the use of modifiers. Make any other changes you think will improve the essay. Work with a partner or small group to revise and edit the essay. Write your revised essay on a separate piece of paper, and compare your response with those made by other pairs or groups of classmates.

See teacher pages for assessment rubrics.

[1]The first thing you should know about butterflies and moths is that they're insects. [2]Like all insects, they haven't got no backbone. [3]They have six legs and two antennae, their bodies are in three sections.

[4]So these are the ways butterflies and moths are alike. [5]They belong to the group of related insects called Lepidoptera. [6]They have an unusualer life cycle than any insect. [7]Because they change shapes—from a caterpillar into a chrysalis into a adult. [8]Moths and butterflies have two pairs of wings. [9]That are covered with delicate, flat scales. [10]The most small wingspan is one-eighth inch and the larger, the Atlas moth, is more than ten inches.

[11]Next, I'm going to tell you how butterflies and moths are different. [12]Butterflies' wings have more brighter colors than moths' wings. [13]Some of the most beautifulest butterflies are the monarchs, swallowtails, and peacocks. [14]Among the most strangest butterflies are the clear-winged butterflies, which have less fewer scales on there wings than any butterfly. [15]At the end of their antennae, butterflies fly during the day and have little knobs. [16]Holding them vertically over their heads at rest, butterflies close their wings.

[17]Most moths aren't hardly as colorful as butterflies. [18]Moths' wings are more dull in color. [19]Although a few are beautifuler than some butterflies. [20]When resting on leaves and bark, their dull gray and brown wings are probably for camouflage. [21]Moths have all different kinds of antennae, but none have no knobs at the end. [22]Moths hold their wings open, flat against the surface at rest.

[23]I can't tell you nothing more about butterflies and moths.

Revising and Editing Worksheet 2

Read the following paragraphs carefully. Correct errors in the use of modifiers, and make any other changes you think will improve the paragraphs. Pay special attention to a strong opening thesis statement and concluding sentence. Write your revision on a separate piece of paper.

See teacher pages for assessment rubrics.

[1]This report is on the Battle of Gettysburg. [2]The most baddest battle in the Civil War. [3]Having decided to invade the North, the Army of Northern Virginia was led by General Robert E. Lee. [4]General George Meade led the Union troops, who had been in charge of the northern army for only five days.

[5]At dawn on July 1, 1863, a small Confederate troop in search of boots for there soldiers ran into a more large Union cavalry troop. [6]When they fought outside of Gettysburg, Pennsylvania, there wasn't no turning back. [7]Gettysburg was one of the most quietest towns, it isn't hardly more than eight miles north of the Maryland border.

[8]Both sides sent for reinforcements. [9]On that first day, the more strong Southern forces pushed back the Northern troops. [10]Union forces digged in at Cemetery Hill and Culp's Hill, south of Gettysburg. [11]The Confederates west of them at Seminary Ridge.

[12]On the second day of battle, results were lesser clear. [13]Ordered to attack Union troops, at three o'clock on the afternoon of the third day, a disastrous charge was led by Confederate General George Pickett. [14]The three-day battle at Gettysburg proved to be the most bloodiest of the war. [15]Twenty-three thousand soldiers from the North were killed, wounded, or missing. [16]The South lost twenty-eight thousand. [17]On July 4, Lee retreated homeward. [18]Prevented from crossing the Potomac, the flooded river held Lee's troops in the North. [19]Lincoln commanded General Meade to attack Lee's army. [20]General Meade didn't never pursue them.

Chapter Review

Exercise A Using the Degrees of Comparison

Edit the following sentences for correct use of modifiers. If you find an error, cross out the word or phrase, and rewrite it correctly on a separate piece of paper. If a sentence is correct, write *C* after the sentence. **Hint:** Some sentences have more than one error.   Suggested corrections are indicated.

1. St. Augustine, Florida, is the ~~most old~~ city in the United States.
   (oldest)

2. Death Valley in the Mojave Desert is the ~~most~~ lowest point in North America.

3. Utah's Great Salt Lake is North America's largest saltwater lake. C

4. Which of these Great Lakes is the ~~largest~~—Lake Erie or Lake Michigan?
   (larger)

5. This is one of the most ~~beautifulest~~ parts of the Appalachian Trail.
   (beautiful)

6. The Mississippi River, which flows more than two thousand miles, is much ~~more~~ longer than the Missouri River.

7. Bituminous coal is mined ~~most~~ frequently in West Virginia than in any other state.
   (more)

8. Of the six New England states, Rhode Island is the ~~smaller~~.
   (smallest)

9. American whaling ships sailed ~~oftenest~~ from Nantucket and New Bedford.
   (most often)

10. Philip likes whale watching more than anyone else in his family.

Exercise B Correcting Misplaced and Dangling Modifiers

On a separate piece of paper, rewrite each sentence to correct all misplaced and dangling modifiers. If a sentence is correct, write *C*.   See Answer Key.

1. Helen found 106 Web sites on the extinction of dinosaurs, looking for information for her research paper.

2. She printed articles from museums and scientific organizations trying to evaluate the information.

3. Reading a natural history museum's home page, new information was discovered.

4. After exploring the Internet for several days, a stack of note cards was piled high on her desk.

5. Before writing her first draft, piles of note cards were sorted.

6. Taken from Internet sources, Helen tried to evaluate the accuracy of the information.

7. She discarded articles printed from possibly unreliable Web sites.

8. Proofreading for errors, the punctuation of her Works Cited list was checked.

9. Listening to the sound of the sentences, her first draft was read aloud.

10. Congratulating herself, her paper was finished by the due date.

Exercise C **Editing Paragraphs**

Edit the following paragraphs to correct all errors in the use of modifiers. **Hint:** Some sentences have more than one error. Some have no errors.

[1]Many cultures consider gold the ~~valuablest~~ [most valuable] of all metals. [2]Gold has been found on every continent, on the ~~most high~~ [highest] mountains, in deserts, and even in the frozen Arctic ground. [3]Spanish explorers [exploring the New World] looted the ~~beautifulest~~ [most beautiful] Aztec gold decorative objects ~~exploring the New World~~. [4]Searching for gold to send home, [European explorers shipped] more than four hundred tons of gold ~~were shipped~~ from the New World ~~by European explorers~~. [5]~~Visiting some of the most famousest museums in the world,~~ [You can see] exhibits of pre-Columbian gold decorative objects [in some of the most famous museums in the world.] ~~can be seen~~.

[6]In some cultures, such as ancient Egypt, gold wasn't ~~hardly~~ the most valuable of metals. [7]In ancient Egypt, silver was called white gold because it was ~~more~~ scarcer than gold. [8]In Babylonia and Sumeria, silver was also the ~~desirablest~~ [most desirable] of all the metals. [9]~~Considered the most precious of metals, the~~ [The] search for gold [, considered the most precious of metals,] has continued. [10]~~Discovering~~ [With the discovery of] nuggets of gold at Sutter's Mill in 1848, the California gold rush brought more than forty thousand gold prospectors to California by land and sea. [11]A similar gold rush occurred three years later in Australia, which, by the way, is the ~~most small~~ [smallest] of Earth's continents. [12]The world's most ~~spectacularest~~ [spectacular] source of gold, however, is in southern Africa. [13]Huge sheets of gold ore [called reefs] have been mined there~~, called reefs~~. [14]Among the other ~~richer~~ [richest] gold-producing nations are Canada and the United States. [15]In the United States, the states where the ~~muchest~~ [most] gold is mined are South Dakota and Nevada.

Choosing the Right Word

Direct students to chapter-specific portfolio projects on Sadlier-Oxford's website.

STUDENT WRITING
Movie Review

Little Tree Grows on Audience
by Jonathan Dewbre
high school student, Dallas, Texas

Movies depicting racial prejudice against Native Americans have been quite prevalent during the '90s—*Dances With Wolves* and *The Last of the Mohicans*, just to name a few. In the fallout of big budget movies, don't dismiss *The Education of Little Tree* as a children's movie.

The Education of Little Tree is set in Oklahoma during the early Depression. Little Tree (Joseph Ashton), a recently orphaned eight-year-old Cherokee boy, is adopted by his grandparents; while there, his grandfather (James Cromwell), grandmother (Tantoo Cardinel), and close friend Willow John (Graham Greene) help him learn about his ancestors and the traditions of the Cherokee people. However, when he is discovered by law enforcement officials helping his grandfather to distill whiskey, he is deemed to be in an unhealthy environment and is sent to a boarding school. Literally stripped of any remnants of his heritage and forced into submission by an oppressive school, Little Tree finds that he is in danger of losing the fight against Americanization.

Little Tree is fundamentally different from other recent movies depicting the conflict between Native and European Americans. For one thing, the movie isn't on a big-budget scale; it relies almost entirely on its actors to carry the story, a potential pitfall since the lead in the movie is an eleven-year-old boy. But, then again, Joseph Ashton is no normal eleven-year-old. Ashton, in a practically seamless performance, manages to convey emotions ranging from joyful discovery to utter despair without seeming deliberate like so many actors his age; one hopes that he won't disappear into child-star limbo land. . . .

The Education of Little Tree sports a well-written script based on the controversial memoirs of Forrest Carter. It doesn't feel the need to include sappy dialogue like *Last of the Mohicans* or a ten-hour buffalo massacre like *Dances With Wolves*; the story is a constantly moving effort, designed to let the audience learn life's lessons along with Little Tree, and it never drags. . . . The direction of *Little Tree* is equally well done; Friendenberg wisely allows the natural beauty of the forests of Oklahoma to carry the viewer's eye while not trying to overwhelm us with it.

Little Tree isn't something one would call a "feel-good" movie, but it leaves the viewer satisfied, which is all the movie really sets out to do. It's alternately humorous, rousing, thought-provoking, and sentimental. Be prepared to shed some tears before it's done—if you're not genuinely moved by the ending dialogue of the film, you've either set barriers between yourself and the movie, or you're dead.

Allow time for students to discuss the student writing. Suggest that they identify its strengths and propose possible improvements. Use the model to introduce the concepts in the chapter.

Jonathan's movie review gives a short summary of the events of the movie. He also explains its unique qualities, analyzes the actor's performance, and praises the script. At the end of the review, he summarizes his opinion concisely.

As you reread the essay, notice that Jonathan has skillfully used only a few words to say a great deal. This chapter will help you focus on using words accurately and concisely in your own writing.

From *A* to *Badly*

● **a, an** Use *a* before a word that starts with a consonant sound. Don't look at the word's spelling; pay attention to its beginning *sound.* Use *an* before a word that starts with a vowel sound, including words that start with a silent *h.*

> **a** camera, **a** history, **a** horrible accident, **a** university
>
> **an** onion, **an** hour, **an** honest answer, **an** X ray

● **accept, except** *Accept* is a verb that means "to receive" or "to agree to." *Except* is a preposition that means "but."

> Everyone agreed to **accept** the judge's decision.
>
> Everyone **except** me stayed late.

● **affect, effect** *Affect* is a verb that means "to influence." The noun *effect* means "the result of an action." The verb *effect* means "to cause" or "to bring about."

> Crossing several time zones may **affect** your sleep.
>
> What are the **effects** of overcrowded schools?
>
> Timeouts are meant to **effect** changes in a child's behavior.

● **all right** Spell *all right* as two separate words. The word *alright* is not acceptable in formal written English.

> Are you feeling **all right** after so little sleep?

● **all the farther, all the faster** Use "as far as" instead of "all the farther." Use "as fast as" instead of "all the faster."

> Two miles is **as far as** he jogs.
>
> The collie runs **as fast as** the boy does.

● **amount of, number of** Use *amount of* when you write about a general quantity of something. Use *number of* to refer to something that can be counted.

> The **amount of** popcorn sold at the theater was huge, even though only a small **number of** people saw the movie.

● **and etc., etc.** *Etc.* (abbreviation of Latin *et cetera*) means "and so forth." Never use the word *and* before *etc.*

> We packed food, water, sunscreen, a first-aid kit, ~~and~~ etc.

● **anywheres, everywheres, nowheres, somewheres** These words are spelled incorrectly. *Anywhere, everywhere, nowhere,* and *somewhere* have no *-s* at the end.

> We saw palm trees **everywhere.** I couldn't see snow **anywhere.**

Read these two sentences:

The crew members pulled their oars *all together.* [*All together* means "in unison."]

By the end of the race, they were *altogether* exhausted. [*Altogether* means "extremely."]

Even though English includes both *altogether* and *all together*, don't assume that it also includes both *alright* and *all right*. There is only one *all right; alright* is not used in formal written English.

● **at** Don't use the word *at* after *where*.

Where is the concert ~~at~~?

● **bad, badly** Use *bad* as an adjective and as a predicate adjective after linking verbs. **Remember:** A predicate adjective describes the subject. Use *badly,* an adverb, to modify an action verb.

Chris feels **bad** about missing the party.

She sings **badly.**

Exercise 1 **Editing a Report**

■ Look for additional editing strategies in **Composition** Lesson 1.3.

Edit the following paragraph to correct all errors in word choice. **Hint:** Not every sentence contains an error; some sentences have more than one error.

¹The change of seasons ~~effects~~ *(affects)* many animals and insects. ²Huge flocks of birds fly from ~~everywheres~~ *(everywhere)* up north to ~~somewheres~~ *(somewhere)* warm so they can survive ~~alright~~ *(all right)* during the winter. ³~~A~~ *(An)* Arctic tern, for instance, flies from the Arctic ~~all the farther~~ *(as far as)* it can go—all the way to the Antarctic.

⁴Some insects (butterflies, moths, locusts, ~~and~~ etc.) also migrate. ⁵Monarch butterflies fly ~~all the faster~~ *(as fast as)* they can—about 12 mph—from Canada to a mountain range in Mexico.

⁶Elk, moose, caribou, ~~and~~ etc., migrate to summer feeding grounds, and other animals migrate to breed. ⁷Both sea turtles and seals come ashore to breed, but ~~a~~ *(an)* eel swims downriver to breed in the ocean.

⁸The salmon life cycle involves ~~a~~ *(an)* unusual migration. ⁹Mature salmon leave the sea to swim upriver to the place where they were born ~~at~~. Their migration is especially difficult because a large ~~amount~~ *(number)* of them are caught by fishermen who watch the migration cycle carefully. ¹⁰Do you suppose the salmon, who lay their eggs and die, feel ~~badly~~ *(bad)* or simply ~~except~~ *(accept)* their life cycle?

From *Beside* to *Further*

● **beside, besides** *Beside* means "by the side of." *Besides* means "in addition to." *Besides* as an adverb means "moreover."

   We picnicked **beside** the river. **Besides** sandwiches, we brought fruit.
   It's too cold to swim; **besides,** we have no sunscreen.

● **between, among** Use *between* to refer to two people or things being compared. You can also use *between* when discussing three or more items if you think only two will be compared at a time. Use *among* to refer to a group or to three or more people or things.

   Just **between** you and me, I can't stand cilantro.
   Can you tell the difference **between** a sonnet, a ballad, and a couplet?
   It's good to be back home **among** family and friends.

● **borrow, lend, loan** *Borrow* means "to take something temporarily that must be returned." *Lend,* the opposite of *borrow,* means "to give something temporarily." Don't confuse *loan* and *lend. Loan* is always a noun in formal written English; a loan is the thing that is lent.

   Howie wants to **borrow** five dollars.
   Sheila **lent** him the money.
   He will repay her **loan** Saturday.

● **bring, take** *Bring* refers to a movement toward or with the speaker. *Take* refers to a movement away from the speaker.

   Karl **brought** me a souvenir. Please **take** this package to him.

● **could (might, should, would) of** Use *have*, not *of*, with these helping verbs.

   Avram **should have** brought his guitar to the party.

● **discover, invent** *Discover* means "to find something for the first time." *Invent* means "to think up and produce something new that didn't exist before."

   When was gold **discovered** in California?
   Carl Magee **invented** the parking meter in 1935.

● **different from** Use *from*, not *than*, after *different*.

   How is a square **different from** a rectangle?

● **eager, anxious** Use *eager* to show hopeful excitement. Use *anxious* to show worry about the future.

   She was **anxious** about the math test.
   They were **eager** for Christmas break.

Editing Tip

Here's a mnemonic device to help you remember that *lend* is a verb and *loan* is a noun. In Shakespeare's *Julius Caesar*, Antony begins his famous speech with this line:

Friends, Romans, countrymen, *lend* me your ears.

At the end of the speech he might have said:

OK, folks, I'm returning your ears. Thanks for the *loan*.

Enriching Your Vocabulary

The Latin verb *praecedere* (from *pre,* "before," and *cedere,* "to go") is the root of several English words. A *precedent* is something that occurred previously or that can serve as a justification or an example. Lawyers look for *precedents* to support their arguments. And when you do your homework, you may find it helpful to review the *preceding* lesson. See Exercise 4.

farther, further *Farther* refers to physical distance. *Further* means "to a greater degree or extent."

> Which is **farther** from Earth—Neptune or Pluto?
> I will study the issue **further** and give you my opinion.

Exercise 2 Choosing the Right Word

Underline the word in parentheses that correctly completes each sentence.

EXAMPLE   Which inventions do you know about (beside, <u>besides</u>) the telephone?

1. In 1608, a Dutch eyeglass maker (<u>discovered</u>, invented) that he could see (<u>farther</u>, further) by looking through two lenses at once.

2. He thought (farther, <u>further</u>) and put one lens at each end of a tube.

3. How is his telescope different (<u>from</u>, than) a microscope?

4. The first toothbrush in 1770 (took, <u>brought</u>) wealth to an ex-prisoner.

5. A friend of Walter Hunt's had (borrowed, <u>lent</u>) him fifteen dollars.

6. (Eager, <u>Anxious</u>) about the debt, Hunt invented the safety pin in 1825 to repay the (lend, <u>loan</u>).

7. In 1870, Thomas Adams (<u>borrowed</u>, loaned) some chicle resin from a friend.

8. Adams would (of, <u>have</u>) preferred to make a rubber substitute but patented chewing gum instead.

9. Others (beside, <u>besides</u>) Eadweard Muybridge helped create motion pictures.

10. What is the difference (<u>between</u>, among) a Polaroid and all other cameras?

Exercise 3: Paragraphs will vary. Give students full credit if they have expressed themselves clearly, answered the questions about their invention, and tried to persuade the president of the company to produce their invention. They should also have written grammatically complete sentences that begin with a capital letter and end with an appropriate end punctuation mark.

■ **To help you start, use the prewriting strategies in Composition Lessons 1.1 and 1.2.**

Exercise 3 Write What You Think

What invention is the world waiting for? Get together with a small group, and choose the invention that interests you. Then write a paragraph in which you persuade the president of a company to produce your invention. Answer these questions about your invention:

> What is it for? Who will use it? What will it look like? How is it different from anything you can buy now?

Edit your paragraph to make sure you've used the right words in the right places.

Exercise 4 Creating Mnemonics

Work with a partner to write a mnemonic device for one or more of the easily confused words in this lesson or the preceding lesson. Create a class book of mnemonic devices for challenging pairs of words.

From *Fewer* to *Of*

◖ **fewer, less** *Fewer* refers to nouns that can be counted. *Less* refers to nouns that can't be counted.

Sean buys **fewer** books. I should eat **less** chocolate.

◖ **good, well** *Good* is always an adjective, never an adverb. *Well*, however, can be both. The adverb *well* means "done in a satisfactory way." The adjective *well* means "in good health."

Sally has a **good** excuse.
She wasn't feeling **well,** so she didn't study as **well.**

◖ **had ought, hadn't ought** Drop the *had*. Use just plain *ought* and *ought not*.

They ~~had~~ **ought** to start early to miss the rush hour traffic.

◖ **hopefully** Use *hopefully* as an adverb to describe the manner in which something is done. Do not use it in place of "I hope."

The boys approached the discount ticket office **hopefully.**

◖ **kind (sort, type) of a** Drop the *a*. Use *kind of, sort of,* or *type of*. But keep in mind that *kind (sort, type) of* can usually be omitted without changing the meaning of a sentence and should be avoided unless it is truly necessary.

This **kind of** ~~a~~ squash tastes like sweet potato.
This squash tastes like sweet potato.

◖ **learn, teach** Don't use *learn* when you mean *teach* or *instruct*. *Learn* is what a student does; *teach* is what a *teacher* does.

I **learned** how to embroider from a Hmong woman who **taught** our class.

◖ **leave, let** *Leave* means "to depart" and "to place." *Let* means "to allow."

When you **leave,** please **leave** the books on the table.
Don't **let** them get lost.

◖ **like, as, as if, as though** Don't use *like* to introduce a subordinate clause. Use *as, as if,* or *as though*. Use *like* to express a similarity.

He looks **as if** he's really sorry.
Carey arrived early, **as** she said she would.
The mime looked **like** a statue.

Step by Step

To decide whether to use *good* or *well:*

1. Decide how the word is used in the sentence.

2. If the word is an adverb (telling how something is done), it can only be *well*. *Good* is never used an as adverb.

3. If the word is an adjective, look at its meaning in the sentence. If it means "in good health," use *well*. For all other meanings, use *good*.

Enriching Your Vocabulary

Some Latin words have made their way into English unchanged. This is the case with *vice versa,* found on page 240, which has as its roots *vicis* (change) and *vertere* (to turn round or about). *Vice versa* is used to indicate that the relations in the preceding statement are reversed. For example, I enjoy talking with my friends and *vice versa.*

of, off of Don't use *of* after the prepositions *inside, outside,* and *off.* Also, use *from,* not *off* or *off of,* when you're referring to the source of something.

I put the milk **inside ~~of~~** the cooler. Please take the cooler **off ~~of~~** the table.
Is this the cooler we borrowed **from** Jee-Young?

Exercise 5 **Choosing the Right Word**

Underline the word in parentheses that correctly completes each sentence.

1. Mr. Weber (learned, <u>taught</u>) us some expressions from other languages.

2. (<u>I hope that</u>, Hopefully,) when you hear the words *joie de vivre,* "joy of life," you feel happy.

3. If I say *mea culpa,* "my fault" in Latin, I have to make (less, <u>fewer</u>) long apologies.

4. *Shalom,* a (type of a, <u>type of</u>) greeting, means "peace" in Hebrew.

5. I feel (<u>good</u>, well) when I hear *Aloha,* Hawaiian for "love."

6. Unless your question is *apropos,* "to the point," you (hadn't ought, <u>ought not</u>) to interrupt.

7. (<u>Let</u>, Leave) us show our support by going *en masse,* "as a large group."

8. Have you ever felt a sense of *déja vu,* (like, <u>as though</u>) something has happened before?

9. When you fill your gas tank (off of, <u>from</u>) a pump, you either pump first and pay later, or *vice versa,* "in reverse order."

10. A crime scene left *in situ,* "in its original place," has nothing removed ____ (from, off of) the scene.

11. When two people speak *tête-á-tête,* they are having a (type of a, <u>type of</u>) private conversation.

12. It is sometimes cheaper to buy lunch (<u>from</u>, off of) the *a la carte* menu so you can pay for food items individually.

13. On an invitation, the letters *R.S.V.P.* stand for the French phrase *répondez s'il vous plait* and they mean that you (<u>ought</u>, had ought) to reply.

Exercise 6 **Creating a Story**

■ To start your story, look for several drafting strategies in **Composition** Lesson 1.2.

Get together with a small group to write the beginning of a story. Try to use at least eight of the words you've studied so far in this chapter. Exchange your story beginning with another group, and check the other group's use of words. Each group should continue the story of the other group. Keep trying to use words you've studied in this chapter. Story beginnings will vary.

From *Real* to *When*

● **real, really** *Real* is an adjective that means "actual." *Really* is an adverb that means "actually" or "genuinely."

> Your news was a **real** surprise. We are **really** disappointed.

● **some, somewhat** *Some* is an adjective. *Somewhat* is an adverb meaning "slightly." Don't use *some* as an adverb.

> Let's think about cooking **some** food.
> The rain has let up **somewhat**.

● **than, then** *Than* is a conjunction that introduces a subordinate clause. *Then* is an adverb meaning "therefore" or "next in order or time."

> She lives closer to our school **than** I do. **Then** why don't we meet at her house?
> First, let's discuss your idea; **then** we'll vote.

● **that, which** Use *which* to introduce a nonessential clause. Use *that* in an essential clause.

> Our math team is going to the state finals, **which** start next week. The team **that** wins the competition will get the trophy.

● **that, who** Use *who* in clauses that refer to people. Use *that* in essential clauses that refer to things.

> Ms. Houlihan, **who** teaches algebra, coaches the math team.
> The calculator **that** I use at school is solar-powered.

● **this here, that there** In standard written English, *this* and *that* are used alone. Drop the word *here* or *there*.

> I'm trying to fix **this** ~~here~~ chair. Please hand me **that** ~~there~~ screwdriver.

● **those, these, them** Don't use *them* as an adjective. Use *those* or *these*.

> Have you read all of **those** books? I've read only **these** two.

● **when, where** When you define a word, don't use *when* or *is when*. *Where* refers to a place. Also, don't use *where* to mean "that."

> INCORRECT   Squaring a number is **when** you multiply the number by itself.
> CORRECT   To square a number, multiply the number by itself.
> INCORRECT   I read **where** the Chinese New Year is this Friday.
> CORRECT   I read **that** the Chinese New Year is this Friday.

Step by Step

To decide whether to use *which* or *that* to introduce a description of a noun:

1. If you can drop the description without destroying the point of your sentence, use *which*.

   My first dog, **which** was a golden retriever, was named Cooper.

2. If dropping the description destroys the meaning of your sentence, use *that*.

   The dog **that** I loved the most was my first.

Exercise 7 Choosing the Right Word

Underline the word in parentheses that correctly completes each sentence.

1. Vincent van Gogh, (which, <u>who</u>) was a Dutch artist, died at thirty-seven.

2. He had tried teaching and preaching but (than, <u>then</u>) turned to art.

■ See Usage Lesson 10.3 for the correct use of *who* and *whom*.

3. He painted for the last eight years of his (real, <u>really</u>) troubled life.

4. I read (where, <u>that</u>) he did eight hundred paintings during (<u>those</u>, them) years.

5. Theo, (that, <u>who</u>) was his younger brother, supported van Gogh.

6. Theo sold fewer (then, <u>than</u>) six of his brother's paintings.

7. (Some, <u>Somewhat</u>) discouraged, van Gogh kept right on painting.

8. (<u>This</u>, This here) is one of his favorites, a painting of his bedroom.

9. I love the swirling stars and moon (<u>that</u>, who) fill his *Starry Night*.

10. Van Gogh created dignified portraits of the workers (which, <u>who</u>) posed for him.

Exercise 8 Editing a Paragraph

On a separate piece of paper, rewrite the paragraph below to correct the usage errors. **Hint:** Some sentences have more than one error. Some have none.

¹Marc and Megan, ~~which~~ [who] is Marc's cousin, are working ~~real~~ [really] hard. ²Megan, ~~which~~ [who] is twelve years older then Marc, is a computer programmer. ³A computer programmer is ~~when~~ someone [who] writes step-by-step directions to run a computer program. ⁴Last week, Megan read on the Net ~~where~~ [that] a software company is sponsoring a contest for a new computer game. ⁵She told Marc about the contest, and ~~than~~ [then] the two of them decided to enter the contest. ⁶Right now, ~~them~~ [those] two are brainstorming ideas. ⁷Marc says their game will be somewhat challenging and also fun. ⁸They are determined to make up a better game ~~then~~ [than] this ~~here~~ popular one, which is all about destroying enemies. ⁹Megan thinks that ~~them~~ [those] kill-the-enemy games cause players to feel ~~some~~ [somewhat] violent in real life. ¹⁰Megan and Marc are planning to create a ~~real~~ [really] exciting adventure game that doesn't involve killing.

Corrections may vary somewhat. Sample answers are given.

Exercise 9 Write What You Think

In a paragraph, state your opinion of the following statement clearly. Support your opinion with reasons, facts, and examples.

Violence in today's movies, TV programs, and computer games has caused an increase in violent behavior in our society. Paragraphs will vary. Give students full credit if they have stated an opinion and attempted to support their opinion. They should also have written grammatically complete sentences that begin with a capital letter and end with an appropriate end punctuation mark.

Revising and Editing Worksheet 1

In the following draft of a book review, correct errors in the choice of words, and make any other changes you think will improve the paragraphs. Work with a partner or small group to revise the paragraphs. Write your revised report on a separate piece of paper, and compare your revisions with those made by your classmates.

[1]*The Diary of a Young Girl* by Anne Frank is a very unusual kind of a diary. [2]It is different than other diaries. [3]Because of the circumstances under which it was written. [4]It is a first-person account of an historical period.

[5]Anne begun writing her diary when she was thirteen. [6]She lived in Amsterdam, Holland. [7]Among 1942 and 1944, Anne and her mother, father, and sister lived in hiding. [8]The Frank family hid because of the affects of the Nazi occupation of Holland. [9]At first, the Nazis would not leave Jews go to public school, drive, play sports, go to the theater, movies, and etc. [10]Then everywheres throughout Nazi-occupied Europe, Jews were sent to labor camps and death camps. [11]Beside the Franks, another family and a dentist hid. [12]They hid in a "secret annex" behind a bookcase. [13]The bookcase was in the building where Mr. Frank had a business at. [14]Miep Gies and another non-Jewish worker brought them food.

[15]Anne's diary ends in August 1944. [16]When Nazis invented them and taked them away. [17]After they leaved, Miep Gies discovered the diary, she put it in a desk to save for Anne. [18]Of the eight people which hid in the annex, only Anne's father survived the war.

[19]I felt badly as I read this diary. [20]Because I knew Anne and the others would not be alright. [21]Anne writes so good about her thoughts and feelings and the details of her life. [22]Cynthia Ozick, an American writer, thinks Anne Frank would of become a great writer if she had lived. [23]If you have not yet read this here diary, I think you had ought to.

Students who have read the diary may wish to expand their edited worksheets with opinions of their own.

Enriching Your Vocabulary

The noun *annex* comes from *annexus*, which is the past participle of the Latin verb *annectere*, meaning "to bind to" or "to tie." A garage is an *annex* to a house. Similarly, an appendix is an *annex* to a book.

Revising and Editing Worksheet 2

In the following draft of a book review, correct errors in the choice of words, and make any other changes you think will improve the paragraphs. Work with a partner or small group to improve the paragraphs. Write your improved report on a separate piece of paper, and compare your revisions with those made by your classmates.

¹Consider all the machines that effect your life at home and in other ways. ²Do you have any idea how they work? ³A real fascinating book about machines is *The Way Things Work* by David Macaulay. ⁴England is where he was born at, but he came to the United States when he was eleven. ⁵Beside being a book, *The Way Things Work* is now on CD-ROM. ⁶Which allows you to look at it on a computer and things move and you can hear stuff.

⁷This here book shows how hundreds of machines everywheres work. ⁸Leave me give you some examples. ⁹Airplanes, parking meters, television, staplers, clocks, synthesizers, and etc. ¹⁰Macaulay's book is a kind of a reference book, it's very different than an encyclopedia. ¹¹It's filled with diagrams and drawings, it learns readers something about the history of each machine and how it works. ¹²And who discovered it.

¹³Beside the factual information, stories and drawings of woolly mammoths appear throughout the book. ¹⁴To explain basic scientific concepts. ¹⁵The mammoth is a extinct animal like an elephant. ¹⁶The mammoth is huge. ¹⁷Them mammoth stories add humor to the book.

¹⁸I think anyone which can read will enjoy this book. ¹⁹The whole idea of how things work is real interesting to think about. ²⁰It makes me want to learn more about everything, and that's a kind of an exciting idea.
Sudents' revisions will vary. See teacher pages for revising and editing rubrics.

Chapter Review

Exercise A Choosing the Right Word

Underline the word in parentheses that correctly completes each sentence.

1. I hope you will (accept, except) my apology.
2. Taryn felt (real, really) (bad, badly) about what had happened.
3. Who will be at the party (beside, besides) Jody and Perry?
4. No one could (have, of) predicted the outcome.
5. (This, This here) medicine has no known side (affects, effects).
6. Ten miles was (all the farther, as far as) she could hike.
7. Are you feeling (all right, alright)?
8. The four candidates argued (between, among) themselves.
9. (I hope, Hopefully,) no one will tell the cook about the (amount of, number of) helpings of dessert I took.
10. This dessert has (less, fewer) calories than ice cream.
11. Austin promised to (learn, teach) us how to change a flat tire.
12. She is much more interested in math (then, than) he is.
13. Mara's nervousness lessened (some, somewhat) after the interview.
14. For someone (which, who) likes cats, (this, this here) book is a good gift.
15. Do you know who (invented, discovered) the bicycle?
16. No one could (of, have) known that thieves were in the museum.
17. Hilarie sat (besides, beside) the river (between, among) her two best friends.
18. Karyn sings (real, really) (good, well) but plays the trumpet (bad, badly).
19. How will the changes in schedule (affect, effect) you?
20. Can you please (lend, loan) me your calculator?
21. Mara doesn't feel (good, well) enough to attend her graduation.
22. How much did you pay for (those, them) hiking boots?
23. Are you finished with the thesaurus I (loaned, lent) you?
24. We would (of, have) arrived on time, but there was a (really, real) big fire, and the highway was closed.
25. Kim (brought, took) dinner with her when she visited her grandparents.

Exercise B Editing a Paragraph

Cross out the words that are used incorrectly, and write the correct words above them. **Hint:** Some sentences have more than one error. Some have none.

[1]Do you know the difference ~~among a~~ **between an** atom and a molecule? [2]Yesterday, Mrs. Oki, ~~which~~ **who** is my science teacher, ~~learned~~ **taught** us the difference. [3]I heard her say ~~where~~ **that** a molecule is the smallest unit of a compound. [4]A molecule cannot be broken down ~~farther~~ **further** and still remain the same compound. [5]Molecules are made up of a combination of atoms, ~~who~~ **which** are smaller ~~then~~ **than** a molecule. [6]For example, the formula for a molecule of water, ~~that~~ **which** is a compound, is H_2O. [7]This ~~here~~ formula indicates that a molecule of water has two atoms of hydrogen and one atom of oxygen. [8]Both carbon monoxide (CO) and carbon dioxide (CO_2) are made up of carbon and oxygen atoms. [9]CO is different ~~than~~ **from** CO_2 because a molecule of CO has one less oxygen atom ~~then~~ **than** CO_2. [10]Chemistry is a kind of ~~a~~ subject that I think is ~~real~~ **really** clear.

Exercise C   Writing Correct Sentences

For each of the words below, write an interesting and complete sentence. Underline the word in each sentence, and then exchange sentences with a partner. Check to see if the underlined words have been used correctly.

EXAMPLE   *teach*
When will you <u>teach</u> me how to change a flat tire?

1. affect	11. learn	Sentences will vary.
2. badly	12. as	
3. farther	13. further	
4. leave	14. among	
5. bad	15. different	
6. besides	16. somewhat	
7. well	17. which	
8. discover	18. loan	
9. except	19. effect	
10. than	20. fewer	

Cumulative Review

Exercise A Using Verbs Correctly

On a separate piece of paper, correct all of the errors in verb usage in the following sentences. Look for incorrect verbs and verb forms, unnecessary shifts in verb tense, and unnecessary use of the passive voice.   See Answer Key.

1. A new school record was set by Carey when the race was swum by her in fifty-eight seconds.

2. After Flora will have dived a dozen times, she becomes dizzy.

3. Flora drunk a glass of water and laid down beside the pool.

4. A towel was brung by the coach, who tells her to set awhile and rest.

5. All of the girls on the swimming team knowed that drinking plenty of water be important; the coach has speaked about it many times.

6. The coach has teached them about the dangers of dehydration.

7. Haven't you did some research and wrote a paper on heat exhaustion?

8. Once I weared heavy clothes and done hours of gardening on a very hot, dry day.

9. When I raised from my knees, I begun to feel weak, and then I faints.

10. Fluids should be gave to people with heat exhaustion, and they should lay flat or with their heads down.

Exercise B Subject-Verb Agreement

Underline the verb in parentheses that agrees with the subject.

1. One of the banjo's strings (is, are) broken.

2. Everyone (sings, sing) loudly, but many (sings, sing) off key.

3. None of the musical instruments (belongs, belong) to the school.

4. Neither the drummers nor the pianist (plays, play) in this piece.

5. Both Alison and Mercedes (has, have) practiced the solo part.

6. Few of the choir members (plays, play) a musical instrument.

7. The band (rehearses, rehearse) during lunch every Friday.

8. Every band member and choir member (is, are) onstage during the concert.

9. John Philip Sousa's "The Stars and Stripes Forever" (is, are) Mr. Marks' favorite march.

10. The audience (stands, stand) and (sings, sing) "The Star-Spangled Banner."

Exercise C **Using Pronouns Correctly**

Underline the pronoun in parentheses that correctly completes each sentence.

1. Maya and (I, me) are tutoring first-graders in an after-school program.

2. The coach gave Jorge and (he, him) the tennis team's schedule.

3. Just between you and (I, me), Diana really likes Vinnie.

4. Aunt Marina in Santa Fe made these mugs for Mia and (she, her).

5. Bernie is the cartoonist (who, whom) I told you about.

6. Do you know (who, whom) has a color printer?

7. Either Jeff or Scott has a radio in (his, their) desk.

8. The editorial is directed to (we, us) ninth-graders.

9. (Us, We) computer club members are writing a program for a game.

10. The essay contest winners, Lauren and (she, her), will read their essays on the school radio.

Exercise D **Using Modifiers Correctly**

Proofread the following sentences to correct all errors in the use of modifiers. **Hint:** Some sentences have more than one error. See Answer Key.

1. The expensivest car isn't always the bestest one to buy.

2. Searching for a good used car, bargains can be found.

3. The most desirablest used car has had a single owner who has taken good care of it.

4. Some cars are driven less than ten thousand miles a year.

5. Suppose you are trying to decide which of two used cars is best.

6. Experienced in fixing used cars, ask a mechanic to check both cars.

7. A skilled mechanic can hear and feel problems gooder than you.

8. Car repair and maintenance, importanter than any class, should be a required course.

9. Being sold by a friend, Lauren is buying a 1986 blue convertible.

10. The convertible is more clean and more shiny than any car she looked at, but it needs a new transmission, brakes, and four tires.

Usage Test

Exercise 1 Identifying Errors

Directions: Each of the numbered items is either correct or contains an error in one of the underlined parts of the sentence. In the answer section to the right of each item, circle the letter of the underlined sentence part that contains the error. If the sentence is correct, circle *E* for NO ERROR.

EXAMPLE   <u>This story is</u> one of the <u>most famous</u> Greek myths. It is the story
               A   B

            <u>where</u> Icarus ignores his father's <u>advice</u>. <u>NO ERROR</u>
             C   D   E

A B Ⓒ D E

1. Minos, the king of Crete, <u>hires</u> the father of Icarus, Daedalus, <u>who</u> is an
                        A   B

   <u>extreme</u> <u>skillful</u> craftsman and inventor.   <u>NO ERROR</u>
      C   D   E

1. A B Ⓒ D E

2. The craftsman's mission, as Minos <u>describes</u> it to Daedalus, is <u>to design</u>
                                    A   B

   a building for the Minotaur, a man-eating monster that <u>have</u> the head of
                                                         C

   a bull and <u>the body of a man</u>.   <u>NO ERROR</u>
                D   E

2. A B Ⓒ D E

3. Daedalus <u>designs</u> a labyrinth, which <u>is</u> a huge maze <u>made</u> up of bewildering
           A   B   C

   passageways. No one who <u>enter</u> the labyrinth can escape.   <u>NO ERROR</u>
                            D   E

3. A B C Ⓓ E

4. After Daedalus <u>finishes</u> the labyrinth, the king <u>refuses</u> <u>to leave</u> <u>Daedalus</u>
                  A   B   C   D

   <u>and his son</u> travel out of Crete.   <u>NO ERROR</u>
       E   E

4. A B Ⓒ D E

5. King Minos imprisons <u>the two of them</u> in the labyrinth, <u>the very same</u>
                            A   B

   one <u>that</u> Daedalus <u>had builded</u>. The walls are too high for an escape, and
        C   D

   the gates are locked.   <u>NO ERROR</u>
                     E

5. A B C Ⓓ E

6. How can <u>him and his son</u> escape? Daedalus, <u>who is terribly clever</u>, asks
                  A   B

   King Minos for his tools and materials. <u>Lying</u>, Daedalus tells the king that
                                           C

   he just wants <u>to keep busy</u> inventing things.   <u>NO ERROR</u>
                  D   E

6. Ⓐ B C D E

7. After <u>carefully</u> observing <u>how birds fly</u>, Daedalus designs <u>two sets</u> of
        A   B   C

   wings made of feathers <u>held</u> together by thread and wax.   <u>NO ERROR</u>
                      D   E

7. A B C D Ⓔ

8. <u>Him</u> and Icarus put on <u>their</u> wings, and Daedalus warns Icarus to
   A   B
follow him, not to <u>set</u> his own <u>course</u>. <u>NO ERROR</u>
             C   D   E

8.(A) B C D E

9. "<u>Be careful</u>," cautions Daedalus, "for if you <u>fly</u> too close to the sun, the
    A   B
heat will <u>sure</u> melt the wax. Then your wings will fall apart, and you
         C
will <u>be drowned</u> in the sea." <u>NO ERROR</u>
       D   E

9. A B (C) D E

10. Icarus <u>foolishly</u> flies <u>higher</u> than anyone else has ever <u>gone</u>, and his
          A   B   C
wings do melt, <u>ignoring his father's advice</u>. <u>NO ERROR</u>
                   D   E

10. A B C (D) E

Exercise 2   Correcting Errors

Directions: The underlined part of the following sentences may contain one or more errors. In the answer section to the right of each item, circle the letter of the choice that correctly expresses the idea in the underlined part of the sentence. If you think that the original wording is correct, circle *D* for NO ERROR. **Hint:** A sentence may have more than one error.

EXAMPLE   Keno and his brothers <u>are my best friends.</u>
           A. is my most bestest friends.   C. are my most best friends.
           B. are my bestest friends.   D. NO ERROR

A   B   C (D)

1. <u>Neither Katie nor him have finished</u> reading *The Adventures of Huckleberry Finn.*
   A. Neither Katie nor he has finished   C. Neither Katie nor he have finished
   B. Neither Katie nor him has finished   D. NO ERROR

1.(A) B C D

2. Dave plays the trumpet <u>real good, much better than me.</u>
   A. really well, much better than I.   C. really well, much better than me.
   B. really good, much better than me.   D. NO ERROR

2.(A) B C D

3. Jed <u>caught the pass and run</u> to the thirty-yard line.
   A. caught the pass and runned   C. catched the pass and ran
   B. caught the pass and ran   D. NO ERROR

3. A (B) C D

4. <u>No one know who is</u> in charge of the election.
   A. No one knowed who is   C. No one know whom is
   B. No one knows who is   D. NO ERROR

4. A (B) C D

5. Until Susie Cook set a new record this year, no one <u>had never come to school</u> every day for four years without an absence.
   A. had never came to school   C. had ever come to school
   B. had ever came to school   D. NO ERROR

5. A B (C) D

6. <u>Maryann and me learned</u> our dog Mollie some new tricks.   6.(A) B C D
   A. Maryann and I taught   C. Maryann and me taught
   B. Maryann and I learned   D. NO ERROR

7. Everyone <u>couldn't hardly wait for their</u> interview results.   7. A B (C) D
   A. couldn't hardly wait for his or her C. could hardly wait for his or her
   B. could hardly wait for their   D. NO ERROR

8. <u>Todd or her usually answer</u> the phone before it rings twice.   8.(A) B C D
   A. Todd or she usually answers   C. Todd or she usually answer
   B. Todd or her usually answers   D. NO ERROR

9. Will you <u>please lie this here pillow</u> in the sun?   9. A B (C) D
   A. please lay this here pillow   C. please lay this pillow
   B. please lie this pillow   D. NO ERROR

10. Rick <u>has never sang no solos</u> with the choir.   10.(A) B C D
    A. has never sung any solos   C. has never sung no solos
    B. has never sang any solos   D. NO ERROR

Exercise 3 Identifying Errors

Directions: In each numbered group of sentences, *one or more* of the sentences may contain usage errors. In the answer section to the right of each item, circle the letter of *every* sentence that contains an error.

EXAMPLE   A. Matt and Nicholas hope to make the varsity team.   A (B)(C) D
           B. Either Guillermo or Glenn think Matisse is the best painter.
           C. No one in these rooms know the answer to your question.
           D. Most of the work is complete.

1. A. She and I are on the student-council nominating committee.   1. A B (C)(D)
   B. The person with the most acting experience is she.
   C. Just between you and me, Sara and ~~her~~ sing off key. she
   D. Lynette sent postcards of San Antonio to Jerry and ~~I~~. me

2. A. Neither Bing nor Daniel rides his bike to school.   2. A B C (D)
   B. Both Juan and Faustino are writing about new vaccines.
   C. Everyone in the marching band is responsible for his or her instrument.
   D. Jessica or her parents ~~prefers~~ rock-and-roll music. prefer

3. A. When Nora had the flu, she just ~~laid~~ in bed and slept. lay   3.(A) B (C) D
   B. Everyone knows how many serious questions have been raised.
   C. Sophia had made extra sandwiches, but David had ~~ate~~ them. eaten
   D. Please sit on the porch with us.

4. A. We ~~hadn't~~ scarcely opened the door when the phone rang. had
   B. Olivia accepted the award for her brother, who is ill.
   C. Marcel cooks worse than anyone else I know.
   D. Mike and Jenny have brought their guitars to the party.

4. (A) B C D

5. A. One of the pipes burst when the ground froze last winter.
   B. Sam and I knew all along that you were only joking.
   C. Mr. Genece ~~learned we~~ students about new developments in genetics. taught us
   D. Without your help, I never would have ~~knowed~~. known

5. A B (C)(D)

6. A. Amy could hardly keep from laughing during the most serious scenes.
   B. Luciano is the tallest and most accurate player on the basketball team.
   C. Hoping to find her dog, ~~the neighborhood was thoroughly searched by Kayla.~~ Kayla thoroughly searched the neighborhood.
   D. Mihal knows more about computers than anyone in the class. else

6. A B (C)(D)

7. A. When it crashed into a bigger ship, the yacht broke in half and sank.
   B. They ran almost two miles together before they spoke to each other.
   C. Lorna has swum fifty laps at the pool.
   D. The two candidates for mayor ~~shaked~~ hands and set down. shook

7. A B C (D)

8. A. Will you please ~~loan~~ me your calculator for an hour? lend
   B. When did Thomas Alva Edison ~~discover~~ the lightbulb? invent
   C. I should have fewer wrong answers than on the last test.
   D. His parents let him stop taking piano lessons.

8. (A)(B) C D

9. A. Issa is one of my friends, whom you would like.
   B. Whom did you say is calling?
   C. Alexis and Aaron are the ones ~~whom~~ have given us their opinions. who
   D. Ms. Rengarajan is the teacher who has taught me the most.

9. A B (C) D

10. A. Gina and Sigrid certainly play table tennis well.
    B. Kristen was ~~real~~ upset when someone took her wallet. really
    C. Guy and his brother live closer to school than I do.
    D. Jason feels ~~worser~~ then he felt yesterday. worse

10. A (B) C (D)

Exercise 4 Correcting Errors

Directions: Look back at each item in Exercise 3, and double-check your answers. Make sure you have identified *all* of the sentences with errors. On a separate piece of paper, rewrite correctly *all* of the incorrect sentences in each numbered item. Write the entire sentence in each and every case.
Hint: A sentence may have more than one error.
See annotations on incorrect sentences above.

Punctuation:
End Marks
and Commas

Direct students to chapter-specific portfolio projects on Sadlier-Oxford's website.

STUDENT WRITING
Expository Essay

Bottled Water: Reasons Vary for Purchasing Thirst Quencher
by Leslie Harrell
high school student, Grosse Pointe Farms, Michigan

It may be free from the faucet, but slap on a label and people will pay for it.

Upon first look, bottled and tap water appear to be the same. They are both clear, refreshing, and wet. Their chemical compositions are both mainly hydrogen and oxygen. But many South students feel that one has the edge in taste that is worth the price.

"I really like bottled water," said Tracy Gehlert. "It tastes better and you can carry it around easily to class."

Bottled water, though just recently seeming to gain popularity, has been around for a long time. The first bottles were sold in 1830 in earthenware jugs, according to the home page [of a major bottled water company. Another company] has been in business for two hundred years . . . .

Bottled water is regulated by the Food and Drug Administration and has to meet all applicable federal and state standards, The Bottled Water home page reports. [One of the major water producers claims that its product] is completely natural and goes through its own filtration process underground . . . . It comes complete with minerals that filter into the water on its fifteen year journey from the French Alps.

"I like the taste of bottled water better than [that of] tap water," said Patrick Spain. "It's fresher and it's colder than water out of the tap."

Some people just don't buy all the hype about bottled water.

"I don't drink bottled water," said Ben Weaver. "There's enough of it in the faucet."

Tap-water drinkers may be happy to know that bottled water is not really any safer than tap water. Health standards for bottled water are no stricter than health standards for public water from the tap, The Bottled Water home page reports. In fact, until 1995, bottled water was not even subject to the same standards as tap water.

Facts or no facts, millions of people keep buying bottled water. The average consumer of bottled water has changed from highly educated, upscale, white-collar North Americans to all social, economic, and age groups, The Bottled Water home page reports. [One major producer] bottles and ships five to six million bottles of natural spring water around the world each day . . . .

Water is essential to the human body. Whether you drink bottled or tap water, get with the flow and join the millions of Americans [who] are switching from soft drinks to water.

Allow time for students to discuss the student writing. Suggest that they identify its strengths and propose possible improvements. Use the model to introduce the concepts in the chapter.

Leslie's article begins with an attention grabber that draws the reader in. She includes facts, statistics, and quotations from people she has interviewed. Her article ends with a call to action.

As you reread the essay above, think about how much more difficult it would be to understand Leslie's message without punctuation! Think about how you use punctuation in the writing you do throughout this chapter.

End Marks and Abbreviations

■ Use a **period** at the end of a statement (declarative sentence) and at the end of a command (imperative sentence).

DECLARATIVE   No one knows who the woman in the *Mona Lisa* is.

IMPERATIVE   Please find out more about Leonardo da Vinci.

■ Use a **question mark** at the end of a direct question (interrogative sentence). An indirect question ends with a period.

DIRECT   Do you know who painted the *Mona Lisa*?

DIRECT   Abby asked me, "Do you know who painted the *Mona Lisa*?"

INDIRECT   Abby just asked me who painted the *Mona Lisa*.

■ Use an **exclamation point** at the end of an exclamation (exclamatory sentence).

Stop that thief! He's trying to steal the *Mona Lisa*!

■ Use a period after many abbreviations.

In general, when you write a paper or report for school or work, avoid using abbreviations. Instead, spell out the word. There are some common exceptions to this rule shown in the following chart.

Periods in Abbreviations				
CATEGORY	**EXAMPLE**			
Initials and Titles	Mr. A. N. O'Hara, Jr. Phyllis A. Washington, Ph.D.			
Times	A.M. P.M. B.C. B.C.E. A.D.			
Others	Inc. Co. Assn. etc. vs.			

■ Some abbreviations should not have a period.

An **acronym** is a word formed from the first letter(s) of several words, such as *NATO* (formed from *North Atlantic Treaty Organization*). Acronyms do not take periods.

The modern tendency is to omit the period following common abbreviations, such as *ft* (*foot* or *feet*) and *lb* (*pound*). Some other common abbreviations that don't take periods include *MPH (miles per hour)*, *AM* and *FM* radio, *TV*, *FBI*, *IRS*, and postal abbreviations for states (FL, OH, TX).

 If you're in doubt about whether to use a period with an abbreviation, check a college or unabridged dictionary, but be aware that even dictionaries differ in how they punctuate some abbreviations, including the abbreviations for United States (*US* or *U.S.*) and United Nations (*UN* or *U.N.*).

■ Beware of sentence fragments. Strategies for correcting sentence fragments appear in **Grammar** Lessons 5.3 and 13.6.

Editing Tip

When an abbreviation comes at the end of a sentence, use only one period.

The movie doesn't start until 10 P.M.

Don't omit a comma, a question mark, or an exclamation point following an abbreviation.

Oh, no! The test begins at 7:30 A.M.!

How can we know what happened in 800 B.C.?

Enriching Your Vocabulary

The verb *abridge* comes from the French *abregier*, which in turn comes from the Latin *abbreviare*, "to shorten." It is usually necessary to *abridge* the text of a novel for recording on audiotape. But something that is *unabridged* has not been condensed. An *unabridged* dictionary is too big to carry in your backpack.

Proofreading a Paragraph

Proofread the following paragraph to add end punctuation marks and periods for abbreviations as needed. If you're not sure whether an abbreviation takes a period, check a dictionary.

¹Have you ever visited Washington, DC **DC or D.C.** ²Last night, I watched a TV program about Washington ³Did you see it, too **?** ⁴If it's on again, be sure to see it **.** ⁵What an interesting city Washington is **!** ⁶Dr A Rogers, the narrator, took us viewers on a tour of the White House **.** ⁷Did you know that the White House wasn't painted white until 1817 **?** ⁸If I were visiting Washington, I'd like to tour the US Capitol **US or U.S.** at the foot of Pennsylvania Avenue **.** ⁹I'd also visit the Smithsonian's two underground museums: the Arthur M Sackler Gallery of Asian Art and the National Museum of African Art **.** ¹⁰Last year, my sister visited the Holocaust Museum, but she didn't have time to see the National Air and Space Museum because her plane left at 1:30 PM **P.M.**

Exercise 2 **Writing Sentences**

Work with a partner or small group to write sentences based on the information in the graph below. Write at least one exclamatory sentence and two interrogative sentences. You don't have to use all of the information.

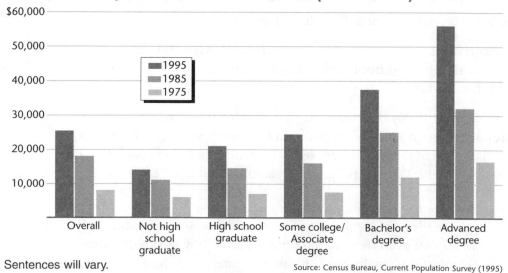

Average Annual Income of Workers 18 Years and Over by Educational Attainment (1975–1995)

Sentences will vary.

Source: Census Bureau, Current Population Survey (1995)

Commas in a Series

Commas signal a slight pause but not a complete stop. They are tricky punctuation marks that involve a lot of rules. In the next few lessons, you'll review the most important rules for using commas.

◆ Use commas to separate items in a series.

Many stylebooks do not require the last comma before the conjuctions.

A **series** contains three or more similar items in a row.

A human eye has a cornea, an iris, a lens, and a retina.

The girls like playing golf, reading books, and riding horses.

◆ Use a comma to separate two or more adjectives that precede and modify the same noun.

The human eye is a **complex, efficient** organ.

However, don't use a comma when the last adjective in a series is really part of a compound noun. You can tell if one of the adjectives belongs to the noun if you can reverse the position of the adjectives.

Whose **red eyeglass** case is this? [*Eyeglass case* is a compound noun.]

■ Mechanics
See also Lesson 14.3, which explains when to use semicolons rather than commas for a series.

Editing Tip

When a coordinating conjunction (such as *and* or *but*) connects a series of items, phrases, or clauses, *don't* add commas. Commas are needed between independent clauses.

Jean dropped a contact lens *and* searched for ten minutes *but* couldn't find it.

Jen dropped a lens, and she couldn't find it anywhere.

Exercise 3 **Proofreading Sentences**

The comma key is broken on her typewriter, so Abby wasn't able to put commas where she needs them. Insert all necessary commas. If a sentence is correct, write C. **Hint:** Not every sentence needs a comma.

1. Color blindness is an inability to distinguish one or more colors. C

2. Some birds, butterflies, and bees are to some extent color blind.

3. Some humans cannot distinguish the colors red, blue, and green.

4. Color blindness affects twenty times more men than women. C

5. Someone with monochromatism sees only black, white, and gray.

6. Picking out socks, coordinating outfits, and choosing new clothes are problems.

Step by Step

To decide whether to put a comma between two adjectives before a noun:

1. Put *and* between them. If *and* makes sense, use a comma.
   [and]
   I felt a sharp, stabbing pain in one eye. [use a comma]

2. If *and* doesn't make sense, don't use a comma.
   ~~and~~
   One tiny eyelash hurt my eye. [no comma]

7. A cab driver, train engineer, or pilot must be able to distinguish colors in traffic signals.

8. Color blindness would be a serious, annoying problem for an artist or fabric designer.

9. The vision of color-blind people is usually not limited in any other way. C

10. The test for color blindness involves detecting a figure in a field of dots, squares, and other shapes.

Proofreading Sentences

Insert all missing punctuation marks, including end marks.

1. A tall, red-haired young woman waited outside the stage door.

2. She huddled under an *enormous* umbrella covered with cats, dogs, and fish.

3. Three young actors, two dancers, and several musicians left the theater.

4. They glanced at her, turned away, and continued their conversations.

5. More actors, stagehands, and musicians emerged and hurried away.

6. She waited, she paced, and she looked at her watch.

7. A strong, wet, icy wind blew her umbrella inside out.

8. The young woman's program slipped and fell and landed in a puddle.

9. Finally, the show's star emerged along with her personal secretary, her dresser, and her understudy.

10. The starstruck young woman rushed forward with her wet program and pen, and begged for an autograph.
   No comma here is acceptable.

Exercise 5 Proofreading a Paper

Students should share their papers with partners.

Take a paper you have written recently or one you wrote last year, and proofread it carefully. Focus particularly on end marks and commas. Check to see whether you have used these punctuation marks correctly. If you decide to make any punctuation changes, be ready to explain why you made each change.

Enriching Your Vocabulary

Both the noun *enormity* and the adjective *enormous* are derived from the Latin adjective *enormis* (from *e*, or "out," and *norma*, or "rule"). *Enormity*, then, is the quality of exceeding the rule or norm or something of immense size. The public may be shocked by the *enormity* of a natural disaster. Similarly, something that is *enormous* is out of proportion to the norm. Most of us occasionally make an *enormous* mistake.

Compound Sentences and Phrases

 Use a comma before a coordinating conjunction (*and, but, or, nor, for, so,* and *yet*) that joins two independent clauses.

    After dinner, Dave washed the pile of dishes**,** and Sara dried them and put them away.

 Use a comma after an introductory participle or participial phrase.

    Terrified, the kitten hid under the bed.

    Terrified by the thunder, the kitten hid under the bed.

 Use a comma after an introductory prepositional phrase or a series of introductory prepositional phrases.

    In short, no one was prepared.

    At 2 A.M. on February 3, a series of tornadoes struck town.

P.S. A comma after a short prepositional phrase, as in the first example above, may not be necessary, but it's never wrong. If you get in the habit of adding a comma after all introductory prepositional phrases, you'll be sure your meaning is clear.

When the subject follows the verb, as in the following sentence, do *not* use a comma after the introductory prepositional phrases.

                V   S

    Behind the mirror in the front hall **is** a treasure **map**.

 Use a comma after an introductory adverb clause.

    If you look at the moon with binoculars, you'll see craters.

Editing Tip

Don't confuse a compound sentence with a sentence that has a compound subject or a compound verb. You don't need a comma between parts of a compound subject or compound verb.

COMPOUND VERB
Hana made the bread into loaves and let it rise near the oven. [no comma]

COMPOUND SENTENCE
Hana made the bread, and we ate it for dinner. [comma]

Exercise 6 Revising Sentences

On a separate piece of paper, revise each sentence so that it begins with an introductory element. Add commas where necessary.
Hint: You may have to add, drop, or change some words.
See Answer Key.

1. The brothers Orville and Wilbur Wright owned a bicycle repair shop in Dayton, Ohio, from 1892 to 1904.

2. The brothers experimented with different designs for an airplane, using the tools in their shop.

3. No one had flown a craft that was heavier than air, although people had flown balloons and gliders successfully.

Writing Hint

When you write paragraphs and essays, try to vary your sentences to avoid singsongy repetition. Use an introductory word, phrase, or subordinate clause to vary sentence beginnings.

4. The Wright brothers designed a power-driven biplane by attaching a homemade engine to a glider.

5. Orville Wright flew the plane 120 feet on December 17, 1903, at Kitty Hawk, North Carolina.

6. The Wright brothers made four flights that day, setting new aviation records.

7. The Wrights became world famous as they made longer flights during the next few years.

8. They founded the Wright Company in 1909, when the U.S. government ordered army planes.

9. You can visit the restored house where Orville was born as well as the Wrights' bicycle shop if you go to Greenfield Village, Michigan.

10. The government established the Wright National Monument in 1927 on more than four hundred acres in Kitty Hawk.

Exercise 7 **Writing a Paragraph**

Work with a partner or small group to write a paragraph of at least five sentences. The paragraph should be based on the following notes. Proofread your paragraph to make sure you've used commas correctly.

Students' paragraphs may vary.

1910—Baroness Raymonde de la Roche of France = 1st licensed woman pilot

1911—1st licensed U.S. woman pilot = Harriet Quimby, magazine writer

April 16, 1912—1st woman to fly across English Channel: Harriet Quimby

July 1, 1912—Quimby killed in crash during Harvard-Boston aviation meet

June 15, 1921—1st licensed African-American woman pilot: Bessie Coleman; killed in air crash in 1926

May 20-21, 1932—Amelia Earhart, 1st woman transatlantic solo, Newfoundland to Ireland, 15 hours

1932—1st woman commercial airline pilot: Ruth Rowland Nichols; held three international records: speed, distance, altitude

1973—Frontier Airlines hires Emily H. Warner, 1st female pilot of U.S. large airline

Dec. 14-23, 1986—Jeanna Yeager with Dick Rutan set records for speed & distance around world nonstop & nonrefueled

---

Sentence Interrupters and Nonessential Elements

Sentence interrupters are parts of a sentence that interrupt the main thought. At the end or beginning of a sentence, use a single comma to set off an interrupter. In the middle of a sentence, use a pair of commas.

- Use commas to set off a noun of direct address, the name of the person being spoken to.

    Sondra, did you know that the Bahamas became independent in 1973?

- Use commas to set off nonessential appositives and appositive phrases.

    The Bahamas are made up of 700 islands and 2,400 cays**, or small islands**.

    Nassau**, the capital,** is on New Providence Island.

- Use commas to set off parenthetical expressions and transitional expressions that interrupt a sentence.

    Christopher Columbus's first stop**, incidentally,** was in the Bahamas.

- Use commas to set off a nonessential adjective clause. Do not use commas with an essential adjective clause.

Every adjective clause is either essential or nonessential. An **essential adjective clause** is necessary to make the meaning of the sentence clear. Usually, it answers this question: "Which one(s)?" (A clause that begins with the word *that* is usually an essential clause.) A **nonessential adjective clause**, on the other hand, adds information, but the sentence makes sense without it.

ESSENTIAL Blackbeard was one of the pirates **who frequented Bahamian waters**.

NONESSENTIAL Blackbeard**, whose real name was Edward Teach,** died in 1718.

ESSENTIAL The Americans **who invaded Nassau in 1776** held it briefly.

NONESSENTIAL You can visit the forts on Nassau**, which were built to defend against a Spanish invasion**.

**MECHANICS
Lesson 13.4**

Some Common Parenthetical and Transitional Expressions

as a result
by the way
for example
for instance
furthermore
on the other hand
incidentally

in fact
moreover
nevertheless
of course

Step by Step

The Comma Test

To decide if an adjective clause should be set off with commas:

1. Try saying the sentence aloud without the adjective clause.

2. If the sentence makes sense without the adjective clause, that clause is *nonessential*. Use commas to set off the clause.

3. If the sentence doesn't make sense without the clause, that clause is *essential*. Do not use commas.

Proofreading Sentences

Proofread the following sentences, adding commas where they are needed. Write *C* if the sentence is correct.

1. Australia‸, which is between the Indian Ocean and the Pacific‸, is the smallest continent.

2. Bangladesh‸, a nation in southern Asia‸, became independent in 1971.

3. Did you know‸, Harold‸, that the Arctic Ocean has ice year-round?

4. Anchorage is Alaska's largest city‸, but not its capital.

5. Santa Fe‸, the capital of New Mexico‸, attracts many artists.

6. The Rio Grande is the river that forms our border with Mexico. C

7. Nova Scotia‸, which French settlers called Acadia‸, is one of the Canadian Maritime Provinces.

8. Iceland‸, a large island in the North Atlantic‸, has geysers.

9. Ms. Wu‸, how can we find out which cities have the most smog?

10. The Hague‸, of course‸, hosts the International Court of Justice.

Revising Sentences

On a separate piece of paper, revise each sentence by inserting at the caret mark (‸) the words in parentheses. Use commas correctly.

EXAMPLE   The river‸ is the Seine River. (that flows through Paris)
The river that flows through Paris is the Seine River.

1. The Sahara Desert‸ *, which is in northern Africa,* is the world's largest desert. (which is in northern Africa)

2. French is the main language‸ *that is spoken in Quebec*. (that is spoken in Quebec)

3. Florence is the city‸ *where da Vinci and Raphael lived*. (where da Vinci and Raphael lived)

4. Many ships have disappeared in the Bermuda Triangle‸ *, a region in the Atlantic Ocean*. (a region in the Atlantic Ocean)

5. The Arctic and Antarctic circles are imaginary‸ *, of course*. (of course)

6. Algiers‸ *, which is the capital of Algeria,* is a port city on the Mediterranean Sea. (which is the capital of Algeria)

7. The Nile River‸ *, which flows north from central Africa to the Mediterranean,* is the longest river in the world. (which flows north from central Africa to the Mediterranean)

8. ‸ *John, in* what part of Norway were your grandparents born? (John)

9. New Delhi‸ *, in fact,* replaced Calcutta as India's capital. (in fact)

10. Both Paul Gauguin and Robert Louis Stevenson chose to live in Tahiti‸ *, a South Pacific island*. (a South Pacific island)

Other Comma Uses

● Use commas to set off *well*, *yes*, *no*, and single-word adjectives that begin a sentence.

> Well, did you hear the good news?
> Yes, I did.   No, I didn't.
> Anxious, she looked at her watch for the twentieth time.
> Excited and happy, we waited to meet the adopted baby.

● Use commas to separate the date and year. No comma is needed between the month and date or between the month and year.

> Malcolm X (then Malcolm Little) was born on May 19, 1925.
> He was born on May 19.
> Malcolm X was assassinated on February 21, 1965.
> He was assassinated in February 1965.

● Use commas following the greeting and closing of a friendly letter.

> Dear Maya,   Sincerely,
> With love,   Best wishes,

Note: A comma may also be used to introduce some short, informal quotations. See Lesson 14.6 for the rules that govern the use of commas and colons in quotations.

Writing Hint

A business letter's form differs from that of a friendly letter (see page 264). Friendly letters have no heading (usually, the writer gives only the date of the letter) and no inside address. In a friendly letter, a comma (not a colon) follows the greeting. The signature is always handwritten instead of typewritten.

Exercise 10 Using Commas Correctly

Circle the letter of *all* the correct answers for each question.

1. Which of the following is an appropriate greeting for a friendly letter? (a) Dear Mr. Tannenbaum: (b) Dear Leila, (c) To whom it may concern: (d) Dear Grandma,

2. Which is an appropriate closing for a friendly letter? (a) Sincerely, (b) Love, (c) Sincerely yours: (d) Yours sincerely:

3. Which of the following sentences is correctly punctuated? (a) Mary Shelley, the author of *Frankenstein*, was born on August 30, 1797. (b) Mary Shelley, the author of *Frankenstein*, was born in August, 1797. (c) Mary Shelley, the author of *Frankenstein*, was born on August, 30, 1797.

4. Which of the following sentences is correctly punctuated? (a) Yes we have no bananas. (b) Yes, we have no bananas. (c) Yes, we have no bananas

Enriching Your Vocabulary

The adjective *apt* comes from the Latin *aptus*, which means "suited, fitted, or appropriate." The class valedictorian offered *apt* advice to the new graduates. *Aptitude*, used in Exercise 11, is derived from *aptus* and the suffix *–tudo* ("condition or quality"). Do you have an *aptitude* for a particular sport?

5. Which date line for a friendly letter is correctly punctuated?
   (a) September 19 1975 (b) May 8, 1986.
   (c) July 1, 1779 (d) November, 18, 1995

Exercise 11 | Proofreading a Friendly Letter

Proofread the friendly letter below. Add commas, periods, and other end punctuation marks where necessary. Correct any run-on sentences and sentence fragments. Be sure to check the spelling, too.

December 18, 2000

Dear Aunt Bea,

Wow! Thanks very much for the new dictionary. What a good birthday present. It's something I've wanted for a long time, but haven't been able to buy for myself. It's certainly a great improvement over Mom's old dictionary, which was printed in something like the Dark Ages.

I'll make good use of the dictionary because I'm trying to study a little for the PSAT exam later this year. Even though everyone says you can't really study for it. PSAT stands for Preliminary Scholastic Aptitude Test. It's a kind of practice test for the Scholastic Aptitude Test. The SAT is important when I apply for college.

Well, how are you? I hope that you, Uncle Rob, Rhea, and Mike have all been well. I know you're always busy, Aunt Bea, and I really admire your ability to work full time and run a house. What's new at work?

Yes, we're all looking forward to seeing you and the family on New Year's Day. I can't wait to impress you with my new vocabulary from the dictionary you sent me.

Much love,
Nina

Exercise 12 | Writing a Friendly Letter

Write a letter to a friend, relative, or pen pal, who lives far away. Tell the person about one or two experiences that you are willing to share with the class. Be sure to ask some questions, too, so that the person you're writing to will write back. Students' letters will vary.

Correcting Run-on Sentences and Sentence Fragments

■ **Use Grammar** Lesson 5.3 for practice in fixing sentence fragments. Use Lesson 5.7 for run-ons.

◖ A **run-on sentence** incorrectly combines two or more sentences. Use the following three strategies to correct run-on sentences.

1. Add end punctuation and a capital letter to break up the run-on sentence.

   RUN-ON   The earliest people were hunters and gatherers, agriculture came later.

   CORRECTED   The earliest people were hunters and gatherers. Agriculture came later.

2. Change the run-on into a compound sentence. Note the different corrections that are possible.

   RUN-ON   Hunters and gatherers roam freely, farmers stay in one place.

   CORRECTED   Hunters and gatherers roam freely, **but** farmers stay in one place.

   CORRECTED   Hunters and gatherers roam freely; **farmers** stay in one place.

3. Turn one of the sentences into a subordinate clause.

   CORRECTED   **Although hunters and gatherers roam freely,** farmers stay in one place.

◖ To correct a **sentence fragment**, use these three strategies.

1. Add the missing subject, verb, or both.

   FRAGMENT   With the cultivation of wild plants.

   CORRECTED   Agriculture began with the cultivation of wild plants.

2. Attach the fragment to a complete sentence before or after it.

   FRAGMENT   Some early farms were in the Southwest. In the land surrounding mesas.

   CORRECTED   Some early farms were in the Southwest in the land surrounding mesas.

3. Drop a subordinating conjunction.

   FRAGMENT   Because the women carried water to mesas.

   CORRECTED   The women carried water to mesas.

Writing Hint

If you always correct a fragment or run-on in the same way, your paragraphs may sound monotonous and singsongy. In a paragraph or essay, read the sentences aloud. See how they sound together. Aim for variety.

Exercise 13   **Proofreading a Paragraph**

Proofread the paragraph on the following page to correct run-ons and fragments. Read your revision aloud to see that the sentences sound smooth together.

[1]What happened to American farms during the last half of the twentieth century? [2]Take a look at the graphs in Exercise 14 ~~,~~ **. As** ~~as~~ the number of American farms decreased, the average size of American farms increased. [3]According to the first graph, there were more than six million farms in the United States in 1940 **.** **Now** ~~now~~ there are fewer than two million. [4]Where did the farms go? [5]Some family farms did disappear **as** ~~. [6]As~~ cities, suburbs, towns, and malls grew into what once were fields. [7]Most of America's farms, however, just got a lot bigger. [8]The second graph shows the acreage of the average farm. [9] **There has been a** ~~A~~ steady increase in farm size from 1940 to 1997. [10]In 1940, the average American farm was 174 acres **;** in 1997 the average farm was 470 acres.

Exercise 14 Writing a Paragraph

Working with a partner, use the graphs below to write at least five sentences. Proofread your sentences to check for the correct use of commas and to eliminate fragments and run-ons. Then exchange sentences with another pair of classmates, and compare what you've written. Students' sentences will vary.

U.S. Farms, 1940–1997

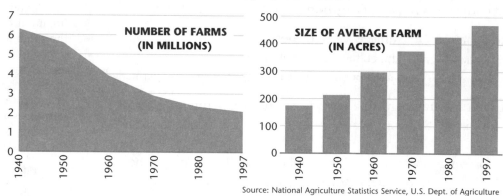

Source: National Agriculture Statistics Service, U.S. Dept. of Agriculture

Exercise 15 Write What You Think

Work with a small group to make two separate charts listing what you think are the advantages and disadvantages of living (1) on a farm and (2) in a city. Write at least one paragraph, clearly stating your opinion about where you would rather live and supporting your opinion with reasons. When you've finished writing, proofread your paragraph to make sure there are no sentence fragments or run-on sentences. Check for correct commas. Answers will vary. Give students full credit if they have stated an opinion and attempted to support their opinions. They should also have written grammatically complete sentences that begin with a capital letter and end with an appropriate end punctuation mark.

Editing and Proofreading Worksheet 1

Correct sentence fragments and run-on sentences in the following paragraphs and make any other changes you think will improve the paragraphs. Check for the correct use of commas, periods, and other end punctuation marks. Proofread carefully. Work with a partner or small group. Write your revised paragraphs on a separate piece of paper, and compare your response with those made by other pairs or groups of classmates.

[1]In many cultures around the world~~their~~ , there are myths about a trickster hero. [2]The Native Americans of the Pacific Northwest, for example, have many stories about Raven. [3]~~Their~~ He is their trickster hero, who can change his shape through magic.

[4]Long ago at the beginning of the world. [5]Raven brought the Indian people the sun, the moon, and fire. [6]In the dark, cold world of earliest times, the people had no fire. [7]All of the people ate raw food and shivered in the cold. [8]Because Raven knew that there was fire up in the sky, , one [9]~~One~~ night he flew up through a hole in the sky to the tent of the sun. [10]He transformed himself into a baby boy and lay outside the tent. [11]The daughter of the skies found him, and brought him into the sun's tent. [12]The baby boy grew quickly. and became [13]~~Became~~ a toddler in four days. [14]Although everyone was kind to the little boy, he cried because he wanted to play with the sun's fire. [15]Raven cried and cried, until finally the sun said he could play with a small stick of firewood.

[16]As soon as he got the fire, the little boy transformed himself into his real shape. Raven held the firestick in his beak and escaped ~~threw~~ through a smoke hole in (the sun's tent. [17]The smoke dyed all his feathers black, ~~and~~ which is why Ravens are still) black to this day. [18]The people who lived in the sky were furious, . They ~~they~~ chased Raven but they could not catch him. [19]Raven found the hole in the sky, dived down to Earth, and carefully lay the stolen fire on dry wood. It ~~it~~ was the first fire on Earth. [20]~~Also~~ Raven also taught the people how to start a fire by rubbing two sticks together.

Editing and Proofreading Worksheet 2

Correct sentence fragments and run-on sentences in the following paragraphs and make any other changes you think will improve the paragraphs. Check for the correct use of commas, periods, and other end punctuation marks. Proofread carefully. Work with a partner or small group. Write your revised paragraphs on a separate piece of paper, and compare your response with those made by other pairs or groups of classmates. Students' revisions may vary. A sample revision is given.

¹Have you ever taken care of a baby or young child? if you have, you know [If] how exhausting babies can be a baby is totally helpless. ²And dependent for [A] [and] survival on a parent or caregiver. ³One of the most difficult problems caregivers face is a baby who seems to cry endlessly. ⁴Its difficult to listen. ⁵To a crying [It's] [to] baby who can't tell you what's wrong.

⁶When babies cry? ⁷Child-care experts advise a process of elimination. ⁸To [, child-care] [to] try to find out what's wrong first check the baby's diaper. some babies object to [. First,] [Some] being wet or in soiled diapers, then see if the baby is hungry; doctors don't [Then] [Doctors] recommend that caregivers try to put newborns and very young babies on a feeding schedule; they should be fed whenever they are hungry. ⁹If a baby feels hot or seems sick, take his or her temperature, of course, and call a doctor.

¹⁰Babies learn to trust the world when they are fed and changed. ¹¹And gently [and] held and cuddled. ¹²Its a good idea to talk, sing, or even read to young babies; [It's] they learn from the sound of your voice. ¹³Some babies fall asleep. ¹⁴When they [when] are gently rocked or rolled in a carriage.

¹⁵It takes a lot of patience, kindness, and energy to raise a baby into a child. ¹⁶It also takes someone to ask for advice. many child-care experts have written [Many] guidebooks on baby care. ¹⁷If you can, buy or borrow one. ¹⁸There are television programs, too. ¹⁹Remember that a newborn human is totally helpless and completely dependent. ²⁰be glad when he or she is old enough to tell you [Be] what's wrong.

Chapter Review

Exercise A **Proofreading Proverbs**

Proofread the following **proverbs**, or wise sayings. Add commas and end punctuation marks as needed.

> EXAMPLE   Too many boatmen will drive the boat up the mountain.

1. Deal with the faults of others as gently as you do your own.

2. A people without history is like wind on the buffalo grass.

3. What does a frog in the well know about the ocean?

4. If you want to get on in the world, first help others to get on.

5. Yes, Virginia, there is a Santa Claus.

6. When the tiger is away, the rabbit is master.

7. So long as there is bread to eat, water to drink, and a bended arm to sleep on, happiness is not impossible.

8. Who knows this morning what will happen tonight?

9. Oh, the good times when we were so unhappy!

10. If two people keep a horse between them, it will be thin; if two people share a boat, it will leak.

Exercise B **Using Commas and End Marks Correctly**

In the following sentences, insert all missing commas, periods, and other end marks.

1. Citrus fruits, tomatoes, and broccoli are sources of Vitamin C.

2. Broccoli, in fact, also contains Vitamin A, calcium, and potassium.

3. Jorge, did we plant the grapefruit tree in May 1996?

4. Yes, it bears grapefruit from about October through March.

5. I like picking strawberries and tomatoes, for instance.

6. Did you know that strawberries are really false fruits?

7. The real fruits of a strawberry are those tiny black specks.

8. When you julienne a raw vegetable, you cut it into thin strips.

9. Parmesan and Romano, for example, are hard cheeses but mozzarella and Monterey Jack are soft cheeses.

10. How lucky we are to have summer fruits available all year! *or* .

Exercise C Revising Sentences

Revise each sentence by inserting the words shown in parentheses at the caret mark. Add commas and end punctuation where necessary. Check to see that your sentences are punctuated correctly.

1. A trio is a group of three; a quartet has four ^ (of course)
   <small>, of course , .</small>

2. Captain Ahab ^ was obsessed with killing the white whale ^ (who commanded the *Pequod*)
   <small>, who commanded the *Peqoud* , .</small>

3. Harriet Beecher Stowe's *Uncle Tom's Cabin* ^ is a powerful antislavery novel ^ (which appeared in 1851)
   <small>, which appeared in 1851 , .</small>

4. When was the Bill of Rights added to the Constitution ^ (Maxine)
   <small>, Maxine ?</small>

5. How did Beowulf ^ kill the monster Grendel ^ (hero of the English epic poem)
   <small>, hero of the English epic poem , ?</small>

6. *Gulliver's Travels* by Jonathan Swift is a satire ^ (that ridicules human weaknesses)
   <small>that ridicules human weaknesses .</small>

Exercise D Proofreading a Paragraph

The following mess of words is a puzzle for you to figure out. Make it into a paragraph by separating it into sentences. Add commas, periods, and other end marks. Be sure to begin each sentence with a capital letter.

when you're looking for a quotation to begin or end an essay you may find exactly what you're looking for in a book of quotations you can usually find several books of quotations in a library or bookstore for example *Bartlett's Familiar Quotations* which is in its sixteenth edition contains more than 20,000 quotations by 2,550 authors you can look up a quotation in two ways in *Bartlett's* if you already know the quotation but want to check the exact wording you can look up one of its main words in the alphabetical index at the back of the book if you're looking for quotations by a specific author check the alphabetical list of authors at the beginning of the book for instance you can find twelve different quotations by Dr Martin Luther King, Jr the entry for every author lists his or her birth and death dates as well as the source and date for every quotation other books of quotations are organized by theme and some books contain only quotations by women African Americans or other special sources

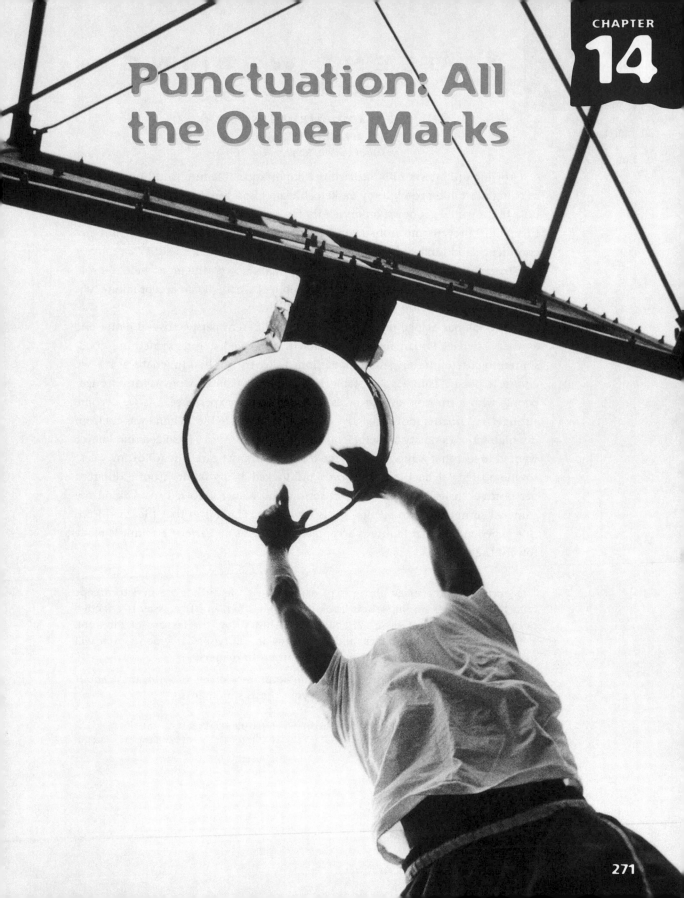

Punctuation: All the Other Marks

STUDENT WRITING
Expository Essay

An Important Lesson
by Mandy Kiaha
high school student, Kamehameha, Hawaii

Growing up, I never fully realized the importance of failure, and I never saw it as being something good. If my basketball team lost a game or if I got a bad grade on a test, I would get down on myself for failing. Not only did blaming myself for the failure prevent me from learning from it and improving, it also hurt my confidence and hindered my development even more. Then, I read *I Can't Accept Not Trying* by Michael Jordan. The author, a well-known athlete, as well as a role model of mine, said it best in this book when he [wrote], "I can accept failure, but I can't accept not trying."

This book has helped me see things from a different perspective—a better one at that. Michael Jordan took failure and transformed it into something good, something useful. He suggested that as long as we try our best in whatever it is we choose to pursue, failure is acceptable. In this respect, failure shapes us into stronger people who learn from and grow as a result of these experiences. As we become stronger and smarter individuals, we become successful in life. When I was cut from my high school's varsity basketball team my sophomore year, I realized that I never wanted to feel that way again, to have that hole in my heart. The following week, I remembered Michael Jordan's words and looked at my failure from a different perspective. Instead of wallowing in sorrow and blame, I vowed to work on my game all summer and to set new goals for myself. The lesson that I learned from this experience is that failure is acceptable as long as an earnest attempt is made toward the goal.

The purpose of the essay above is to explain how the author learned to accept failure. She names an important book that helped her, but the essay is effective because the author relates an anecdote that shows how the lessons of the book influenced her. Facts, statistics, and anecdotes are all types of evidence that will make your writing more effective and interesting to readers.

As you learn more ways to use punctuation accurately in this chapter, think about using anecdotes like this one to support your thesis statements.

Allow time for students to discuss the student writing. Suggest that they identify its strengths and propose possible improvements. Use the model to introduce the concepts in the chapter.

Colons *MRT/CLIPP*

A colon (:) signals that something will follow: a list, a long quotation, or a formal statement.

◀ Use a **colon** before a list of items, especially after the words *the following* or *the following items*.

COLON   Among Dickens's most popular novels are the following**:** *A Christmas Carol*, *Great Expectations*, and *A Tale of Two Cities*.

Exception: Do not use a colon when the list follows the main verb of a sentence or a preposition.

NO COLON   The main characters in *A Tale of Two Cities* are Sydney Carton, Lucie Manette, and Charles Darnay.

◀ Use a colon before a formal statement or quotation and before a long quotation that is set off as a block (any quotation of more than three lines).

The editor points out why *A Tale of Two Cities* is unique among Dickens's novels**:** "It is the one work in the whole series that fully merits the title of a 'historical' novel."

When a long quotation (more than three lines) is set off as a block, indent the quotation, and don't use quotation marks.

A Tale of Two Cities begins with a long run-on sentence that states a series of **paradoxes:**

> It was the best of times, it was the worst of times, it was the age of wisdom, it was the age of foolishness, it was the epoch of belief, it was the epoch of incredulity, it was the season of Light, it was the season of Darkness, it was the spring of hope, it was the winter of despair. . . .

◀ Use a colon to emphasize a word or a phrase.

Madame Defarge and her husband resemble two of Shakespeare's most famous characters**:** Lady Macbeth and Macbeth.

◀ Use a colon in these situations: (1) between the hour and minutes, (2) between the chapter and verse in a reference to the Bible, and (3) after the greeting of a business letter.

8**:**30 A.M.   Genesis 12**:**1–3   Dear Accounting Department**:**

Editing Tip

Many people confuse colons and semicolons. Although these two punctuation marks look alike and their names are similar, they are *not* interchangeable. Colons and semicolons do totally different work. Lesson 14.3 gives the rules for using semicolons.

Writing Hint

You can also use a comma to introduce a short quotation, but always use a colon before a long quotation and in formal writing.

Enriching Your Vocabulary

The noun *paradox* closely resembles its Greek root *paradoxos*, which means "unbelievable" or "beyond what is thought." In a country as wealthy as the United States, hunger is a *paradox*.

■ **See Mechanics Lesson 14.2 for additional information on using colons in business letters.**

Exercise 1 Adding Colons to Sentences

Insert colons where they are needed in the following sentences. **Hint:** Not every sentence requires a colon. In sentences 8 and 9, accept a comma or a dash as well as a colon.

1. The two cities in Dickens's tale are Paris and London.

2. The novel deals with these issues: love, justice, mercy, and loyalty.

3. In the preface, Dickens acknowledges Thomas Carlyle's *History of the French Revolution*.

4. A maid accidentally destroyed Carlyle's manuscript of that history by throwing it into a fire.

5. Here is Dickens's stated purpose: "It has been one of my hopes to add something to the popular and picturesque means of understanding that terrible time. . . ."

6. Chapter 3 opens with this line: "A wonderful fact to reflect upon, that every human creature is constituted to be that profound secret and mystery to every other."

7. Among the novel's memorable minor characters are Miss Pross and Jerry Cruncher.

8. Cruncher holds two jobs: an odd-job man by day and a body snatcher by night.

9. Readers can never forget Madame Defarges's hobby: knitting.

10. The novel ends with Carton's words: "'It is a far, far better thing that I do, than I have ever done; it is a far, far better rest that I go to, than I have ever known.'"

Exercise 2 Writing a Journal Entry

What is your schedule for Monday, a typical school day? Tell what you do during the day; begin each entry with the time. Write complete sentences.

EXAMPLE   *7:15 A.M. I wake up, eat breakfast, and get dressed.*
Students' answers will vary.

Writing Business Letters

If you want to request information or an interview, you can write a **letter of request**. Do you want to order a sweatshirt for your brother? If there's no toll-free number, write an **order letter**. If something you've ordered arrives in the wrong color or size, write a **letter of complaint**.

🖊 When you write a business letter, follow the proper form for style, spacing, and punctuation.

A business letter has six parts. Each part is labeled in the model letter below. This letter follows the **full block style** in which every part of the letter begins at the left-hand margin.

Writing Hint

A business letter should be clear and brief. Be sure to include all necessary information. Check your spelling, punctuation, and grammar, too, especially if you're applying for a job. Remember that your letter advertises you.

2210 Nashville Avenue
New Orleans, LA 70115
December 19, 2003

Heading
Writer's address and date

Customer Service Department
APL Music Service
P.O. Box 871149
Indianapolis, IN 46291–0149

Inside Address
Name of person or department
Company name
Street address
City, state and ZIP code
(no comma after state)

Dear Customer Service Department:

Salutation
followed by a colon

I am a new member, and my account number is 801562–42M.

On October 30, I mailed you a coupon for the three free CDs I am entitled to receive after buying one CD at regular club prices. I had already purchased one CD at regular club prices. I am enclosing a photocopy of the coupon, which shows the three CDs I asked for.

I have heard nothing from you about these three free CDs. Please tell me when I will receive them.

Body

Sincerely,

Amie Moriani

Amie Moriani

Closing
followed by a comma

Handwritten signature
followed by typed name

Understanding Business Letter Form

In the space provided, write the letters of *all* of the correct answers for each question. Some questions may have more than one correct answer.

_____d_____ 1. Which of the following is an appropriate greeting for a business letter? (a) Dear Mrs. Mikala, (b) Dear Ms. Mikala, (c) Dear Ms. Mikala; (d) Dear Mrs. Mikala:

_____b, c_____ 2. Which is an appropriate closing for a business letter? (a) Sincerely yours: (b) Sincerely yours, (c) Yours truly, (d) Sincerely;

_____b_____ 3. Which of the following comes right below the inside address? (a) the heading (b) the salutation (c) the body of the letter (d) the signature

_____b_____ 4. What goes on the *first* line of the three-line heading? (a) your name (b) your street address (c) your city, state, and ZIP code (d) your telephone number

_____d_____ 5. Which is the correctly written *last* line of an inside address? (a) June 21 2000 (b) June 21, 2000 (c) Del Mar, CA, 92014 (d) Del Mar, California 92014

_____d_____ 6. Which of these are important in a business letter? (a) accuracy (b) clarity (c) correct letter form and grammar (d) all of the above

Exercise 4 Writing a Business Letter

Write a business letter for one of the situations suggested below. Use the full block style shown on page 275. Use today's date in the heading. Proofread your letter for business letter form, grammar, punctuation, and spelling.

1. You are ordering a $12.95 sweatshirt with the logo of your favorite team. Write to Sports Clothing, Inc., at 87-62 Jamaica Avenue in Westbury, New York. The ZIP code is 11590. Tell the size, color, and team, and enclose a money order with your letter.

2. Your sweatshirt has arrived, but it's the wrong team. Write a letter of complaint to the same company (address above). Ask the customer service department to send you the right sweatshirt and to tell you how to return the wrong one.

3. You are writing to Dr. Carlos Eckels, Director of the Museum of Science in your community (or in a nearby city). Make up an address for the museum. You want to interview Dr. Eckels for a paper you're writing about a science program for preschool children. Identify yourself, tell why you are writing, and tell him that you'll call in a few days to make an appointment for the interview.   Students' letters will vary.

Semicolons

A **semicolon** (;) signals a pause that is longer than a comma's pause but shorter than a period's.

● Use a semicolon to join independent clauses in a compound sentence when you are not using a coordinating conjunction.

SEMICOLON   For more than fifty years, Ellis Island was an immigration station; it closed in 1954.

COMMA   For more than fifty years, Ellis Island was an immigration station, **but** it was closed in 1954.

● Use a semicolon before a conjunctive adverb or transitional expression that joins independent clauses. Use a comma after the conjunctive adverb or transitional expression.

Ellis Island was abandoned for decades; **however,** some of the buildings have been carefully restored.

● Use a semicolon to separate items in a series when one or more of the items contains a comma.

Uncle Ned's grandfather from Kiev, Russia; Frank's great-grandmother from County Cork, Ireland; and JoAnn's great-grandparents from Naples, Italy, all passed through Ellis Island.

Exercise 5 Using Semicolons and Colons

Some of the following sentences need a semicolon; others require colons. Review the rules for colons in Lesson 14.1, and then add the proper punctuation marks. If a sentence is correct, write C.

1. Samuel Ellis, a farmer, owned Ellis Island in the early 1700s; the U.S. government bought it in 1808.

2. Ellis Island is in New Jersey waters; however, an 1834 agreement brought it under New York jurisdiction.

3. The first stop for twelve million immigrants was Ellis Island; 98 percent of them entered the United States.

4. They came for many reasons: to escape religious persecution or starvation, to find a better way of life, and to be reunited with family.

5. Steerage passengers went through Ellis Island; first-class passengers did not.

6. Doctors examined new arrivals for infectious diseases; some were sent back home.

Some Common Conjunctive Adverbs

accordingly	meanwhile
also	moreover
besides	nevertheless
consequently	otherwise
furthermore	still
however	then
indeed	therefore

Some Common Transitional Expressions

as a result	in other
for example	words
for instance	on the other
in addition	hand
in fact	that is

Editing Tip

When these same words (conjunctive adverbs and transitional expressions) are sentence interrupters, they're set off on both sides by commas.

Our view, however, was blocked by a steel beam. We couldn't, as a result, see home plate.

Enriching Your Vocabulary

The Latin roots of the noun *jurisdiction* are *juris* (law or right) and *dictio* (the act of saying). Thus, *jurisdiction* means "the legal power to rule on a matter" or "the power to exercise authority." The approval of a nominee to the Supreme Court falls within the *jurisdiction* of the U.S. Senate.

7. Government officials denied entrance to the following: criminals and the insane.

8. At its busiest, Ellis Island had thirty-five buildings; the main building has been carefully restored.

9. President Johnson declared Ellis Island a National Historic Site in 1964. In 1989, the Museum of Immigration opened. C

10. There you can see photographs, passports, and other documents; you can listen to tapes of immigrants' Ellis Island memories.

Exercise 6 ▪ Using Punctuation in Compound Sentences

On a separate piece of paper, combine each set of independent clauses into a compound sentence. Do *not* use coordinating conjunctions. Check your combined sentences for proper punctuation.   See Answer Key.

1. An immigrant is someone who comes to live in a new country. An emigrant is someone who leaves a country.

2. American Indians are native Americans. Every other American is an immigrant or a descendant of immigrants.

3. The first colonists were English. Later immigrants came from other Western European countries.

4. Some came to escape religious persecution. However, most sought a better economic opportunity.

5. As the country expanded, immigrants moved west to find land. For instance, Danes, Norwegians, and Swedes staked out farms on the Great Plains.

6. During the 1840s and 1850s, about 1.5 million Irish arrived. They came to escape the potato famine.

7. From the 1880s to the 1920s, 4.5 million Italians arrived. During the same period, 2.5 million Jews immigrated.

8. Communists took over Cuba in 1959. As a result, about 700,000 Cubans moved to the United States.

Exercise 7 ▪ Write What You Think

Some people think the government should allow more legal immigrants to enter the United States. Others feel that there should be fewer legal immigrants.

Write what you think about the number of legal immigrants. State your opinion clearly, and support it with reasons and evidence.   Answers will vary. Give students full credit if they have stated an opinion on one of the issues and attempted to support the opinion. They should also have written gramatically complete sentences that begin with a capital letter and end with an appropriate punctuation mark.

Underlining (Italics)

If you're writing by hand or on a typewriter, use underlining to indicate italics. But if you're writing on a computer, you can actually use italic type. (*Italic type is the slanted type that looks like this*.) Use underlining or italics, not both.

◖ Use underlining (or italics) for the following kinds of titles and names:

BOOKS	*The Odyssey Up from Slavery Pride and Prejudice*
MAGAZINES	*Sports Illustrated Scientific American*
NEWSPAPERS	*USA Today The Washington Post The Los Angeles Times*
PLAYS	*The Piano Lesson Romeo and Juliet The Miracle Worker*
MOVIES	*2001: A Space Odyssey The Empire Strikes Back E.T.*
TV/RADIO SERIES	*60 Minutes Masterpiece Theatre*
WORKS OF ART	Georgia O'Keeffe's *Red Poppy*
	Vincent van Gogh's *The Starry Night*
SHIPS, PLANES,	*H.M.S. Titanic Spirit of St. Louis*
SPACECRAFT	*Apollo 13* the space shuttle *Atlantis*

◖ Use italics for foreign words and expressions that are not commonly used, and for words, letters, and numbers referred to as such.

FOREIGN WORDS	*E pluribus unum* means "out of many, one."
	I listed my studies at the *Instituto Internacional* on my résumé. [The word *résumé* is French, but is commonly used and should not be italics]
WORDS AS WORDS	Is *advice* or *advise* the right word for this sentence?
LETTERS	How many *s*'s are there in your name?
NUMBERS	What is the next ordinal number after the number *9*?

Editing Tip

Not all titles are italicized. Many kinds of titles (short stories, poems, songs, and others) belong in quotation marks (see Lesson 14.5).

Exercise 8 Revising a Report

Read the following review. Add underlining to indicate italics, and check for mistakes in spelling and punctuation.

[1]The Disney Studio's animated movie <u>The Lion King</u> was a box office hit, but the Broadway musical is an even bigger hit. [2]The Broadway show, <u>The Lion King</u>, got all <u>A</u>'s from reviewers; <u>magical</u> is the word they use most often to describe the show. [3]It's such a sellout that a cartoon in <u>The New Yorker</u> magazine suggests a ticket to the show as an appropriate

gift for a newborn baby. ⁴In <u>The New York Times</u> and other newspapers, scalpers advertise tickets for three hundred dollars and up.

⁵<u>The Lion King</u> on Broadway adds gorgeous African music and dance plus highly imaginative staging and costumes. ⁶Perhaps someday there'll be a movie version of this Broadway version of the Disney movie. ⁷(Where will it all end?)

⁸The concept of talking animals with human emotions, so basic to both versions of the hit, isn't new. ⁹It's found in Rudyard Kipling's <u>The Jungle Book</u> (talking tropical animals) and in Richard Adams's <u>Watership Down</u> (talking rabbits)—and even in Beatrix Potter's <u>The Tale of Peter Rabbit</u> (more talking rabbits).

¹⁰Adaptations of books are sometimes—but not always—a winning formula for stage and screen. ¹¹Consider these big winners: <u>West Side Story</u> (based on William Shakespeare's <u>The Tragedy of Romeo and Juliet</u>), <u>My Fair Lady</u> (based on George Bernard Shaw's play <u>Pygmalion</u>), <u>Les Misérables</u> (based on a novel by Victor Hugo), and <u>Mary Poppins</u> (based on a series of children's books by P. L. Travers). ¹²In contrast to the musical and movie based on the sinking of the <u>Titanic</u>, an event that actually occurred, all of these hit plays sprang from the writers' imaginations.

Exercise 9 **Writing Brief Reviews**

On a separate piece of paper, write a brief review of (1) your favorite movie, (2) your favorite television series, and (3) your favorite book. Explain as specifically as you can why you've chosen each one as the best. Write one or more paragraphs for each of the three works. Share your reviews to see if anyone else has named your favorites. Check each other's paragraphs for the correct use of italics and other punctuation marks. Reviews will vary. Each student should write one or more paragraphs for all three reviews.

Quotation Marks

● Use **quotation marks** for titles of short works.

POEMS	"Courage" "Mending Wall" "The Road Less Traveled"
SHORT STORIES	"The Most Dangerous Game" "Through the Tunnel"
ARTICLES	"Michigan Starts the New Year in Style"
	"An Interview with Maya Angelou"
SONGS	"Lift Ev'ry Voice and Sing" "Candle in the Wind"
SINGLE TV PROGRAMS	"Shirley Temple: The Biggest Little Star"
PARTS OF BOOKS	Chapter 3, "A New Nation"

P.S. It isn't easy to remember which kinds of titles are italicized and which go in quotation marks. If you're not sure about which one to use, check a punctuation guide such as this book or a book such as *The Chicago Manual of Style* or *Words into Type.*

● Use quotation marks at the beginning and end of a direct quotation.

When a direct quotation is an entire sentence, begin with a capital letter. Introduce a short, one-sentence quotation with a comma. When only a word or two is quoted, use a lowercase letter if the quoted words do not begin the sentence.

> Of the Louisiana Purchase, H. W. Elson writes, "The bargain was a great one for America."
>
> H. W. Elson called the bargain that America got "a great one."

Exercise 10 **Punctuating Sentences**

Add or change punctuation marks in the following sentences. If a sentence is punctuated correctly, write *C*.

1. Tennyson's poem "The Eagle" contains this memorable

    image: The wrinkled sea beneath him crawls. . . ."

2. "My candle burns at both ends; / It will not last the night, . . . "
    wrote the American poet Edna St. Vincent Millay.

3. Edgar Allan Poe's raven keeps repeating one word: "Nevermore."

4. In her essay "Choice: A Tribute to Dr. Martin Luther King, Jr.," Alice

    Walker writes, "He gave us back our heritage."

Editing Tip

Do not use quotation marks for an indirect quotation.

DIRECT
"Please close the door," she said.

INDIRECT
She asked me to close the door.

Quotation Marks with Other Punctuation Marks

• **Periods** and **commas** always go inside closing quotation marks.

• **Semicolons** and **colons** always go outside closing quotation marks.

• **Question marks** and **exclamation points** go inside closing quotation marks if the quotation is a question or an exclamation. They go outside if the whole sentence is a question or an exclamation.

■ For placement of quotation marks in dialogue, see Lesson 14.6.

5. "The Dynasty: The Nehru–Gandhi Story" is a TV documentary about India's independence.

6. Anne Morrow Lindbergh wrote: "The wave of the future is coming and there is no fighting it."

7. What do you think "the pursuit of happiness" means? C

8. I really enjoyed reading Anton Chekhov's short story "The Bet."

9. "Song of Myself," Walt Whitman's poem, begins with this line: "I celebrate myself, and sing myself. . . ."

10. In *The Way to Rainy Mountain*, N. Scott Momaday writes: "Tai-me came to the Kiowas in a vision born of suffering and despair."

Exercise 11 **Write Your Own Exercise**

On a separate piece of paper, write one or more complete sentences on each topic in the numbered items below. Leave out all punctuation marks. Then exchange papers with a classmate, and see if you agree on how to punctuate each sentence. See the summary on page 281 about where to place other punctuation marks in relation to quotation marks. See Answer Key.

1. a song that's popular now (Mention the title and the performer.)

2. a direct quotation (an actual quotation or a made-up one) at the beginning of a sentence

3. a chapter title from a book and a summary of what's in the chapter (Use this book if you wish.)

4. a poem you've read and your thoughts about it (Mention the poem's title and author.)

5. a song that's been around a long time and the reason for its popularity

6. a newspaper or magazine article and your thoughts about it (an actual article or a made-up title)

7. a short story you've read and your thoughts about it (Mention the title and author.)

8. a TV program (a single episode, not a series) you watched last week and your thoughts about it (Make up a title for the program if you can't remember it.)

9. an indirect quotation

10. a direct quotation that's not a whole sentence (Make one up, and use it within a complete sentence.)

Punctuating Dialogue

Dialogue is the words the characters in a novel say. The words that identify the speaker (*he said, she said*) are called a **dialogue tag**. Follow these rules for punctuating dialogue and direct quotations.

Enriching Your **Vocabulary**

The noun *dialogue* comes from a Greek verb, *dialegesthai*, meaning "to converse." The prefix *dia* tells us that at least two individuals are involved. A *monologue*, on the other hand, is spoken by one person. Hamlet's most famous *monologue* begins "To be, or not to be."

◖ Begin a new paragraph every time the speaker changes.

◖ Place quotation marks at the beginning and end of a speaker's exact words.

   "Nori, it's time for you to learn some origami**,**" Mrs. Muro said.

◖ When a dialogue tag interrupts a quoted sentence, begin the second part of the quotation with a lowercase letter.

   "Maybe**,**" Nori said, "you can teach me how to make a paper crane?"

If the second part of a divided quotation is a complete sentence, it should begin with a capital letter.

   "Do your homework," Nori's mother said. "Grandmother might teach you when you're through."

◖ When a direct quotation comes at the beginning of a sentence, use a comma, question mark, or exclamation point—but *not* a period—to separate it from the dialogue tag that follows.

   "Of course, I will**,**" Mrs. Muro answered.

◖ Commas and periods always go *inside* the closing quotation marks.

   "While you wash the dishes, I'll get my papers**,**" Grandma said.

◖ When the speaker's words are a question or an exclamation, place the question mark or exclamation point *inside* the closing quotation marks.

   "Do you remember how you cried when the paper cranes got wet**?**"
   "Yes **!**" laughed Nori, remembering.

Writing Hint

To write natural-sounding dialogue, use sentence fragments, contractions, and slang words and expressions. Also, don't overuse *said*. Try to use verbs that express the speaker's tone of voice, such as *whispered, laughed, complained,* and *insisted*.

◖ When the quotation itself isn't a question or exclamation, place the question mark or exclamation point *outside* the closing quotation marks.

   Who said, "I have but one life to give for my country"**?**   ✗
   Please stop saying "It's all your fault"**!**

◖ When the quotation is a question use a question mark inside the closing quotation mark. Place a period after the dialogue tag that follows.

   "Didn't you think they were beautiful**?**" she said**.**

Exercise 12 Writing a Dialogue

Work with a partner or small group to create one or more of the following dialogues. Write the dialogue on a separate sheet of paper, following the conventions for punctuating dialogue. Find a partner or partners to role play your dialogue for a small group or the whole class. Students' answers will vary.

1. Write a conversation between two space visitors watching a football game (or any other sport) for the first time.

2. Write a dialogue in which two people are in conflict. Some possibilities include: a brother and sister, a boyfriend and girlfriend, two good friends.

3. Write a conversation involving three friends that you might overhear in a store, on a bus, in the school cafeteria, or after school.

Exercise 13 Punctuating Dialogue

On a separate piece of paper rewrite the following dialogue. Add all the appropriate punctuation marks. See Answer Key.

¹Tina and Lou are waiting for the school bus. ²Last night I read an article about a girl who's the kicker on her high school football team Tina told Lou. ³Really! he exclaimed. ⁴I don't believe you! ⁵Really, Tina insisted. ⁶Her name is Anna Lakovitch, and she goes to a private high school. ⁷She's the captain of the school soccer team, too, which is probably why she's such a good kicker. ⁸Hmphhh! Lou snorted. ⁹I can't believe they'd let girls play on a school varsity team. ¹⁰Tina's voice rose And why not, Lou? ¹¹If girls want to play football, they should play with other girls, not guys. ¹²They don't belong on a guy team, he growled. ¹³Well, her teammates like having her there. ¹⁴She scores points for them. ¹⁵And do you know what? she asked. ¹⁶Lou grunted What? ¹⁷Her football team nominated her as homecoming queen Tina announced and she won. ¹⁸She was crowned during half-time—wearing her football uniform!

Exercise 14 Write What You Think

Write one or more paragraphs in which you state your opinion clearly on these three questions. Support your opinion with well developed reasons and evidence.

• Should girls and boys play on the same varsity high school team?

• Should laws be passed enforcing a girl's right to try out and play for a school's varsity team?

• Is it inappropriate in some sports to have girls and boys on the same team? If so, which ones? Answers will vary. Give students full credit if they have stated an opinion on each of the three questions and attempted to support their opinions. They should also have written grammatically complete sentences that begin with a capital letter and end with an appropriate end punctuation mark.

Apostrophes

Apostrophes (') are used in contractions, in the possessive forms of nouns and indefinite pronouns, and in three kinds of plurals.

■ Use an apostrophe to show where letters, words, or numbers have been omitted.

you're   I'd   who'll   they're   we've   class of '99
o'clock   o'er   goin'

■ Add an apostrophe and -s ('s) to a singular noun to show possession.

an hour's wait   our neighbor's dog
Charles's report   the bus's ignition

Exception: To make pronunciation easier, add only an apostrophe after ancient Greek names of more than one syllable and after the names *Moses* and *Jesus*.

Hercules' labors   Moses' brother   Jesus' sermon

■ To show possession in a plural noun that ends in -s, add only an apostrophe (').

students' reports   two dollars' worth
the neighbors' dogs   the Fernandezes' car

■ Add an apostrophe and -s ('s) to show possession in a plural noun that does not end in s.

women's wages   children's drawings
geese's feathers

Editing Tip

One of the most common spelling mistakes is to put apostrophes in possessive personal pronouns. Don't! These pronouns show possession *without* an apostrophe.

hers   his   yours
its   ours   theirs

■ Use an apostrophe and -s ('s) to show the possessive form of indefinite pronouns.

everyone's papers   someone's wallet   anybody's turn

■ Use an apostrophe and an -s ('s) to show a plural in three special cases: (1) to form the plurals of letters, (2) to form the plurals of numbers, and (3) when words are referred to as words.

The word *accommodate* has two c's and two m's.
Laura's phone number has five 6's and two 7's.
That sentence uses too many *and*'s.

When you write about decades, both 1990s and 1990's are acceptable.

Write the contraction for these words.

1. I would _____ I'd _____   6. they are _____ they're _____

2. you are _____ you're _____   7. who is _____ who's _____

3. we will _____ we'll _____   8. I am _____ I'm _____

4. she would _____ she'd _____   9. is not _____ isn't _____

5. it is _____ it's _____   10. will not _____ won't _____

Exercise 16 **Correcting Apostrophes**

Read the following paragraphs. Correct all errors in the use of apostrophes. Also correct spelling mistakes. **Hint:** Not every sentence contains an error; some sentences have more than one.

¹One of the most popular winter ~~sport's~~ sports is skiing. ²(Note, by the way, that the word *skiing* has two ~~is~~ *i*'s but *skier* has only one.) ³The latest "snow toy" on ski ~~resorts~~ resorts' slopes is the skiboard. ⁴Skiboards come in pairs (one for each foot), and they're hardly longer than a ~~skiers~~ skier's boots. ⁵~~Theyre~~ They're not ~~everyones~~ everyone's idea of what to do on a mountain; in fact, skiboarders endure many skiers wisecracks. ⁶But ~~theyre~~ they're just plain fun, one writer reports, and can improve a ~~skiers~~ skier's balance. ⁷~~Heres~~ Here's how to turn: Just tip a skiboard on ~~it's~~ its edge a tiny bit. ⁸You can do practically anything on skiboards you can do on skates: ~~trick's~~ tricks such as skiing backward, spinning, even dancing.

⁹An older "snow toy" is the snowboard (both feet on a single board), which has been around for many years. ¹⁰A ~~snowboarders~~ snowboarder's movements resemble a ~~surfers~~ surfer's or a ~~skateboarders~~ skateboarder's balancing act. ¹¹In fact, a snowboard looks like a longer, foot-wide version of a skateboard minus ~~it's~~ its wheels. ¹²One seventy-three-year-old snowboard manufacturer says that "boarding" is easy. ¹³"I tell people that if they ~~cant~~ can't learn in two hours, they should forget it."

Editing and Proofreading Worksheet 1

Add punctuation marks to the following paragraphs. Correct all run-ons and sentence fragments, and make whatever other changes you think will improve the paragraphs. (In this retelling of a myth, the word *Thunders* and the names of animals function as proper nouns and are therefore capitalized.)

Hint: Look for errors in spelling and verb usage. Students' revisions will vary. A sample revision is given.

[1]Do you know the Cherokee myth about the origin of fire? [2]Before there was fire, the animals complained they ~~was~~ *were* very cold. [3]The Thunders sent lightning to make the first fire in the base of a hollow tree, ~~the tree~~ *which* was on an island far, far away.

[4]I will go get fire said Raven because I am so strong and I can fly far. [5]But the fire in the base of the tree scorched Raven and blackened his feathers*, so* [6]Raven ~~flyed~~ *flew* home without the fire.

[7]Then Screech-Owl volunteered, but the fire and smoke burned his eyes. [8]Hooting Owl and Horned Owl each tried, but neither could reach the fire*;* they both came back with ashy circles around their eyes.

[9]Next, these two snakes tried*:* tiny Black Racer and huge Blacksnake. [10]They failed*, too.* [11]"I will succeed where all of you have failed*,*" Blacksnake boasted. [12]But he fell into the burning tree*,* [13]~~Barely~~ *barely* managing to escape.

[14]Now all of the other birds, other snakes, and four-footed animals refused to go. ¶ [15]"I will bring back fire*,*" announced Water Spider quietly. [16]From her spidery silk, she ~~weaved~~ *wove* a tiny bowl*, and* ~~she~~ tied ~~the tiny bowl~~ *it* to her back*.* *Then* ~~and~~ she walked on the water to the island*, and from* *From* the grass around the tree*,* she picked up one coal of fire*,* ~~and she~~ put it in her bowl*, and* ~~she~~ came back*.* ~~and thats~~ *That's* how fire entered our world. ¶ [17]"Hooray!" they cheered, ~~welcomeing~~ *welcoming* Water Spider home. [18]"At last, we can stay warm in this freezing world."

Editing and Proofreading Worksheet 2

Help improve this first draft of a story beginning. Add punctuation marks wherever necessary, and make whatever other changes you think will improve the student's story. Correct run-on sentences and fragments and add paragraphs signs (¶). **Hint:** Watch out for spelling mistakes, too, and change some of the *said's*.

"Let's [,] [urged]
¹~~Lets~~ hurry [,] Margo ~~said to~~ Bill [or] ~~well~~ miss the beginning [¶] ["Don't]
"we'll ["Don't] [""]
[reassured her] "[doesn't] [7:30] [there're]
~~said~~. ³ [~It ~~doesnt~~ start till 730. ⁴You know ~~therere~~ at least fifteen minutes of

["] [governess's]
previews [¶"] ⁵But I love the music from The King and I! ⁶Did you know it was

based on a real ~~governess~~ autobiography, a book called Anna and the King of

[there'll] [It's]
Siam? ⁷Besides, I'll bet ~~therell~~ be lots of people in line. ⁸~~Its~~ opening night,

[don't] ["] ["]
parking will be a problem, and I ~~dont~~ want to sit in the front row [¶] ⁹Not to

["]
worry, Margo. ¹⁰What's your favorite song from the movie? Bill asked. ¹¹Before

[song's] ["]
she could answer, Bill boomed the ~~songs~~ first lines [,] Shall we dance? On a bright

["]
cloud of music, shall we fly? ¹²Margo joined him with the rest of the song. ¹³Bill

[¶"] ["] ["] ["]
laughed, turning to look at her. ¹⁴Bill! she yelled. Watch out! ¹⁵A car was backing

["] ["] [shouted]
out of a driveway just ahead of them. ¹⁶We're going to hit it! she ~~said~~. ¹⁷Bill

[and leaned]
slammed on his brakes. ¹⁸~~Leaned~~ on the horn. ¹⁹He wrestled with the steering

[Their]
wheel as Margo braced for the crash. ²⁰~~They're~~ car jumped the curb and

[¶]
bumped to a stop against a hedge. ²¹The other car kept going and drove away.
["] ["] [breathed] ["] ["] ["] [answered]
²²Wow, that was close! Bill ~~said~~. ²³Are you OK, Margo? [¶] ²⁴I think so [,] Margo ~~said~~ [:]
[Her]
~~her~~ voice quavered and her hands shook.

Revisions will vary. You may wish to have students complete the story.

Chapter Review

Visit us at
www.sadlier-oxford.com

Exercise A Using Colons and Semicolons

Insert colons and semicolons where they belong in the following sentences.
Hint: Some sentences need more than one punctuation mark.

1. Jana has lived in three cities: Budapest, Hungary; New York City, New York; and San Diego, California.

2. Hemingway's title comes from these lines by John Donne: "Do not ask for whom the bell tolls; it tolls for thee."

3. The bus will leave promptly at 7:00 A.M.; don't be late.

4. Egg prices vary from state to state; they also vary according to demand.

5. Sound travels faster at higher elevations; in fact, at 36,000 feet, sound travels eighty miles an hour faster than at sea level.

6. Two of the earliest American Indian cultures include the following: the Clovis Culture (about 11,200 years ago) and the Folsom Culture (about 10,900 years ago).

7. In 1932, Amelia Earhart became the first woman to fly solo across the Atlantic; it took her about fifteen hours.

8. What comes after this line from Isaiah 2:4 in the Bible: "And they shall beat their swords into plowshares. . ."?

9. Betsy Ross supposedly designed the first American flag; however, no one knows if this is true.

10. The world's busiest airports include O'Hare in Chicago, Illinois; Harts Field in Atlanta, Georgia; and Dallas/Ft. Worth Airport in Texas.

Exercise B Using Italics and Quotation Marks

Should you use underlining (italics) or quotation marks? Insert the appropriate punctuation for each item. Make sure you place quotation marks in the right place in relation to other punctuation marks. Before you start, review the summary in the side column on page 281. Underlined words or phrases indicate italics.

1. Have you read Marjorie Kinnan Rawling's novel The Yearling?

2. My favorite song from the Broadway play Oklahoma! is "People Will Say We're in Love."

3. "The Pedestrian," a short story by Ray Bradbury, is set in a frightening future.

4. The movie <u>Apollo 13</u> is based on the near-disaster of the <u>Apollo 13</u> spacecraft.

5. Mark Hamill is the actor who played the young hero in the 1977 movie <u>Star Wars</u>.

6. Every Sunday morning, reporters on <u>Meet the Press</u> interview someone famous.

7. In his essay "Shooting an Elephant," George Orwell tells about an experience he had as a police officer in Burma.

8. In the chapter entitled "Pulling Up Roots" from her book <u>Passages</u>, Gail Sheehy writes that before the age of eighteen, teenagers have a clear motto: I have to get away from my parents.

9. Richard Wright's autobiography <u>Black Boy</u> appeared in 1945.

10. "Ice" is the title of this week's episode of <u>The X-Files</u> TV series.

Exercise C Adding Punctuation to Dialogue

Read the following dialogue. Insert quotation marks, other punctuation marks, and paragraph symbols (¶) where they are needed. See Answer Key.

¹Have you seen my sneakers? Laura asked. ²No, I haven't seen them, her younger brother Gabe answered. ³Why? he added sarcastically. ⁴Do you think I've hidden them? ⁵Don't be so smart, Gabe, she sighed. ⁶I know I left them right here by the couch. ⁷So, Laura, he asked why don't you put your shoes in the closet when you take them off—like I do? ⁸Everyone can't be as neat and perfect as you are, Gabe. ⁹Laura's voice had an edge to it. ¹⁰How did Gabe always manage to be so annoying? ¹¹Will you two please stop arguing all the time! Mom called from the kitchen. ¹²You left your sneakers under the kitchen table, Laura. ¹³And Gabe's right. ¹⁴Stop leaving your clothes all over this apartment.

On a separate piece of paper, continue the dialogue between Laura and her brother Gabe.

Capitalization

STUDENT WRITING
Research Paper

Jefferson Davis, Abraham Lincoln, and the American Revolution
by Greg Ruttan
high school student, Lake Oswego, Oregon

The Civil War can be seen, in part, as a debate over what the Founding Fathers would have wanted. Neither the North nor the South rejected America's revolutionary heritage. Both Lincoln and Davis saw themselves as [men] following in the Founding Fathers' footsteps, and both of their positions would have [found] support among some of America's Founding Fathers. However, Lincoln supported more the Federalist point of view with his insistence on the power of the federal government, while Davis took the traditional Anti-Federalist view of the federal government being subordinate to the states. Prior to the Civil War, this clash of philosophies had been a part of American politics, even before the death of the Founding Fathers. The conflict between Andrew Jackson and South Carolina over nullification is a good example of this conflict. However, after the Civil War, the debate between the Federalist and Anti-Federalist philosophies ceased. The federal government was supreme. Lincoln and Davis not only alluded back to the Founding Fathers, but through military means they [also] settled the debate the Founding Fathers had been unable to resolve between the Federalists and the Anti-Federalists. Reprinted with permission of *The Concord Review*.

This excerpt is the concluding paragraph from a research paper that identifies the political and ideological similarities between the government leaders of the Revolutionary War and those of the Civil War. This paragraph summarizes the writer's main arguments and restates the paper's thesis statement.

You will learn about the use of capital letters in this chapter. The excerpt above is a good example of how frequently you may be called on to use these rules in your own writing.

Allow time for students to discuss the student writing. Suggest that they identify its strengths and propose possible improvements. Use the model to introduce the concepts in the chapter.

Proper Nouns and Proper Adjectives

Remember that a **proper noun** (Lesson 4.1) names a particular place, person, thing, or idea and that a **proper adjective** (Lesson 4.4) is the adjective form of a proper noun. Both proper nouns and proper adjectives begin with a capital letter.

🔹 Capitalize the names of people.

   Marie Curie   Albert Einstein   George Washington Carver

🔹 Capitalize geographic names.

PLANETS, CONSTELLATIONS	Earth Mars the constellation Big Dipper
CONTINENTS	North America Asia Australia Antarctica
ISLANDS	Haiti Hawaiian Islands Sicily Manhattan
COUNTRIES	United States Mexico India Israel Italy
STATES	Texas California New York Maine
CITIES	Los Angeles El Paso Detroit
BODIES OF WATER	Caribbean Sea Nile Lake Erie
LOCALITIES, REGIONS	Mount Rainier the Northeast
	the Far West the South
STREETS, HIGHWAYS	Speedway Overlook Road Fifth Avenue
BUILDINGS	the Eiffel Tower Rockefeller Center
PARKS, MONUMENTS	Lincoln Monument Grand Canyon

Note: In the examples above, articles (*the*) and short prepositions (*of*) that are part of the name are *not* capitalized.

🔹 Capitalize proper adjectives formed by proper nouns.

   European   Shakespearean   Danish   French   American

Exercise 1 Proofreading Sentences

Insert capital letters where they belong in the following sentences. To indicate a capital letter, use the proofreading symbol of three underscores beneath the letter (t̲).

   EXAMPLE   Tornado warnings are in effect throughout the northeast.

1. Look for the bright stars in the belt of the constellation orion.

2. The danube river bisects the city of budapest, hungary.

3. Is madras on india's eastern or western coast?

4. An ocean liner on the st. lawrence seaway passes through many locks.

Editing Tip

Don't capitalize words such as *north*, *south*, *east*, and *west* when you're talking about compass directions. Capitalize these words only when they refer to regions of a country.

Look in the **northeast** after sunset.

A blizzard is expected in the **Northeast**—specifically, in Vermont and New Hampshire.

Also, don't capitalize a common noun that refers to a proper noun.

We hiked for a day in the **Rocky Mountains**. Below the frost line, the **mountains** were covered with wildflowers.

5. In 1911, the american explorer hiram bingham discovered machu picchu, a ruined incan city in peru.

6. Through a telescope, you can easily observe saturn's rings.

7. Which city is the capital of new mexico: albuquerque or santa fe?

8. Glacier national park spans both sides of the canadian border.

9. How does a shakespearean sonnet differ from an italian sonnet?

10. Settlers in the south and west supported jacksonian democracy.

Exercise 2 **Writing a Biography**

Work with a partner or small group to write a one-paragraph biography based on the following notes. You do not have to use all of the information. First, capitalize all the words on the note card that should be capitalized. Then write your biography on a separate piece of paper. Proofread it carefully to make sure that you've written complete sentences and that you've capitalized all the words that need capitalizing.   Students' paragraphs will vary.

> herman melville [1819-1891]—american novelist & short story writer
>
> born new york city; dutch and english ancestry
>
> father died when melville was 12; quit school at 15; worked at odd jobs
>
> 1839-1844 mostly at sea: first as cabin boy on ship to liverpool, england; then 2 years on whaling ship; spent time in tahiti & other islands in pacific ocean
>
> wrote several novels based on sea experiences
>
> married & bought farm near pittsfield, massachusetts
>
> worked for 19 years as inspector in u.s. customs house in battery park, new york city
>
> died in poverty

Exercise 3 **Writing Paragraphs**

For a geography project, you've been asked to trace your "life route" on a map. Write two or more paragraphs that include all of the following information:

• the city, state, and country where you were born

• cities, states, and countries where you have lived

• where you have traveled and where you would like to travel

• where you would like to live someday

You may wish to have students exchange papers with a partner, and check to see that the partner has written complete sentences and correctly capitalized words.

Titles

● Capitalize titles and abbreviations of titles only when they are used before names. Also capitalize abbreviations of academic degrees after a name.

| Senator John Glenn | a United States senator |
| Howard Esquinez, M.D. | a family practice doctor |

A few important titles are generally capitalized even without a person's name: *the President of the United States; the Prime Minister; the Pope; the Chief Justice of the Supreme Court.*

● Capitalize a word that shows a family relationship only when it is used before a name or when it is used as a name.

Grandpa Max   Aunt Ada   his stepfather   my aunt

"How does my pie taste, Grandmother?"

● Capitalize the first and last words and all important words in the titles of works.

Note: Unless they appear as the first word in a title, do not capitalize the following small words: articles (*a, an, the*), coordinating conjunctions, and prepositions with fewer than five letters.

BOOKS	*The Catcher in the Rye* *Julie of the Wolves*
PERIODICALS	*The Washington Post* *National Geographic*
STORIES, ESSAYS	"Through the Tunnel" "On Civil Disobedience"
POEMS	"Stopping by Woods on a Snowy Evening"
PLAYS	*The Skin of Our Teeth* *The Tragedy of Romeo and Juliet*
TV SERIES	*I Love Lucy* *Live from the Met* *Meet the Press*
WORKS OF ART	*Sunflowers* *Madame Cézanne in a Red Dress*
MUSICAL WORKS	Brahms's First Symphony "Michelle"
MOVIES	*Beauty and the Beast* *It's a Wonderful Life*

Exercise 4 **Proofreading Sentences**

Insert capital letters where they belong in the following sentences. To indicate a capital letter, use the proofreading symbol of three underscores beneath the letter (m̲).

1. Delores read aloud Robert Frost's "the death of the hired man."

2. We watched an incredible game on Channel 3's *monday night football* broadcast.

Remember that forms of *be* are verbs. They require capitals in titles of works.

Do you know the poem "No Man is an Island"?

3. I remember how uncle max piled too much food on everyone's plates.

4. The mayor appointed commissioner estella brown as chairperson.

5. The musical *kiss me, kate* is based on Shakespeare's *the taming of the shrew.*

6. During the seventh-inning stretch, fans sing, "take me out to the ball game."

7. Every Friday, *wall street week* reports financial news.

8. In the original *star trek* series, James Kirk was captain of the *enterprise.*

9. The pair of skaters from Quebec skated to the theme from *gone with the wind.*

10. One of the Beatles' most popular songs is "yesterday."

Exercise 5 **Proofreading a Paragraph**

Work with a partner to insert capital letters where they belong in the following paragraph. To indicate a capital letter, use the proofreading symbol of three underscores beneath the letter (p).

[1]Leslie went to the library to look for sources for her research paper, "the cuban missile crisis." [2]First, she checked for articles in the *encyclopedia britannica*. [3]She also looked at the "cuba" entry in the *encyclopedia americana*. [4]Next, she checked the *reader's guide to periodical literature*. [5]Using a microfilm machine, she took notes from "a new resolve to save the old freedoms" in the November 2, 1962, issue of *life* magazine. [6]"the lessons learned" in the November 12, 1962, issue of *newsweek* contained several good quotations. [7]In the library's online catalog, Leslie discovered two promising books. [8]The first, *thirteen days* by u.s. attorney general robert f. kennedy, provided an eyewitness account of the crisis. [9]She also took some notes from *force and statecraft* by gordon a. craig and alexander l. george. [10]When she explored the Internet for information, Leslie couldn't tell which sources were biased and which were objective.

Exercise 6 **Writing About Relatives**

On a separate piece of paper, write two paragraphs. Each paragraph should focus on a different relative. You can write about a relative you know or an ancestor who is no longer living. Tell some important facts or a brief story about each relative. Be sure to explain how each person is related to you. When you have finished writing, proofread your paragraphs carefully to make sure you've used capital letters correctly.   Students' paragraphs will vary.

First Words, Organizations, Religions, School Subjects

🖊 Capitalize the first word in every sentence. Capitalize the first word in a direct quotation when the quotation is a complete sentence. But do not capitalize the first word in an indirect quotation.

DIRECT   Ms. Weil said, "Now we'll play Scott Joplin's 'Maple Leaf Rag.'"

INDIRECT   Ms. Weil said that now the band would play.

If a quoted sentence is interrupted, begin the second part with a lowercase letter.

"Now," said Ms. Weil, "let's play Scott Joplin's music."

Note: When you're quoting lines of poetry, follow the poet's style. Some modern poets, notably the American E. E. Cummings, don't follow the usual rules for using capital letters.

🖊 Capitalize the names of languages, nationalities, peoples, races, and religions.

Schools in Bhutan teach English as the official language.

The three Tibetan Buddhist monks are creating a sand painting.

🖊 Capitalize the names of groups, teams, businesses, institutions, and organizations.

Save the Children   New York Jets   University of Illinois

🖊 Capitalize the names of school subjects that are followed by a number. Capitalize the names of all languages.

Tara is taking Algebra 2, English, world history, and journalism.

Some style books capitalize the terms *Black* and *White* when referring to people's race; some do not. Whichever style students follow, have them use it consistently.

Exercise 7 **Proofreading Sentences**

Insert capital letters where they belong in the following sentences. To indicate a capital letter, use the proofreading symbol of three underscores beneath the letter (w̲).

1. do you know who said "all's fair in love and war"?

2. at ohio state university, she majored in english and french.

3. patrick henry said, "it is natural for man to indulge in the illusions of hope."

4. the american league and national league baseball teams that train in florida play each other in the grapefruit league.

5. after graduating from college, amy plans to join the peace corps.

6. christopher columbus introduced the hammock, a native american invention, to europeans.

7. in *the power of myth*, joseph campbell advises, "follow your bliss."

8. for generations, people of croatian descent have been fishing in louisiana oyster beds.

9. the canadian eskimos prefer to be called inuit, which means "the people."

10. valentine's day is the feast day of st. valentine, a catholic saint.

Exercise 8 **Create Your Own Exercise**

On a separate piece of paper, write one or more complete sentences in response to each numbered item. When you've finished writing, exchange your sentences with a partner. Proofread each other's sentences for correct use of capital letters.   Students' answers will vary. See Answer Key.

1. Tell what school subjects you plan to take next year.

2. Tell which sports you like to watch on TV and who your favorite teams are.

3. Define a word or expression that comes from a language other than English, and identify the language.

4. Name three charities that you would donate money to if you could.

5. Name two teams that you follow, and give your opinion of their abilities.

6. Tell something about your ancestry (your grandparents and great-grandparents). If you can, tell where your ancestors were born.

7. Write a sentence in which you quote a speaker or writer. You may quote someone you know (a friend or relative) or someone famous.

8. Take the same quotation that you wrote in question 7, and turn it into an indirect quotation.

9. Write one fact about a religious holiday (how or when it's celebrated), and identify the religion.

10. As part of the United States census every ten years, people are asked to identify their race. Write a sentence telling which categories (or choices) you think should be listed on the census form.

I and *O*; Historical Events, Documents, and Periods; Calendar Items; Brand Names

◖ Capitalize the words *I* and *O*.

The first-person pronoun *I* is always capitalized. So is the poetic interjection *O*, which is rarely used today. The modern interjection *oh* isn't capitalized unless it's the first word in a sentence.

> One of Walt Whitman's poems about Lincoln is titled "**O** Captain! My Captain!"
>
> Oh dear, this book is overdue and, **oh**, the fine is twenty-five cents.

◖ Capitalize the names of historical events, documents, and periods.

HISTORICAL EVENTS	World War II Battle of Gettysburg D-Day
SPECIAL EVENTS	Superbowl Sunday Mardi Gras
DOCUMENTS	Bill of Rights Emancipation Proclamation
PERIODS	the Middle Ages the Mesozoic Era the Renaissance

◖ Capitalize calendar items but not seasons.

CALENDAR ITEMS	Chinese New Year St. Patrick's Day Tuesday, October 6
SEASONS	spring semester autumn leaves a mild winter

When you refer to a century, however, do not use capital letters.

> twenty-first century architecture   music of the sixteenth century

◖ Capitalize brand names for manufactured products.

> Netscape Navigator   Ford Taurus

But do *not* capitalize the common noun that follows a brand name.

> a bar of Ultra-clean soap   a tube of Sparkle toothpaste

Enriching Your Vocabulary

The verb *emancipate* comes from the Latin *emancipare* and means "to set free from the power of another." Near the end of his life, George Washington *emancipated* his slaves. The noun *emancipation* can be traced to the same Latin root and means "the act of setting free." The *emancipation* of the serfs in Russia took place in 1861.

Exercise 9 ## Proofreading a Paragraph

Insert capital letters where they belong in the following sentences. To indicate a capital letter, use the proofreading symbol of three underscores beneath the letter (f̲̲̲).

¹Mara has to write a research paper about some aspect of the french revolution. ²She's trying to limit her topic by exploring the Internet, using microsoft internet explorer. ³When she searched for the french revolution, she found thousands of articles. ⁴To narrow her search, she

added other key words: declaration of the rights of man and citizen, committee of public safety, and the revolutionary tribunal. ⁵she checked *encarta*, a CD-ROM encyclopedia, for information about the reign of terror, the name given to the period when thousands were guillotined. ⁶Exploring further, she discovered that bastille day on july 14 marks the beginning of the french revolution. ⁷She considered writing about the influence of the american revolution but decided that was too complicated. ⁸Somewhere in her paper, she wants to use this quotation by the frenchman Alexis de Tocqueville: "Never was any such event . . . so inevitable yet so completely unforeseen." ⁹Mara is writing her first draft on an ibm computer, and she is using a hewlett packard printer. ¹⁰She's using microsoft word 97 as her word-processing program and copying her draft on a xerox copier.

Exercise 10 Writing a Paragraph

Work with a partner to write one or more paragraphs on a separate piece of paper. Itemize the food you'd buy to feed ten of your friends at a birthday party. Mention the brand names of products. Be sure to write in complete sentences. Proofread your paragraphs for complete sentences and for the use of capital letters. Compare the foods you've chosen with the foods chosen by your classmates.   Students' paragraphs will vary.

Exercise 11 Proofreading Sentences

Proofread the following sentences for the correct use of capital letters. Use these proofreading symbols: a slash (to indicate lowercase) and three underscores (to indicate a capital).   In sentence 3, lowercase *fourth* is also acceptable.

Winter = lowercase letter   kraft cheese = capital letter

1. Lara bought a dozen Eggs and a package of Sabrett Hot Dogs.

2. Tony wrote, "i always buy a lot of fresh fruit in the Summer."

3. Every fourth of july, the supermarket runs out of hot dog buns.

4. Kevin buys Water and Juices instead of pepsi or other soft drinks.

5. For memorial day, Julio bought chickens to barbecue.

Editing and Proofreading Worksheet 1

Proofread and revise the following paragraphs. Correct sentence fragments and run-on sentences, eliminate wordiness, and make any other changes you think will improve the paragraphs. Write your revised report on a separate piece of paper. **Hint:** Watch out for spelling mistakes, too.

Students' revisions will vary. A sample revision is given.

[1]william carlos williams, m.d., was a rare combination—a poet and a member of the american medical association. [2]he was born in 1882 in rutherford, new jersey. [3]williams was an averege (average) student at the horace mann school in new york city. [4]he graduated from the university of pennsylvania in philadelphia. [5]after graduating from college, he enrolled in a school of dentistry.—[6]but later switched to a medical school.

[7]at nineteen, williams met fellow college freshman ezra pound, who would become an important poet. [8]when he was a medical intern in 1909, williams [9]payed (paid) to publish his first book of poems. [10]ezra pound criticized williams's poems for their old-fashioned rhythm. [11]williams never reprinted them; he called them "artificial."

[12]young dr. williams married florence (flossie) herman in 1912 after flossie's sister turned him down. [13]the couple settled in rutherford, where williams had his home and office at 9 ridge road for forty years. [14]he delivered babies, tended the sick, [15]and wrote poems about everyday things and people.

[16]in *the autobiography of le roi jones*, the african american poet, amiri baraka, praised williams's natural rhythms: "he knew american life had outdistanced the english rhythms and their formal meters. . . ." [17]baraka went on to praise williams's use of "the language of this multinational land."

[18]two of williams's most famous poems are "the red wheelbarrow" and "spring and all." [19]*paterson* (1945), his book about a small new jersey city, includes not only history but also poems, documents, newspaper clippings, and letters.

Editing and Proofreading Worksheet 2

Work with a partner or small group to proofread and revise these paragraphs. Correct sentence fragments and run-on sentences, improve word choice, eliminate wordiness, and make any other changes you think will improve the paragraphs. Write your revised report on a separate piece of paper, and compare your response with those made by other pairs or groups of classmates. **Hint:** All the place names in this exercise are spelled correctly.

Students' revisions will vary. A sample revision is given.

[1]during world war II, nazi german troops invaded many european nations. [2]including austria, czechoslovakia, poland, denmark, holland, luxembourg, and france. [3]in may 1940, retreating british, belgian, and french soldiers huddled on the beach at dunkirk, a small french seaport on the english channel. [5]they were waiting to be evacuated. [6]german troops surrounded dunkirk; german planes bombed the city and the soldiers.

[7]from may 16 to june 14, more than 850 ships came to the soldiers' rescue. [8]some were british navy ships, but most were small boats. [9]british civilians sailed across the english channel to dunkirk, [10]they were a vast armada of barges, ferries, fishing boats, tugboats, lifeboats, rowboats, yachts, and motorboats. [11]Even a thames river sightseeing boat made the trip [12]ordinary british citizens who owned these small vessels risked their ~~lifes~~ lives. [13]some were killed when german planes sank their boats. [14]the rescuers brought more than 338,000 allied soldiers safely back to england. [15]"operation dynamo," as the rescue mission was called, ended on june 14. [16]when the germans captured dunkirk and the remaining soldiers.

[17]in a speech to the british parliament, which is like the united states congress, prime minister winston churchill said that the evacuation of dunkirk must not be thought a victory. [18]"wars are not won by evacuations," churchill said. [19]he vowed, however, that britain would continue fighting germans everywhere ~~everywheres~~ and would never surrender.

Motivated students may wish to learn more about Operation Dynamo by reading *Dunkirk: The Complete Story of the First Step in the Defeat of Hitler* by Norman Gelb. It was published in 1989 by Morrow Publishing Company in New York City.

Chapter Review

Visit us at
www.sadlier-oxford.com

Exercise A Proofreading Sentences

Insert capital letters where they belong in the following sentences. To indicate a capital letter, use the proofreading symbol of three underscores beneath the letter (b).

1. which of these great lakes is larger—lake erie or lake superior?
2. Like many other state capitols (the building in which state legislatures meet), the state house in boston, massachusetts, has a gold dome.
3. mount vernon, george washington's home, is on the potomac river in virginia.
4. niagara falls has two parts: the american horseshoe falls and the canadian falls.
5. if you fly over mount whitney, you are above the highest peak of the sierra madres in northern california.
6. the shoshones, a native american people, live mostly in idaho, nevada, utah, wyoming, and california.
7. during the precambrian era, what's now the state of florida was underwater.
8. the sears tower in chicago was once the world's tallest building.
9. which four united states presidents have their faces carved on mt. rushmore national memorial in the black hills of south dakota?
10. the mississippi river flows from northern minnesota to the gulf of mexico.

Exercise B Proofreading a Paragraph

Proofread the following sentences for the correct use of capital letters. Use the proofreading symbol of three underscores to indicate a capital (s).

¹the scottish novelist and poet robert louis stevenson created a fictional island. ²he named it treasure island. ³in stevenson's novel, it is a small island off the coast of mexico. ⁴on the island are three hills: foremast hill, mizzenmast hill, and spyglass hill. ⁵a pirate, captain flint, buries his treasure on the island. ⁶bill bones, his first mate, draws a map to show where it's buried. ⁷years later, someone discovers the treasure map at the admiral benbow inn in black hill cove in western england. ⁸jim hawkins (the narrator), squire trelawney, and dr. livesey set sail on the *hispaniola* to find

the island and the buried treasure. ⁹aboard ship are one of captain flint's crew members—long john silver—and some other old pirates. ¹⁰to find out what happens, read stevenson's classic novel, *treasure island*.

Exercise C Proofreading Paragraphs

Insert capital letters where they belong in the following sentences. To indicate a capital letter, use the proofreading symbol (h).

¹during world war II, carl gorman was one of four hundred navajo code talkers in the united states marines. ²gorman was born on the navajo reservation in chinle, arizona. ³like many native americans, he'd been forced to attend a government boarding school as a boy. ⁴there, he was forbidden—even punished—for speaking his native language. ⁵when the united states entered world war II, gorman was thirty-four. ⁶he was too old to serve in the military. ⁷in 1942, the marines were recruiting native americans who could speak both english and navajo fluently. ⁸the navajo language has no alphabet and is extremely complex. ⁹military experts had determined that only about thirty people in the world besides the fifty thousand or so navajos knew how to speak the language. ¹⁰mr. gorman lied about his age to enlist in the marines. ¹¹he became the oldest of the navajo code talkers. ¹²since the language has no words for modern weapons, the navajos used native words to stand for weapons. ¹³a bomber was *jay-sho*, or "buzzard," for example, and a fighter plane was *da-he-tih-hi*, or "hummingbird."

¹⁴throughout the war, the code talkers served on the front lines. ¹⁵when the Marines invaded guadalcanal in august 1942, gorman and other navajo volunteers relayed orders and reported troop movements by radio. ¹⁶the japanese code breakers could never figure out what the guttural sounds of the navajo language meant. ¹⁷on iwo jima, saipan, taiwan, and other islands in the pacific ocean, the navajo marines used the only american military code that was never broken.

Spelling

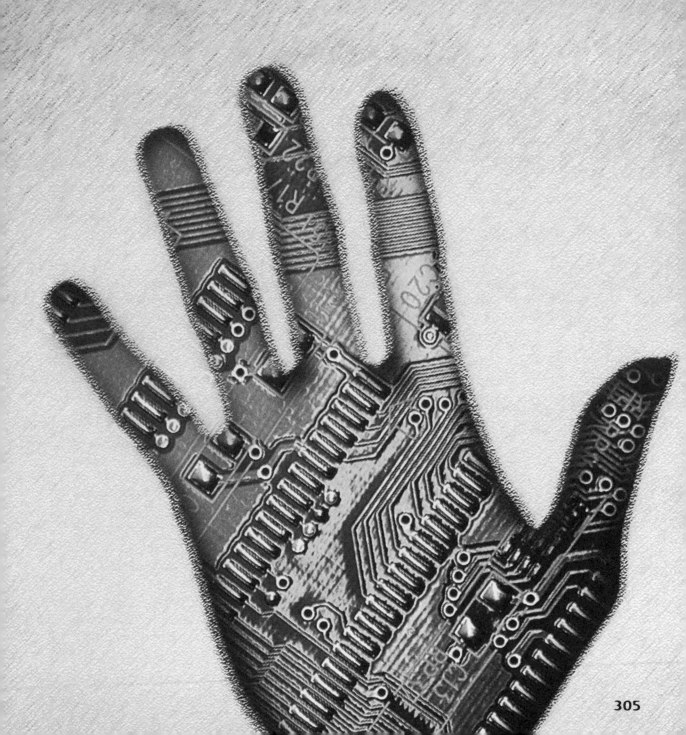

Direct students to
chapter-specific
portfolio projects
on Sadlier-Oxford's
website.

STUDENT WRITING
Persuasive Essay

Computer Course Should Be Optional
by Leslie Miller
high school student, Pottsville, Pennsylvania

Although some students could benefit from taking computer courses in school, these classes should remain electives and not become requirements for receiving a high school diploma.

One main reason for this is that not all students have the need for a basic computer course. Unlike the material in the English, math, and science departments, many students already know many of the concepts that would be taught in one of these computer classes. This would make such classes boring and pointless for these students. Such a situation may lead to an undesirable scenario, one in which students who really do need the basic knowledge find themselves being disturbed and distracted by their peers.

Also, the fact that some students have prior knowledge of computers may force the teacher to accelerate the pace of the class. This also may lead to certain students not receiving all the training they need to use the computer.

Another negative effect of basic computer courses becoming mandatory for graduation is the time they would take up in the schedule of the student who wants to take more academic courses. Many courses, especially AP and advanced courses, are only offered during certain periods of the day. If a student were forced to choose between a computer course and an academic course, [he or she] would obviously have to choose the computer class, because it would be a required course. This would mean that the student would miss out on other challenging academic work merely to take a basic computer course.

Finally, requiring computer courses would force out some of the other programs and classes which use computer labs. In order to get all the students in who need the basic class, certain classes might have to be canceled or reduced to only one period a day. This would limit opportunities for students who want to take advanced computer classes, computer art classes, and other courses in which computers are needed on a daily basis. . . .

Some may say that classes must be mandatory to advance students in this world where technology is rapidly progressing. However, students have already proven that they can and will learn this technology without school courses. Most youths can grasp the concept quickly and can easily operate these machines. Therefore, requiring computer classes would simply waste students' precious class time.

The persuasive essay above is clearly organized. The first paragraph states the writer's opinion, then each following paragraph states a reason that supports the opinion. Transition words (*one, also, another,* and *finally*) lead a reader through the argument. The writer ends the essay with a restatement of her position.

Part of the power of this or any essay is the accuracy of the spelling. As you do the exercises in this chapter, use the spelling rules to make your own writing powerful.

Allow time for students to discuss the student writing. Suggest that they identify its strengths and propose possible improvements. Use the model to introduce the concepts in the chapter.

Using a Dictionary

You may never compete in a spelling bee, but in school and in the world of work, spelling counts! One way to improve your spelling is to read a lot; another way is to refer to a dictionary often.

◖ If you're in doubt about how to spell a word, use a dictionary.

Besides showing each entry word's definition and etymology (word history), a dictionary gives many kinds of spelling help:

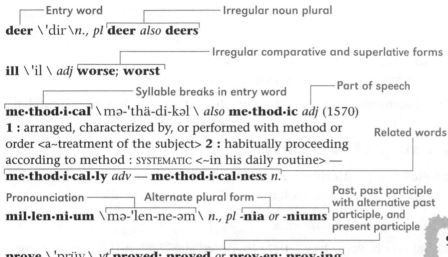

—from *Merriam-Webster's Collegiate Dictionary*, Tenth Edition

In doing the following exercises, use a college dictionary to find or check your answers.

 You may not be sure of the spelling of a word, but you probably have a good idea. Look in the dictionary for what you think the spelling of the word is. If the word isn't there, try looking up other possible ways of spelling it. Ask yourself, "What other letter or letters make the sound I'm looking for?" If you can't find a word after several tries, ask someone for help.

Spelling Tips

1. Learn what a new or unfamiliar word means. When dealing with two words that look similar but have different meanings, you need to know which meaning goes with which spelling.

2. Learn to pronounce and spell a new word by syllables or word parts. Slurring leads to misspelling.

3. Whenever you misspell a word, add it (spelled correctly) to your proofreading log. Underline the "hard spot," the letter or letters that caused you trouble.

 Using a Dictionary to Check Spelling

Write the letter of the correct spelling in the blank. If you're not sure of the correct spelling of a word, look up the item in a dictionary.

_____c_____ 1. (a) simillar   (b) similer   (c) similar   (d) simmilar

_____c_____ 2. (a) unecesary   (b) unnecesary
                (c) unnecessary   (d) unecesary

_____c_____ 3. (a) accidently   (b) acidentally
                (c) accidentally   (d) accidentaly

_____d_____ 4. (a) embarass   (b) embarras   (c) embaras   (d) embarrass

_____c_____ 5. (a) believible   (b) beleivable   (c) believable   (d) believeable

_____a_____ 6. (a) disappearance   (b) disappearence
                (c) dissapearance   (d) disapearance

___a or b___ 7. (a) judgement   (b) judgment   (c) judgemint   (d) judgmint

_____a_____ 8. (a) preferred   (b) prefered   (c) prefferred   (d) preffered

_____b_____ 9. (a) responsability   (b) responsibility
                (c) responsiblety   (d) responsabilty

_____a_____ 10. (a) accommodate   (b) acommodate   (c) accomodate   (d) acomodate

Exercise 2   **Using a Dictionary**

Answer the following questions on a separate piece of paper. If you're not sure about how to spell your answer, look the word up in a college dictionary.

1. What is the plural of *datum*?   data

2. Assume that you have to hyphenate the word *sufficient* at the end of a line. Show all the points where you could place a hyphen.   suf- or suffi-

3. How do you spell the plural of *sheep*?   sheep

4. How do you spell the two-bladed tool that you use to cut paper or cloth?   scissors

5. How do you spell the word that describes two lines that never meet?   parallel

6. If you are measuring a room to buy a new carpet or rug, what are the two dimensions you need to measure?   length and width

7. How do you spell the past tense and past participle of the verb *pay*?   paid

8. When a word has alternate spellings, the one listed first in a dictionary is the preferred form. Write the spelling that is preferred in the United States.

     a. <u>catalog</u> *or* catalogue   d. theatre *or* <u>theater</u>
     b. <u>traveler</u> *or* traveller   e. <u>cooperate</u> *or* co-operate
     c. <u>indexes</u> *or* indices   f. grey *or* <u>gray</u>

9. If you have three brothers and they're all married, what do you call their wives when you refer to them as a group?   sisters-in-law

10. How do you spell the long, thin pasta that is not linguine and is often served with tomato sauce and meatballs?   spaghetti

Spelling Rules

English spelling is so irregular that it's useful to learn the few rules you can depend on—even though these rules have exceptions.

● Write *i* before *e* except after *c*.

Note that most of these words have a long *e* sound.

FOLLOW RULE	achieve	believe	chief
	niece	piece	
AFTER C:	ceiling	conceit	deceive
	receive	receipt	
EXCEPTIONS:	either	neither	leisure
	seize	weird	

● Write *ei* when these letters are not pronounced with a long *e*, especially when the sound is a long *a* as in *neighbor* and *weigh*.

	height	their	foreign	forfeit
SOUNDS LIKE *AY*:	eight	freight	neighbor	reign
	sleigh	veil	weigh	

● Watch out for words with more than one syllable that end with the sound *seed*. Only one word is spelled with *-sede*. Three words end in *-ceed*. All other words end in *-cede*.

-SEDE	supersede			
-CEED	exceed	proceed	succeed	
-CEDE	concede	intercede	precede	recede	secede

Exercise 3 Remembering Spelling Rules

Work with a partner or small group to complete each item below. Then compare your answers with those of others in your class. See Answer Key.

1. Write a mnemonic device (see the Writing Hint) to help you remember the three words that end in *-ceed*.

2. Write all of the one-syllable words that end with *-eed*. How many can you think of? Check your list with a partner or small group.

3. Write a definition for each of the words that ends with *-cede*: *concede, intercede, precede, recede, secede*. Then use each word in a sentence.

Writing Hint

A good way to remember something is to make up a mnemonic, or memory, device. Here's a nonsense sentence to help you remember the exceptions to the *i*-before-*e* rule:

"**Either weird** sister can **seize** a lizard at **leisure**, but **neither** ever tries."

Proofreading a Newspaper Column

The newspaper that published the following letter needs a better proofreader. Find and correct all of the spelling mistakes in the two letters below. **Hint:** You should find 23 errors.

Dear Doctor Diet:

¹Is it ~~conciet~~ conceit that motivates my ~~neice~~ niece, who's always on a diet? ²Can she really ~~beleive~~ believe that if she wears a size eight dress, she's too fat?

Worried in Wisconsin

Dear Worried in Wisconsin:

³Many teenagers are unduly concerned with ~~thier~~ their ~~wieght~~ weight, but others who aren't concerned should be. ⁴The ~~cheif~~ chief worry for dieters is that they ~~wiegh~~ weigh too much for ~~thier~~ their ~~hieght~~ height, and often they do. ⁵Unfortunately, many dieters ~~decieve~~ deceive themselves by thinking they can ~~acheive~~ achieve popularity, happiness, and success if they look like the models on TV and in magazine ads.

⁶The key to a healthy body ~~wieght~~ weight is ~~niether~~ neither dieting nor diet aids. ⁷I've been giving these same two ~~peices~~ pieces of advice to my ~~pateints~~ patients for years. ⁸To ~~succede~~ succeed in reaching your ideal weight, eat a diet that is long on fruits, vegetables, and grains and short on fats; and equally important, get out and exercise during your ~~liesure~~ leisure time. ⁹~~Wierd~~ Weird crash diets—including the currently popular high-protein ~~protien~~ diet—play havoc with the body, and often the ~~wieght~~ weight loss is only temporary. ¹⁰So tell your ~~neice~~ niece to put down that piece of cake or pie, ~~sieze~~ seize her sneakers, and go for a walk or bicycle ride or play tennis with a ~~freind~~ friend.

Doctor Diet

Prefixes and Suffixes

Prefixes and suffixes are groups of letters that change a word's meaning. A **prefix** (such as *dis-*, *il-*, *mis-*, and *un-*) is added to the beginning of a word; a **suffix** (such as *-er*, *-ly*, *-ment*, and *-ness*) is added to the end.

- Adding a prefix does not change the spelling of the original word.
    disappear   illegible   mistrust   unusual

- If a word ends in *-y* preceded by a consonant, change the *-y* to *i* before adding a suffix.
    business   carrier   happiness   loneliest   tried
    EXCEPTIONS: dryness   trying   flying

- If a word ends in *-y* preceded by a vowel, keep the *-y*.
    joyous   **buoyant**   employer   stayed
    EXCEPTIONS: laid   said

- Adding the suffix *-ly* or *-ness* does not change the spelling of the original word.
    carefully   lateness   really   stillness

If a word ends in two *-l*'s, drop one of the *l*'s before adding *-ly*: dull + ly = dully.

- Drop a word's final silent *-e* before adding a suffix that begins with a vowel. **Note:** American dictionaries give *likable, lovable, movable,* and *sizable* as preferred spellings but do also include *likeable, loveable, moveable,* and *sizeable.*
    creative   likable   loving   provider   mistaken   Students should be consistent in whichever spelling they choose.

- Keep the final silent *-e* if the word ends in *-ge* or *-ce* and the suffix begins with *a* or *o*.
    changeable   courageous   noticeable   outrageous

- Keep the final silent *-e* before adding a suffix that begins with a consonant. **Note:** American dictionaries give *judgment* as the preferred spelling but also include *judgement.*
    amazement   boredom   hopeful   placement   statehood
    EXCEPTIONS: argument   ninth   truly   wisdom

- Double the final consonant in some one-syllable words when the suffix begins with a vowel. Doubling occurs when the word ends in a consonant preceded by a single vowel.
    hopping   planning   redder   shopping   sitter   winner

- Double the final consonant in some words of more than one syllable. Doubling occurs if the word ends in a single consonant preceded by a

Some Prefixes and Their Meanings

Prefix	Meaning
circum-	around
dis-, un-	the opposite
il-, im-, in-, ir-	not
post-	after
pre-	before
re-	again
sub-	below
super-	above, beyond

Some Suffixes and Their Meanings

Suffix	Meaning
-able	capable of being
-ate, -en, -fy	become, make
-dom, -hood	state of being
-er, -or	a person who
-less	without
-ment	state or condition of
-ous, -ful	full of

Enriching Your Vocabulary

The adjective *buoyant* is derived from the Spanish verb *boyar* (to float). In addition to its literal meanings of "floating" or "capable of keeping something afloat," *buoyant* may be used in the figurative sense of "cheerful" or "light." The *buoyant* snorklers bobbed in the waters of the bay. The party guests were in a *buoyant* mood.

single vowel *and* the new word is accented on the second syllable.

controller   occurrence   referral   submitted

Do *not* double the final consonant when the new word is not accented on the second syllable: *preference, reference.*

 You don't have to memorize all of these rules and their exceptions. When in doubt about how to spell a word, check your dictionary.

Exercise 5 Adding Prefixes and Suffixes

Write the word that results when the following prefixes or suffixes are added.

1. occur + -ing   occurring

2. pay + -able   payable

3. il- + legal   illegal

4. im- + mobile   immobile

5. note + -able   notable

6. occasion + -al   occasional

7. argue + -ment   argument

8. sincere + -ity   sincerity

9. pre- + caution   precaution

10. mean + -ness   meanness

11. encourage + -ment   encouragement

12. careful + -ly   carefully

13. submit + -ed   submitted

14. luxury + -ant   luxuriant

15. full + -ly   fully

16. dis- + appear   disappear

17. un- + necessary   unnecessary

18. nine + -ty   ninety

19. ir- + responsible   irresponsible

20. love + -able   lovable

Exercise 6 Create Your Own Exercise

Write ten sentences in which you use at least ten words that contain prefixes or suffixes or both. Spell some of these words incorrectly. Then exchange papers with a classmate. Proofread each other's sentences to find and correct all of the spelling errors. Students' sentences will vary.

Exercise 7 Writing New Words

Hold a contest. In ten minutes, write as many words as you can that contain one of the prefixes or suffixes (or both) that are listed in the side column on page 311. Get together with a small group to compare your lists. See if you can define all of the words you've listed. **Hint:** Look up the prefix or suffix in a college dictionary for help. Students' answers will vary. Give full credit if they write 10 new words.

Noun Plurals

For any noun, start with the singular form, and follow the directions below to form the plural.

Making Nouns Plural		
KINDS OF NOUNS	**WHAT TO DO**	**EXAMPLES**
Most nouns	Add -s to the singular.	computer**s**, tower**s**, landslide**s**
Nouns that end in -s, -x, -z, -ch, -sh	Add -es to the singular.	bus**es**, kiss**es**, fox**es**, waltz**es**, inch**es**, dish**es**
Family names	Follow the two preceding rules.	the Washington**s**, the Fox**es**, the Church**es**, the Horowitz**es**
Nouns that end in -y preceded by a consonant	Change the -y to i, and add -es.	bab**ies**, worr**ies**, lad**ies**, flurr**ies**
Nouns that end in -y preceded by a vowel	Add -s.	monkey**s**, turkey**s**, toy**s**, boy**s**, valley**s**
Most nouns that end in -f	Add -s.	chief**s**, roof**s**, belief**s**, proof**s**, tariff**s**
A few nouns that end in -f or -fe	Change the -f to v and add -s or -es.	thie**ves**, shel**ves**, lea**ves**, li**ves**, wi**ves**
Nouns ending in -o preceded by a vowel	Add -s.	radio**s**, zoo**s**, patio**s**
Most nouns ending in -o preceded by a consonant	Add -es.	hero**es**, tomato**es**, potato**es**, tornado**es**
Most musical terms ending in -o	Add -s.	soprano**s**, alto**s**, solo**s**, cello**s**, piano**s**
Compound nouns	Make the most important word plural.	attorney**s** general, **men**-of-war, passer**s**by, sister**s**-in-law
Letters, numbers, and words referred to as words	Use an apostrophe ' + -s.	*A*'**s**, *3*'**s**, no *if*'**s**, *and*'**s**, or *but*'**s**
Irregular plurals, foreign plurals, and words that stay the same for both singular and plural	No rules apply! Memorize these forms.	children, mice, women, men, feet, teeth, geese, series, oxen, data, alumni, sheep, deer, species

Editing Tip

Even if you're writing on a computer, you still need to proofread your papers carefully, because a spell check program won't catch *every error*. For instance, it won't point out that you've written *there* when you should have written *their*; and it won't catch proper nouns that are misspelled.

Exceptions:
A few nouns have two acceptable forms: hoo**fs** or hoo**ves**, scar**fs** or scar**ves**, dwar**fs** or dwar**ves**.

Exceptions:
memo**s**, silo**s**
A few nouns have two acceptable forms: volcano**s** or volcano**es**, mosquito**s** or mosquito**es**, flamingo**s** or flamingo**es**.

Exercise 8 Forming Noun Plurals

Write the plural form of each noun. If you're unsure of the correct form, check a dictionary to see if it lists irregular plurals or alternate plural forms. If no plural form is listed, follow the rules in the chart on page 313.

1. video _____videos_____
2. child _____children_____
3. rodeo _____rodeos_____
4. Willis _____Willises_____
5. great-grandmother _____great-grandmothers_____
6. finch _____finches_____
7. half _____halves_____
8. studio _____studios_____
9. strawberry _____strawberries_____
10. ox _____oxen_____
11. brother-in-law _____brothers-in-law_____
12. Gutierrez _____Gutierrezes_____
13. woman _____women_____
14. waltz _____waltzes_____
15. adviser _____advisers_____
16. ditch _____ditches_____
17. cargo _____cargoes or cargos_____
18. soccer ball _____soccer balls_____
19. referee _____referees_____
20. tape recorder _____tape recorders_____
21. volcano _____volcanoes or volcanos_____
22. kilometer _____kilometers_____
23. Chefitz _____Chefitzes_____
24. secretary of state _____secretaries of state_____
25. square foot _____square feet_____

Exercise 9 Writing with Noun Plurals

You have just won an essay contest. The first prize is a ten-minute spending spree in the store of your choice. There's no dollar limit. You can buy as many items as you can gather up during the ten minutes, but there's only one catch: You have to buy two of every item you choose.

Write several paragraphs in which you give the following information:

1. what kind of store you'll shop in

2. what you'll put into your shopping cart

3. what you'll go for first, second, and third

Remember to choose two of every item. When you've finished writing, check to see that all noun plurals are spelled correctly. Students' paragraphs will vary. Make sure that they've spelled noun plural forms correctly.

Editing and Proofreading Worksheet 1

Correct any spelling and punctuation errors that you find in the following business letter. Make any other changes that you think will improve the letter. Be sure to follow the business letter form that appeared in Lesson 14.2. Make up the rest of the heading, inside address, and any other details that you need. Write your revised letter on a separate piece of paper.

Revisions will vary. A sample revision is given. Students should correct all spelling errors and errors in letter form.

_____ Students should _____

_____ write an address. _____

February
~~Febuary~~ 9, 2001

_____ Students should _____

_____ add an _____

_____ inside address _____

Dear Mrs. Eliot:

    receive   possibility

¹I would like to ~~recieve~~ some information about the ~~posibility~~ of a

hoping
summer job in your company. ²I am ~~hopeing~~ to apply for one of your

internship positions.

        please   and
³Can you tell me when the summer internship begins ~~⁴And~~ when it will

end. believe   exceptionally   well
⁵I ~~beleive~~ I'm ~~exceptionaly~~ ~~good~~ qualified to work in your office. ⁶I

            keyboarding. My   legible
have had a year of ~~typeing, my~~ teacher says my handwriting is ~~legable~~

keyboarding
and my ~~typing~~ skills are excellent.

                    experience
⁷I have had a lot of ~~expereince~~ working with photocopying and fax

          , computers,   electric typewriters   designed   filing
machines. ⁸~~Computers~~ and ~~electrics typewriter.~~ ⁹I ~~designd~~ a new ~~fileing~~

system for the student council this year. ¹⁰I can give you several

recommendations.
~~recomendations from freinds and relatives who like me a lot.~~

      there   applications   . You
¹¹Are ~~their~~ ~~applicationes~~ I should complete? ¹²Please write or call, ~~you~~

          during the day or evening at 555-9706.
can reach me at home. ¹³~~I'll be real dissappointed if I don't hear from~~

Thank you for considering
~~you soon.~~   me for a summer internship.

      sincerely
Yours ~~sincerly,~~

Add handwritten signature.
Add typed name.

Editing and Proofreading Worksheet 2

Revisions will vary. A sample revision is given. Students should correct all spelling errors.

Revise the following paragraphs. Correct all spelling errors, sentence fragments, and run-on sentences. Feel free to make any other changes that you think will improve the paragraphs. **Hint:** You should find 28 spelling errors.

[1]Beatrix Potter is famous for ~~writeing~~ (writing) and illustrating books for ~~childs~~ (children).

[2]Growing up in one of London's wealthy families~~.~~, [3]Beatrix had no ~~freinds~~ (friends) and did not go to school. [4]A governess taught her lessons in a schoolroom at home.

[5]Her younger brother, Bertram, ~~he~~ was the only child she ever saw. [6]Beatrix and Bertram amused ~~themselfs~~ (themselves). [7]They kept pets and ~~carefuly~~ (carefully) observed and drew them.

[8]The ~~Potteres~~ (Potters) spent their summers outside of London (in the country). [9]~~They went to the country.~~ (they went) [10]First, to Scotland, later to the ~~beautyful~~ (beautiful) Lake District in northern England. [11]By the time she was twelve, [12]Beatrix was ~~recieving~~ (receiving) private drawing lessons. [13]She made ~~sketchs~~ (sketches) of ~~foxs~~ (foxes), rabbits, ~~mouses~~ (mice), ~~cockroachs~~ (cockroaches), and other ~~animales~~ (animals and). [14]~~She~~ was ~~happyest~~ (happiest) when she was drawing.

[15]As she grew older, [16]~~She~~ (she) pursued her interests in art, geology, botany, and archaeology. [17]She was in her ~~twentys~~ (twenties) when she sold her first drawings to a publisher. [18]That was her first ~~sucess~~ (success), [19]~~Unusual~~ (unusual) for ~~womans~~ (women) in wealthy English ~~familys~~ (families). [20]She ~~supplyed~~ (supplied) additional drawings, [21]~~Which~~ (which) the company published as ~~greating~~ (greeting) cards and book ~~ilustrations~~ (illustrations).

[22]In 1893, Beatrix wrote to the five-year-old son of her former governess. [23]Her letter began, "My dear Noel, I don't know what to ~~right~~ (write) to you, so I shall tell you a story about four little rabbits whose names were Flopsy, Mopsy, Cottontail, and Peter." [24]The letter contained drawings, ~~two~~ (too). [25]Five years later, Beatrix borrowed the letter from young Noel. [26]From the letter's story, she wrote and ~~ilustrated~~ (illustrated) her ~~extremly~~ (extremely) ~~successfull~~ (successful) first book, *The Tale of Peter Rabbit*. [27]If you ~~havent~~ (haven't) met Peter Rabbit yet, try reading aloud his story (or a different one from Potter's ~~serieses~~ (series) of little books) to a young child.

Chapter Review

Visit us at
www.sadlier-oxford.com

Exercise A Spelling with Prefixes and Suffixes

On a separate piece of paper, create fifteen new words from the following prefixes, words, and suffixes.

PREFIXES		WORDS		SUFFIXES	
dis-	re-	imagine	appear	-ment	-ing
un-	mis-	admire	like	-ed	-ance
il-	in-	amaze	excite	-able	-ation

Exercise B Spelling Noun Plurals

In the space provided, write the plural form of each of the nouns listed below.

1. memory _____memories_____   6. silo _____silos_____

2. leaf _____leaves_____   7. monkey _____monkeys_____

3. belief _____beliefs_____   8. cliff _____cliffs_____

4. series _____series_____   9. hero _____heroes_____

5. species _____species_____   10. tomato _____tomatoes_____

Exercise C Choosing the Correct Spelling

Look carefully at each choice and then choose the correct spelling of each word. Write the letter of the correct spelling in the blank.

___a___ 1. (a) grammar (b) grammer (c) gramar (d) gramer

___c___ 2. (a) privelege (b) privalege (c) privilege (d) privalige

___c___ 3. (a) prefered (b) preffered (c) preferred (d) prefferred

___b___ 4. (a) receed (b) recede (c) riseed (d) resede

___a___ 5. (a) recommendation (b) reccommendation
      (c) reccomendation (d) recomendation

___c___ 6. (a) dissapearance (b) disapearance
      (c) disappearance (d) disappearence

___b___ 7. (a) temperment (b) temperament
      (c) tempermant (d) tempermint

___c___ 8. (a) liesure (b) leizure (c) leisure (d) liezure

___a___ 9. (a) separate (b) seperate (c) seperit (d) separrate

___d___ 10. (a) imediately (b) imediatly
      (c) immeditely (d) immediately

Exercise D **Proofreading Paragraphs**

Proofread the following paragraphs to correct all spelling errors. **Hint:**
The word *résumé* is spelled correctly. You should find 25 spelling errors.

¹When you're looking for or applying for a job, one of the things you'll
need is a résumé. ²A résumé lists information about you and about your
work history. ³Here is the kind of information you should include: your
name, ~~adress~~ address, and ~~telefone~~ telephone number; your education; your work history,
including the ~~companys~~ companies or persons you've worked for. ⁴You should also
include two references. ⁵These are names and phone numbers of people
who know you ~~personaly~~ personally and can ~~recomend~~ recommend you.

⁶It used to be that résumés were ~~allways~~ always on ~~peices~~ pieces of paper that you
would mail to a company or take in person to a job ~~interveiw~~ interview. ⁷Some
résumés still are paper ones, but more and more of them are electronic.
⁸The Internet is used increasingly by employers to ~~advertize~~ advertise jobs. ⁹Job
seekers e-mail ~~there~~ their résumés to companies.

¹⁰More than half of the ~~bigest~~ biggest companies in the United States use
computers to scan the ~~thousends~~ thousands of résumés they ~~recieve~~ receive. ¹¹The
computers search for keywords to find job hunters who have the
~~experiance~~ experience and education the company is looking for. ¹²Also, there are
employment ~~agencys~~ agencies that ~~specialise~~ specialize in finding jobs for clients by ~~useing~~ using
the Internet.

¹³~~Heres~~ Here's some advice from these employment agencies. ¹⁴Use light-
colored paper; avoid graphics. ¹⁵Spell every word ~~corectly~~ correctly. ¹⁶Describe your
~~personel~~ personal characteristics, such as "good memory," "high energy," or
"~~responsable~~ responsible and dedicated." ¹⁷List the specific skills that will make you a
good ~~candadate~~ candidate for the job. ¹⁸~~Eventualy~~ Eventually, if you are chosen for an
interview, a real person—a ~~hireing~~ hiring manager—will talk to you in person.
¹⁹An ~~efective~~ effective résumé can help you get that interview.

Cumulative Review

Exercise A Punctuation Marks

Add end marks and commas where they belong in the following paragraphs, and correct any spelling errors. Use the proofreading symbols shown below.

capital ≡	question mark ?	comma ∧	semicolon ⦂
period ⊙	exclamation point !	colon ⊙⊙	apostrophe ⌄
quotation marks ⌄ ⌄		italics tête-á-tête	

¹Every year at the Santo Domingo Pueblo near Santa Fe New Mexico the Pueblo Indians celebrate an ancient ritual. ²The Corn Dance lasts a ~~hole~~ whole day. ³About a thousand dancers chant, pray, and dance to complex drum rhythms. ⁴The Corn Dance is an ancient, sacred ceremony during which the Pueblo Indians pray for rain and a good harvest. ⁵At least one adult from each family participates in the dance, and ~~childs~~ children are taught the dance steps in school. ⁶Some dancers wear ~~strikeing~~ striking costumes. ⁷A few men are covered with white body paint and have corn husks standing on top of ~~there~~ their heads. ⁸These dancers, who represent dead spirits, weave in and out of the other dancers. ⁹The others ignore the spirit dancers, for ~~theyre~~ they're supposed to be invisible. ¹⁰Each dancer wears shell jewelry and holds or wears an evergreen bough, which symbolizes rebirth. ¹¹Young ~~womans~~ women wear flat blue wooden headdresses that symbolize the mesas and the rain-giving clouds.

Exercise B Capitalization

Add capital letters where they are needed in the following expressions. To indicate a capital letter, use the proofreading symbol of three underscores beneath the letter (f̲).

1. this year's spring vacation
2. *the los angeles times*
3. dr. janice beckerman
4. english, math, and art
5. the american red cross
6. the united nations
7. the french ambassador
8. in the city of victoria on vancouver island
9. a paint store on euclid avenue
10. the rio grande
11. world history 101 and algebra
12. the world's tallest building
13. uncle leo, aunt dora, and sam

CUMULATIVE REVIEW

14. a ski resort in <u>new</u> <u>mexico</u>
15. the best <u>restaurant</u> in town
16. the middle <u>ages</u>
17. the song "<u>somewhere</u> <u>over</u> the <u>rainbow</u>"

18. <u>charley's</u> <u>hamburger</u> <u>heaven</u>, my favorite café
19. <u>st.</u> <u>patrick's</u> day
20. the <u>bill</u> of <u>rights</u> at the end of the <u>constitution</u>

Exercise C Spelling

On a separate piece of paper, rewrite each sentence, correcting the misspelled words.

1. Five ~~foriegn~~ ~~frieghters~~ achieved ~~unbeleivable~~ speeds despite the fact
   foreign   *freighters*   *unbelievable*
   that their cargos ~~wieghed~~ two thousand tons.
                      weighed

2. The police chief's niece has few ~~freinds~~ because she's ~~to conceited~~.
                                      friends   *too* *conceited*

3. ~~Ninty~~-eight ~~sliegh~~ dogs sledded to the North Pole.
   Ninety   *sleigh*

4. The seven ~~sister-in-laws~~ ~~succeeded~~ in ~~seceeding~~ from serious squabbles.
              sisters-in-law *succeeded*   *seceding*

5. In the hospital's newborn nursery, ~~bannana boxs~~ of ~~bountyful~~,
                                        banana *boxes* *bountiful*
   ~~beautyfull~~ ~~babys~~ bawl and babble.
   beautiful *babies*

Exercise D Proofreading a Passage

Add all of the missing punctuation marks and capital letters to the words below. Use the proofreading symbols shown on page 319, and write the correctly punctuated and capitalized passage on a separate piece of paper.

one of robert frost's most popular poems is "stopping by woods on a snowy evening" when i first read this poem in *the poetry of robert frost*, i thought it was perfectly easy and simple, it's about a horse and a person who stop to watch some woods on a snowy day, on looking at the poem more closely, however, i found that there's much more than just the poem's literal meaning, for example, in the final stanza, what promises does the speaker have to keep and what does the word sleep mean? i think that the dark woods and the snow symbolize death, and that the promises symbolize the speaker's commitment to life, do you agree or disagree with this interpretation?

Mechanics Test

Exercise 1 Identifying Errors

Directions: Each of the numbered items is either correct or contains an error in one of its underlined parts. In the answer section to the right of each item, circle the letter of the sentence part that contains the error. If the sentence is correct, circle E for NO ERROR.

EXAMPLE   Before Walt Whitman began <u>writing American</u> poetry looked   (A) B C D E
                              A

<u>and sounded</u> very much like British poetry. <u>American</u> poets used
     B   C

traditional meters<u>, rhymes,</u> and stanza forms. <u>NO ERROR</u>
           D   E

1. <u>Whitman's</u> parents had <u>ancestors who</u> arrived early in the history of the   1. A B C D (E)
      A   B

United States. <u>His</u> father's ancestors were English<u>; his</u> mother's were
          C   D

Dutch. <u>NO ERROR</u>
            E

2. Did you know that Walt Whitman was born on <u>May 31,</u> 1819, <u>he</u> grew up   2. A (B) C D E
                                          A   B

on his <u>father's</u> farm in <u>West Hills, Long Island,</u> with eight brothers and
          C   D

sisters. <u>NO ERROR</u>
              E

3. In 1823, Whitman's family moved to <u>Brooklyn</u>, which was then a separate   3. A (B) C D E
                                          A

city just across the <u>East river</u> from <u>New York</u>. Whitman dropped out of
                 B   C

school when he was <u>eleven and got</u> a job as an office boy. <u>NO ERROR</u>
                      D   E

4. For ten years, Whitman worked as a <u>journalist; then</u> he left to travel to   4. A (B) C D E
                                          A

New Orleans, <u>the Great lakes,</u> and <u>Niagara Falls.</u> He returned to Brooklyn,
              B   C

where he became the editor of a <u>newspaper, *The Freeman.*</u> <u>NO ERROR</u>
                                   D   E

5. Walt Whitman loved to walk on the <u>beachs of Long Island</u> and to roam   5. (A) B C D E
                                          A

the woods and <u>fields. Although</u> he never went to <u>college, he</u> read great
                  B   C

<u>works: the</u> Bible, Shakespeare's plays, and the poetry of Homer and
     D

Dante. <u>NO ERROR</u>
            E

6. His main <u>activity, however, was</u> writing poems in the <u>simple, natural</u>
                           A   **B**

rhythms of the way people <u>talked, he</u> filled many notebooks with his
                                     C

<u>poems.</u> <u>NO ERROR</u>
 D   **E**

6. A B Ⓒ D E

7. In 1855, he paid out of his own pocket to publish a collection of

<u>his poems; he</u> titled his book <u>*Leaves of Grass.*</u> For the rest of <u>his life,</u>
     A   **B**   **C**

Whitman kept <u>reviseing</u> his book through nine editions. <u>NO ERROR</u>
                 D   **E**

7. A B C Ⓓ E

8. Not <u>everyone who</u> saw his book realized <u>its</u> worth, <u>but</u> the great
        A   **B**   **C**

American essayist Ralph Waldo Emerson did. *Leaves of Grass*, Emerson

wrote to Whitman, is <u>"the most extraordinary piece of wit and wisdom</u>
                                                                           D

<u>that America has yet contributed."</u> <u>NO ERROR</u>
                                    E

8. A B C D Ⓔ

Exercise 2   Correcting Errors

Directions: In the following sentences, the underlined part may contain *one or more errors*. In the answer section to the right of each item, circle the letter of the choice that correctly expresses the idea in the underlined part of the sentence. If you think that the original version is correct, circle D for NO ERROR. **Hint:** A sentence may have more than one error.

EXAMPLE   "Will you please shut the door <u>when you leave</u>"? she asked.   A B Ⓒ D
                 A. when you leave." she asked.   C. when you leave?" she asked.
                 B. when you leave," she asked?   D. NO ERROR

1. <u>Bill's French poodle is eager,</u> friendly, and affectionate.   1. A B C Ⓓ
   A. Bill's french poodle is eager,   C. Bill;s french poodle is eager;
   B. Bills' French poodle is eager,   D. NO ERROR

2. They saw <u>eighty fameous Italian paintings</u> in a single museum.   2. Ⓐ B C D
   A. eighty famous Italian paintings   C. eightey famous Italian paintings
   B. eighty famous italian paintings   D. NO ERROR

3. We are <u>hopeing to visit Emily Dickinsons home</u> in Amherst,   3. A B Ⓒ D
   Massachusetts.
   A. hoping to visit Emily Dickinsons home
   B. hopeing to visit Emily Dickinson's home
   C. hoping to visit Emily Dickinson's home
   D. NO ERROR

4. You'll need to measure the <u>frame in inchs, not foots.</u>   4.Ⓐ B C D
   A. frame in inches, not feet.   C. frame in inches; not feet.
   B. frame in inches, not foots.   D. NO ERROR

5. I couldn't see <u>anyone when I opened the door, but</u> I heard a door slam.   5. A B C Ⓓ
   A. anyone; when I opened the door, but
   B. anyone, when I opened the door, but
   C. anyone when I opened the door; but
   D. NO ERROR

6. On the shelf <u>in the closet are: two umbrellas,</u> three tennis rackets, and a   6. A Ⓑ C D
   box of photographs.
   A. in the closet: are two umbrellas,   C. in the closet, are two umbrellas,
   B. in the closet are two umbrellas,   D. NO ERROR

7. The <u>Empire State building is on Fifth avenue</u> in New York City.   7.Ⓐ B C D
   A. Empire State Building is on Fifth Avenue
   B. Empire State Building is on Fifth avenue
   C. Empire State building is on Fifth Avenue
   D. NO ERROR

8. <u>Ms. Rogers named the following students for the team: Roger, Akiko,</u>   8. A B C Ⓓ
   <u>Roxanne, and Jorge.</u>
   A. Ms. Rogers named: Roger, Akiko, Roxanne, and Jorge for the team.
   B. The students named by Ms. Rogers are: Roger, Akiko, Roxanne and Jorge.
   C. Ms. Rogers named the following students for the team, Roger, Akiko,
      Roxanne and Jorge.
   D. NO ERROR

9. He <u>recieved an invitation to his friends'</u> anniversary party.   9. A B Ⓒ D
   A. recieved an invitation to this friends
   B. received an inviteation to his friends'
   C. received an invitation to his friends'
   D. NO ERROR

10. <u>Because everyone is planing to come to the party.</u>   10.Ⓐ B C D
   A. Everyone is planning to come to the party.
   B. Because everyone is planning to come to the party.
   C. Everyone is planing to come to the party.
   D. NO ERROR

Exercise 3 Identifying Errors

Directions: In each numbered group on the following page, *one or more* of the
items may contain errors. Circle the letter of *every item that contains an error*. If
you think all four items are correct, circle E for NO ERROR.

EXAMPLE   A. Watch out for that truck!   A B(C)(D)E
B. Hal asked the librarian if he could borrow ten books.
C. Because she hadn't received any mail for four days.
D. Jason and Mary share an office they can't come in on the same day.
E. NO ERROR

1. A. "Have you ~~recieved~~ your grade yet?" Emily asked. received   1.(A) B (C) D E
   B. "No, I haven't," Ed replied. "Have you?"
   C. Emily shook her head. "Not yet, but I'm ~~hopeing~~ for a really hoping
   good grade."
   D. "I know you studied a lot," Ed told her.
   E. NO ERROR

2. A. The main branch of Cuyahoga ~~savings bank~~ is downtown. Savings Bank   2.(A)(B)C D E
   B. Have you read ~~macbeth~~ by William Shakespeare.– Macbeth/?
   C. Nora's cousin, who's a doctor, works at Mt. Sinai Hospital.
   D. I addressed my letter to Judge Anna Suarez and sent it to her at the
   United States Federal Court Building.
   E. NO ERROR

3. A. Phyllis searched for her lost earring; Sophie found it.   3. A (B) C D E
   B. Please bring the following ~~items~~ a flashlight, a sleeping bag, and a radio. items:
   C. At 8:30 A.M. tomorrow, the marathon runners start.
   D. We wanted to arrive early; however, we were two hours late.
   E. NO ERROR

4. A. "Where are you going"? she asked. going?" she   4.(A)B C (D) E
   B. "I'm headed for the library," he answered.
   C. "Would you like to come with me?"
   D. "I can't," she replied, "because I'm babysitting\ babysitting."
   E. NO ERROR

5. A. He received several good reviews for his writing.   5. A B (C)(D) E
   B. The recipe calls for three ripe tomatoes and two potatoes.
   C. You'll find ~~sheeps~~ and goats in the childrens petting zoo. sheep
   D. Please ~~except~~ my sincere ~~apologys~~.   accept/apologies
   E. NO ERROR

Exercise 4 Correcting Errors

Directions: Look back at each item in Exercise 3, and double-check your answers. Make sure you have identified *all* of the sentences with errors. On a separate piece of paper, rewrite every incorrect sentence in each numbered item correctly. **Hint:** A sentence may have more than one error.
Correct answers are indicated next to the sentences above.

Glossary

active voice   the form of a verb that shows the subject performing an action.

adjective   a word that modifies (tells more about) a noun or pronoun.

adjective clause   a subordinate clause that modifies a noun or pronoun.

adjective phrase   a prepositional phrase that modifies a noun or pronoun.

adverb   a word that modifies (tells more about) a verb, an adjective, or another adverb.

adverb clause   a subordinate clause that modifies a verb, an adjective, or another adverb. In an **elliptical adverb clause**, some words are omitted (or understood).

adverb phrase   a prepositional phrase that modifies a verb, an adjective, or another adverb.

agreement   the correct relationship between subjects and verbs in number and person or between pronouns and antecedents in number and gender.

anecdote   an incident that actually happened, often based on personal experience or observation. It is one type of evidence that may be used in persuasive writing.

antecedent   the word or words that a pronoun replaces.

appositive   a noun or pronoun that identifies or explains the noun or pronoun that precedes it.

appositive phrase   a phrase made up of an appositive and all of its modifiers.

articles   three common adjectives. *A* and *an* are **indefinite** articles; *the* is the **definite** article.

body   the part of an essay that explains the information introduced at the beginning of the essay.

character   a person who appears in a story; an element of all fiction.

chronological order   the order in which events occurred; a method of organizing used by writers of fiction and nonfiction.

clause   a group of words that contains a subject and a verb but that does not express a complete thought. There are several types of clauses: **independent**, **subordinate**, **essential**, **nonessential**, **adjective**, **adverb**, and **noun**.

clause fragment   a subordinate clause incorrectly punctuated as a sentence. It does not express a complete thought.

clincher sentence   a restatement or summary of the main idea of a paragraph that was expressed in the topic sentence. It ends the paragraph.

clustering   a step in the prewriting process; the method of generating ideas for writing by creating a diagram to explore a topic, to break a large topic into smaller parts, or to gather details (also called **mapping** or **webbing**).

coherence   the logical organization of ideas.

collective noun   a noun that names a group of people or things.

common noun   a noun that names a general, rather than a particular, person, place, thing, or idea.

compare   to identify the way two or more topics are similar.

complete predicate   in a sentence, the verb and all its modifiers (such as adverbs and prepositional phrases), objects, and complements.

complete subject   the simple subject of a sentence and all its modifiers (such as adjectives and prepositional phrases).

complex sentence   a sentence that has one independent clause and at least one subordinate clause.

compound-complex sentence   a sentence that has two or more independent clauses and at least one subordinate clause.

compound noun   a noun that consists of two or more words. It may be hyphenated, written as one word, or written as two words.

compound sentence   a sentence that has two or more independent clauses and no subordinate clauses.

compound subject   two or more subjects sharing the same verb.

compound verb   two or more verbs sharing the same subject.

conclusion   the part at the end of an essay that summarizes the main ideas.

conjunction   a word that joins other words or groups of words. There are three kinds of conjunctions: **coordinating**, **correlative**, and **subordinating**.

conjunctive adverb   an adverb (such as *however*, *moreover*, and *therefore*) used to combine two simple sentences into a compound sentence.

connotation   the emotional associations attached to a word.

contrast   to identify the way two or more topics are different.

coordinating conjunction   a conjunction (such as *and*, *but*, and *for*) that joins words or groups of words that are of equal importance.

correlative conjunctions   a pair of conjunctions (such as *either . . . or* and *neither . . . nor*) that are always used together.

dangling modifier   a modifier that does not describe or limit any word or group of words in a sentence.

declarative sentence   a sentence that makes a statement and ends with a period.

degrees of comparison   the forms of a modifier that indicate the extent of a quality. The three degrees are **positive** (used to describe one thing), **comparative** (used for two things), and **superlative** (used for three or more things).

demonstrative pronoun   a pronoun (such as *this*, *that*, and *those*) that points to a specific thing or person.

denotation   the meaning of a word given in a dictionary.

dialect   a way of speaking in certain regions or among certain groups of people.

direct object   a noun or pronoun that receives the action of an action verb. It answers the question *whom* or *what* following the verb.

discuss   to write about a topic in any way you choose. This is a key word to look for in an essay test question; it tells you how to approach the topic.

double negative   two negative words used together incorrectly to convey a negative meaning.

drafting   in the writing process, the step of putting thoughts into sentences and paragraphs.

editing   the process of correcting grammatical and usage errors in a piece of writing.

elaboration   the process of adding details to support the main idea.

emphatic form   a verb form that is made up of the verb *do* and another verb to provide emphasis.

essay   a piece of writing on a limited topic. All essays have an **introduction**, a **body**, and a **conclusion**.

essential clause   a clause that adds information necessary to understand the sentence. It is not set off by commas.

evidence   information supplied to support an opinion. Types of evidence include **anecdotes**, **incidents**, **examples**, **facts**, **quotations**, and **statistics**.

example   a type of evidence used as an illustration to support an opinion.

exclamatory sentence   a sentence that expresses strong feeling and ends with an exclamation point.

explain   to help a reader understand something by giving reasons or information. This is a key word to look for in an essay test question; it tells you how to approach the topic.

expository paragraph   a paragraph that explains or informs.

fact   a statement that can be proven. It is a type of evidence used to support an opinion.

fragment   a group of words that is not grammatically complete and is incorrectly punctuated as a sentence.

freewriting   a step in the prewriting process; the method of generating ideas for writing by recording ideas for a specified time without stopping, while ignoring grammatical and mechanical rules.

gerund   a verb form that acts as a noun and always ends in *-ing*.

gerund phrase   a phrase made up of a gerund and all of its modifiers and complements. The entire phrase functions as a noun.

grammar   in any language, the rules that govern how words are arranged to form meaningful structures.

imperative sentence   a sentence that commands or makes a request. It ends with either a period or (if the command shows strong feeling) an exclamation point.

incident   a ministory that has a plot, characters, and a setting. It is a type of evidence that can be used to support an opinion.

indefinite pronoun   a pronoun (such as *everyone*, *all*, and *none*) that refers to an unspecified person or thing or that expresses an amount.

independent clause   a clause that has a subject and a verb and expresses a complete thought (also called **main clause**).

indirect object   a noun or pronoun that answers the question *to whom*, *for whom*, *to what*, or *for what* following an action verb.

infinitive   a verb form that is almost always preceded by the word *to* (the *sign*, or *marker*, of the infinitive). In a sentence, an infinitive can act as a noun, adjective, or adverb.

infinitive phrase   a phrase made up of an infinitive and all of its modifiers and complements.

intensifier   an adverb that answers the question *to what extent*.

intensive pronoun a pronoun that ends in -*self* or -*selves* and adds emphasis to a noun or pronoun.

interjection a word that expresses mild or strong emotion. It has no grammatical connection to the rest of the sentence.

interrogative pronoun a pronoun (such as *who, whom*, and *whose*) that begins a question.

interrogative sentence a sentence that asks a question and ends with a question mark.

inverted sentence a sentence in which the verb comes before the subject.

irregular verb a verb that does not form its past and past participle by adding -*d* or -*ed* to the present tense.

linking verb a word that joins the subject of a sentence with a word that identifies or describes it.

loaded words words that carry positive or negative connotations that may sway emotions.

mechanics the correct use of capital letters and punctuation marks.

misplaced modifier an adjective or adverb placed far from the word it modifies.

modifier a word that describes or limits another word or group of words. Adjectives and adverbs are modifiers.

nonessential clause a clause containing information that is not necessary for the sense of the sentence. It is set off by commas.

noun a word that names a person, place, thing, or idea. Nouns that name ideas are **abstract nouns**. **Concrete nouns** name things that can be seen, heard, smelled, tasted, or touched. There are four types of nouns: **proper**, **common**, **collective**, and **compound**.

noun clause a subordinate clause that functions as a noun.

noun of direct address a proper noun that names the person being spoken to. It has no grammatical relation to the rest of the sentence.

paragraph a block of text that includes a sentence stating the main idea and other sentences supporting that idea. There are four types of paragraphs: **descriptive**, **expository**, **narrative**, and **persuasive**.

paraphrase to restate in your own words every idea in the same order as in an original source.

participial phrase a phrase made up of a participle and all its modifiers and complements. The whole phrase acts as an adjective.

participle a verb form that acts as an adjective (modifies a noun or a pronoun). **Present participles** always have an -*ing* ending. **Past participles** of regular verbs end in -*d* or -*ed*, but those of irregular verbs have different endings.

parts of speech the eight categories into which English words are classified according to their function in a sentence.

passive voice the form of a verb that shows a subject receiving an action.

personal pronoun a pronoun (such as *I, we, she, he*, and *you*) that refers to the speaker or to another person. The personal pronouns have **subject**, **object**, and **possessive forms**.

persuade to try to make someone agree with your opinion or to take action.

persuasive paragraph a paragraph that aims to convince the reader that the writer's opinion is correct or to take action.

phrase a group of related words that has no subject or predicate. There are several types of phrases: **adjective**, **adverb**, **appositive**, **gerund**, **infinitive**, **participial**, and **prepositional**.

plot an element of fiction; the sequence of events in a fictional work.

point of view an element of fiction; the perspective of the person who tells the story.

predicate the part of the sentence that tells what the subject does, what it is, or what happens to it. A predicate may be **simple** or **complete**.

predicate adjective an adjective that follows a linking verb and modifies (or describes) the subject of a sentence.

predicate nominative a noun or pronoun that follows a linking verb and renames or identifies the subject.

prefix a meaningful group of letters added at the beginning of a word to form a new word.

preposition a word that connects another word in a sentence to a noun or pronoun (and its modifiers, if any) to form a prepositional phrase.

prepostitional phrase a phrase that begins with a preposition and ends with an object (a noun or pronoun). There are two types of prepositional phrase: **adjective** and **adverb**.

prewriting the step of the writing process that includes all the thinking, planning, and organizing that is done before writing begins.

primary source an original text or document, such as a literary work, diary, letter, speech, interview, or historical document.

principal parts the four basic forms of a verb. They are the **present**, the **present participle**, the **past**, and the **past participle**.

pronoun a word that takes the place of a noun or another pronoun. There are seven kinds of pronouns: **personal**, **indefinite**, **demonstrative**, **interrogative**, **reflexive**, **intensive**, and **relative**.

proofreading a step in the writing process; reading a piece of writing to look for and correct mistakes in spelling, punctuation, and capitalization.

proper adjective an adjective formed from a proper noun. It begins with a capital letter.

proper noun the name of a particular person, place, thing, or idea.

quotation exact spoken or written words. It is a type of evidence used to support an opinion.

reflexive pronoun a pronoun that ends in *-self* or *-selves* and refers to an earlier noun or pronoun in the sentence.

regular verb a verb that forms its past and past participle by adding *-d* or *-ed* to the present.

relative pronoun a pronoun (such as *who*, *whom*, *that*, and *which*) that introduces an adjective clause.

revising the process of improving the content, organization, and style of a piece of writing.

run-on sentence a sentence made up of two or more sentences that are incorrectly run together as a single sentence (also called **stringy sentence**).

secondary source a writer's comments on a primary source. Some types of secondary sources are reference books, biographies, works of literary criticism, and textbooks.

sentence a grammatically complete group of words that expresses a thought. A sentence may be **simple**, **compound**, **complex**, **compound-complex**, **declarative**, **exclamatory**, **imperative**, **interrogative**, or **run-on**.

sentence fragment a group of words that is not grammatically complete and is incorrectly punctuated as a sentence.

setting an element of fiction; the place and time of the events in a story.

simple predicate a verb or verb phrase that tells something about the subject of a sentence.

simple sentence a sentence that has one independent clause and no subordinate clauses.

simple subject the key word or words in the subject of a sentence.

spatial order a method of organizing a piece of writing in which the writer describes the physical placement of someone or something (for example, from left to right or from inside to outside).

statistics facts expressed in numbers. Statistics are a type of evidence that may be used in persuasive writing.

subject the part of the sentence that names the person, place, thing, or idea the sentence is about. A subject may be **simple** or **complete**.

subject complement a noun or pronoun (**predicate nominative**) or an adjective (**predicate adjective**) that follows a linking verb and is necessary to express a complete thought.

subordinate clause a clause that has a subject and a verb but that does not express a complete thought (also called **dependent clause**).

subordinating conjunction a conjunction (such as *that*, *although*, *because*, and *unless*) that introduces an adjective or adverb clause.

suffix a meaningful group of letters added at the end of a word to form a new word.

summarize to give the most important ideas in your own words. This is a key strategy to use in writing a research paper.

synthesize to put together to form a new whole.

theme an element of fiction that conveys a message (for example, about people or life).

thesis statement a summary of an essay's main or controlling idea (also called **opinion statement** or **position statement**). It belongs in the introduction and may be one or two sentences.

topic sentence a sentence that states the main idea of a paragraph. In an essay, it also ties the paragraph in which it appears to the preceding paragraph.

usage in any language, the customary rules governing the use of words and groups of words to communicate ideas.

verb a word that expresses an action or a state of being. Some **action verbs** express an action that can be observed; others express an action that usually cannot be seen. **Linking verbs** join the subject of a sentence with a word that identifies or describes it. A **verb phrase** contains a main verb plus one or more **helping** (or **auxiliary**) **verbs**.

verb tense a form of a verb that expresses the time an action is, was, or will be performed. The three **simple tenses** are **present**, **past**, and **future**. The three **perfect tenses** are **present perfect**, **past perfect**, and **future perfect**. Each tense also has a **progressive form** made up of a helping verb and the present participle (the *-ing* form).

***you* understood** the understood subject of a command or request (an imperative sentence).

Index

phrases
   adjective, 125
   adverb, 125
   colons to emphasize, 273
   in combining sentences, 137–38
   gerund, 133
   infinitive, 135
   intervening, 191
   participial, 127, 128
   prepositional, 125, 128
   verb, 77, 127, 191
place, transitional words and
   expressions to show, 27
plagiarism, 64
planes, italics for titles of, 279
play titles
   capitalization of, 295
   italics of, 279
plot in literary analysis, 55
plot summary in literary analysis,
   54
plural nouns
   apostrophes in, 285
   spelling of, 313
plural pronouns, 215
plural subjects, 191
plural verbs, 191
poems
   capitalization in lines of, 297
   capitalization of titles of, 295
   quotation marks for titles of,
      281
point-by-point method of
   organizing a compare and contrast
   essay, 48–49
point of view in literary analysis,
   56
position statement in persuasive
   writing, 43
positive as degree of comparison,
   221–24
possessive nouns, 133
   apostrophes in, 285
possessive pronouns, 75, 133
predicate(s), 101–2
   complete, 101
   simple, 101
predicate adjective, 81, 117
predicate nominative, 117, 207
   noun clause as, 155
prefix, 311–12
prepositional phrase, 125, 128
   comma to set off introductory,
      129, 259
preposition(s), 87–88
   compound, 87
   defined, 87

distinguishing between adverbs
   and, 125
   ending sentence with, 87
   object of, 155, 209
present participles, 127, 173
   as adjectives, 173
   as verbs, 173
present perfect tense, 183
present tense, 55, 183
   literary present, 183
prewriting
   brainstorming in, 10
   clustering in, 10–11
   for compare and contrast essay,
      47–50
   defined, 9
   for essay questions, 69–70
   for expository writing, 64–65
   5-W and How? questions in, 11
   freewriting in, 10
   for literary analysis, 54–56
   mapping, 10–11, 39
   for narrative writing, 39
   for persuasive writing, 44–45
   Venn diagram in, 48
   webbing in, 10–11
   writer's notebook in, 9
primary source, 61
principal parts of verbs, 173, 175
problem-solution research report,
   59
progressive form, 183
pronoun(s), 16, 26, 75–76
   agreement with antecedent, 215
   appositive/appositive phrase as,
      139–40, 213
   capitalization of *I*, 299
   defined, 75
   demonstrative, 75
   indefinite, 75, 193–94, 215
   intensive, 75
   interrogative, 75
   object, 209–10
   personal, 75
   plural, 215
   possessive, 75, 133
   as predicate nominative, 117
   reflexive, 75
   relative, 147
   singular, 215
   subject, 207–8
proofreading, 18–19
   of compare and contrast essay,
      51
   of essay questions, 70
   of expository writing, 66
   of literary analysis, 58

of narrative writing, 40
   of persuasive writing, 45
   and spell checking, 313
   symbols for, 18
proofreading log, 18, 19, 307
proper adjectives, 81, 293
proper nouns, 73, 293
publishing, 19
   of compare and contrast essay,
      51
   of expository writing, 66
   of literary analysis, 58
   of narrative writing, 40
   of persuasive writing, 45
   suggestions for, 19
punctuation marks. *See*
   apostrophes; colons; commas;
   ellipsis points; exclamation points;
   hyphens; italics; periods; question
   marks; quotation marks;
   semicolons
   proofreading for, 18
purpose, 13, 65

Q

question marks
   after abbreviations, 255
   to end interrogative sentence,
      99, 255
   with quotation marks, 283
questions. *See also* interrogative
   sentences
   5-W and How?, 11
   direct, 255
   indirect, 255
quotation marks, 281–82
   at beginning and end of direct
      quotations, 281–82
   at beginning and end of
      speaker's exact words, 283
   enclosing single words, phrases,
      and short sentences in, 55
   with other punctuation marks,
      283
   for titles of short works, 279,
      281
quotations
   capitalization for first words of,
      281, 297
   colon to introduce, 273, 281
   commas to introduce short
      informal, 263
   direct, 297
   ellipsis points to indicate
      omissions, 55
   in expository writing, 30
   indenting block, 273
   indirect, 297

quotations (*continued*)
  italics for long, 55
  in persuasive writing, 31
  in supporting main idea, 23

R

raise, rise, 181
real, really, 241
reasons
  in persuasive writing, 43
  in supporting main idea, 23
reflexive pronouns, 75
relative adverbs, 147
relative pronouns, 147
religions, capitalization of names of, 297
repetition
  avoiding, 32
  eliminating, 119
request, letter of, 275
research paper, 58–66. *See also* expository writing
revising, 15–17. *See also* editing
  of compare and contrast essay, 51
  of essay questions, 70
  of expository writing, 66
  of literary analysis, 57
  of narrative writing, 40
rise, raise, 181
run-on sentences, 113–14
  correcting, 265

S

school subjects, capitalization of, 297
science research papers, 58
secondary source, 60
second person, 191
-sede, spelling rules for, 309
semicolons, 277–78
  in combining sentences, 111
  before conjunctive adverb that joins independent clauses, 277
  in correcting run-on sentences, 113
  to join independent clauses in compound sentence, 277
  with quotation marks, 283
  to separate items in series when one or more of the items contains a comma, 277
  before transitional expression that joins independent clauses, 277
sentence(s). *See also* combining sentences
  clincher, 21, 22–23
  complex, 157

compound, 111–12, 145, 157, 259
compound-complex, 157
declarative, 99, 255
defined, 99
ending with prepositions, 87
exclamatory, 99, 255
imperative, 99, 255
interrogative, 99, 255
inverted, 107
need for subject and predicate in, 101–2
run-on, 113–14
simple, 157
testing for, 103
topic, 21, 22, 32
varying beginnings and structure of, 129–30, 159–60, 259
sentence completeness, 16
sentence fragments, 99
  correcting, 103–4, 265
sentence interrupters, commas with, 261–62
series
  commas in, 92, 257–58
  semicolons in, 277
set, sit, 181
setting in literary analysis, 56
ships, italics for names of, 279
short stories
  capitalization for titles of, 281
  quotation marks for titles of, 281
should, should of, 237
simple predicate, 101
simple sentence, 157
simple subject, 101
simple tenses, 183
singular pronouns, 215
singular subject, 191
singular verb, 191
sit, set, 181
some, somewhat, 241
somewheres, anywheres, everywheres, nowheres, 235
songs, quotation marks for titles of, 281
sort, sort of a, 239
source card, 62
spacecraft, italics for names of, 279
spatial order, 26
  in descriptive writing, 29
spell checking, 313
spelling, 309–14
  with *-cede, -ceed,* and *-sede,* 309
  to form plural nouns, 313

of gerunds formed from verbs ending in *-e,* 133
getting information on, from dictionary, 307
i before *e* except after *c,* 309–10
of past participles, 173
with prefixes, 311
of present participles, 173
proofreading for, 18
with suffixes, 311
split infinitives, 135
standard English, 99, 177, 223
statistics
  in expository writing, 30
  in persuasive writing, 31, 43
  in supporting main idea, 23
Step by Step, 10, 48, 83, 85, 103, 107, 115, 133, 151, 197, 207, 209, 211, 221, 239, 241
steps in process, chronological order for, 26
story map, 39
style in revising, 15
subject, 101–2
  complete, 101
  compound, 105–6, 197
  finding, 107–8
  noun clause as, 155
  plural, 191
  simple, 101
  singular, 191
  understood, 107
subject complements, 117
  predicate adjectives as, 117
  predicate nominatives as, 117
subject pronouns, 207–8
  as appositives, 213
  who as, 211
subject-verb agreement. *See* agreement
subordinate clauses, 145, 147, 149, 151–52, 155. *See also* adjective clauses; adverb clauses; noun clauses
  in combining sentences, 151–52
  in complex sentences, 157
  in compound-complex sentences, 157
  in correcting run-on sentences, 113, 265
  in varying sentences, 159
subordinating conjunctions, 89, 149, 151
suffix, 311–12
summarizing, transitional words and expressions to show, 27
summarizing information, 63

superlative as degree of
  comparison, 221–24
synonyms, 26

T

take, bring, 237
teach, learn, 239
teams, capitalization of names of,
  297
tense. *See* verb tense
than, then, 241
that, which, 241
that, who, 241
that there, this here, 241
the, 81
them, those, these, 241
theme in literary analysis, 57
then, than, 241
these, them, those, 241
thesis statement
  in essay, 32
  in essay test, 69, 70
  in expository writing, 64
  in literary analysis, 54
  in persuasive writing, 43
this here, that there, 241
those, these, them, 241
time
  transitional words and
    expressions to show, 27
  use of colon between hour and
    minutes, 273
time order, 38
titles, 295–96
  capitalization in, 295
  italics for, 279
  quotation marks for, 279, 281
topic
  breaking down, 10
  choosing, 10
  narrowing, 9
topic sentences, 21, 22, 32
transitions, 26, 47
  list of common, 27
  use of semicolons before, 277
  using clear, 48–49
transitive verbs, 115
TV/radio
  capitalization of titles of, 295
  italics for titles of series of, 279
  quotation marks for titles of
    programs on, 281
type of a, 239

U

unclear comparisons, avoiding, 223
underlining. *See* italics
understood subject, 107

unity, 21–25
  skills for maintaining, 22
usage, glossary of, 235–42

V

Venn diagram, 48
verb(s), 16, 77–78
  action, 77, 115
  compound, 105–6, 259
  defined, 77
  emphatic form of, 183
  helping, 77, 173
  irregular, 175–82
  linking, 77, 115, 117
  past participle as, 173
  plural, 191
  present participle as, 173
  principal parts of, 173, 175
  regular, 173–74
  singular, 191
  transitive, 115
  using vivid, 77
  voice, 185–86
verbals, 127
  gerunds as, 133–34
  infinitives as, 135–36
  participles as, 127–28
verb phrase, 77, 127, 191
verb tense, 77, 183–84
  future, 183
  future perfect, 183
  literary present, 183
  past, 183
  past perfect, 183
  perfect, 183
  present, 55, 183
  present perfect, 183
  simple, 183
voice
  active, 185
  passive, 185

W

webbing, 10–11
well, commas to set off, 263
well, good, 239
when, where, 241
which, that, 241
who, that, 241
who/whom, 147, 211–12
*Wiring Schools to the Internet is
  Essential to the Way Kids Learn,* by
  Al Gore, 41
wordiness, eliminating, 26, 33, 119
words
  choice of, in revising, 15
  colons to emphasize, 273
  connotations of, 42

denotations of, 42
determining part of speech for,
  93
inserting single, in combining
  sentences, 85–86
loaded, 44
words as words
  apostrophes to form plurals of,
    285
  italics for, 279
Works Cited list, 64
would, 237
would of, 237
writer's notebook, 9
Writing Hint, 13, 21, 29, 51, 55, 56,
  73, 81, 87, 99, 105, 119, 125, 127,
  135, 149, 155, 177, 181, 183, 185,
  207, 213, 215, 223, 259, 263, 265,
  275, 283, 309
writing process
  drafting in, 13–14
  prewriting in, 9–12
  proofreading in, 18–19
  publishing in, 19
  revising and editing in, 15–17
writing strategies
  for coherence, 26–28
  eliminating wordiness, 119
  for unity, 21–25
writing style, 13

Y

year, commas to separate, 263
yes, commas to set off, 263
you, as the understood subject, 107